The
Swim Coaching
Bible

VOLUME II

Dick Hannula
Nort Thornton

Editors

Human Kinetics

Library of Congress Cataloging-in-Publication Data

The swim coaching bible, volume II / Dick Hannula, Nort Thornton, editors.
  p. cm.
  ISBN 978-0-7360-9408-5 (soft cover) -- ISBN 0-7360-9408-3 (soft cover)
1. Swimming--Coaching. I. Hannula, Dick, 1928- II. Thornton, Nort, 1933-
  GV837.65.S95 2012
  797.21--dc23
                                2011048356

ISBN-10: 0-7360-9408-3 (print)
ISBN-13: 978-0-7360-9408-5 (print)

The web addresses cited in this text were current as of February 2012, unless otherwise noted.

Acquisitions Editor: Tom Heine; **Developmental Editor:** Laura Podeschi; **Assistant Editor:** Tyler Wolpert; **Copyeditor:** Amanda M. Eastin-Allen; **Permissions Manager:** Martha Gullo; **Graphic Designer:** Fred Starbird; **Graphic Artist:** Tara Welsch; **Cover Designer:** Keith Blomberg; **Photographer (cover):** Adam Pretty/Getty Images; **Photographer (interior):** Harrison Stubbs/Freediving Marine Videography, unless otherwise noted; **Photo Asset Manager:** Laura Fitch; **Visual Production Assistant:** Joyce Brumfield; **Photo Production Manager:** Jason Allen; **Art Manager:** Kelly Hendren; **Associate Art Manager:** Alan L. Wilborn; **Illustrations:** © Human Kinetics, unless otherwise noted; **Printer:** United Graphics

Human Kinetics books are available at special discounts for bulk purchase. Special editions or book excerpts can also be created to specification. For details, contact the Special Sales Manager at Human Kinetics.

Printed in the United States of America   10   9   8   7   6   5   4   3   2   1

The paper in this book is certified under a sustainable forestry program.

Human Kinetics
Website: www.HumanKinetics.com

United States: Human Kinetics
P.O. Box 5076
Champaign, IL 61825-5076
800-747-4457
e-mail: humank@hkusa.com

Canada: Human Kinetics
475 Devonshire Road Unit 100
Windsor, ON N8Y 2L5
800-465-7301 (in Canada only)
e-mail: info@hkcanada.com

Europe: Human Kinetics
107 Bradford Road
Stanningley
Leeds LS28 6AT, United Kingdom
+44 (0) 113 255 5665
e-mail: hk@hkeurope.com

Australia: Human Kinetics
57A Price Avenue
Lower Mitcham, South Australia 5062
08 8372 0999
e-mail: info@hkaustralia.com

New Zealand: Human Kinetics
P.O. Box 80
Torrens Park, South Australia 5062
0800 222 062
e-mail: info@hknewzealand.com

E5148

Contents

◆ PART THREE ◆

TEACHING STROKE TECHNIQUE

◆ PART FOUR ◆

TRAINING FOR OPTIMAL PERFORMANCE

◆ PART FIVE ◆

FINAL TOUCHES FOR PEAK PERFORMANCE

Preface

Dick Hannula AND Nort Thornton

The Swim Coaching Bible, Volume II, is not a revision but rather is an entirely new book. Why publish a completely new edition of *The Swim Coaching Bible*? Since the first volume was published more than 10 years ago, swimming records have gotten faster and coaching techniques have been constantly evolving. The time is right for an all-new volume that includes many new coach–authors and topics. Every coach who contributed to the first volume and is included in this volume writes on a new topic. The one exception is Bill Sweetenham, who requested to write about his original topic because he had so much new information to add.

When we started coaching swimming, very little published coaching information was available. We learned mostly through observing the fastest swimmers and talking with other coaches. Coaching clinics and books were gradually added to the mix but they developed slowly. *Swimming World (Junior Swimmer)* was not yet published, at least when one of us started coaching. The greatest moments in developing new coaching ideas were when four or more of the most successful coaches in an area got together for an ideas session. Now we bring together in one book 25 successful coaches who each condense the most important information on their topic into a single chapter. The new and the experienced coach alike now have immediate access to a coaching reference full of information that, in the old days of coaching, took a lifetime to learn.

The Swim Coaching Bible, Volume II, is a complete reference book. Each chapter is based on the successful coaching experiences of the authors—and what a lineup of great coaches! At least 15 of the coach–authors have coached world record holders or Olympic champions; their bios are success stories of great achievements. The new chapter topics cover the essence of what it takes to be a successful coach.

We are very pleased to bring you the second volume of *The Swim Coaching Bible*. We believe it will prove to be the most valuable reference in the library of every swimming coach.

Acknowledgments

We would like to acknowledge and thank all the chapter authors of *The Swim Coaching Bible, Volume II*, for contributing their great knowledge and experience, as well as Harrison ("Skip") Stubbs for allowing us to use his stunning photography. All of these individuals were willing to share their talents and to give back to the entire swimming community. Their time and effort have made this book a success.

—Dick Hannula and Nort Thornton

PART ONE

ESTABLISHING PRIORITIES

1

Developmental Stages of Competitive Swimmers

John Leonard

The stages of an athlete's career in the sport of swimming are diverse. This chapter lists the experiences that are normal from the time a future swimmer starts swimming lessons through all levels of competitive swimming. Competitive swimming results in a very positive experience, but a swimmer may have to overcome challenges at each stage along the way; this chapter details these challenges. First, we take a look at a typical swim family and the stages of their involvement in the sport. Later, we provide some recommendations for swimmers, their parents, and their coaches.

STAGES OF DEVELOPMENT

One of the most remarkable things about the sport of competitive swimming is its complexity. The following fictional story of a brother and sister traveling the road to swimming success illustrates what swimmers commonly experience in each stage of competitive swimming.

Swimming Lessons

Two athletes, one boy and one girl, first led to a swimming pool by their mom at 4 to 7 years of age, begin swimming lessons and learn to appreciate their time in the water. They find, as most humans do, that water is endlessly fascinating and fun to be in.

Swim Team

A few years later, the children or their mom discover the swim team. For a few carefree afternoons a week in the summer, they enjoy new friends and new skills and learn to become better performers in the pool.

The boy discovers swim meets, where he can race his buddies and see who is the fastest. It's simple, direct, and fun and an uncomplicated way to enjoy the water and race! The girl is intrigued by the idea that there are right and wrong ways to do things on the swim team, and an authoritarian figure called a coach notices that the girl is interested in learning to do things correctly. Mastering the sport is more important to her than simply racing.

Novice Swimming

Later that year or the next, the boy and girl discover that a year-round USA Swimming team exists in their community. Their mom signs them up for the novice age-group team where, for the first time, they learn that swimming can be serious and the coaches treat teaching and learning technique as the most important part of the process. One coach in particular says that swimming is a technique-limited sport, so one needs to master the techniques of good swimming. For the boy, this goes in one ear and out the other, but the girl catches on immediately and decides that she will become a master of the sport. Swim meets keep the boy in the sport. Good practice sessions keep the girl in the sport.

Age-Group Swimming

After a year of novice swimming, the young swimmers graduate to the age-group team, which has participation requirements. Swimmers are expected to attend five practices per week. Also, the amount of practice time increases from 45 minutes per day to 90 minutes per day. The children carpool to practice with other swimmers and swap stories and tips in the car. They make new friends—lots of them.

The boy and girl become more proficient at their strokes, starts, and turns, and later in the year they travel with their parents to an overnight meet in another town and stay in a hotel with their teammates. Both the socializing and the sport become more appealing and increasingly affect their lives. They find that their friendships are focused on other swimmers, who understand their new world. Their mom and dad are happy because they are also good students who make the most of their limited study time.

High School Swimming

A few years of age-group swimming go by, and suddenly a few of their older friends are missing for part of the year to take part in high school swimming. A whole new world of sport opens for the pair of young athletes.

The young man and woman enter the world of high school sports. The high school swimming experience is fun for both because it provides a team experience with teammates who are the same sex and close to the same age. The competition is exciting because, unlike in club swimming, the races are shorter and have a sprint emphasis and the meets are completed in a couple hours or less. A school letter jacket also increases social recognition in the high school community.

Their swimming coach in high school is an English teacher who swam on a team at one time and enjoys coaching but is also so busy with teaching and family that he doesn't have much time to spend learning more about the sport today. In addition, he coaches the students for only a short season.

For the young lady, the high school season runs from September through November, and for the young man, from December through early March. They have dual meets, conference meets, and, if they make it, a state championship meet. During the rest of the year they train with their club coach, a highly trained American Swimming Coaches Association level 4 USA Swimming coach who is a full-time coaching professional.

After a year of high school and year-round swimming, the young man decides that the sport is too much work for too little reward. Although he continues to swim in high school because he enjoys the racing, being with his friends, and the more relaxed atmosphere of the high school team, he decides that the high-intensity training of weeks and sometimes months on end without a swim meet in USA Swimming is just not for him. It's too much continuous effort with too little of what he likes—the racing! He becomes a 12-weeks-a-year swimmer. During the rest of the year, he works part time and studies hard for college admission.

His sister, meanwhile, becomes whole-heartedly involved in her sport. She trains Monday, Wednesday, and Friday from 5:30 to 7 a.m., Monday through Friday from 4 to 7 p.m., and Saturday from 7 to 11 a.m. With all this training, her times improve dramatically and she becomes good enough to compete in junior nationals for her USA Swimming club and is one of the best swimmers in her state high school meet.

Her brother enjoys the casual atmosphere of the high school team and the racing. However, she finds it too casual and not focused enough on goals and achievement and believes that her high school practices are too limited to enable her to attain her high-level competitive goals. Some conflict exists between her club coach and high school coach as to the type of training she should be doing. This sets up some uncomfortable moments for the young lady during the course of her high school career because she has to get along with both coaches.

The high school dual meets rarely present good competitive opportunities for her, but the district, regional, and especially the state meet are the best swim meets she attends all year. They lead to recognition at school and are exciting, with lots of enthusiastic fans and people who care about all the effort she is putting in to being the best she can be. She desperately wants to do well at her state championship meet and knows that college recruiters will be there to see her swim and consider her for a college scholarship.

Her brother, being a male and a late developer, continues to get faster. He lifts weights at home and after school year round. By the time he's a senior, he is one of the fastest athletes in the state in the 50 free and he's getting offers of college scholarship.

This seems totally unfair to the girl, who has put in five times the amount of work. However, her times seem to have leveled off and have improved very slowly during the past 2 years. She gets a few scholarship information requests, but because she swims the mile and the 500, she has fewer opportunities than her sprinter brother to score points in meets and the scholarship offers are fewer and for less. She drowns her unhappiness in a few more milkshakes, and the extra couple of pounds she puts on do not help her improve. But her club coach has done a great job and she has wonderful strokes and, despite a few extra pounds, she continues to put forth good swimming times and competitive results—at least enough to encourage her to continue.

Collegiate Swimming

At the end of their senior year in high school, the young lady enrolls in a small private college at the Division III level with a coach she really likes and a team of girls she relates to instantly. The good community feeling she gets from the girls and the coach is the determining factor in her choice. Her brother decides to swim in college at the Division I level. He receives books and the promise of a partial tuition scholarship at State U, which he chooses based on the positive impression of their nationally competitive football games and the great recruiting weekend he had when he visited. He really likes the guys, and if the coach seems pretty demanding, well, no big deal, he can live with that—it's the guys that he'll be with that count. Plus, by staying in state, he saves his parents a lot of money.

In college, the young man really likes hanging out with the guys and, while he has a hard time handling the amount of swim training they do, he really enjoys all the time in the weight room. His strength levels soar and his improvement is dramatic. When the university team has a dual meet, it's very competitive and he has to swim faster than ever before to not let his team down. The social and academic sides of college are more demanding than high school and require good decisions and time management. He has always been responsible and he learns to handle the academic and social expectations in college, although he is not surprised when some of his freshman teammates quit the team with low grades or are academically ineligible at the end of the year. He makes note that all the talks his parents gave him about maturity were not far off the mark. He swims fast, and at the conference meet the coach tells him that he'll have a partial tuition scholarship in the coming year.

Meanwhile, his sister is having a hard time relating to the new coach that she liked so much during her visit. She discovers that the young coach is nowhere near as professional as her club coach and that the team is restricted in how much they can train with the coach preseason, and she is mortified to discover that much of her training preseason has to be done on her own to comply with NCAA Division III rules. Not many of the girls are as serious about swimming as she is, and they are more like her high school team than her club team, which does not make her happy. Around Christmas, she tries to put on a dress that she wore on occasion in high school and discovers that it no longer fits. An older girl says, "Well, you've put on the freshman 15, like most of us do. Don't worry; you'll get rid of it next year." She has indeed gained 15 pounds (6.8 kg) by overeating due to her unhappiness and homesickness. Over the Christmas holidays, she vows to lose it all. She goes on a stringent diet, eating barely 1,000 calories a day, increases her training level at home with her beloved club coach, and swims 10 kilometers per practice to help lose the 15. Her club coach notes her hard work and praises it while asking himself why she is so much slower with a few extra pounds. He has no idea that she is severely restricting her calories.

She loses the 15 pounds, plus another 5. She is excited about and even obsessed with her weight from them on. She puts a scale in her dorm room and weighs herself day and night. She is mortified one evening after splurging on a cheeseburger, fries, and milkshake and discovers she has regained the additional 4 pounds she had lost since coming back to the dorm. She decides "I can't keep all this in my stomach," goes into the bathroom, and sticks her finger down her throat to vomit. She then gets back on the scale and is pleased with her self-control when she finds she has lost 3 pounds by the next morning. She drags her tired body off to practice, where she can barely swim because she lacks calories to burn. That pattern continues for the rest of the semester. She performs terribly at her conference meet and is even more unhappy when her brother texts her with his great results. "How does he earn that?" she asks herself.

Luckily, her college coach recognizes the problem when she repeatedly disappears into the bathroom immediately after eating meals on the team's conference swim trip. He gets professional help for her during the spring of her freshman year and she talks to her parents about her problem. During her first summer back home, she regains her equilibrium with healthy eating and a dose of training with her club coach. By August, she and her brother, who took the summer off from swimming but lifted weights every day, are ready and eager to return to college.

As their college careers continue, both settle into routines that accommodate their various interests. The young man gradually makes an ever-increasing commitment to his sport, and as his male body evolves from boyhood to manhood, his sprint abilities increase proportionately. In time, he becomes a marginal swimmer at nationals, and finally, in his junior year, gets to make a consolation final and come back and swim at night. By his senior year he's a top eight finalist at NCAAs and is widely recognized as one of the top male sprinters in the NCAA.

Meanwhile, his sister pays constant attention to her eating issues and, in conference with her college coach and in deference to her maturing body, decides to drop the mile and the 1,000 and concentrate downward on the 500, 200, and 100 freestyles and discovers her talent for sprint butterfly. She qualifies for NCAA Division III nationals and is a relay contributor throughout her career at the Division III level. During her senior year she is recognized as the top student–athlete of her college class. Immediately after her last college race, she declares her retirement from the sport and is happy and proud when she reflects on all she has both accomplished and overcome.

Postgraduate Swimming

Her brother, meanwhile, has a few courses to finish up in order to graduate at the end of his 4-year eligibility and Olympic Trials are just 18 months away, so he decides to stay in training and swim through so he can say he swam at Olympic Trials. Along the way, he improves considerably and finishes in the top eight in both the 50 free and the 100 free at the trials, though he does not make the Olympic team. After a couple of free months with no swimming and no job, he decides to try professional swimming and gets a small contract with a swimsuit company, which provides the funding to pay for his living expenses. He gets to try the FINA World Cup series of professional races in Europe and over an 8-week period gets to see some of the great capitals of Europe and race the great swimmers of the world. He enjoys this greatly and has some moderate success, so he continues for the next 3 years. He makes a U.S. World Short Course Championship team and has the joy of representing his country in a world competition.

One more Olympic Trials come around and he is happy to compete, though nervous, and makes finals once again, and once again just misses the team. After watching his sister rise rapidly in the business world using the work ethic she gained through her swimming, he decides it is time to hang up his Speedo and retires after the trials. He periodically thinks about returning for one more try during the next 4 years, but he doesn't do it.

Masters Swimming

Four years later, both brother and sister are in their early thirties. She is married and has just had her first child; he is engaged and is doing well in his business. Within 6 months of each other and encouraging each other all the way, they decide to get back into the water to stay in shape. Six months after that, for a lark, they decide to try a swim meet and join U.S. Masters Swimming and attend their first meet.

He struggles with an extra 20 pounds he's put on since his retirement from competitive swimming but really enjoys the racing, so he decides to start attending masters team practice four times per week instead of two. She doesn't care much about the racing, but the other three ladies in her relay really need her—two are close to her age and one is old enough to be her mother—and she enjoys the sense of community in the masters team and having other moms to talk to about something other than children. She ups her practice schedule similarly to his and becomes a four-times-a-week masters swimmer.

Repeating the Cycle

Four years later, the woman puts her child into swimming lessons. Two years after that, she watches proudly as her son completes his first 8-and-under swim meet.

Ten years later, after his first two children have tried every sport except swimming, the man has the surprise of his life when his young son comes to him one evening and says, "Dad, Mom told me you used to be on the swim team. Is that right? There's a team down at the summer pool, and I'd like to join and see how good I am. I think I'd like the racing!" The circle is unbroken.

DEVELOPMENTAL ADVICE

The previous life scenario is entirely fictitious, of course, but it is very typical in many respects. Parents, coaches, and the athletes themselves must expect and prepare for these challenges and others when they participate in swimming. The sections that follow advise parents, athletes, and coaches on how to prepare for and deal with the ups and downs of this challenging yet rewarding sport.

For Swim Parents

Following is some advice to parents on each phase of the developmental process—or at least those phases in which the parent is largely involved.

Swimming Lessons (Ages 3 to 7)

- Select a quality learn-to-swim program for your child.
- Focus on who will teach your child to swim rather than on who offers swimming lessons.
- Ask "In your program, how long does it take the average child to go from being scared and terrified to swimming 25 yards freestyle with rotational breathing?"
- Ask for references from satisfied clients.
- Generally, you will get what you pay for. Many places offer inexpensive swimming lessons. You want your child learn to swim to be safer around the water. You can pay for lessons for many months and your child never learns to swim. This changes inexpensive swimming lessons into a very expensive waste of time and effort, and your child will pick up bad habits.
- Expect lessons to cost between $80 and $120 for a set of 10 lessons. Expect that it will take 40 to 80 lessons to achieve the milestone listed in the third bullet point.
- Let the teacher teach. If your child has special needs, the instructor needs to know. Otherwise, stay out of it.
- Look for attention to detail in the teacher. Swimming is a technique-limited sport. If the child is not taught proper technique, it will be damaging for a lifetime. You may not know what proper technique is, but you know when someone is paying attention to detail.
- Your child will not always be happy during lessons. Most people aren't happy when they are asked to do something new. Console yourself that you are giving your child a life-saving and life-enriching skill and that eventually they will be very happy that you did make them go to lessons and stick with it.
- Thank the instructor daily. Very few, if any, earn much money giving swimming lessons. It's a labor of love and passing on the skills of something that they themselves love. Appreciation in the form of a simple "thank you" is a great reward for most of these dedicated teachers.

Age-Group Swimming (Ages 8 to 12)

- Select an age-group program for your child.
- Interview a number of teams and coaches about what they do and what they can do for your child.
- Ask about what the team emphasizes in the early years. The answer you want to hear is technique, technique, technique. The answers you don't want to hear are speed, speed, speed or winning.

◆ Ask about the practice schedule. When first coming from a learn-to-swim program, expect three to four practices per week. In a year or two, perhaps four to five practices per week. By ages 11 to 12, perhaps five to seven practices per week. Each practice should last for 45 to 60 minutes (some very talented and advanced swimmers may be invited to do more) and gradually increase.

◆ Understand the purpose of swim meets. They are there to test what the child learns in practice. Coaches who are on the right track teach calm, cool, collected behavior at meets and the ability to both have fun when racing and analyze the results of the techniques used in the race. Coaches who emphasize winning do your child no service.

◆ Expect your coach to ask your child to swim all the events. Focusing on a few things they do well early in their career is shortsighted. The breaststroker at age 10 may well be the best distance swimmer by age 17. You cannot tell what can develop, so the child should keep developing all strokes as long as possible.

◆ Be a parent. Take care of the parental things and let the coach coach. This is equally true in practice and at swim meets. If you have questions or comments, talk to the coach and listen to the coach's response. Talking to your child about it sets up a destructive conflict for your child. Talking to other parents about it is similar to asking your neighbor how to pull your decayed tooth: not wise. Ask the coach.

◆ Support the total success of the team. This is not an individual sport. Eventually, your child will be deeply affected by the degree of success or lack thereof of their teammates. It takes a team to succeed in this sport. You cannot do it with a selfish "me first" approach.

◆ Do ask the parents of teenagers what they went through in the sport. You can learn from their experience. The longer you are in the sport, the more you learn to relax, have a sense of humor, and enjoy it! Your child may sometimes try to impress you with how hard it is. They are truly not complaining; they are usually bragging. Learn to discern the difference. The relevant question is not whether they are having fun every day (no one ever does) but whether it is a satisfying experience. If they want to go to practice, all is well. Sometimes in the earliest years, parents have to enforce the commitment the child has made in joining the team by taking them away from the computer or TV, putting them in the car, and saying "We're going to practice." Eventually, the swimmer should be eager to go.

Late Junior High School and Early High School (Ages 13 to 15)

◆ Junior high or middle school are typically the feather gatherer years. Many schools offer an endless variety of opportunities for children to be involved after school. Many swimmers can become distracted by these opportunities in the short term and lose focus on their sport. As a parent, the temptation is to discourage these activities, but it's best to let them try other activities and find out for themselves what they're most passionate about.

- High school swimming is both the greatest boon to a swimming career and a very dangerous phase. We hope that every child will try high school swimming. The in-school recognition is spectacular, and the identity this provides the swimmer in school is irreplaceable. On the other hand, the coaching may or may not be consistent with their year-round coaching, and in some states the rules are quite restrictive. In addition, in some cases, competition can be less strong for much of the year. This gives the weaker year-round swimmer a chance to shine, but it can lead the stronger year-round swimmer to develop poor habits as they dominate their events without as much challenge.

- Encourage the high school coach and the club coach to communicate and collaborate for the benefit of the athlete. In some communities, this is a big challenge. Parents can help here.

- Understand that every athlete develops at a unique pace on an individual maturation cycle. Patience is needed to allow that to happen. Some swimmers attain success at a young age and some develop their potential in high school and even in their college years. Every swimmer should focus on great technique and consistent and persistent training through the extended developmental years. This approach will reward the swimmer with the best results in the long run.

- Understand that in the teen years and beyond, the swimmer will not be doing best times on almost every swim as they may have done at an earlier age. With age it gets harder to get faster, and improvement takes hard, quality practice. Improvement will be slow and best times may be seen only once or twice a season. This is entirely natural; do not fret. It teaches the great life lesson that big rewards require concentrated, persistent effort.

- In these years, a shift will occur. The coach, rather than the parent, will become the primary focus and feedback unit in the athlete's team. Likely, the child wants to put some distance between child and parent; this is okay. Let the sport become their sport rather than "our sport." They're doing the swimming; let them own it.

- You have now been involved in swimming for a while and have had some experiences. Use those experiences to help parents who are new to the sport.

Late High School (Ages 16 to 18)

- Recognize that both the coach and the athlete's peers supplant the parent as the primary other for the swimmer; again, this is natural. The most important feedback at this stage may come from peers. If the athlete has been well coached, it's entirely possible that even the coach is reduced to a resource person at this stage.

- The wise parent stays in the background at this stage. Attend practices rarely, if ever, and attend meets when asked by your child. If they would prefer you not be there, accept this graciously. It is entirely possible that your presence puts unwanted pressure on your child.

- They will need tremendous help with college selection. This needs to be done in conjunction with professional help from the school guidance counselor and from the year-round and high school coach serving as the experts in which college program your athlete will fit into well.
- Sit back and enjoy the results of all your hard work as a parent. These can be enjoyable years!

College (Ages 19 to 24)

- Once the swimmer has left home for college, your role is reduced to a support function. Interestingly, every college swimmer seems to want their parents to be at a fair number of swim meets. It is very enjoyable to take a road trip and watch your child compete. They may not have wanted you there in high school, but once away at college, having Mom and Dad in the stands is much more important. Odd but true.
- Recognize that best times at this mature physical stage will be the hard-won result of a great deal of effort and concentration and are likely to happen once or twice a year when shaved and tapered. However, it is likely that racing skills are finely tuned and are a focus, and even small technical improvements will be celebrated with enthusiasm by athlete and coach.

Congratulations, Mom and Dad! Great job!

For Athletes

Following is some advice for the young athlete at each stage—or at least each stage in which they are conscious of the process.

Age-Group Swimming (Ages 8 to 12): Learning to Learn, Learning to Train

- Things take time. Don't be in a rush.
- Learn the basic body positioning skills and good breathing technique for each stroke first.
- Get to practice. The most important part of success is showing up.
- Pay attention to your coach. Learn to learn.
- Watch your better teammates. What can you learn from them? (Coaches, you need good role models in the water!)
- Pay attention to detail. Learn to do things correctly.
- Respect your teammates. Give them your effort to improve.
- Respect your competitors. They drive you to improve.
- Concern yourself with your own improvement. Don't compare yourself with others. People change and mature at different rates, but it all evens out.
- Be a good team member. Cheer for and encourage your teammates.

Late Junior High School and Early High School (Ages 13 to 15): Learning to Train, Learning to Compete

- Live in the here and now. Don't worry about yesterday or tomorrow but rather fully experience today and now. It's the only place you can positively influence your life and sport.
- Train for the purpose of race preparation. Don't train just to train. Relate everything you do in training to how it will help you race.
- Work on your intention. Do you intend to constantly improve? If you do, you can measure every decision you have to make against that intention. Do what fits your intention.
- No one can prosper in a vacuum. Make the team around you, from your parents to your friends, to your teammates to your coaches and everyone else involved, part of your support team. Thank them appropriately. If they are not on your support team, why would you want to be around them?
- Chase one rabbit. Coach Confucius said "He who would chase two rabbits will catch neither." This is great life advice. What's your one rabbit today? This week? This month? This year?
- Hidden training—how you eat, sleep, rest, and think—will profoundly affect your success. Do it well.
- No one race or swim meet will determine the success of your swimming career. It's a long journey. Make the journey, not the destination, the thing you value.
- Everyone can set goals. Can you determine what it takes to get there? Use your support team, especially your coach, to determine the process goals you need to reach your achievement goals (in all of life, not just swimming).

Late High School (Ages 16 to 18): Learning to Compete, Learning Independence

- Setbacks and hardships occur. The key life skill to learn is resilience. Get up and bounce back. Stay focused.
- Everyone wants to go to heaven. No one wants to die. If you want to go to heaven, you have to do what is required, even when it's not what you want to do.
- Be a motivation machine. Let success motivate you to do even better and drive you. Let failure or difficulty redouble your enthusiasm and energy for the journey. Be extra energetic in going after what you want. Everything that happens can energize you; let it.
- Learn to do what you need to do first and what you want to do later on.
- Avoid cranial–rectal insertion disease. Don't spend all your time dwelling on your own hardships and challenges. The best cure is to do something for someone else so you can see someone besides yourself.
- Competition means "to strive with." You need good competition in order to improve. Race and train with people who are better than you.

- Keep it friendly. This is just swimming, after all. Always be a good sport and be a good sport in all ways.
- Enjoy the process. It's likely the last time in your life that you'll have the freedom to train when, where, and how you wish. Twenty years from now, you'll kill for more time to train. Be grateful for the time and opportunity.

College (Ages 19 to 24)

- If you are still swimming as a primary occupation, congratulations!
- Cherish the wonderful opportunity to be your best.
- You're a more mature human being. This will have profound implications for changes in your training and racing. More time will be required for recovery, and more attention to rest and resilience will be necessary.
- Increased strength may also indicate a need for stroke changes. Be open to it.
- In some sprint cases, racing may *be* training. That's different, but fine.
- Tapers likely will require more time and attention.
- Best times will be hard fought for and well earned. Congratulate yourself.

Masters Swimming (Ages 25 and On)

- If you can train continuously and not take a couple years off, you can maintain quality performance for a very long time.
- Because masters swimming is relatively new, no one knows much about the limits. Performances are amazing today and likely will be more so tomorrow.
- As you age, your aerobic capacity will stick with you but your neuromuscular performance may not stick as well, and reversibility will be faster than it was when you were younger. If you use speed work and then take a break, that's the capability you will likely lose first and it will be the hardest to regain.
- Thirty minutes of exercise every day is better than three hours per day three times per week. Consistency counts.
- Training with friends is more fun than training alone. It's probably worth the effort to find a group you can participate in. Friends sustain us.
- It's a great journey. Enjoy it.

For Coaches

In today's world of swimming, coaches face numerous and diverse challenges. Following are some things that coaches need to consider in their own development.

- Coaching is not a well-paid profession. If money is important to you, this may not be the best way for you to earn a living. Consider owning and running a learn-to-swim program. Because everyone needs to learn to swim but only a few choose competitive swimming, your range of clients will be much larger. If you can earn a living by running a swim school, it relieves the pressure of having to earn a living coaching and you feed your swim team with well-prepared swimmers.

- Understand that you are selling something that is completely counter to current American culture. Our sport demands long-term patience and commitment, whereas current culture glorifies immediate gratification. Our sport demands hard work, whereas current culture glorifies ease of life. You'll have to either educate your families about patience and disciplined pursuit of a goal or have a really small team. Of course, every market has a place for the counterculture. And culture changes, fads decline, and the eternal values of our sport endure. Fortunately, many parents understand the need for their children to be involved in something to counter current trends.

- Twenty-five years ago, parents sided with the teacher when their child got in trouble at school. Today, they side with their child and the teacher is the bad guy. The same is true with coaches. Gaining parental support and trust has never been harder, and you'll have to work at it every day. Let parents be on deck during practice (as long as they don't interfere) so they can appreciate what you bring to their child every day and put their trust in you.

- Loyalty is hard to come by. You train an assistant coach well and soon they are out the door, down the street, and running their own program that competes with yours. Train them anyway. Have your assistants sign noncompete contracts that your lawyer has drawn up. Well-trained assistants make or break you as a coach. Take the time to train them and educate them, and be direct with them about loyalty. Hire well and keep your best staff.

- Be patient in the long term and impatient in the short term. Short-term impatience means that you demand and expect a lot from your athletes. Nothing is a larger compliment, but you'll have to explain that to them. You will get what you expect from children. High expectations usually become realized. On the other hand, have long-term patience. Development takes more time now than ever before because more and more young people come into programs with poor, underdeveloped skills. Know where you are going with your team and your athletes and be unrelenting yet patient in order to get there.

- Set goals for yourself, your team, and your athletes. A rocket to the moon is off course 99% of the time, but it self-corrects because its computer knows where it is supposed to go. Make sure your mental computer and those of your staff and parents and athletes know where to go in the sport and outside of it.

- Coach as if every athlete will be with you forever, even though in today's mobile society they probably won't be. There are no short-term, easy solutions. Don't focus just on speed work with that great 11-year-old because she might move next year and so you want her to be fast this year. Do the aerobic base work that you'd do if she was going to be with you until age 18. And trust that your colleague in Tacoma, Washington, who has an athlete moving to you in Philadelphia next year, is doing the same with *his* great 11-year-old!

- Leave the woodpile higher than you found it. You'll change jobs—once, twice, maybe 10 or more times. Develop a reputation for always leaving a program much better than you found it. Be a program builder, not a program user.
- Remember that coaching is a people business. Walk away from your computer and spend time talking with your athletes. Decades from now, they will remember what you had to say and that you listened to them. Leave that legacy rather than a bunch of electronic scratches on a hard drive.
- Make parents your allies. All around the world, in every culture and every society, just about the only thing the entire human race shares is that we love our children. Make this the center-point of your coaching. You want the best for your athletes and so does every parent. Figure out how to be allies, not adversaries.

CONCLUSION

Competitive swimming is a great sport in which to learn lifelong skills. Most likely, the benefits won't come in the form on the financial rewards of professional swimming; that is reserved for a select few in the sport. The benefits come from experiencing personal achievement through persistent, intensive effort over a long period of time. This carries over into academic achievement, professional success, and relationships. Former swimmers continue to state that competitive swimming was their best preparation for the ups and downs of life and for a healthy and productive existence.

Happy coaching!

2

From Youth to Senior in Competitive Swimming

Bill Sweetenham

Every competitive swimmer must prepare for the transition from one level of swimming to another. Proper transition from youth through senior competition makes it more probable that the transitions will be uncomplicated and smooth and will lead into successful national and international competition. The basic skills that a swimmer learns as an age-group athlete allow both athlete and coach to move through the passage of maturation on to the youth level. The youth level occurs roughly from ages 13 to 17, or until the swimmer enters open senior competition. A transportable set of skills and wide range of experiences will allow the athlete the flexibility to easily adapt to the new challenges before them in open competition.

This all-important journey from an age-group swimmer to a committed, competition-based senior and open-age athlete is extremely challenging. It teaches many life lessons and is an extremely positive experience that provides rewarding opportunities both in the sport and in the athlete's outside endeavors.

HOW A GOOD YOUTH PROGRAM CAN GUIDE ATHLETES TO SENIOR SUCCESS

Past observations and experience clearly indicate that, for the vast majority of successful athletes, moving forward is the most important element in an athlete's long-term development and career plan. Every swim teacher, coach, parent, club, and associated supporter should aim to encourage, help, and develop young people to become senior-age, competition-based swimmers. Very few experiences in life are more rewarding than seeing a mature athlete whom you have assisted significantly through the development process achieve this high standard.

The development and transition of an athlete from a recreational age-group swimmer to a committed, mature senior swimmer is not always linear in terms of measurable improvement in competition. It is vital for the complete growth of the athlete that much more than improvement in competition times or podium results are taken into account when forming observations, confidence, and measurements. Competition times and podium results are extremely positive and necessary measurements, but they are definitely not the only ones that determine the rewards of an athletic and personal journey. Improved stroke technique, better work habits, and more personal commitment, for example, while less quantitative and thus more difficult to identify, are just as imperative to development.

The coach, club, and program all need clearly stated objectives, goals, processes, and desired outcomes, and those who sign up for the program must understand how these things will contribute to their long-term personal growth. Far too often, a lack of understanding and appreciation of the club model results in limitations on the long-term career goals of program participants. Youth-age athletes often leave the sport due to the frustration they feel at the lack of direction, leadership, and harmony in their club.

The club board, directors, committee, parents, and coaching staff must all clearly understand and appreciate the value of having role models of youth and senior athletes in the club program. Role modeling clearly benefits age-group athletes and parents. This aspect of the club's development is sometimes overlooked or ignored.

This oversight can potentially inhibit the growth of the individual athlete, coach, and club. More often than not, this occurs when the club has a young or inexperienced coach or a club committee directed by age-group parents. Despite the recognized success and contribution of national and state academies or institutes, universities, and regional and state high-performance programs, clubs and club growth play the main role in a country's sustainable and repeatable success at every level of competition.

Clubs or programs that fail to address as a recognized priority the transition of athletes from youth level to senior level will soon become the limiting rather than the deciding factor in the success of the team and the individual athletes. This applies to national and international winning success rates as well as the overall growth of the sport.

Coaches or clubs that are unwilling or unable to successfully address this transition must offer the youth athlete an opportunity for release and pathway to a program that can provide this transition, and must do so in a positive, unselfish manner and without restrictions or hesitation. Grapes should not be allowed to die on the vine. Coaches and athletes must choose programs wisely! Athletes should choose a club, coach, and program that fosters a wide variety of experiences, encourages individual growth and development, and has a positive, supportive team environment. A club and program must understand that each athlete has different and specific needs and drives.

A poorly chosen club, coach, or program can negatively affect enjoyment, process, longevity in the sport, and the final result and personal growth. A good decision provides a positive result in all of these areas and will provide success for life. This also applies to coaches and their choice of position, club, and workplace.

It has always been my conviction that the club programs that are sustainable and successful are committed to producing great athletes and people. They achieved this outcome by promoting a pathway that allowed swimmers to develop from the early age groups through senior athletes. High-level open performance achievements became inevitable due to a quality control system that is secondary to this pathway.

All swimmers should be developed as though they will become an Olympic champion and senior athlete. Not everyone can achieve Olympic representation, but everyone can be developed and their skills can be enhanced as if this is the desired outcome. In any program, a swimmer must be developed progressively and systematically as a total athlete and person. However, we have all witnessed the overaggressive age-group program that is focused only on a short-term gain, gratification, and recognition to the detriment of individuals and their long-term development and longevity in the sport. This must be avoided at all costs if the transition from age-group to youth and from youth to senior is to be successful.

Several options are available for youth athletes or parents looking to make the right choice. Athletes and parents must consider club attributes such as location; available pool space and time; all-weather training in year-round facilities; sports science and sports medicine support; available and appropriate competitions; strength and conditioning facilities; and experienced, knowledgeable, and driven coaches.

Athletes and parents can choose from several types of programs.

1. **A senior university or institute program that incorporates sport as well as long-term academic career goals.** This is a great choice because it offers peer leadership, academics, and usually some form of lifestyle support. However, if not chosen wisely, the program can expose the negative sides of these three attributes as well. The youth athlete must have the courage and the conviction to not compromise or place at risk their career goals.

How the youth athlete has been prepared with independent leadership skills often means the difference between success and failure in this environment. The athlete must understand that they must make this environment work for them and not against them. The home coach and program must instill these skills in the young athlete as the athlete moves on to a senior program.

2. **A long-term total athlete and personal development program that guides swimmers through the challenges and obstacles of age, youth, and senior ranks.** This program will include a significantly large number of athletes of all ages and varying skill and talent levels. It suits the senior athlete who thrives in a massive team environment and is happy to be part of a recognized and supportive club program. This situation usually suits the individual who has progressed through the different squads of the club. This club is usually close to the swimmer's home base and provides all of the associated benefits of location, team support, and a supportive environment. Note the model in figure 2.1.

3. **A program based on high performance comprising only senior athletes.** This type of program is a variation of programs 1 and 2 and could focus on either males or females or could be event specific. For example, it could be a sprint program for women or a breaststroke individual medley program for men. It could also be an event-specific program that includes both males and females. The athletes must choose a multidimensional and fully integrated program that offers the greatest chance for ultimate success. The choices are many for any youth athlete pursuing a career in senior and open competitive swimming.

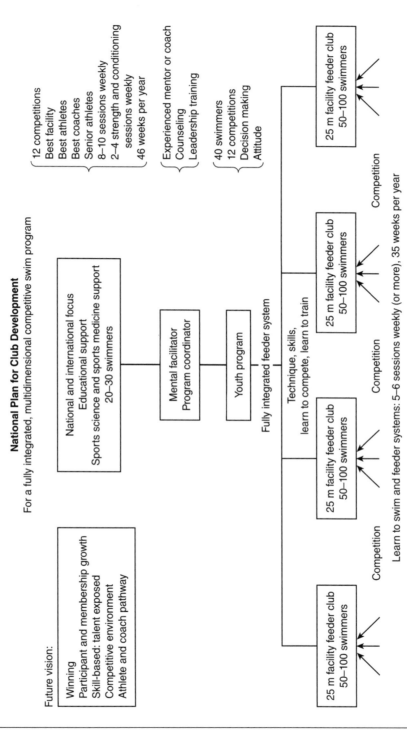

National Plan for Club Development
For a fully integrated, multidimensional competitive swim program

Future vision:

Winning
Participant and membership growth
Skill-based: talent exposed
Competitive environment
Athlete and coach pathway

National and international focus
Educational support
Sports science and sports medicine support
20–30 swimmers

Mental facilitator
Program coordinator

Youth program

Fully integrated feeder system

Technique, skills,
learn to compete, learn to train

12 competitions
Best facility
Best athletes
Best coaches
Senior athletes
8–10 sessions weekly
2–4 strength and conditioning
sessions weekly
46 weeks per year

Experienced mentor or coach
Counseling
Leadership training

40 swimmers
12 competitions
Decision making
Attitude

25 m facility feeder club
50–100 swimmers

25 m facility feeder club
50–100 swimmers

25 m facility feeder club
50–100 swimmers

25 m facility feeder club
50–100 swimmers

Competition

Competition

Competition

Competition

Learn to swim and feeder systems: 5–6 sessions weekly (or more), 35 weeks per year

FIGURE 2.1 National plan for club development for a fully integrated, multidimensional competitive swim program.

4. **A "one size fits all" program.** In this program governed by mass mediocrity, the vast majority of participants tend to overcompete, underprepare, or undertrain and, as a result, underperform. These programs usually have extremely limited pool space and facilities and are driven by recreation, participation, socialization, entertainment, swimming for safety, and the values and priorities of associated aquatic sports. A definite need exists for these programs and variations of them. However, they are not the youth-to-senior transition program for any athlete who wishes for more than very general outcomes.

As an example, if the club or the athlete's objective is repeatable excellence as a senior or youth athlete, then the model in figure 2.1 (page 19) should not be compromised.

SENIOR GROUPING AND TALENT DEVELOPMENT

Senior grouping permits like-minded and similarly talented swimmers to train together for the best results. Put like with like! Athletes of similar commitment, skill, talent, and fitness should train and prepare together and should not be distracted by swimmers of a lower commitment level. The reverse of this theory also applies.

- *Commitment* is the amount of time and effort an individual puts into swimming. It is subjective but easily recognizable by every coach.
- *Skill* is learned, taught, and practiced to perfection. Great programs and coaches emphasize skill enhancement and perfection (turning, starting, finishing, core strength, flexibility, breathing patterns, attendance, and so on) over skill acquisition.
- *Talent* is God given or inherited from parents and is best described as accelerated rate of learning (athlete), accelerated rate of teaching (teacher), and accelerated rate of change and adaptation (coach).
- *Fitness* is applied attitude to skill, talent, mental strength, and work ethic.

See figure 2.2 for an example grid illustrating groupings based on both fitness and talent levels. Following are some guidelines for such a model.

- For the top boxes, do more swim practice rather than less. For the bottom boxes, do less swim practice rather than more.
- Avoid at all costs having the above practice with the below or vice versa.
- Fitness combines attitude and speed.
- All groups (all four boxes) in a systematic and positive learning and teaching environment must possess high skills. (Skill is the non-talent-driven aspects of learning and performance such as turning, starting, breathing patterns, and so on.)

High talent High fitness	Low talent High fitness
Low talent Low fitness	High talent Low fitness

FIGURE 2.2 An example of senior grouping based on swimmers' talent and fitness levels.

- There are no excuses for poorly prepared or poorly developed skills!
- All students learn and practice skills to perfection.
- Talent is 80% or more genetic. Talent was once recognized, but it can also be developed.
- It is always possible to add fitness and speed to efficiency and skill but extremely difficult to do the reverse.
- The lower category is focused on fun (e.g., a recreational social group). These swimmers should be developed separately and accordingly.
- Students categorized in the lower squares will look to surf clubs, school, and swimming-associated sports for health, safety, and entertainment rather than participate in committed, competitive swimming activities.
- Focus on realistic but positive long-term plans when developing athletes; do not confuse this with short-term recognition and success.
- Swimmers and coaches should be superior in every possible way and never give less than 100% in all areas of the sport.

In figure 2.2 athletes in the bottom half should never be expected to prepare and train with athletes in the top half unless compromised results are desired.

As mentioned earlier, every club swimmer must be prepared to continually improve his or her performance from the youth to the senior years. Athletes have no excuse for coming through maturation with anything other than outstanding background preparation and excellent skill-based performance.

I have never met or seen an athlete without talent. However, I have witnessed many programs, athletes, and performances where less-than-ideal skills were evident. Skills should be of the highest level in all matured athletes. Skills (turning, starting, breathing patterns, and so on) are not necessarily seen only in genetically gifted athletes; they can be taught, developed, and learned independent of genetic talent. A golden rule is to never place skill acquisition ahead of skill perfection.

It has been my experience that talent is most often possessed by athletes who learn at an accelerated rate. Similarly, a talented teacher or coach will teach at an accelerated level.

All athletes in a coach's care must have the very highest levels of skill. With this in mind, I strongly believe that work ethic and mental performance can influence the ability of the athlete to transition from youth to senior. Without either, all the skill in the world will not be enough for success.

Table 2.1 on page 22 provides examples of athlete evaluations. Athletes A, B, and C considered their abilities in each of these areas at the beginning of the season and scored themselves between 1 (poor) and 10 (perfect). At the end of the season, the coach also scores each athlete based on their performance throughout the year and tallies up the end result (less than 10 is low; 10 to 19 is average, and 20 to 30 is high). Athlete A originally ranked herself on the low-to-average end but achieved higher results. Athlete B also ranked himself on the lower end and achieved low results. Athlete C ranked herself on the higher end and achieved high results. Athlete C's end result is the desired outcome and is achievable by all. Coaches should ask their athletes

TABLE 2.1 Key Areas for Athlete Development

Rank 10 as perfect and 1 as poor or failing. The end result is out of 30 total.

		Talent • Inherent skill • Learned skill	Work ethos • Able to • Willing to • Able and willing to	Mental strength • Performance under pressure • Attitude • Prepared in adversity	End result
Athlete A	**Athlete evaluation**	4	5	5	14
	Coach evaluation	5	8	7	20
Athlete B	**Athlete evaluation**	5	3	5	13
	Coach evaluation	6	2	4	12
Athlete C	**Athlete evaluation**	8	9	7	24
	Coach evaluation	9	9	8	26

to evaluate themselves at the beginning of the season using this table. Athletes should be brutally truthful or the end result will be far more damaging than the evaluation.

IDENTIFYING A QUALITY SENIOR PROGRAM

The dedicated and committed senior swimmer must find a program that is worth consideration. What attributes identify such a program?

1. The experience, knowledge, and enthusiasm of the head coach and the harmonious working relationship of the coaching and support staff
2. The support program associated with the swim team, including pastoral care and academic, sport science and medicine, strength and conditioning, and personal growth opportunities
3. How the program positively interfaces with and supports the national team effort at the international level

SKILLS DISPLAYED IN A QUALITY SENIOR PROGRAM

A swimmer who is committed to attaining the elite level of competition should require these team essentials when moving to a new club. Every coach can commit to adhering to these principles in order to provide a team environment that will enable his or her swimmers to reach the top level of competition.

1. Individual swimmers and the team maintain self-discipline with no intervention from the coach or staff.

2. The team has great leadership and is organized and the management has a no-fuss approach.

3. Distractions are minimal.

4. The opportunity for quality sleep, rest, and nutrition is available.

5. Low-emotion and low-stress recreation activities exist.

6. The program has an appropriate competition calendar that can be customized to fit the requirements of the individual athlete and the team.

7. Punctuality is expected and respected. Flexibility that doesn't compromise the athlete or the team is allowed. Senior athletes have a more individual approach to training compared with youth-age athletes.

8. All swimmers leave on time for repeats.

9. Turning is executed so that in freestyle and backstroke the time differential from hand entry (last) to feet touch is under 1 second; for individual medley, and in breaststroke and butterfly, the time differential from hand touch to feet touch is under 0.8 second.

10. Swimmers have narrow differentials in time and stroke count from the first half of the race to the second half of the race.

11. Swimmers never fade or get passed in the last 50 meters of any competition. They consistently perform fast with low emotion, are well rehearsed, and perform efficient heats under pressure situations. The program has a 200 or 400 down approach for the 200-meter athletes in preference to a 50-meter up approach.

12. At training, the athletes have a strong kick into and out of turns.

13. Swimmers in the program have fast dolphin kicking and streamlining skills under and above the water.

14. All swimmers are aware of their turning and starting skills [i.e., speed (time) and distance from feet leaving the wall to head surface].

15. All swimmers are capable of achieving their race speed and race stroke rates within two to four strokes (maximum) from a start or turn.

16. The coach constantly provides stroke rate evaluations, in particular for sprint (50, 100, and 200) swimmers.

17. In all turns and, more importantly, finishes, finger-tip touches (not the palms of the hands) are used. Breaststroke and butterfly performances can display reduced and changing techniques at slow speed (it is advisable to avoid this in heat and semifinal situations); however, poor skills are never displayed at any speed.

18. Finishes are accelerated but hold stroke length.

19. In freestyle, breaststroke, and butterfly, all athletes breathe (head up) after they touch the wall.

20. Poor training skills equal poor race pace results—if it has not been consistently achieved in training (and at a higher level than expected), then it most certainly

will not be achieved under pressure in competition. This is understood by the team and coaching staff and is continually and positively reinforced at practice.

21. There is a sense of urgency and athletes and staff understand
    - precision under pressure,
    - preparation under pressure,
    - accuracy under pressure, and
    - the difference between speed and effort and efficiency.

22. Every swimmer is aware of their individual maximum heart rate (not by any formula but by accurate and repeated measurements in maximum training sets).

23. The training environment is happy and challenging.

24. The coach has an open mind and is creative and innovative. The athletes are (without indulging and pampering) made to feel special. The coach is highly energetic and a great psychologist.

25. All athletes know their 10 best performances, heats, and finals, and every athlete has race-day schedules for warm-up and state of readiness. Finals are won by the clinical execution of easy, unemotional, well-rehearsed, well-planned, and flawless heat and semifinal performances. Apart from World Long Course and the Olympics, every competition is in itself a preparation for a higher form of competition.

BODY AWARENESS IN A QUALITY SENIOR PROGRAM

In addition to training in a strong club environment, senior athletes must become aware of their individual needs to train and perform at their best. Athletes must be able to determine when they are responding well to increased high-intensity training and when they need to introduce more rest and recovery. Much of this can be measured.

Senior athletes who are pursuing small improvements in speed performance certainly need to be aware of how the body is responding to the training stimulus. Given that they usually have a skill and aerobic background, senior athletes will physically respond much more quickly to any previously exposed training zones and energy systems. This is a fantastic advantage of becoming a senior athlete.

However, like any high-performance machine, the body requires precision monitoring, tuning, and maintenance. The most significant and measurable applied performance improvements of the recent coaching era have come, I believe, from increased coaching knowledge regarding individual recovery (physical and mental) skills. This vastly improved knowledge and experience has greatly assisted the coaches who are willing to substantially increase the volume of applied and specific race speed and race pace training in workouts and practice sessions.

Increased recovery and increased race pace and speed training have improved performances tremendously. Just as high-performance engines and machines need monitoring gauges to scientifically guide and govern stress, wear, and tear, so do senior athletes who are going to push the boundaries of physical and mental limits.

Our simplest gauges in sport tend to be nutrition (blood profiles), lactates, heart rates, and the athlete's perceived exertion and feelings of readiness.

Here is a great training set that produces readings on race speed, race pace, breathing patterns, athlete readiness, and maximum heart rate and lactate measurements. It can also test recovery skills and evaluations.

A total of 8 sets of 4 × 50

6 × (4 × 50 – 3 @ 1:00 @ 200 race pace average; 1 @ 1:30 dive @ 200 race pace average less 1.5 seconds). Measure speed, stroke rate, breathing patterns, stroke length, lactate, and heart rate after the fourth and sixth sets.

2 × (4 × 50 – dive @ 1:30 @ max speed and effort). Measure lactate and heart rate after each set. This should provide information on maximum lactate and heart rate. When lactate measurement isn't available, measure all of the other indicators.

The athlete should be reasonably fresh to do this workout, and it should be followed by a recovery workout in the next workout or practice. This workout is a great training set and can be repeated several times. The following are suggested variations.

1. Complete the last two sets of 50s as a secondary lactate removal set done in either kick or swim—perhaps even pull.

    2 × (4 × 50 @ 1:30; 1 @ 200 race pace average, 1 @ plus 2 seconds, 1 @ plus 4 seconds, 1 @ plus 6 seconds over race pace average)

2. During tapering, the set can be modified by doing fewer sets, or fewer race pace repeats, or both.

    6 × (4 × 50; 3 @ 1:00 @ race pace, 1 @ 1:30 recovery)

This set can be manipulated many ways to suit the needs of the athlete or the periodization cycle of the season or training phase. The senior athlete will more than likely require more rest and adaptation time and undergo a significantly longer period of race preparation than youth and age group swimmers. Only individual experience and logical, systematic experimentation can be applied to this situation.

CHANGES IN MOTIVATION FROM YOUTH TO SENIOR LEVELS

As athletes reach maturation and look toward a journey as a senior athlete, their priorities change significantly. The days of a carefree age-group athlete having fun and simply enjoying their sport may change over the next few years. They may start comparing their competitive swimming lifestyle with the lifestyles of their nonsporting or nonswimming friends. Athletes must have a clearly identified pathway that includes recognizable and tangible benefits.

These benefits may appear to the athlete in many forms, and each athlete may view and value them differently. It is crucial that a coach understand the needs, motives, and incentives of the individual. The athlete is in total control, and the coach provides choices and advice. For some athletes, this may be the first and most significant independent decision and period of change they have dealt with. The coach must provide leadership in this situation.

The team goal can be paramount, but coaches must clearly understand and accept that each individual has needs, dreams, and desires that produce strong motives. The team structure must allow for and promote this, whether it is a team or individual effort.

Motives, once identified, facilitate and create drives. The stronger the drive, the more likely the athlete has the ability required to achieve success. The drive within the individual will then determine positive performance and lifestyle behaviors. The coach must understand the mind and heart of the athlete. The coach must be accepting of the needs, motives, incentives, and behaviors of the athlete and create an environment where these will grow in a team concept. The coach must be able to positively influence the individual attributes of every athlete in their care.

A major change in coaching psychology occurs between the precocious age-grouper and youth athlete and the senior swimmer. Every athlete is an experience of one. In most situations, the youth-age athlete enjoys the increased affiliation and acceptance by their peer group within the team and the coaching staff. This affiliation and the strong need for excellence in performance and skill become exceptionally strong motivators.

Youth-age athletes are also strongly driven by the stress and excitement of both training and competition. This occurs over time with influence by the coaching staff, the environment, and peer group athletes. These incentives are very different from the participation, recreation, and social involvement associated with age-group swimming. Success for the team and individual is always an important factor, but at the youth age it is less significant.

For the adolescent athlete, independence becomes more of an incentive and a need. From approximately 16 to 20 years of age, and to some degree depending on the social and performance background of the individual, an athlete's needs, motives, drives, and incentives will almost certainly change.

The senior swimmer will look more toward success that will bring financial gain and independence. Enthusiasm for excellence as an incentive must be carried over from the youth ages. Each senior athlete must have strong, recognizable desires to be the best that they can be in terms of total development. Winning can be part of that, but it must be realistic. Winning is being the best that one can be and significantly contributing to a team success through one's performance. Thus, there is an "I" in "TEAM":

(T)ogether
(E)ach
(I)ndividual
(A)chieves
(M)ore

This is an exceptionally strong incentive for the senior athlete, whereas the youth athlete in most cases thinks only in terms of personal outcomes (i.e., "me" and "mine").

PATHWAY TO THE PODIUM IN NATIONAL AND INTERNATIONAL COMPETITION

Bridging the gap between youth and senior swimming can be a challenge. A gap analysis establishes with utmost honesty exactly what an athlete's current situation is and exactly where, how, and more importantly when the athlete will achieve the desired outcome. It is then simply a matter of establishing the processes (training, competition, lifestyles, strength, nutrition, and so on) that need to be systematically put in place to achieve this outcome. Coaches should have a backup plan and put a timeline on every aspect of the plan.

Tables 2.2 (page 28) and 2.3 (page 29) are examples of a pathway from youth level to senior level for high-performance swimming. A pathway indicates the time results that are necessary to compete at a specific level; these are targets to be reached if an athlete is on the path to compete at that particular level. However, this pathway can be manipulated for a higher or lower standard to suit the individual. If it is to be a "pathway to podium" or national to international pathway, targets could include a top three at world championships, the Olympics, or the World Long Course. If the pathway is for a less-talented athlete, the top 25 in world rankings column could be changed to be the top 40. I have purposely left out the European Open Championships and focused this youth-to-senior pathway on the world level, and as such European success can and will occur as a byproduct of this clearly directed performance pathway. As a result, for instance, Britain achieved European senior champions and European junior champions en route to a much-improved world-level result. This occurred for Britain in what could be described as the first time in the modern era of world swimming (i.e., the past 30 to 40 years).

This pathway can be modified to suit any situation and athlete. It is first a pathway from youth to senior; a simple upgrade makes it a pathway to the podium. This gives the athlete clear indications of achievable pathways. I have purposely selected an alternative pathway. International point score equivalents may be added to this pathway, but not used a substitution, because ranking standards are far superior indicators. The only challenge remaining is to identify winning times in 2016 (one must think ahead) and prepare the 16- and 18-year-olds with a pathway to winning performances. The pathway can be modified to meet the needs of a particular team. For example, a team may need to create a pathway with qualifying and placing time standards for the state high school meet, sectional club championship, or university Division I, II, or III championship meets.

My experience, research, and observations confirm that three distinct windows of opportunity exist during which one can influence real change in an athlete's development in swimming:

1. **6 to 10 years of age:** skill acquisition and enhancement
2. **Maturation (onset):** aerobic and technique essential for skill consolidation and success in endurance events
3. **Approximately 18 years of age (completion of major growth):** achievement of real speed and sprint capabilities

TABLE 2.2 European Guideline Evaluation Times for Males

Males	16 and under	17–18 years	19–20 years	21–22 (23) years	Top 16 WR	FINA	Eighth into WLC final 2007	Variances
50 FS	0:24.41	0:23.53	0:23.13	0:22.45	0:22.41	0:22.35	0:22.31	
100 FS	0:53.63	0:51.36	0:50.95	0:49.56	0:49.18	0:49.23	0:48.87	
200 FS	1:57.00	1:52.64	1:52.53	1:48.77	1:48.29	1:48.72	1:48.47	
400 FS	4:08.23	3:58.70	3:58.01	3:51.04	3:48.56	3:49.96	3:48.72	
1500 FS	6:28.82	15:44.98	15:45.12	15:15.46	15:09.12	15:13.16	15:02.16	
100 BF	0:57.83	0:55.47	0:54.71	0:53.21	0:53.01	0:52.86	0:52.26	
200 BF	2:09.06	2:02.87	2:01.79	1:58.64	1:57.47	1:57.67	1:56.47	
100 BK	1:00.51	0:58.17	0:57.07	0:55.50	0:54.87	0:55.14	0:54.92	
200 BK	2:10.55	2:05.64	2:03.91	2:00.70	1:59.63	1:59.72	1:59.52	
100 BR	1:06.95	1:03.91	1:03.72	1:01.65	1:01.32	1:01.57	1:01.11	
200 BR	2:25.31	2:19.48	2:18.37	2:14.37	2:13.12	2:13.69	2:12.44	
200 IM	2:12.28	2:07.11	2:05.65	2:02.40	2:01.55	2:01.40	2:00.53	
400 IM	4:40.68	4:31.08	4:27.44	4:21.13	4:18.20	4:18.40	4:17.73	

	EYOF QT eighth average	EJC QT eighth average	FINA B times	Top 25 WR (2 per nation)	Top 16 WR (2 per nation)	FINA A times	Eighth into WLC final 2007	
Numbers								
Names								

FS = freestyle; BF = butterfly; BK = backstroke; BR = breaststroke; IM = individual medley; EJC QT = European Junior Championships qualifying times; EYOF QT = European Youth Olympics qualifying times; FINA = qualifying time A to enter; FINA A times= qualifying times above A that permit entry; FINA B times = qualifying times below A that may permit entry; WR = world rank; WLC = World Long Course. All world rankings are based on annual world ranking.

6 to 10 Years of Age   The first window of opportunity occurs from 6 to 10 years of age. During this time, core skill behaviors and habits can be positively patterned and retained in a young person's memory. Core skills, habits, and techniques learned well or poorly at this age will more than likely remain with the child athlete throughout their career. Memory patterns practiced continually at this age become embedded and are very difficult to alter. At this age, athletes should learn skills extremely well so that they do not need to be retrained later on. For long-term development, retaining is highly preferable to retraining. This is why it is so important that the athlete and

TABLE 2.3 **European Guideline Evaluation Times for Females**

Females	14 and under	15–16 years	17–18 years	19–20 (21) years	Top 16 WR	FINA A	Eighth into WLC final 2007	Variances
50 FS	0:27.51	0:26.73	0:26.32	0:25.61	0:25.27	0:25.43	0:25.10	
100 FS	0:59.92	0:57.65	0:57.17	0:55.79	0:55.23	0:55.24	0:54.61	
200 FS	2:10.43	2:05.00	2:03.47	2:00.16	1:59.39	1:59.29	1:58.71	
400 FS	4:32.65	4:22.06	4:20.05	4:13.77	4:10.48	4:11.26	4:08.38	
800 FS	9:21.60	8:56.67	8:54.04	8:41.43	8:36.30	8:35.98	8:31.53	
100 BF	1:04.78	1:02.47	1:01.43	0:59.43	0:59.02	0:59.35	0:58.82	
200 BF	2:21.86	2:18.06	2:15.42	2:11.68	2:09.71	2:10.84	2:09.21	
100 BK	1:07.41	1:04.73	1:03.86	1:02.26	1:01.56	1:01.70	1:01.23	
200 BK	2:23.82	2:20.39	2:17.38	2:13.34	2:12.47	2:12.73	2:11.20	
100 BR	1:15.35	1:12.37	1:11.43	1:09.67	1:08.73	1:09.01	1:08.49	
200 BR	2:41.50	2:35.98	2:33.40	2:30.19	2:28.46	2:28.21	2:27.62	
200 IM	2:27.05	2:21.29	2:19.97	2:16.05	2:15.22	2:15.27	2:15.08	
400 IM	5:08.99	4:58.63	4:55.06	4:46.51	4:44.04	4:45.08	4:44.34	

	EYOF QT eighth average	EJC QT eighth average	FINA B times	Top 25 WR (2 per nation)	Top 16 WR (2 per nation)	FINA A times	Eighth into WLC final 2007	
Numbers								
Names								

FS = freestyle; BF = butterfly; BK = backstroke; BR = breaststroke; IM = individual medley; EJC QT = European Junior Championships qualifying times; EYOF QT = European Youth Olympics qualifying times; FINA = qualifying time A to enter; FINA A times= qualifying times above A that permit entry; FINA B times = qualifying times below A that may permit entry; WR = world rank; WLC = World Long Course. All world rankings are based on annual world ranking.

parents select a learn-to-swim and junior squad swim program in which the staff is capable and quality is far more important than quantity.

Maturation   The second influential period in an athlete's long term-development is maturation. Given that the student has practiced exceptionally good, well-supervised skill enhancement for some 4 to 6 years, maturation is the time for consolidation and aerobic development. A more influential and significant approach to developing core skills (which commenced at the learn-to-swim level) and strength and conditioning is required. I have found that a top-and-tail approach works best. In this approach, at maturation the swimmer is exposed to considerable and appropriate aerobic development without ignoring raw speed. Aerobic training at maturation allows the body to adapt and adjust to this stimulus.

Aerobic swimming is moderate-effort swimming repeats over all distances during which the athlete uses perfect technique and skills. This type of training should be in all strokes where technique is never exposed to failure from intensive training sets. Twenty- and 25-meter training competitions should be included in practice, provided that stroke length and technique controls are put in place so it does not become a matter of how fast the swimmer can windmill their arms. Always compete in the 50-meter butterfly to prevent windmilling and to promote and develop underwater dolphin kick skills. This is especially valuable in short-course 50-meter butterfly.

Maturation is a crucial stage for every swimmer who wishes to enjoy a career in the 200-meter and up events. If the coach and athlete fail to take advantage of this window, more often than not the swimmer will need to focus on speed and sprint events rather than endurance-based events during the third age window, around 18 years of age.

Approximately 18 Years of Age The third level of opportunity occurs at approximately 18 years of age. At this age, a proper strength program will enable the swimmer to make considerable strength gains that will result in improved speed. This period also permits more specialization of events.

Exceptions to this model will occur, but I have found that the exceptions can suffer a short life span and slow rate of improvement after an initial period that may have been successful.

Should all three stages be addressed, there is no valid reason—apart from individual opportunity and motivations—why small and continued improvements in speed performance cannot be achieved well into the athlete's thirties.

Statistical analysis shows that, for the majority of athletes with successful performances (winning and podium) at the Olympics, 22 years is an extremely significant age. Athletes who achieve podium success after age 22 likely have tasted victory at this level before or at age 22. Obviously, the women's endurance events (400 individual medley and 800 freestyle) provide opportunities at a much younger age.

A difference exists between fitness-based speed and speed based on technique and skill; both are required for success as a senior athlete. Speed that is identified and measured before 17 to 19 years of age is primarily attributable to technique and the athlete's white fibers (fast-twitch fibers that enable the muscle to fire rapidly). Speed further developed after 18 to 19 years of age can usually be attributed to enhanced skill and technique, white fibers, and training and coaching.

A well-prepared and systematically developed athlete possesses the ability to transfer stroke efficiency across all speeds. In this regard, the athlete has the ability to change gears (speeds) while maintaining efficiency.

Figure 2.3 shows an assumed journey of a 13-year-old female swimmer recording a time of 58.5 and how quickly the swimmer should advance to be on a pathway to the podium. One would expect at least a 2.5-second improvement in the first 6 years and another 2.5-second improvement in the next 3 years to attain a 5-second improvement over 9 years. This improvement would put the athlete at the podium level.

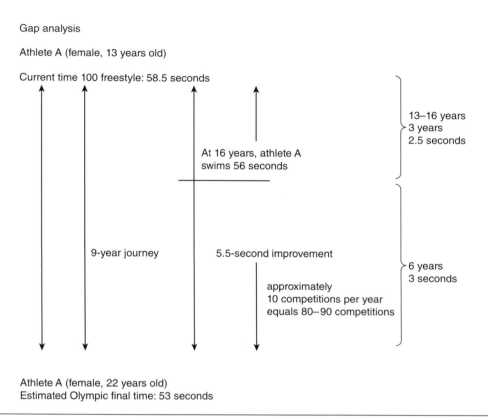

Gap analysis

Athlete A (female, 13 years old)

Current time 100 freestyle: 58.5 seconds

At 16 years, athlete A
swims 56 seconds

13–16 years
3 years
2.5 seconds

9-year journey

5.5-second improvement

approximately
10 competitions per year
equals 80–90 competitions

6 years
3 seconds

Athlete A (female, 22 years old)
Estimated Olympic final time: 53 seconds

FIGURE 2.3   Long-term athlete career and personal growth chart.

In another situation, after only 3 years the swimmer has achieved an improvement of 3 seconds. This leaves 6 more years to achieve an improvement of only 3 seconds. If approximately 8 competitions are held per year for 6 years, the athlete has approximately 40 to 48 competitions to improve approximately 3 seconds in order to reach an Olympic final or podium result.

Olympic talent, whether individual or team, can be identified 6 years out from an Olympics. This is halfway between the earlier Olympic cycle and the targeted Olympics. Figures 2.4 to 2.7 beginning on page 32 present detailed statistics regarding identification, completed in 2006, that look at country and event opportunities for 2012.

This is further evaluated by identifying 16- to 19-year-old athletes per event and country who achieved semifinal status or top 16 world rankings at the Beijing Olympics. This is followed up by studying world rankings to confirm how often an athlete competes within 2% of this world ranking zone in the immediate 4-year cycle and leading into the next Olympics with this in mind.

The 2004 British Olympic training camps in Cyprus proved highly successful. Even though she was not on the team, 2008 Olympic dual gold medalist Rebecca Adlington attended the camps to experience an Olympic preparation opportunity and trained with current representative Rebecca Cooke and coach Stephen Hill. Adlington's coach, Bill Furniss, was on the team. The lesson was to use this gap analysis to identify and provide for the needs of the athlete and coach.

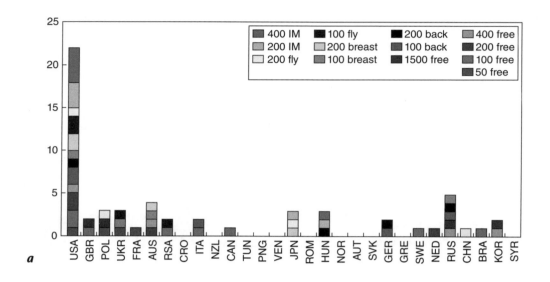

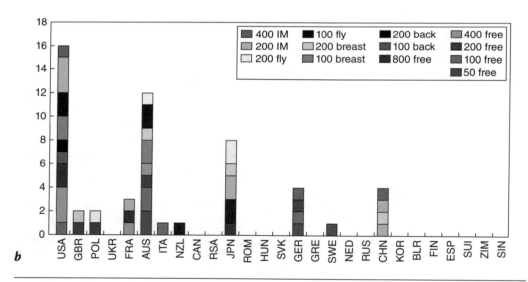

FIGURE 2.4 Top four world rankings in 2006: *(a)* male; *(b)* female.

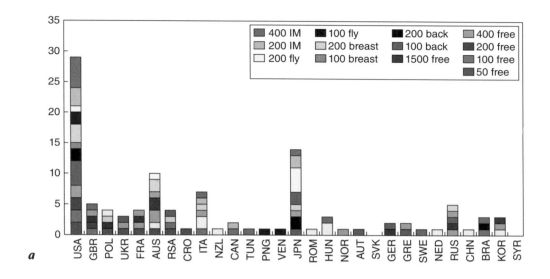

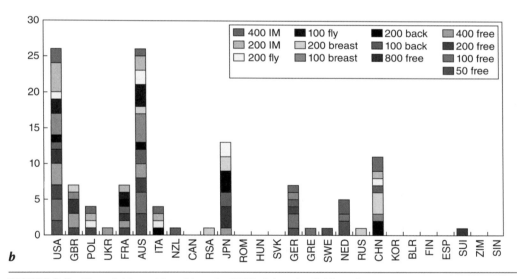

FIGURE 2.5 Top eight world rankings in 2006: *(a)* male; *(b)* female.

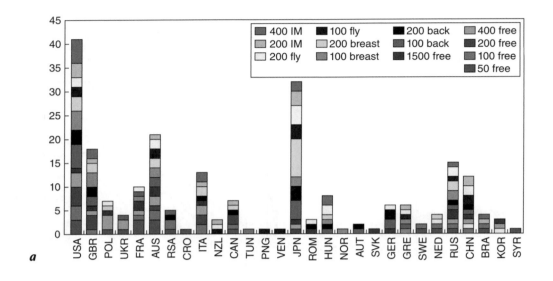

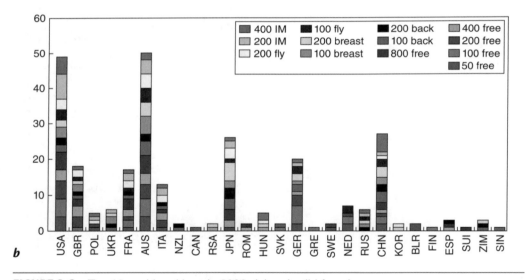

FIGURE 2.6 Top 16 world rankings in 2006: *(a)* male; *(b)* female.

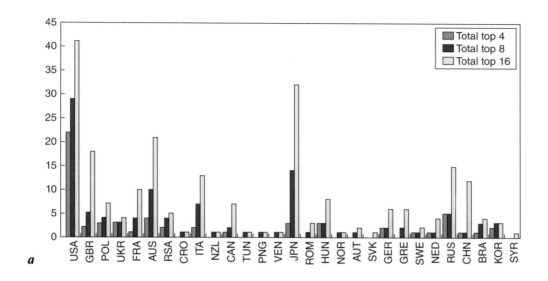

a

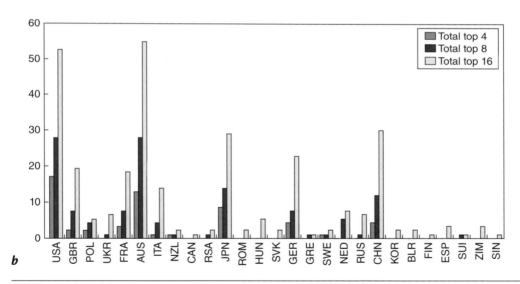

b

FIGURE 2.7   Top 4, 8, and 16 world rankings in 2006: *(a)* male; *(b)* female.

To determining who has a reasonable chance to be on an Olympic team, 6 years out from the Olympics coaches identify and convert (using figures 2.4 through 2.7) opportunities, athletes, and events into reality. It is then a matter of converting youth athletes to senior athletes by providing opportunity and support. This process converts potential into podium and places reality ahead of hope. I have successfully repeated this many times in my coaching career and have been able to seize the moment by carefully planning 6 years in advance.

A country's future potential in swimming performance can be identified by observing whether the country's second or third entry in any Olympic event is 19 years of age or younger and makes a semifinal at the World Long Course level. This is a clear indication, especially if it happens en masse, that the athlete and country will be a major threat at the next Olympics. This also applies to relay makeup. This model and gap analysis can be applied to any athlete or team in any event or competition.

NUTRITION AND STRENGTH AND CONDITIONING TESTING FROM YOUTH TO SENIOR LEVELS

Proper nutrition provides the athlete with an adequate supply of energy to perform the task at hand and enables the athlete to recover sufficiently after exercise. To enable their athletes, every coach should be aware of the best and latest nutritional research.

In addition to promoting proper nutrition, coaches should engage the athlete mentally and physically through strength and conditioning testing. The coach should select two or three (or more if desired) exercises (two upper-body exercises and one lower-body exercise) that are controllable and accurately measure total weight lifted in a set number of repetitions in a given period of time. For example, 12 bench press repetitions in 1 minute 30 seconds at 60 kilograms equals 720 kilograms of total weight. The total weight lifted in that test, by a swimmer with a body weight of 80 kilograms, results in a power ratio of 9 (720 divided by 80).

Improvement can be measured by

1. improvement in strength,
2. loss of body weight (better nutrition), or
3. a combination of both.

This test can also be completed on a swim bench. The athlete uses maximum effort on 10 butterfly pulls; the result is divided by body weight. In addition, this test can be performed while swimming by utilizing power racks using time, stroke rate, and resistance with body weight ratio. Swimmers can then be ranked (only using ratio) using these figures. At the peak of the season and before taper and race preparation, a competition can be conducted within the team and awards (e.g., Team Ironman award or Team Male Gladiator award) for best ratios on combined exercise scores can be presented. This is a very positive way of having all athletes work on power per unit of body weight. These awards would be highly recognized, rewarded, and treasured.

I have also presented an Excalibur award to the athlete or athletes who improved the most. More often than not this goes to a new youth swimmer who has room for improvement or an older senior high achiever who had lost their way a little but found their way back to mental and physical strength.

This mental and physical testing occurs at the peak of land-based evaluations (over a one-week period) toward the end of the strength and conditioning phase. The athlete is tested across all practiced strength and conditioning exercises. The highlight for my team is usually a chin-up test of 10 sets of 10 full chin-ups in 4 minutes. The concept is that the swimmer must be an athlete first and a swimmer second at this stage of preparation. Coaches and athletes should build mental strength and superiority on land before introducing this aspect to the pool. This process also promotes technique-based speed in preference to, but as well as, fitness-based speed.

TIPS FOR COACHING YOUTH ATHLETES TO SENIOR ATHLETES

Every coach will be more effective if they adopt the following tips consistently and persistently.

1. Praise the athlete and criticize the fault or flaw. Allow and encourage ownership and decision making.
2. Coach the person. Train the event. Develop the skills. Provide leadership and opportunity.
3. Redirect when necessary.
4. Simplified, a coach trains age-group and youth athletes; in addition, they coach senior athletes.

These tips cannot always be executed in age-group and youth programs, but they are necessary in open and senior group situations.

LEADERSHIP FROM YOUTH TO SENIOR LEVELS

Leadership is earned and deserved; it is never given. It can be successfully developed to differing degrees in every athlete on every team. A great author, Napoleon Hill, once wrote, "You must train the fitness of your mind to match the fitness of your body" (Hill, 1928). I have always struggled to understand this because I have always believed, probably due to my perceived disadvantaged roots, that quite the opposite is true; that is, you must train the fitness of your body to match the fitness of your mind.

I don't want to be arrogant, but I like to believe that I am mentally the strongest person I have ever known. I always attempt to pass this on as a skill to all athletes and staff that I work with in business, family, and sport. The behavior of athletes and staff is absolutely essential in sustaining the key aspect of a winning culture. In

---

Something to Think About Now! The inconvenience of status quo in the past has to be outweighed by the convenience of change for the future if winning is to be the outcome.

---

today's sporting world, we continue to observe an era of athlete advisory groups, athlete empowerment, key performance indicators, accountability and responsibility, branding and sponsors, athlete managers, and focused strategic planning and direction.

Some degree of leadership is required by every staff and team member. A greater amount of leadership is required of the actual team leader. The team leader must listen to consensus, negotiation, and consultation, but only they can make the final decision. Disciplined decision making is of little consequence unless it is accompanied by accountability by all parties. Everyone must continually develop trust and respect and share the responsibility of leadership.

In every single team that I have worked with, the team is divided as shown in figure 2.8. The goal is to move the middle 40% of the team up so that 60 to 70% of the total team has a "will win" approach. This is not at all easy because the pressure and temptation is to drop 1% to the 40% who can't.

Moving this 40% up requires great organization, effective and efficient management, and really great leadership. If leadership can be sold to the youth athletes when they join the team, you likely can reduce the bottom 40% to 30% and move the middle 40% up to join the top 20%. It is possible but extremely challenging, and the determining factor is whether individual in the growth group buy into leadership. Culture and behaviors are the keys to this change. Learning is change, and change is education.

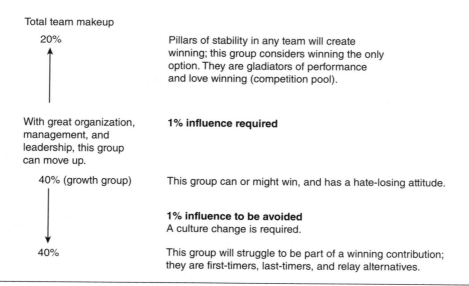

FIGURE 2.8 Total team makeup.

WINNING FROM YOUTH TO SENIOR LEVELS

Winners don't have to be number one in the competition, but this should always be the goal. Winners train and compete at their highest effort. When every team member is a winner, the environment produces champions. I believe that a winner displays the following characteristics.

- A winner takes responsibility for their own performance and doesn't make excuses. Remember, a reason is an excuse and no excuse is a reason.
- A winner welcomes obstacles and setbacks as challenges rather than fears them as barriers.
- A winner competes with pride, intensity, and toughness every time the situation calls for it, not just when circumstances are ideal.
- A winner uses competition and pressure to their advantage rather than as a distraction.
- A winner doesn't necessarily finish first, but they get the best out of themselves in an effort to be first. You can win and not be a winner.
- A winner reacts to a disappointing performance with greater determination the next time rather than with shattered confidence and loss of enthusiasm.
- A winner leads with action and leadership.
- A winner makes decisions with precision and accuracy.
- A winner understands that asking for help is a strength.

A winner doesn't accept a bad performance; they know that they can do better and continue to try to do it. If an athlete wants to consistently be a winner and have repeatable excellence, they will give these guidelines some serious thought and in the future will try to correct anything that negatively influences their performance.

The following is true of successful people:

- They practice to be able to do their absolute best under the worst possible conditions.
- They practice and race well some of the time. Great athletes practice and race great all of the time.
- They do not rely on God-given talent alone, but add self-discipline and attitude to create a greater and more complete athlete.
- They are not the most talented, but are the best-prepared talent.
- They are not those with the will to win, but rather are those with the will to prepare to win.
- They are always enthusiastic.
- They are confident of giving their best in competition because they consistently give their best in practice.
- They can seize the moment.

- They do not accept the status quo.
- They remain focused on the job at hand and are never distracted.

A coach should ask the developing youth athletes who are entering the senior squad to confidentially answer in writing the following questions:

1. Who is the greatest athlete in any sport that you know of?
2. Who is the very best swimmer that you have seen or know of?
3. Who is the athlete who will cause you the greatest challenge this season or year?
4. Who is the person you most admire in any field of endeavor?

The athletes who wrote down their own name four times can likely become winners. A coach will need to do some serious work with the others. Eventually, but sooner rather than later, a coach will have to teach the athlete to beat a serial winner if they are of the caliber and talent. Very few coaches are capable of teaching winning! It must start at the youth level before the athlete breaks into international open competition or the more gentle national market.

The coach should then ask the athletes who, other than themselves, is the toughest, most challenging athlete they will compete against this year. Whoever they name, the coach should then ask, "If I asked that athlete who their biggest challenger would be, would that person name you?" If the answer is no, a problem exists with the athlete's ability to win. The information gleaned from this exercise will help the coach form a winning strategy to help the swimmers on the team.

When training winning, coaches should put in place a three–two–one strategy. In this strategy, the athlete competes in three events at their level of competency. They should come in the top three placings and, as such, should be open to correction and advice regarding their execution of the events. Then, the athlete competes in two events that are below their level of competency. In these events, the coach challenges them to take risks and learn (e.g., swim too fast or too slow early in the race, practice race pace for a longer event, change stroke ratings, and so on) but still expects winning results rather than a strategic winning performance. Finally, the coach enters the athlete in one event in which the athlete faces unwinnable odds. In this situation, the coach offers the athlete unconditional support and the athlete learns that the coach is with them in their toughest and most demanding situation. Every youth and senior athlete has a right to be challenged with a winning performance, even if it is not a winning result. This is where both coach and athlete learn the vital lessons about the individual before any form of rationalization is allowed to take place. The coach should ask, "Am I the best person to coach this individual athlete?" and should not rationalize the answer.

CHANGES IN PHYSICAL PREPARATION FROM YOUTH TO SENIOR LEVELS

The youth swimmer moving on to senior swimming should recognize the changes in the intensity of the training and the commitment level required. The following testing and tips can benefit both coach and swimmer moving to senior swimming.

Testing for Youth to Senior Swimmers

Minimum and maximum refer to minimum stroke count and effort and maximum speed.

1. Add the time and stroke count together. Then try to reduce this value by manipulating balance by alternating speed or stroke length or both. The objective is efficiency.

2. Try doing the same by completing 12 × 50, commencing personal best + 12 seconds, and reducing by 1 second per 50. Then identify the inefficient speed or breakdown of either value and incorporate this value into the training load. This covers all training zones, energy systems, and race pace and speeds.

3. Move this forward using the process in figure 2.9. This is best done by adding the 50s from test 2 together: 12 + 11, 10 + 9, and so on; speed + stroke + heart rate for the 100-meter test as an example only. Then try to reduce. The test can be extended to 200 meters as well.

4. Once again, this can be extended by adding the lactate value or replacing heart rate with a lactate value. One can also replace heart rate or lactate with stroke rate.

FIGURE 2.9   The addition of heart rate to the minimum and maximum efficiency test.

All of these tests provide a comprehensive athlete profile that can be graphed and regularly tested against to check recovery and improvements in performance and adaptation. By adding any combination, one can create a comparison that identifies areas where improvement is required or where breakdowns in efficiency or fitness or both are causing problems or failure in another area (figure 2.10).

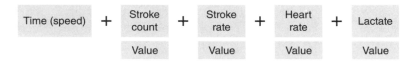

FIGURE 2.10   The addition of stroke rate and lactate to the minimum and maximum efficiency test.

5. 7 × 200 step test incorporating the above values.

6. Individual checking speeds (for more information on this subject, see my book, *Champion Swim Training*, published by Human Kinetics in 2003).

7. To improve the underwater dolphin kick, swimmers should always compete in the 50-meter butterfly in minor meets (short course especially). Swimmers should reduce stroke and speed using the underwater dolphin kick variances.

12 Tips for Youth Swimmers Moving to the Senior Level

Following are tips for youth swimmers who are moving on to the senior level.

1. Choose the program and coach that are right for you. Consider all options and respect your talent. Be happy in your choice and your environment.

2. Do not seek easy options, exceptions to team guidelines and protocols, or compromise.

3. Be prepared to commit to a team approach and unconditionally support the team objectives.

4. Develop the identified weakness of the team so that they become your personal strengths. Be the most skilled swimmer in any pool at any time.

5. Commit to a healthy lifestyle outside of the pool. Love your family and be happy. Make the environment work for you, not against you.

6. Pursue and develop personal leadership skills. Do not be distracted, and control your emotions.

7. Increase your percentage of race speed and race pace while not ignoring other training zones and energy systems. Improve your recovery techniques.

8. Pursue repeatable excellence in all that you do.

9. Be punctual and work on skill refinement outside of normal training hours.

10. Be superior in every possible way and respect your teammates and opposition.

11. Improve or eliminate your weaknesses and maintain your strengths.

12. Be accountable and responsible. Give and receive trust and respect it. Know your job. Competition is just another day at the office.

PREPARING FOR A QUALITY SENIOR PROGRAM

Preparation is, without question, the most significant area of progressive development and change in the last 8 to 10 years of competitive swimming. Recovery skills, both physical and mental, have advanced tremendously in water workouts, in weekly training cycles, and on land. This does not mean that shortcuts exist. Some continue to train with easy and enjoyable processes that have devastating outcomes.

Training sets for the senior swimmer need to focus on race- and competition-specific adaptations. In many cases, this means moving away from the single-focus sets that the athlete performed as an older age-grouper and developing youth athlete. Specificity of training stimulus becomes a major emphasis, which is a change from the general conditioning and background work the athlete completed during longer periods of stimulus before this period. Coaches must learn to read the athlete and differentiate options of training and energy zones and training speeds to best suit the individual.

Without going into too much detail, we now have complex training sets, lactate removal sets, secondary sets, and lactate removal sets in kick and swim along with combination sets. As an example, how many individual and team workouts should a coach design that contain three training speeds and two energy systems followed by a secondary kick removal set? This is quite common now and helps the senior and youth athlete accomplish more in a weekly cycle and provides the advantage of quality recovery. The advance of race stroke rate through tethered and speed assisted swimming are great tools in a smooth transition from youth to open.

Where the youth swimmer once heard the terms fast, easy, and moderate, they now hear much more descriptive terms such as beats below maximum heart rate, race stroke, rate differentials of 50, 100 and 200, lactates, and so on. The youth swimmer must know and understand these terms before moving to the senior ranks. In these ranks, sprint and speed sets are accurately governed by stroke rates and endurance-based sets are governed by heart rates. Lactates can cover both when required. One should take into account the improved and increased percentage per total volume of race speed and race pace work.

A coach must ask, "What have I done differently this year that is an improvement on last year, and how will I move the program forward next year using the same philosophy?" A coach should not accept the level that any athlete is prepared to give at any point in time if it is not in line with agreed outcomes. Will a coach be a better coach tomorrow because of what he or she did or did not do today? The coach is fully responsible for ensuring that the athlete rises to the realistic expectations of the coach and program in each practice and competition and is totally responsible for the training, competition and training processes, behaviors, performances, attitudes, activities, and all other actions of the athletes in his or her care.

The winning leadership of the head coach and team staff drives the winning and high-performance culture and strategies of the program and club and the winning attitudes of the athletes. This is an enormous benefit for the emerging senior athlete.

Eventually, a coach must ask, "Of the total number of athletes I have coached, how many have I successfully taken on the complete journey?" At the conclusion of an athlete's career, both the coach and the athlete must know unconditionally, without reservation or rationalization, that the athlete achieved their maximum potential in every measurable area.

CONCLUSION

This chapter covers some of the significant areas that can positively influence athletes facing the challenge of transitioning from youth to senior. This transition can be complicated and challenging because it often coincides with the transition from national to international and with changes in academic and lifestyle situations. With great management, instinctive coaching, and knowledge of coaching art and science, this transition should be an outstanding and rewarding journey of discovery and opportunity for both athlete and coach.

Given that all things are equal and that the right program, coach, and club have been identified, the major challenge for the youth swimmer to successfully convert to the senior level will be precise and accurate decision making under pressure with minimal intervention from the coach. Every athlete will be an experience of one.

3

Putting the *We* in Team

Jack Bauerle

I have been extremely fortunate over the years to have been a part of many very good teams and some great ones. The difference between the two was not necessarily how they performed at the end of the year but rather how they performed every day during the year. We all know that the level of success achieved at a championship event is earned in the many days, months, and sometimes years preceding the meet. Swimming is classified as an individual sport, which I think is accurate, because when the starting gun goes off, eight swimmers in eight lanes separated by lane lines race to turn off the clock as fast as possible and beat as many other swimmers as they can in the process. Although swimming is an individual sport by definition at race time, all the time spent training and preparing leading up to the race is very team oriented. The quality and effort in the sets required in training are the result of team commitment. The strength of a team depends on the less talented swimmer applying pressure to higher-level swimmers, who in turn apply pressure on up the ladder to the top swimmer; in other words, when a slower swimmer attains more speed, it provides incentive to the rest of the members of the team, and the team grows stronger. Extraordinary effort comes from team application.

CREATING A COHESIVE TEAM ATMOSPHERE

Throughout the years, coaches, athletes, alumni, parents, and folks in general have commented that they admire our team and how well our group conducts itself in and out of the pool. In my opinion, this is the best compliment that a coach can get. Having a team act and conduct themselves properly is very similar to preparing a team to race fast; it takes time, effort, communication, and direction. As a coach and leader of a team, you need not only to set the expectations that you want the team to adhere to, you need to communicate why these expectations are important and provide some detail on how the team is going to get there. The coach needs to provide the team with a roadmap that includes expectations for everything from performance to school to life outside of the sport. A good coach is able to communicate to the athletes both in a group setting and, more importantly, on an individual level.

As we all know, creating a cohesive team atmosphere is easier at some times than others. Creating a team atmosphere can involve large events such as team retreats or seminars with outside professionals, or it can be as simple as posting a sign. A few years ago we posted signs that read "Honor your teammates with your attitude and effort." We posted them on both sides of the locker room door so our athletes could read the saying before and after the workout. It is a simple message that carries great meaning. We feel that if an athlete's attitude and effort are in order, then everything else will fall into place. The sign is a simple way to communicate a team slogan each day without daily discussions.

Team meetings are always an important way to communicate to the group as well as to individuals. At times team meetings are just about logistics—when to meet the bus for an upcoming meet, or a reminder about some upcoming event. Our team meetings never last very long; after a certain time the message becomes diminished. I have always found that frequent shorter meetings are more effective then fewer longer ones. The older the group, the more communication is needed regarding why we do things a certain way and why doing it that way is important.

One of the best things a coach can do during meetings is praise individual athletes in front of the group. We do this after each competition. We recognize not only their times but also their efforts—things like touching another swimmer out at the finish, a hard-fought race, or someone swimming an event that is not their best to help the team. All are important items that, when recognized, motivate the individual swimmer by making them feel their importance and remind others of what is important to the team. On the flip side, when a team has great leadership, team meetings can be kept to a bare minimum. Our team in 2000, which won our second of three consecutive national championships, featured two of our all-time great and trusted seniors, Kristy Kowall and Courtney Shealey. That year we had a total of three team meetings, and one was at the beginning of the season. During that stretch of time the team was on cruise control and I did not dare disrupt it with meetings.

We also recognize individual academic accomplishments in front of the team. We mention anything from acing a test to being named an NCAA postgraduate scholarship winner. Athletes that are involved in community service are also acknowledged. Recognizing athletes' academic, athletic, and service achievements in front of their peers is a powerful way to reinforce what is important and honors each individual's hard work and dedication to the task.

Team meetings can include a number of topics. On the occasion that negative issues need to be addressed, we finish the meetings with a plan to turn the negative issue into a positive learning experience and we make sure that everyone knows not to let whatever happened happen again.

As a coach it is also important to be a good listener and to really try to see things from an athlete's perspective, whether or not you agree. This will allow you to deal with any questions or issues that have surfaced and to head off or anticipate anything that may come up in the future. Anticipation and planning for issues almost always produce better results for everyone involved.

One thing I always make an effort to do is to speak and listen to each athlete at some point during the day. It does not have to be much at times, but to have some level of interaction or conversation with each individual each day helps me and the athlete stay in tune with each other. Some athletes need more individual face time with their coaches and others simply do not. All people and athletes are different, and being able to notice and accept the various needs of some swimmers is an important tool for every coach to have. I have a big glass jar of gumballs in my office just so that swimmers can come in there to get one and we can talk for a minute. Some swimmers come in every day and others only on occasion, but they all know that they can come into my office and get a gumball at any time and have a safe place to talk about anything that is on their mind.

WE VERSUS I

As the title of this chapter suggests, I like to use *we* in place of *I*. For example, "We need to be faster on the last one here" instead of "I want to you to be faster on the last one here." Of course, on occasion I want to use the pronoun *I* and it is important that I do, but for many things, especially regarding training and workout, *we* is a small but important distinction that places a little more ownership back in the athlete's hands and makes them think, *I need to do this last one faster so that we—the team, everyone here—can achieve our goals.*

I have been around long enough that I have a lot of stories and examples to share in order to express my point. These stories often praise past athletes and illustrate something special that that athlete did in a certain situation. In knowing that they could be a part of a story in the years after they leave Georgia, the athletes know that their efforts and successes will always be a part of the history and pride of the program. We are all stewards of the program; swimmers and coaches came before us and other swimmers and coaches will come after we leave, but while we are here it is our job to continue to be the best possible team in every way. The legacy that each team leaves is important, and when the time comes to carry the torch it is our responsibility and honor to not only continue the traditions and accomplishments of teams past but hopefully raise the standard even further.

One of my favorite stories that I enjoy sharing took place at Purdue University during the 2005 Women's NCAA Championships. We were the favorites going into that year, and as it turned out we not only won our fourth NCAA team championship but did something that had never been done before: win all five relays (that was a special team). We had many great swimmers that year, and we were especially loaded with sprint freestylers. During the first day, our 200 free relay qualified first and four of our swimmers seeded in the top eight of the 50 free (first, third, seventh, and eighth). One of our sprinters that swam on the morning relay surprisingly did not make it back for a second swim in the individual event. After talking with my staff and all of the team members involved, I knew that we had a big decision to make. The sprinter that missed consolation finals in the morning was a great relay swimmer, and everyone agreed that she would do well that night. I believe all the talks and examples about teamwork and sacrifice paid off at this point. Samantha Arsenault, one of our seniors and captains and a member of the 2000 Olympic team, was seeded seventh in the 50 that night but was not on the morning relay. Samantha came to me and explained that she wanted to be on the 200 free relay because she earned her spot in finals, but I suggested that it would be better for the team if the athlete who was on the relay in the morning and did not make it back at night swam as part of the relay at night. Samantha knew as I did that having this athlete swim on the relay at finals would give her the confidence to perform better during the remainder of the meet, which would help the team achieve the goal of a team championship. She voluntarily gave up her spot on the relay for another team member because she believed that it was the right move for the team. Knowing what is best is one thing; actually giving up the spot is quite another. This was an important decision because it was still the first day of the meet and this relay had a great shot at winning and a chance of setting a record. The relay did go on to win and set an NCAA and American record in the process. Samantha finished the meet with a seventh-place finish in the 50 free and tenth-place finishes in both the 100 backstroke and 100 free. She was also the backstroker on both of our championship medley relays. Samantha's experience on the Olympic team and her years swimming with us helped her recognize and act upon the team need over her own. Samantha also was a finalist for NCAA Woman of the Year, so it was no surprise to me that she handled the situation with that level of maturity.

As coaches we all have stories and examples of the ideals that we want to instill in our team. I believe that just telling a group that they need to practice teamwork is fine to a point, but for them to really understand what it all means, a coach needs to use stories and examples to relate the word to the action. Stories do not have to be about something that happened to you or even your team; they could come from anywhere. However, examples that you give to your group that involve past team experiences or current team members work the best. You get to send two messages at once: you get to praise the athletes (past and present) in front of their peers, and you get to give real-life examples of the ideals that you want to instill.

It is difficult to list everything that we discuss, but a lot of effort is spent talking about behavior and attitude—things like keeping a positive attitude no matter what, taking ownership of your training, and paying attention to the various details that will help you become a better swimmer. A team is only as strong as its weakest link; every team member has a job to do, and no job is any less important than the others. This approach gives each team member a purpose and a stake in the team's overall success. We also mention to the group that everyone needs to be prepared to handle some adversity along with the successes at meets. Successes are easy to deal with, but adversity is more complicated; no meet is perfect, and any meet will have some level of difficulty attached to it no matter what.

BECOMING A SUCCESSFUL TEAM

A team's success is directly related to its confidence. Groups do a variety of activities to build trust and confidence, and the activities are generally helpful and enjoyable for everyone involved. I have found that the number one thing that builds confidence in swimmers is training hard and training with a purpose. The reality is that performance is related to the training that was done in relation to the event. One of the wonderful things about our sport is that many ideas and theories exist regarding training, and all of them can lead to fast swimming in the end. We have a number of great coaches in the United States, and we do a fantastic job of learning from each other and communicating about the things that we each do regarding training. This is a strength of our organization in general. No matter how the training is structured, a certain level of work has to be a part of the equation. Successful teams train with a common goal and a shared belief in the program, each other, and themselves. Good team members recognize others' needs and successes and respect one another's efforts in making themselves and thus the team better. When a group of individuals are encouraged by their coaches and peers, it builds a sense of urgency and responsibility to the cause and to the group. This can lead to some amazing progress in an individual's training, which will boost an athlete's confidence more than anything else.

CONCLUSION

The team provides an atmosphere of togetherness, a sense of duty and respect that allows its members to cultivate a sense of pride in themselves and others. This is done not only through successes in the end but by completing the journey the right way, as a team, and they will remember and cherish the journey for the rest of their lives. Their willingness to work as a team will serve them well.

4

Mastering Swimming Through the Years

Bob Miller

The notion of prolonged physical fitness has undergone a major transformation over my lifetime. Prolonged physical fitness used to be considered essential in preparing for athletic performance, but usually only for the duration of an athletic career. The college physical education classes of my era taught that strenuous exercise could be dangerous as one ages, and we were taught never to compete with younger athletes. However, the success of older athletes in masters swimming and other sports has proven that these concepts are false.

Exercise—and even vigorous exercise—is now recommended for all ages. Exercise is recommended in order to counter the obesity trend in Western society. Also, research now shows that exercise improves length of life, quality of life, and resistance to a variety of diseases.

I believe that swim coaches can be better coaches if they take time to exercise. They will have greater longevity in the sport and more energy for every daily training session. Coaches who train and swim will have a greater appreciation and understanding of the stresses of training as it applies to their swimmers. Each year, an increasing number of swim coaches swim or run in the early morning hours before clinics and swim meets. More and more coaches are becoming aware of the need to exercise for their own well-being.

Readers of this book include swimmers of all ages and the parents of swimmers in addition to coaches; these lifelong exercise and personal fitness recommendations apply to them as well. Parents that make personal physical fitness a goal can be better role models for their swimming children. They will also enjoy the health benefits that contribute to better understanding the training challenges that their swimming child is experiencing. Swimmers can begin to understand the need to continue their fitness goals beyond the closing of their club, high school, and college swimming careers.

A BRIEF BACKGROUND

To convince you of my qualifications to write on mastering swimming through the years, here I summarize my athletic and training life. At the time of this writing, I am 82 years young and still swimming daily. This life of training is unique in that it has continued through every decade to the present without significant interruptions.

My experience started as an age-group swimmer, and then I became a college swimmer who competed in the NCAA National Championships. After college, I swam in all Army swim meets and then trained for and competed in the modern pentathlon for more than 7 years. The pentathlon training required a heavy emphasis on swimming and running. During these years I qualified for two Pan American Games (1954 and 1958) and the 1956 Olympic Games. These were years of intensive double workouts and I was in the best condition that I ever experienced. Pistol shooting, fencing, and equestrian were the other disciplines of the pentathlon. The training regimen included at least 2 hours of training in all five disciplines during major training. My athletic experience was in swimming, and I was only an average runner. I had to put extra training into my running to become competitive in the pentathlon. I found out that improvement in running carried over to a stronger swimming performance. Most swim coaches now recognize this carryover and incorporate running into their training in the early swimming season.

After the Army years, I started my swim coaching career at the Cascade Swim Club in Seattle, Washington. It stretched through 6 decades and included beginning swimmers through Olympic medal winners. The most noteworthy were Lynn Colella, silver medal in the 200-meter butterfly at Munich (1972), and Rick Colella, bronze medal in the 200-meter breaststroke at Montreal (1976).

My goal was to maintain my speed and training times for as long as possible as I aged. This is what I experienced, and it illustrates the possibilities of mastering swimming through the years. I found that I could and did train at the same level in swimming to at least age 50. In masters nationals, at age 45, I equaled or bettered all my best college times. These were in the 200-yard backstroke and the 200- and 500-yard free. At the same time in life, I ran a marathon around Stanley Park in Vancouver, British Columbia, in 2 hours and 50 minutes. I was essentially able to retain both my swimming and running speeds to age 50. When I turned 55, my speed slowed down a bit but my endurance held up well. I could still repeat 10 × 200 yards on a 3-minute send-off and hold 2:30s. My heart rate did not change when compared with the same set when I was younger. The slowdown began at age 60 and, even though anticipated, was not abrupt. It was not until age 78 that I noticed a sudden slowdown. At age 77, I was able to break a world record in the 200-meter backstroke at the U.S. Masters Swimming world championship. Most of my swim workouts were about 3,000 yards on 5 or 6 days a week. I try to keep up the same yardage on 5 days a week. My send-off time for 10 × 200 yards is now 3:30 descending to 3:10.

One mistake that I believe that I made was not doing enough speed work in my training or enough dryland strength training. Increasing training in these areas may have helped maintain my swimming speed over a longer period. Seniors can still bulk up muscle mass by pressing iron. According to a recent NPR article, Dr. David Heber, UCLA Center for Human Nutrition, states that the "average male weighing 180 pounds (81.6 kg) after age 60 can lose as much as 10 pounds (4.5 kg) of muscle mass over a decade" (Neighmond, 2011). The article continues by citing new research from the journal *Medicine & Science in Sports & Exercise*, which shows that lifting weights after the age of 50 can help prevent age-related muscle loss (Peterson, 2011).

UNITED STATES MASTERS SWIMMING

Mastering swimming through the years depends on swimmers' extending their fitness endeavors beyond their college or high school years. Elite competitive swimmers who meet the standards established by USA Swimming can receive some financial assistance to continue their training in their postgraduate years. These swimmers train to compete in international competitions, including the Olympic Games. United States Olympic Committee professional and postgraduate training centers now exist in Fullerton, California; Charlotte, North Carolina; and North Baltimore, Maryland. All centers are staffed by experienced Olympic swimming coaches.

However, the majority of postgraduate swimmers never fall into this category of elite swimmers. United States Masters Swimming (USMS) provides the opportunity for these individuals. USMS started when I was more than 40 years old and has continued to grow rapidly. It was founded in 1970 by Captain Ransom Arthur, a San Diego physician. That year, Ransom asked John Spannuth, president of the American Swim Coaches Association, to hold the first U.S. Masters Swimming national championship. Since then, USMS has evolved into a nationwide organization of more than 42,000 adult swimmers. The archives of USMS include a listing of the top 10 all-American and all-star masters swimmers throughout the years. For more information related to these records, visit www.usms.org. The International Swimming Hall of Fame now recognizes hall of fame selections in masters swimming.

USMS provides the organization nationwide and lists the clubs providing masters swimming throughout the United States. Although some adults make swimming their primary exercise through YMCAs and fitness clubs without actually joining masters swimming, masters swimming clubs are large and growing in number.

The largest dropoff in masters swimming participation is in the 20- to 40-year age group. Normally, at this stage of life, marriage, starting a family, and pursuing a professional career are dominating factors. Many athletes in this age range can squeeze in daily training for personal fitness, but it is often intermittent. Most will gradually start back into consistent training as their jobs become more secure and their families mature.

Everyone has their own reason to swim for exercise. Health, fitness, friendship, fun, the excitement of competition, travel, and coaching are common reasons. The majority of adult swimmers who choose swimming as their primary exercise don't enter swimming competition, at least early on, but many are soon drawn into some competition on an intermittent basis. Many of the benefits of masters swimming apply to both those who compete on a regular basis and those who choose not to compete.

Many masters swimmers are interested in a regular routine of training and working out with friends. Research has shown that interval training has benefits over simple lap swimming; most masters swimmers use structured workouts of interval training. In addition, good technique is very important for swimming success. Masters swimmers can continue to improve technique by working with competent coaches.

Competition and the instruction of a coach provide good motivation to train more intensively. Competition at the masters level is separated by age groups, usually in 5-year spans. About 30% of masters swimmers compete in swim meets on a regular basis; these swimmers can select from a good number of meets. Masters swimming meets are offered in short-course yards, short-course meters, long-course meters, and open-water swims in lakes, rivers, and saltwater. U.S. national championships are held for both short-course yards and long-course meters each year. The U.S. Masters Swimming world championships are held every 2 years. More than 7,000 swimmers participated in the 2007 world championship meet held at Stanford University; it was the largest swim meet of any kind ever held in North America.

In most cases, placing in any event of a masters swimming competition is not as important to the swimmer as the time. The time measures individual improvement and can indicate quite accurately how long a swimmer can maintain speed and endurance. The time can give the swimmer an immediate reward and the incentive to continue the swimming training program.

AGING AND SWIMMING

Even later in life, many athletes equal or surpass their previous best times. Dara Torres is a good example. She placed second in the 50-meter free at the 2008 Beijing Olympic Games, her fifth Olympic Games, at age 41. At the time of this writing, she has qualified for the 2012 Olympic Trials. At age 43 she swam a 50-meter free in 0:25.9 to meet the qualifying standard. Torres is the first woman in history to swim in an Olympic Games past age 40.

Another great example is Jeff Farrell, a 1960 Olympic gold medalist in Rome, who in his early 60s was breaking masters swimming records with times not far off the best of his college years. In 1997 Farrell broke the masters swimming record for the 60- to 64-year-old age bracket with a 0:23.28 time. His best college time was 0:22.50 in 1960. In 37 years he had slowed only 0.78 second in the 50-yard free. This is only about 21 thousandths of a second per year over 37 years.

The question that remains is when the speed-versus-age curve catches up to world-class athletes. Mark Spitz attempted a comeback for the 1992 Olympics. He failed to make the qualifying time for the Olympic Trials and was 4 seconds over his best time that he made in the 1972 Olympics. After close to a 20-year layoff, Spitz found that he could not regain his Olympic-record conditioning.

Although much about aging remains unknown, it seems that many problems that occur with aging come from disuse. The amount of time that can be given to training is an important factor for all ages and levels of swimmers, but it is especially important as you age. Every swimmer should monitor the number of workouts, the length of workouts, and the frequency of intense training sets in order to determine what works best. Part of the equation is available time and part is how successful you desire to be in swimming competition. To adapt through every decade of life, each swimmer should schedule their time effectively based on their goals for their swimming program. The frequency, the length, and the intensity of workouts can be organized so as to maintain a high level of fitness throughout life. These will need to be adjusted as the swimmer ages.

Research is somewhat scarce in regards to how much exercise adults can adapt to as they age. Statistics are increasingly available on adults in their 40s, 50s, and 60s, and research on exercising adults in their 70s, 80s, and 90s is now becoming available. Too often the general public perceives older adults performing intensive exercise routines as aberrations and not the possible norm. This is slowly changing. As previously mentioned, it seems that adults can benefit from exercise at any age as long as they are medically capable.

Thomas Cureton, a pioneer in researching physical fitness through the aging process, authored or coauthored 50 books on the subject. In 1944, he founded the Physical Fitness Research Laboratory in the Department of Physical Education at the University of Illinois, where he was a professor. He lectured on physical fitness around the world, usually doing nonstop exercise and running during the lectures (he did this before aerobics was a known word). He was a swimmer and runner in his youth, and in his later years he was a champion masters swimmer and once held 14 world records. He died at age 91. Cureton influenced countless adults to start and then maintain a fitness program throughout life.

I have used my lifetime experience with training as an example because few statistics are available regarding uninterrupted training from youth to the age of 82. But here I provide another example: a swim coach friend who is 83. He was a high school and college swimmer but not a national-level competitor. When he was in college, his resting heart rate was 84 beats per minute and he was diagnosed with high blood pressure. After college, from age 21 to 32, he played basketball, softball, and slow-pitch baseball on a weekly basis in their respective seasons but he did not exercise consistently. At age 32, he attended lectures by Thomas Cureton at the local Y and high school and started a lifelong program of aerobic exercising. Over several years, he gradually increased his running to where he was running seven days a week for a total of 50 miles (80.5 km) and swimming 5 days a week for 1 mile (1.6 km) per session. I trained with him at swim meets and clinics over those years. He swam an occasional masters swim meet and ran in masters track and open road races. After age 50 he also competed in triathlon and ran a marathon. He was able to match a college swim time at age 45 and retained running speed to age 50. He could maintain his interval swim sets from his 40s to his 60s and his endurance running into his 60s. His swim set times were noticeably slower in his late 60s, and now, at age 83, the send-off time for repeat 200s is 30 seconds slower than the 40-to-60 age period. Today, at age 83, he swims 2,000 meters three times a week and uses a treadmill or elliptical machine on the other 4 days of the week, plus performs 50 minutes of resistance exercises three times a week. Injuries have reduced his jogging to 4 miles (6.4 km) a session. His resting heart rate is now normally 52, and his blood pressure is normal with no medication.

I believe that every adult can learn from such examples. One problem with running as the primary or only avenue of exercise is injuries over the long term. The coach in my example didn't start running until age 32 and had to limit his running starting at age 51 because of injuries. Most who have competed in running have had to eliminate or reduce their running program after many years of use. I had to stop all running permanently at age 68 because of damage to my hip. Not so with swimming. I had a hip replacement at age 71 and swam up to the day of the surgery. The incision healed in 10 days and I returned to swimming immediately. After another 6 months of swimming, I entered and won a couple events at the U.S. Masters Swimming national championship. The great advantage of swimming is that it can usually be continued when injuries occur. Swimming gives the joints of the legs a needed rest from stress. (The swimming pool has been used extensively by runners and bikers to maintain aerobic levels while recovering from an injury.) Swimming is one activity that adults can continue throughout all ages with little danger of serious injury.

As athletes age, they must pay more attention to how they feel and what their body tells them. A younger athlete may train with a minor injury, but the older athlete should consider taking a day or two off. Older athletes should also cross-train more often. Cross-training gives your muscles a break and relieves boredom. Instead of only swimming, ride a bike, walk, hike, or play tennis. Triathlon is growing in popularity. It is now estimated that 500,000 adults in the United States are involved in triathlon training. Many masters swimmers are drawn into the triathlon through their cross-training activities. Being able to swim well is essential for success in the triathlon and to ensure your safety in the sport.

In order to maintain a high level of fitness in swimming, you must train intelligently. A few masters training tips could keep you training efficiently well past your 40s:

1. Start your swim training gradually. Too much too soon will result in muscle pain and discouragement.

2. Stay in shape. Once you start, don't stop. When you stop training for 2 weeks, for example, it takes 2 days of training to make up for every 1 day off. This viewpoint will keep you in training and help you avoid most layoffs.

3. Do some resistance training along with your swimming.

4. Competing as a masters swimmer will motivate you to improve your training habits.

5. Swim to keep in shape and look physically fit.

CONCLUSION

The following quotation is from the *Harvard Men's Health Watch*: "Many forms of exercise reduce stress directly, and by preventing bodily illness, exercise has extra benefits for the mind. Regular physical activity will lower your blood pressure, improve your cholesterol, and reduce your blood sugar. Exercise cuts the risk of heart attack, stroke, diabetes, colon and breast cancers, osteoporosis and fractures, obesity, depression, and even dementia (memory loss). Exercise slows the aging process, increases energy, and prolongs life" (2011).

This chapter details the beneficial results of lifelong exercise through some real-life examples. It is my hope that all coaches, parents, and swimmers who read this will heed the need to start and maintain an exercise program. Swimming should be the cornerstone of the training method you select. The key words are "Do it!" It takes an often uncomfortable period of time as you start your program, but once the routine is established, you will look forward to every training session and the fitness results achieved.

5

Building a Team
in a Disadvantaged Area

Jim Ellis

I have been involved with aquatics and education for more than 30 years. Coaching swimming and teaching math required many of the same skills. Ultimately, these skills led to the development of my coaching philosophy. During these 30-plus years, participation of minority and disadvantaged athletes in aquatics, specifically competitive swimming, has been discussed at length. Many believe that African Americans can't swim competitively because of our physical characteristics, but nothing could be further from the truth. African Americans have been swimming for fun and competition for decades.

THE PHILADELPHIA DEPARTMENT OF RECREATION

Several factors helped slow the development of high-level competitive swimming in our community. When a young, talented African American swimmer came along, he or she was recruited by a coach of a major swim club, which was usually a white team, and given the opportunity to swim in that program, where he or she became very successful. The result of this practice is that swimmers were removed from the community, where they could have been a role model for other young swimmers. The original team was then denied the opportunity to grow with the athlete and develop more talent using the advanced athlete as a role model. This was one of the driving forces in the development of the Philadelphia Department of Recreation (PDR), which inspired the Hollywood film *Pride*. I wanted to prove society wrong on both accounts and show that first, African Americans can swim, and second, that they could do it with a program in their own community with an African American coach.

Establishing a thriving program in a disadvantaged community certainly comes with unique challenges, but these issues can be overcome with careful planning. Over the years, PDR was able to develop a culture of success that ultimately transformed the team into a truly unique model. Once the program produced a good product, it did not matter that our members were disadvantaged or minorities. Our swimmers were intelligent, well spoken, and conducted themselves in a manner that left no doubt that we were to be taken seriously. What mattered was that something good was taking place and others wanted to be a part of PDR.

PDR was a testament to how careful planning leads to success despite impediments. Of course, having a full understanding of what constitutes success is important in the planning process. Is success having a million-dollar house? Does success mean owning several expensive cars? Is success reaching the Olympics? Can success also mean obtaining college scholarships (see the list on page 65)? Perhaps success can be the discipline gained through training and understanding one's limitations. Perhaps success can be providing a life-altering reality of what the outside world has to offer. Whatever the definition, success begins with a well-developed plan that leads to a well-run program staffed by caring, knowledgeable adults with the active or sometimes passive support of family members. At PDR we came to understand that some things constituted success and some things were the result of success—a very important nuance that makes all the difference.

After starting PDR in a disadvantaged inner-city community, I realized that swimming could also bring serious social and cultural changes to the participants and community. Our success helped dispel a stereotype that African Americans can't swim competitively. This was accomplished by setting the achievement bar very high and through travel to various meets, exposing swimmers and parents to different lifestyles. My goal at PDR was not to have a few kids swimming competitively but to have a team swimming on the national and international level. We wanted our athletes to represent our country at the Olympics. This was the team goal, and everyone was committed to this goal. Along the way, each individual would achieve their own personal goals. PDR was a success; it achieved the following:

- PDR swimmers made top-16 age-group rankings.
- A PDR individual held a national age-group record that stood for 19 years.
- PDR swimmers held several national top-16 relay records.
- PDR currently has a few swimmers on the all-time top 100 list.
- PDR swimmers made the national junior team, Pan-Pacific team, and World University games.
- PDR scored in the top 10 at junior and senior nationals.
- Several PDR swimmers achieved top-25 world rankings.

Along with all the national achievements, our swimmers achieved their personal best times year after year and enjoyed the experience of being involved with a program that strived to make every day positive. This garnered a great sense of pride among everyone in the program. The training sessions were intense each day, and success in the pool extended outside the pool as well. Academic achievement improved across the board, and we even had a competition for achieving the highest score on the SAT exam. As an aquatic instructor, coach, and educator, I saw that young people will rise to meet whatever expectations are set before them.

In my math classes I saw the same results year after year because I refused to accept that my students could not excel in math. We could do math at a high level because we set high expectations and had a plan and stuck to what worked. Sound familiar? Having a plan and high standards worked in the classroom and pool for exactly the same reasons: no mystery, trickery, cheating, or sleight of hand—just good old hard work, dedication, and enthusiasm.

VARIABLES OF SUCCESSFUL DEVELOPMENT

Several variables affect the successful development and continued success of a program in a disadvantaged area.

- ◆ Why do you want to be in that community?
- ◆ What facilities are available?
- ◆ What are the funding sources?
- ◆ How is your programming structured?
- ◆ What is your training philosophy?
- ◆ What do you want to get out of competition?

Many are not clear on what constitutes a disadvantaged community as related to aquatics. A disadvantaged community is one that has very few usable swimming pools and the community has limited or no access to those pools. A disadvantaged community also swims or thinks of swimming for 2.5 months out of the year. In these communities, pools are open only in the summer months, or the ones that are open year round are not maintained to a degree that the community members want to swim in them during the dark, cold fall and winter months. These conditions negatively affect the growth of swimming as a sport or as a vehicle for maintaining health and providing job opportunities in aquatics. Some of the reasons for this situation are economic, political, and cultural factors and lack of education.

Why This Community?

You must ask yourself several questions to determine the path to success. If this community lacks well-run swimming pools and the hours that these pools are available for use are limited, if the community does not have a history of swimming in their schools, if their recreational swimming time is seasonal, and if well over half the community is on public assistance, how and why would you start a competitive swimming program in this neighborhood and hope to sustain it long enough to get results?

Are you familiar with the culture of the community, and are you willing to deal with and work with the community members to establish and build a swimming culture, something that will be very beneficial for everyone involved? If your answer is no, then you are in the wrong business and will likely fail. If you are reading this passage, then your answer is likely yes, and you believe that

1. everyone needs to know how to swim no matter what their economic status is in life,
2. swimming will make for a much healthier community,

3. swimming will expose the community to jobs in the aquatic field, and

4. an untapped pool of talent is waiting to be discovered.

The athlete just needs to be sold on the sport and then given a fair chance to grow and develop through proper training, education, and access to the water and an attitude of "Yes, I have the desire to help others succeed."

Welcome to the world of aquatic professional coaching!

The Importance of Facilities

First, you need to secure a facility or facilities. This is essential. The amount of pool time that you have will determine the type of program you will be able to offer. As mentioned earlier, this is the main deterrent to establishing a swimming program in a disadvantaged community. This will be the most difficult area to navigate.

If you find a facility, you will have to make sure that maintenance will be sufficient throughout the year. In the beginning, you must establish the hours that you want to operate and the amount of chemicals and supplies needed to operate a clean and healthy environment for your patrons. These factors also help determine how much to charge your members. If you can get pool time at one facility, great, but you might have to use several in order to get enough time to run a full-fledged program.

Funding: Need We Say More?

Once you have secured your facility or facilities, a major piece of your operating budget will be in order. The other components are a little simpler.

- How many staff members will you need?
- What are the salary ranges necessary to attract qualified staff and the number of hours they need to work to carry out your proposed program?
- What are your equipment costs for competitive training, swimming lessons, assorted aquatic classes, and recreational activities?

Once these figures are set you can determine how many self-pay swimmers you need to carry to meet the budget. If you find that the community will have a difficult time meeting your fees, you will have to refine your patron revenue stream. A deeper understanding of your community demographics—such as how many families are on assistance and how many children in the local schools in your area are getting subsidized lunches—will help determine whether you need a sliding-scale membership program and what the scale range will be. This information will also likely be necessary for grant writing, donation appeals, partnership appeals with local businesses, or meetings with philanthropic individuals to obtain funding to get you started.

You may also want to look at running a few team-operated fundraisers during the year. A word of caution is in order regarding team fundraisers: These are difficult and can be problematic and often yield poor cost–benefit results. Many schools and other organizations are using the same traditional methods, so you end up going after the same dollars with the same pitch or washing a lot of cars for little money and getting fat on unsold candy bars. When and if you choose fundraising, you need to be very creative. You want a project that will not consume too much time. Remember, after practice the swimmers still have schoolwork and family responsibilities to fulfill. If you follow the team fundraising approach, choose something the whole family can get involved with and that will not be overly burdensome. Yes, this process requires quite a bit of advanced thinking and planning, and you may need to come up with several scenarios.

Programming: The Nitty Gritty

The three components of successful programming are

1. a learn-to-swim program,
2. a parent booster program, and
3. an age-group team.

Learn-to-Swim Program

The learn-to-swim program will be the driving force of your whole program. The goal of the learn-to-swim program is to reach a large cross-section of community members, and this will be the starting point for building a swimming culture in the community. The learn-to-swim component will bring the most revenue to your club.

For team building, the following classes work well:

1. Parent and tot
2. Preschool
3. Elementary school
4. Preteen (age 11–14)
5. High school
6. Adult

Although all groups are important for purposes of competition, I limit the focus to the groups that directly feed into the team. For the preschool group, I offer as many classes per week as time allows. This group receives two 40-minute classes per week for 8 weeks. The emphases of the class are water safety and basic skills. I try to get them swimming as quickly as possible using whatever strategies work and keep it fun. Once the child can swim 15 yards and complete a few other skills, they graduate to the mini team. The same concept is used with the elementary and preteen groups. The primary focus is to get the youngsters swimming as quickly as possible and to have fun while doing it.

I like to graduate and move a whole class together along to the team if possible. I facilitate this in the screening sessions at the start of classes. When the swimmers are graduated to the team, they are simply moving on to advanced swimming lessons, but we want to start building the team concept as quickly as possible with the swimmers and their parents. All activities from this point on are group activities. The swimmers now attend 2 to 3 days of classes per week, and classes range from 1 to 1.5 hours depending on physical development and skill level. This area of the program should be the largest group. You must have a very diverse and strong base, without which you will have difficulty maintaining and sustaining a productive program. Your base will allow the development of a nucleus of swimmers that grow in your program using your methods of drill and stroke technique for years to come. With this strong core it will be easier to add swimmers from other backgrounds to the group. This will also make quadrennial planning much easier.

Quadrennial planning is simply the development of a strong age-group team over a period of 4 years. With such a strong group you will start attracting more high school swimmers as well, and from that group you will find a few swimmers that have the talent and desire to pursue senior-level swimming.

Parent Booster Program

Your second component is your parents group, booster club, or advisory board. This group will need as much education as your swimmers, probably more, and are important for several reasons. They will help take some of the day-to-day work away from the coaching staff. Some parents in financial need can earn credit toward their bill by doing a few jobs that the coach would normally do. The parent group will also be the source of officials for your team when you attend swim meets or host your own. Trained timers and stroke and turn and starter referees are all required to run a meet and will be part of the programming. You will also need parents to operate computers and run the electronic score board and timing equipment. This group will also be instrumental in running your local fundraiser, chaperoning team trips, and planning and running social activities for the team. Once the parents become comfortable with these activities, some of them will want to get involved with the local swim committee. This is where your parents can participate on various committees with the possibility of eventually participating on the national level. Finally, if they are busy and occupied, they have less time to tell you how to coach the kids!

Age-Group Team

The age-group team is the nucleus of future senior team members. The program must be fun in order to retain them in swimming, and it must be a graduated learning process with heavy emphasis on technique.

Training

Forming your training group from your learn-to-swim program will be a very important but exciting time for you. This is the payoff from the hard work spent developing your learn-to-swim group. A good age-group training program will lay the foundation for a very successful senior training group. Several things to consider when choosing swimmers for this group are skill, desire, willingness to work or to stay on task, enthusiasm, positive attitude, parental support, and ability to set goals.

This will be an exciting time for the coaching staff because you will now have to deal with new challenges. When working with an age-group training group, you will be faced with the problem of youngsters maturing at different rates. This will create several subgroups in your overall training group. I find this to be challenging but very stimulating.

The training areas that I thought were important and that were emphasized at PDR were

- consistent stroke mechanics (with all strokes);
- starts, turns, and finishes;
- relay starts and finishes;
- race strategies;
- meet preparation; and
- individual medley training (including a lot of switching sets, dryland training, and, most important, aerobic development).

At PDR we did many long swims on the clock in order to improve aerobic and mental endurance. One of the other reasons that PDR was a successful swimming program was that we made pride in the preparation a working part of our training. As I like to say, we enjoyed preparing to do battle.

Another factor that contributes to a successful program is role models. Our up-and-coming swimmers trained in the pool with the swimmers that were winning and meeting goals; they came through the program doing the same drills and workouts. Younger swimmers could reach out and touch them, talk with them, joke with them, complain with them, and plan ways to outsmart the coach with them. They were teammates even though they were at different levels.

This approach, if implemented in a progressive manner over a period of time, yields tremendous results and leads to the natural development of a senior-level training group. The group will have come from your learn-to-swim program and they will all speak the same training language and know all the drills. When you speak they will have the same picture in their mind's eye. Of course, they may not like the picture you draw or their mind's eye may need glasses, but that is what coaching is all about!

When the swimmer advances to the senior training group, not much changes from what we did in the age-group program except that time commitments increase and attention to detail is heightened. We now train 9 to 10 sessions per week, with a 90% attendance requirement for competition and travel. Our most advanced swimmers self-regulate to a more rigorous attendance requirement because they desire to reach the highest levels of accomplishment. The test sets, kicking sets, pulling sets, and drill sets at this level require use of training equipment such as paddles, fins, pull buoys, sneakers, t-shirts, and bands. We also increase education for the parent and swimmer on such topics as nutrition and puberty (the body changes that take place); stretching, warming up, and cooling down before and after each race; pace work; and what I call "swimulator" swims and tubing work. College plans, tapering, and the mental approach to competition are all discussed with the parent and swimmer. The most important issue for PDR was learning how to compete while under a full training load during the season. The ability to maintain a high level of training during the season was one of our strongest assets, and it is my belief that this allowed us to make 80% of our junior national and senior national cuts unshaved.

Competition

The other important factor in senior swimming and swimming for PDR was the selection of competitions and their timing. This may be the last piece but serves as the evaluation of all the work you and your swimmers have completed in the weeks leading up to competition. When choosing a meet to attend, several things must be considered:

- Where is the meet located?
- What are my objectives for the meet?
- Where does it fall on our training schedule?

By keeping these three things in mind, you will have a good chance of having a very successful meet. Selection of the venue goes a long way in ensuring your swimmers and parents come away with a positive experience. Sitting in a dimly lit pool that has poor-quality water and air is not a pleasant experience and will not lead to a positive overall outcome. Remember, you must know your success benchmark! The purpose for attending the meet is very important and is something that should be explained to both your swimmers and the parents.

Another important part of competition is self-esteem. Remember, disadvantaged youth are traveling to a community that is totally different from what they are used to; they are being placed in a highly competitive, sometimes even hostile, environment. As a coach it is imperative that you prepare your athletes and parents for performing in this type of environment. PDR had to deal with this in our early years of development. Once we became established and began swimming at higher-level meets and making national standards, the transition was much easier and we had the advantage of having role models to help the new parents and swimmers along.

CONCLUSION

The first objective of PDR was to bring the sport of competitive swimming to the inner-city community in a totally new and unique way and to prove that an inner-city team with an African American coach can compete at the highest level of swimming, not just locally but nationally and internationally. Other predominantly African American teams existed, but none had this as their goal. One purpose of this goal was to keep our top swimmers in our community as role models for future generations; it would also help build tradition and establish a legacy for years to come. And it did. Following is a list of the prestigious colleges and universities attended by PDR swimmers.

Columbia University	Cornell University	Dartmouth University
Duke University	Florida State University	Fordham University
Howard University	Johns Hopkins University	Lafayette University
LaSalle University	Miami (FL) University	North Carolina A&T
Northwestern University	Penn State University	Princeton University
Rutgers University	Seton Hall University	Swarthmore University
Towson University	University of Connecticut	University of Georgia
University of Pennsylvania	University of Pittsburgh	University of Rhode Island
University of Texas	University of Vermont	University of Virginia
West Chester University	West Virginia University	

Once this goal was achieved, another milestone occurred. Not only did PDR become a successful competitive swimming program that was started and sustained in an inner-city community, PDR also went from being a 100% African-American team to a completely diverse group of athletes. This was not included in any of my quadrennial plans, but it proved to be a great asset to the growth of the program. PDR was 30 years ahead of its time! Our diversity took us to another level and made us realize that we were in a position to create social and cultural change on a large scale—an effect that is just starting to be looked at by educational institutions and corporations looking for different and new ways to support programs for youth and educational institutions.

PART TWO

LEADING YOUR PROGRAM
TO ITS FULL POTENTIAL

6

Applying Science to Your Coaching

Jan Prins

There was a time when coaches were successful primarily because of their ability to motivate athletes to train harder. This was very much the case in sports such as running and swimming, where it appeared that longer hours and harder effort directly translated to success.

Times have certainly changed. Although the ability to instill the necessary drive into an athlete remains essential, many now acknowledge that successful coaching must include a working knowledge of human motion, specifically sport biomechanics and exercise physiology.

In competitive swimming, the scientific principles governing human aquatic motion and the application of efficient stroke mechanics are now seen as key factors in the ability to swim fast. Increases in muscular strength and cardiovascular conditioning, although important, play a secondary role, particularly as a swimmer advances to increasingly elite levels of performance.

This point was made increasingly clear with the recent unveiling, promotion, and timely demise of high-tech racing suits. The synthetic fibers of the suits altered a swimmer's buoyancy and body contours to the point where superior conditioning played a decidedly less important role. In light of these observations, this chapter focuses on some of the more important anatomical and biomechanical factors that contribute to efficient swimming.

WHEN TO APPLY SCIENCE: THE IMPORTANCE OF PRIORITIZING

Swimming, as with all human activity, is a result of a complex interplay between posture, muscle and joint interactions, and synchronous bilateral motion. When we observe the stroke mechanics of the great swimmers, it is clear that not every world-class swimmer uses textbook stroke mechanics.

The somewhat amusing quote "Swimmers swim fast in spite of their coaches" rests on the observation that many great swimmers appear to be violating some of the more obvious tenets of good propulsion as they surge past their more technically correct rivals. Often, this is because of superior conditioning. However, in many cases, what we may assume to be a serious stroke defect could very well only slightly detract from the overall performance.

With this in mind, we need to develop an awareness of which factors actually contribute to efficient swimming and which are less likely to affect the final performance. In short, we need to develop a list of priorities for evaluating swimming performance. Once it is clear which elements of the stroke should be addressed early and immediately, we will be more successful in introducing an orderly progression to teaching efficient stroke mechanics and will be able to properly diagnose and fix those movements that need correction.

Although we don't have all the answers, ongoing research in swimming stroke mechanics and the knowledge of how research can be applied has better equipped us to put this knowledge to practical use.

BASIS FOR EFFECTIVE MOTION

What can biomechanics do for swimming stroke analysis? Biomechanics uses the disciplines of anatomy and physics to examine motion. To understand how we can apply biomechanics to develop more efficient swimming propulsion, we must observe how our musculoskeletal system allows us to move through the water.

It is good to remind ourselves of a well-established axiom: "We train movements, not muscles." We have a limited number of skeletal muscles, approximately 640, but we are capable of producing a vast range of motions. To produce a specific movement, especially movements that are repeated as in swimming, a series of coordinated signals from the brain must be sent to the muscles. Furthermore, the timing of the signals to the muscles is critical. This muscle activation, termed a patterned sequence, determines which muscles come into play and when.

For efficient joint motion, the rotating limb segments must be maintained at optimal positions with respect to each other. This spatial orientation is vital because muscles do best when they pull in specific directions, and these directions are determined by the relative positions of the bones to which the muscles are attached.

Attempts to apply muscle tension either by repositioning portions of the body, as in consciously rolling the hips, or by holding a specific set of joints in a predetermined place, as in extending the chest forward when lying prone in the water, will affect the timing of muscle activation.

THE MUSCULAR FRAMEWORK FOR SWIMMING

For the voluntary or skeletal muscles to generate and transmit force, one end of the muscle must be anchored to a stable base, usually a bone or set of bones. The stable end is usually closer to the spine and is referred to as the origin of the muscle. It is also referred to as the proximal attachment, in contrast to the opposite end, which is referred to as the distal attachment. The movements of the shoulder offer an excellent example of this point. Because the primary function of the shoulder muscles is to move the arm, their distal attachments are all on the upper arm: the humerus. The proximal attachments (again, the ends located closer to the center of the body) of the larger prime mover muscles of the shoulder, in this case the pectoralis major and latissimus dorsi, are both attached to the stable base of the ribs and spine. The base of support of the smaller muscles, the deltoid and rotator cuff muscles, is on the shoulder girdle (the clavicle and scapula).

This information helps us understand a number of biomechanical applications, such as how muscular torque affects certain phases of stroke mechanics and the basis of spine stabilization for swimming.

THE INTERPLAY BETWEEN PROPULSION AND RESISTANCE

When we observe good swimming technique, we can deduce two things:

1. To be able to swim faster, we must exert sufficient muscular force to overcome the resistance of the water.

2. In order to avoid expending excess effort, we must reduce the existing resistive forces.

Let us briefly examine the roles of propulsive and resistive forces as they affect efficient swimming.

Propulsive Forces

Dynamic fluid forces are present when a swimmer travels through the water. Although this is a rather dull description of the elegant, rhythmic movements of each of the four competitive strokes, the fact remains that we move through the water by exerting a combination of two types of propulsion.

Drag forces are used to pull and push an object forward through the water. Swimmers use propulsive drag forces to engage the water and move their bodies forward. Lift forces also propel bodies forward, except lift forces work in a more complex way. Much has been written and debated about the extent to which each type of force contributes to each competitive stroke. However, it is clear that both forces are used when we swim. The predominance of one over the other depends on which of the four competitive strokes we are examining and on the manner in which the hands and feet engage the water during the course of each stroke cycle.

Most of the current literature that describes propulsive forces in swimming examines the pull patterns transcribed by the hands when viewed from different underwater positions. Because of the complexity of the task—hydrodynamics are a notoriously difficult field of study to quantify—precise empirical determinations remain elusive.

What is clear, however, is that during efficient swimming the positions of the wrists and hands constantly transition or change as the extremities move through the water according to the dictates of the stroke.

Experience has taught us that the ability to engage the water with the hands and feet, the elusive "feel for the water," is best studied by observing and comparing the pull patterns of swimmers of varying degrees of ability. Traditionally, the two views that provide the most information are a head-on (frontal) view and a sideways (lateral) view. Thanks to software advances, we are able to view the paths transcribed by the hands and feet when swimmers are tracked from underwater. The following figures are images captured from video footage that has been subjected to software enhancements. What we observe from these images are the two-dimensional trails of the fingertips and elbows as they move in the selected pull patterns. These trails enable us to track selected anatomical landmarks in real time.

In figure 6.1 we see the trails traced by the fingertips when swimming freestyle. The almost vertical initial path of the fingertips clearly shows what the path of the hands would look like when an early vertical forearm is incorporated into the catch phase of the pull.

In figure 6.2 we see a frontal view of the butterfly stroke. In this example, we are able to detect a discrepancy between the motions of the right and left hands, starting with the entry and continuing on to the initial phase of the pull. It is apparent that although the hands entered the water simultaneously, the left hand entered at a point that is outside the line of the shoulders and consequently shows a much more abbreviated path as it tries to match the position of the right hand midway through the pull.

These images are two-dimensional depictions of motion that is taking place in three dimensions. This is a critical point, the misunderstanding of which has spawned, among other notions, the theory of the S pull. Fortunately, we are now older and wiser with respect to this idea and realize that trying to consciously transcribe these convoluted paths during the underwater pull does not produce optimal results.

FIGURE 6.1 Frontal view of freestyle with video trails.

FIGURE 6.2 Frontal view of butterfly with video trails.

© Jan Prins

© Jan Prins

FIGURE 6.3 Lateral view of the paths of the elbow and hand in freestyle, swum with a high elbow.

© Jan Prins

FIGURE 6.4 Lateral view of the paths of the elbow and hand in freestyle, swum with a dropped elbow.

Two examples of how we can use video trails to our advantage when observing swimmers from a lateral view are shown in figures 6.3 and 6.4. Again, although the trails do not reflect the three-dimensional nature of the paths of the hands, useful information can be extracted when the two pictures are compared.

In figure 6.3 we see the path of the elbow as the hand moves through the catch and initial underwater pull. It is evident that as the hand heads downward and backward, the elbow is held high in a relatively stationary position, first moving forward as part of the overall motion of the body.

In contrast, figure 6.4 illustrates the path of the elbow when it mirrors the path of the hand, indicating the absence of a high elbow.

Because a critical component of swimming is an awareness of the positions of a swimmer's hands and feet during all phases of the stroke cycle, video trails help track the motion of selected points of the body by tracing a continuous path as the motion takes place. This provides coaches and swimmers with a tool for increasing awareness of stroke mechanics.

Resistive Forces

When we float on the surface of the water, the only force we have to contend with is buoyancy. When we start moving, however, the forces produced by the water become dynamic and we have to deal with forces that oppose forward motion and that will decelerate forward movement if sufficient propulsive forces are absent. Known collectively as drag forces (see formula on page 79), they can be placed in three categories (form drag, surface drag, and wave drag), each of which can dramatically affect swimming efficiency.

Form Drag

Drag forces slow a swimmer down in numerous ways. Some are obvious, whereas some are harder to detect unless viewed underwater from the appropriate vantage point. One of the most dramatic examples of how drag forces, in this case form drag, affected the outcome of a race is found in the men's 100-meter butterfly at the Beijing

Olympics. The slight elevation of Milorad Čavić's head as he was in the final millimeters of reaching for the touch pad was apparently sufficient enough to increase drag forces and slow his progress to the point where Michael Phelps, swimming in the adjacent lane, despite taking an extra stroke, was able to hit his electronic touch pad more forcefully and thereby register his completion of the race one one-hundredth of a second sooner!

Following with this example, let's examine form drag—also called shape drag for purposes of swimming analysis because the shape of the body as it moves through the water can produce immediate and far-reaching results. When the water moves over a swimmer's body in a smooth, unbroken path, it is referred to as laminar flow. The molecules of water flow over the body with minimal interruption. When the shape of the object changes to where the molecules start colliding more frequently with the body and themselves, the result is deceleration. If the molecules of water have less surface area to bounce against, drag will naturally be reduced.

To reduce form drag, we need to be conscious of what a swimmer looks like from a frontal view. When observing a swimmer from a head-on position, a cross-sectional area that is as small as possible should be presented for forward motion. When viewed laterally, all body segments should be maintained as close to the longitudinal axis of the body as possible given the constraints of the each stroke. One example of using this knowledge to our advantage is to maintain the head in close alignment with the arms during the push-off. Some coaches allow swimmers to drop their heads below the longitudinal alignment of the arms when streamlining off the wall. This alteration in profile clearly adds to the frontal cross-sectional area of the body and should be discouraged, regardless of whether select elite swimmers are doing it instinctively.

Surface Drag

Surface drag, better known in swimming terms as skin friction, is the result of the friction between the surface of the swimmer's skin and the water. We have long known the importance of reducing this component of drag. Even though we are still somewhat in the dark about the extent to which shaving reduces skin friction, the end result is the perception of moving through the water more smoothly. The reduction of surface drag contributed to the success of high-tech racing suits as many new world records were attained.

Wave Drag

Wave drag is the third type of drag force. Awareness of this factor has revolutionized swimming in the past few years. Wave drag occurs at the interface between two fluids and comes into play when we are swimming close to the surface. Humans will never be able to swim fast enough to reach a state of hydroplaning, but it is surprising how long it took us, in the context of competitive swimming, to realize that the key to efficient propulsion lies in staying underwater for as long as the rules will allow. By using an undulating dolphin kick while remaining deep enough to minimize the retarding force of wave drag, swimmers have entered a new and exciting phase in speed progression.

STABILIZATION OF THE SPINE AND THE ROLE OF THE TRUNK IN SWIMMING

During the past few years, the function of the trunk and spine in swimming has gained attention. First, we outline spinal stability at it applies to human motion. In any activity that involves using our extremities to move in space, such as running or swimming, the trunk must remain stable while the arms and legs are used for propulsion.

To accomplish this motion, a transfer of kinetic energy takes place. The energy originates at the stable end of the body and moves up the kinetic chain to amplify the end result. Briefly explained, the body can be viewed as a series of links, or segments, connected by the joints. When functioning effectively, this link system can help transmit the forces generated by the muscles, which are attached to these links. By invoking what is called the segmental interaction principle, the forces acting between the segments of a body transfer the potential and contractile energy generated by the muscles during the motion through the segments, and the final result is an increased application of force. This is what takes place when, for example, a swimmer's hand is pulled through the water.

How does this apply to swimming stroke mechanics? First, we need to remind ourselves that when floating in the water, ground reaction force is not present. That is, we do not have the luxury of starting out, with the exception of when pushing off the wall or launching off the blocks with our feet planted against an immovable surface. Without this stable base, our ability to impart force is significantly decreased.

A pilot study conducted at our laboratory demonstrated what takes place when ground reaction force is progressively decreased (Prins, 2007). Using high-speed video cameras, a subject was filmed while performing an overhand throwing action using a water polo ball. When measuring the velocity of the ball at the moment it left the thrower's hand, the results were very predictable. As shown in figure 6.5, the ball velocity was highest when the subject stood on land with her feet in a power

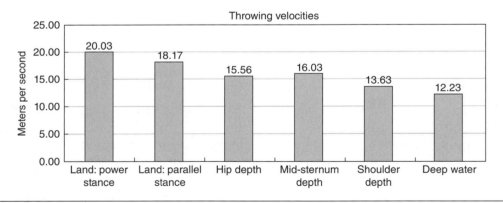

FIGURE 6.5 Comparison of throwing velocities while standing on land or in varying depths of water and when floating in deep water.

Reprinted, by permission, from J.H. Prins, 2007, "Swimming stroke mechanics: A biomechanical viewpoint on the role of the hips and trunk in swimming," *Journal of Swimming Research* 17: 39-44.

stance (i.e., one foot in front of the other). The lowest velocity was recorded when the subject floated in deep water using a flotation vest.

This study confirms what our intuition tells us. In order to exert the highest throwing velocity, we must start with the most stable base we can muster—in this case, standing firmly on the ground. When we attempt to throw while floating unsupported in deep water, the primary base of support is located in the region of the spine and hips, which provides the sole platform from which to initiate muscular forces. This does not imply that the hips should remain immovable. They must, however, provide the necessary base of support to allow for maximum force to be exerted at the other end of the link.

THE BIOMECHANICAL IMPLICATIONS OF CONSCIOUS BODY ROLL

Body roll plays an integral part when swimming freestyle and backstroke because, when swimming these two strokes, the torso rotates around the longitudinal axis of the body. The underlying question is whether hip action is accomplished

1. by conscious, voluntary hip rotation performed either immediately before or during the movements of the arms, or
2. as a consequence of what the arms are doing (i.e., during the hand entry and arm extension, the torso begins and continues to roll without additional conscious motion).

And—this is important—the trunk ceases to roll at the conclusion of the extension phase, immediately before the initiation of the catch phase of the pull.

As discussed previously, when floating on the surface, no ground reaction force is available. In the absence of firm footing, the trunk has to provide the stable platform for the muscles that control both the upper and lower extremities to generate propulsive forces.

We are not suggesting that the hips be held in a rigid, fixed position during swimming because holding any part of the body in a relatively immovable position is clearly unwarranted. Furthermore, voluntarily contracting the anterior abdominal or posterior trunk muscles with the intent of preventing the rotation of the trunk is unnecessarily fatiguing and will interfere with rhythmic, bilateral movements of the arms and legs. Observing the longitudinal motion of the hips in elite freestylers from an underwater lateral view demonstrates the extent to which the torso rotates around a longitudinal axis.

When observing elite competitive swimmers—competing in events ranging from 50 meters to 1,500 meters—it becomes evident that the shorter the event, the flatter and more stable the body position. This reduction in body roll is not performed consciously but rather stems from the need to apply more powerful muscular pulling forces when pulling in an attempt to swim faster. Based on this evidence, we can state that it should not be a question of how much a swimmer's hips should roll but of how much emphasis on active hip rotation should be recommended. Our contention is that recommending conscious rolling of the hips and torso during the course of a stroke cycle is not conducive to the optimal application of force.

TORQUE AND SWIMMING

When we rotate our arms and legs around a joint axis, we exert torque. Torque is the angular equivalent of force. It has two components: the applied force, which is the amount of force applied, and the force arm, which is the perpendicular distance from the axis of rotation to where the force is applied. To move our limbs, we exert internal torque as the muscles exert force on the bones to initiate movement. The internal torque must be greater than the torque that is produced externally, which corresponds to the external load, which is the weight of the limb plus the load. For example, in the shoulder joint the attachments of the muscles to the bones, with few exceptions, are located at very short distances from the axes of rotation. This means that their force arms are relatively very small. Therefore, because torque is the product of force multiplied by the force arm, the internal torque must exceed the external torque for the limb to move. Because the external force arm is many times larger than the internal force arm, the muscle force that is needed to overcome any external load must be disproportionately large. These requirements will vary as the segmental angles change; nevertheless, the end result is that the muscles controlling arm action at the shoulder must work extremely hard to both initiate and sustain motion.

Because the straight-arm recovery in the freestyle is a popular topic of discussion, let's use it to illustrate how torque plays a role in determining how much work is required to perform a straight-arm versus bent-arm high-elbow recovery. Although freestylers have always varied in the degree to which they allow their elbows to flex during the arm recovery, the prevailing recommendation has been to hold the arms in as relaxed a fashion as possible during the above-water phase of the stroke. If the arm is held with minimal tension, we see the typical appearance of the high-elbow recovery. Conversely, the straight-arm recovery requires conscious extension at the elbow joint throughout the entire time the arm is carried over the water. Because the trajectories of the hands vary during these two movements, we need to examine the differences in the torque exerted by the shoulder muscles when performing the two distinct styles of recovery.

When moving an arm that is performing a high-elbow recovery, are these muscles required to exert the same effort as when the arm is held fully extended? After all, the mass of the arm has not changed; the difference is in whether it is held outstretched or kept closer to the shoulder joint as it travels through the arc-like pattern of the arm recovery.

The simple answer is that a difference exists because of a concept referred to as the moment of inertia. Moment of inertia refers to the manner in which the mass of an object, in this case the arm, is distributed relative to its axis of rotation. When the arm is outstretched, it has a larger moment of inertia and, consequently, is more resistant to being moved around the prescribed arc of motion. The greater resistance implies that more muscular work is needed. Therefore, the farther we stretch the arm out, the more effort is required from the shoulder muscles.

If any are reluctant to accept this concept, we have only to examine the way we instinctively bend our elbows when carrying a load. Regardless of how heavy it is, we know intuitively that we must bend our arms. We are simply reducing the moment of inertia so as to reduce the external torque and the ensuing demands we place on the muscles responsible for carrying an external load.

To illustrate this concept we examine the frontal views of a freestyler who is using both the high-elbow and straight-arm recovery. Using a grid that is superimposed on the photographs (figure 6.6), we can arrive at an approximate difference in the moment of inertia of the arm during the respective recoveries. At the instant the arm is in line with the shoulders, an approximately 20% difference exists in the distance the hand is extended laterally.

In addition to the increased demands the straight-arm recovery places on the shoulder muscles, another factor figures prominently into overall efficiency. The arm and hand develop angular velocity as they travel around this curved path. When applied to swimming, the further away the hand is from the shoulder, the larger the angular velocity—that is, the faster the hand is moving around the curve. Therefore, when the elbow is held straight, the recovering hand travels at a higher angular velocity compared with the rate at which the hand travels with the high-elbow recovery. The increase in hand velocity increases the risk of the hand entering the water too quickly, potentially affecting the effectiveness of the catch.

We also know that slowing a fast-moving limb segment is extremely demanding for the muscles and joints because decelerating a fast-moving limb segment requires eccentric muscle contractions. Muscles contracting in an eccentric mode have been shown to have the potential to generate higher contractile forces and are subject to increased stresses. Consequently, the kinematics of the straight-arm recovery, manifested by the increased angular velocities and decelerations of the arm, have the potential to place increased demands on both the muscles and supporting soft tissue. In light of the literally thousands of strokes that are taken by a competitive swimmer, one can expect the incidences of undesirable clinical conditions to increase when adopting this change in style.

© Jan Prins

FIGURE 6.6 Frontal views of the freestyle arm recovery with elbows held in two distinct positions: *(a)* high elbow and *(b)* straight arm.

HIGH-SPEED VIDEOGRAPHY AND MOTION ANALYSIS

As research equipment evolves, so does biomechanics. As far as swimming is concerned, the digital age has revolutionized our ability to capture images and evaluate the resulting data. What took weeks or even months to do before can now be done almost immediately, given the necessary resources. Although the hardware and software used in the laboratory for research in biomechanics is still beyond the average team budget, a greater availability of recording tools now exists, which has generated more creative ways of looking at swimming stroke mechanics.

The use of high-speed cameras is a recent development. With swimmers swimming faster, we see an increased blurring of hands when filming at standard frame rates (30 frames per second). High-speed digital cameras can capture images at 100 frames per second or faster and produce much clearer images, resulting in a more accurate interpretation of the results.

One of the exciting aspects of motion analysis is the ability to combine a selected video clip, enhanced by superimposed segmental lines or "stick figures," with graphs of the selected parameters. When we can visually equate what is taking place with changes, for example, in displacements and velocities, we have a much clearer idea of how changes in underwater motion affect overall performance.

Current research in our laboratory using synchronized, high-speed cameras has resulted in two important findings. Figure 6.7 is a picture of a report generated using

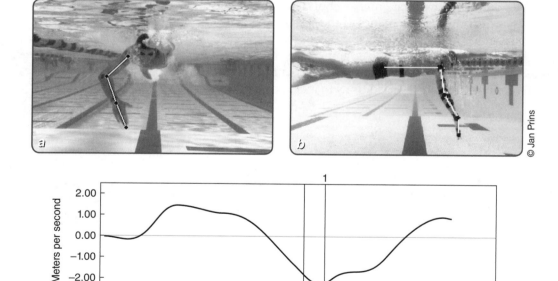

FIGURE 6.7   Freeze frame of a motion analysis report showing synchronized (a) frontal and (b) lateral views of freestyle, combined with a (c) velocity–time graph for hip velocity in the longitudinal plane of motion.

motion analysis software. It combines two synchronized views of a freestyle swimmer with an accompanying graph that shows the linear velocity of the hip during a single underwater pull. The vertical line on the graph is synchronized with the corresponding motion on the video clip.

The first finding is that the peak hip velocity during the stroke cycle occurs not at the latter stages of the underwater pull, but during the middle third of the stroke. The second finding, as shown in the frontal view of the figure and repeated by the majority of the swimmers participating in our initial study (26 subjects), shows that the degree of elbow bend assumed during this middle phase appears to be more of an obtuse angle (greater than 90 degrees).

Not surprisingly, both of these findings are closely tied to increasing underwater propulsive forces of the pull. As discussed earlier, we now believe that the majority of our potential for swimming faster is the result of using propulsive drag forces. The generic formula for drag force (F_D) is as follows:

$$F_D = \tfrac{1}{2} \, C_D . r . Ap . V^2$$

While the two variables we have control of in the formula are the cross-sectional area (Ap) of the limbs (primarily the hands and feet) and the velocity (V^2) at which these segments are moved underwater, it is the velocity that should be our focus. We stated in the previous section that according to the dictates of angular motion, a hand traveling over a path when held farther from the shoulder will have a higher linear velocity. Consequently, as this formula shows, we are capable of exerting higher propulsive drag forces when pulling with a straighter arm. As a reminder, to avoid imposing intolerable internal loads on the shoulder joint, we do not want to pull with a fully extended arm.

This discussion should immediately prompt the question, "How does this tie into the age-old dictate that we should hold our arms at a 90-degree elbow bend in the middle portion of our stroke?" Although a detailed explanation is beyond the scope of this chapter, the reason as to why we cannot continue to make this assumption is clear. We bend our elbows to minimize the work imposed on our shoulders when trying to overcome a fixed external load or resistance. Carrying a heavy weight and climbing out of the pool are examples of our response to overcoming a fixed resistance. However, the water is not a fixed resistance, necessitating that we employ the formula described above when attempting to move ourselves when immersed in a fluid.

Although this statement may sound simplistic, it has far-reaching ramifications. When viewed in the context of swimming, it now appears that the instinctive tendency of elite swimmers to ignore the recommendation to hold the elbow at 90 degrees in the middle phases of the freestyle and backstroke has a biomechanical explanation. This provides us with a scientific clarification to support what a few insightful coaches have been quietly advocating the last few years.

OTHER RESEARCH EQUIPMENT

Three other avenues for investigating swimming stroke mechanics warrant mention, all of which necessitate the installation of specialized apparatus and the reliance on software written explicitly for interpreting the resulting data.

Computational Fluid Dynamics   With increased application of computational fluid dynamics (CFD), researchers are examining fluid flow around a swimmer's body. The data for CFD studies are obtained from modeling; computers simulate drag and propulsive forces around the body. The advantage of CFD is that it can simulate the interaction of the water around a swimmer and examine areas of study such as the generation of vortices and how effectively the varying layers of the water surrounding a swimmer can either assist or slow forward motion.

Particle Image Velocimetry   Also a relatively new technology, this was developed for observing the flow patterns around fish and insects. Lasers are used to track the movements of particles, usually glass beads, polystyrene, or aluminum flakes, as they travel around the moving object. The technique has been refined so that fluid flow, including vortices, can be observed. Recent attempts to apply the technology to a swimmer's hand have produced encouraging results, but much needs to be done before the technology can be applied to more substantial views of a swimmer's body.

Swimming Velocity Meters   A number of groups, both research and commercial, use swimming velocity meters to record swimming speeds. When using a swimming velocity meter, a swimmer pulls a fine wire cable that is attached by a belt to a direct current generator mounted on the pool deck. The fluctuations in the swimmer's overall speed are recorded and synchronized with a video camera. The motion of the body performing the stroke is recorded via tension in the cable, which is used to analyze changes in stroke mechanics. The equipment is relatively inexpensive and easy to set up, but many who have used this technology have noted that the interpretation of the graphs is contingent on the periods of time during each stroke cycle when the tension on the cable is not constant. This variability in tension is due to the overall fluctuations in forward motion of the body, which is inherent in all swimming strokes.

CONCLUSION

As we learn more about the application of biomechanical principles as they affect swimming, it is important to use these principles to better explain stroke mechanics. However, caution is recommended because it is easy to introduce ideas and terminology that may appear technically accurate but could be misleading. Statements such as "lead with the hips" are not only ambiguous but are scientifically unsound when taken literally.

We must remember that while we continue to experiment, we need to tread carefully when proposing untested ideas. We must remain aware of the anatomical and biomechanical implications of what we recommend, particularly when it leads to alterations in the thousands of repetitive movements performed at every workout.

7

The X Factor Revisited

George Block

In 1971, the great Dr. James Counsilman gave one of the most famous talks in swimming, "The X Factor." In his speech, Counsilman pondered the secret to success in developing coaches and asked, "Is there any one factor or trait that determines a successful swimming coach?"

Counsilman reviewed the effects of intelligence, personality, leadership, good looks, desire, and energy on the success of a potential coach. None proved to be the master trait of a successful coach. He went on to critique his own academic preparation of future coaches. He looked at the need for coaches to master physiology, biomechanics, research, and nutrition, and found that only the mastery of psychology was predictive of success in the coaching ranks.

The psychology that Counsilman believed to the key to success in coaching was not textbook Psychology 101. In his discussion of intelligence, Counsilman said, "Intelligence has a lot to do with success in coaching … (but) the type of intelligence I am speaking of … could better be called a type of perception."

SKILLS FOR SUCCESS IN COACHING

In 1971, Counsilman was, as always, about 25 years ahead of his time. In 1996, Dr. Daniel Goleman published *Emotional Intelligence*, which defined exactly the special intelligence, or perception, that Counsilman had mentioned. In 1998, Goleman followed up with *Working With Emotional Intelligence*, which echoed almost verbatim Counsilman's thoughts.

On Goleman's website (danielgoleman.info), he points out—as Counsilman did in 1971—that "business leaders and outstanding performers are not defined by their IQs or even their job skills, but by their 'emotional intelligence': a set of competencies that distinguishes how people manage feelings, interact, and communicate. . . . Emotional intelligence is the barometer of excellence on virtually any job. . . . It counts more than IQ or expertise."

Goleman's *Working With Emotional Intelligence* was one of the first books to catalog a list of teachable and learnable skills that, once mastered, would allow anyone to succeed at the highest levels in his or her profession. *Working With Emotional Intelligence* should be on the must read list of any coach.

The 12 personal competencies and 13 key relationship skills that Goleman describes in his book are echoed by list after best-selling list of master traits of success: 7 *Habits of Highly Successful People* (Covey, 1989), *20 Immutable Laws of Leadership* (Gwaltney, 2009), *21 Irrefutable Laws of Leadership* (Maxwell, 1998), and *17 Indisputable Laws of Teamwork* (Maxwell, 2001). [Maxwell may have been the master list maker. He also published *25 Ways to Win With People* (2005) and *Today Matters* (2004).]

Coaches can and should browse through the management section of any bookstore to find list after list of the same traits of success that Counsilman first alluded to in 1971. These books should be part of our self-improvement process, if we can be honest enough to assess ourselves critically

However, the traits listed by Counsilman and others are not traits at all. They are tools—tools of the profession of coaching. All coaches are physiologists, biomechanists, researchers, managers, nutritionists, politicians, and even psychologists. But the tools of the coach do not determine what kind of athlete is developed any more than the tools of the carpenter determine what kind of house is built, or the musical instrument determines the song, or the instruments of the surgical suite determine the outcome of the surgery. The product of the tools is in the hands of the carpenter, musician, physician, artist, or coach. The effective use or application of tools determines the result.

The X Factor

Counsilman considered many tools and traits in an attempt to determine what makes up the X factor in coaching.

Counsilman believed in four professional coaching tools:

1. Physiology
2. Biomechanics
3. Psychology
4. Organization

Counsilman also believed that every coach must have eight human traits:

1. Love and affection
2. Security
3. Status
4. Achievement
5. Affiliation
6. Recognition
7. Self-esteem
8. Challenge

THE COACH'S X FACTOR

The X factor that contributes to the success of a coach is somewhat elusive. However, it is an essential ingredient in separating the great coach from the average coach. Perhaps we can discover the coach's master skill, that elusive X factor, by looking to the hard sciences: physiology, stroke mechanics, and nutrition.

Physiology   What coach hasn't been both befuddled and amazed by the swimmer who has only kicked all season long yet achieves personal bests at the end of the season? And who hasn't been frustrated by the swimmer who just can't seem to make practice but still achieves breakthroughs at the championship meet? The master skill is not physiology.

Stroke Mechanics   Every coach knows that stroke mechanics set the limits of a swimmer's performance. The swimmer can't achieve beyond his or her skill level… except when they do. As the performance pyramid gets progressively higher, technical aberrations get fewer and farther between but, even in the finals of the Olympic Games, they don't disappear entirely. Biomechanics might be the ceiling of performance, but it isn't the floor.

Nutrition   Every 4 years we hear about the latest Olympic champion who is fueled by junk food. No one doubts the importance of nutrition. The prevalence of dietary supplement use among world-class swimmers shows that they generally recognize how important proper nutrition is. But the best nutritionist isn't the best coach. In fact, many more swimmers eat their way off of the podium than onto it.

If the master skill for coaching success isn't found in the hard sciences, perhaps we should look to the social sciences: management, political science, and psychology.

Management   A top manager will be very successful. She will have a large, well-organized team and a profitable swim school that feeds both money and swimmers into her team, and her parents' group will be organized to support her efforts. Do the best swimmers always come from the largest clubs? Sometimes, but not always.

Sometimes they come from the absent-minded professor whose pool deck and garage is filled with homemade gimmicks, computers, and notepads. These researchers (both formal and informal) have pushed American swimming forward. They nearly always produce provocative ideas and occasionally produce the best swimmers.

Political Science   Politically skilled coaches generally secure facility time by working with school districts or city councils. They turn dysfunctional team boards into networking and meet-organizing machines. They create strong, team-first environments and produce quality swimmers on a regular basis—but so do small-team loners.

Psychology   What about Counsilman's master skill of psychology? All coaches believe that we are psychologists, perhaps even psychiatrists, but we are still waiting for the first psychologist to appear on an Olympic coaching staff. Great performance may be incompatible with great psychology because the balanced life that is so valued in the mental health world is incompatible with the passion needed for the highest levels of success in any endeavor.

We have all seen swimmers succeed beyond their conditioning, stroke technique, and nutritional habits. We have seen champions come from large teams, small teams, great facilities, and dungeons. Great swimmers have been produced by full-time, well-trained professional coaches and by semiretired part-timers. So what do these coaches have in common?

Swimmers can succeed beyond their training and technical skills, but they never succeed beyond their level of belief. The late, great Richard Quick, former collegiate and Olympic coach, said, "I believe in belief." He knew that a swimmer had to believe it before he could achieve it. Thus, he knew that coaches often had to act as belief bridges, believing for their swimmers until their swimmers could believe in themselves.

The great coaches all have strong belief systems. Counsilman called this their concept, or black box. He said that every coach has a concept with their own model of how the human system works—the physiology, neurology, and psychology—and the coach works with that concept to produce swimmers. The great coaches spend significant time building and refining their concept and passionately believe in it.

So what is this great, belief-transmitting skill? The master skill that I see in the great coaches is evangelism. Evangelism is generally associated with words and phrases such as missionary zeal, purpose, or activity; militant zeal for a cause; and zealously preaching, promulgating, and disseminating. This paints a clear picture of every great coach. They are missionaries. They are zealous, purposeful, and active. They are continuously preaching, promulgating, and disseminating. This evangelism is how belief gets transmitted.

Every coach has his or her own beliefs. They can be, and usually are, very different. But every successful coach has studied the sport and developed a belief system that can be passionately evangelized to swimmers, parents, and administrators.

How do coaches evangelize? Some preach, some joke, and others whisper, but every swimmer is a doubter who must see and touch it before they can believe it. This is where coaching comes in.

Self-confidence comes from doing things we have never done before. Belief comes from doing things we were sure we could never do. Successful coaches build self-confidence by allowing swimmers to do things they have never done before and then create belief by moving swimmers to accomplishments they were sure were impossible. How do coaches do this? In as many ways as there are coaches. They do it more, then harder, then faster. They do it with race pace and short rest and overcompensation and specificity. They do it on dry land, with weights, medicine balls, body weight, and tubes. They get every motion perfect or they confound motor learning with speed and complexity. Some simply know how and when to rest.

No one way exists, but their way exists. The best coaches develop their way deliberately, believe in it passionately, and evangelize both that belief and that passion.

CONCLUSION

What is the X factor that separates the best from the rest? The best coaches are passionate believers, and they evangelize that belief to their swimmers by acting as belief bridges until the swimmer can passionately believe in himself. Quick was right to believe in belief, and so was Counsilman. Belief is the best psychology.

8

Planning for Success

Stephan Widmer

This chapter is about you, the coach who wants to move forward with your teaching methods. By buying this book you have passed the first and most important test: You are ready to learn. A successful coach constantly endeavors to become a more adept and competent professional. Progress and education are a continuous journey.

The goal of a successful coach is to learn and grow with their athlete in pursuit of a breakthrough in performance. Every situation provides opportunities for coaches, athletes, and support staff to learn and modify their approach based on the analyzed outcomes. These changes don't have to be enormous or dramatic, but it is valuable to ensure that they are part of a daily process of growth.

It is important to be totally honest with yourself, stick to your core principles, and wisely address the areas that demand your attention. All athletes have very different personalities, and, as mentors, coaches have to find out what triggers each individual. It is equally important to discover what triggers you personally as a coach on your own journey to change. This chapter shows you what you can do to bring about positive change. Celebrate change as an opportunity to grow!

The key focus of this chapter is the little things that, when added together, can make a dramatic difference. Essential core principles are highlighted, and the advice won't get too complicated. Swimming is not easy. Winning is not easy. Improving is not easy. But improving 100 little things by 1% is easier than improving one thing by 100%. As all the 1% improvements start to add up, you will recognize that you've made progress, and from that small step forward your confidence will grow. This confidence can be enough to make you improve another 1%, and from there success can breed more success.

AN INTRODUCTION TO PLANNING FOR SUCCESS

To understand the present of a person, you need to look at their past; if you would like to know about their future, look at their present. This is the story of the professional development and growth that have helped me to become the coach I am today.

I grew up in Switzerland and started coaching in Uster, a city near Zürich. I always had great support from the club manager, Philippe Walter. Philippe believed that anything is possible. One year into my coaching I was selected as a Swiss team coach for the 1994 world championships in Rome. These world titles were vital to my decision to endeavor to become a world-renowned coach. At these championships I started dreaming about coaching athletes to a world-class level. However, I had a strong feeling that I couldn't achieve my dreams in my home country and decided to change my environment. I believed strongly in my Swiss education and increasingly in my professional abilities, but I needed bigger daily challenges in a professional environment.

The Swiss swimming situation was not encouraging; only one Swiss swimmer has won an Olympic medal (Étienne Dagon over 200-meter breaststroke at the 1984 Los Angeles Olympic Games). It was time to move on, so I decided to leave my harbor. I knew this was the right decision, but it was nonetheless tough. I quit two jobs, both of which I loved, and I left behind my family, my friends, and my culture to follow my dream. Travelling backpacker-style around the globe, I visited the best swimming nations in the world. On this journey to the unknown I met Scott Volkers, a coach who produced an Australian Olympic gold medal and a world record.

At the time I lacked one crucial part, the discovery of which made me the coach I am today. Scott guided me toward an "anything is possible" attitude! I worked as his assistant coach in Brisbane, the capital city of Queensland, Australia, from 1997 to 2000. Today I call Scott a great friend, coaching peer, and mentor. Had I never left my home country, I would have never arrived at my new home in Brisbane and would not have been exposed to such a high level of expertise in coaching world-class athletes. I had a strong feeling to follow my dream, and through one leap of faith and a lot of hard work I find myself at the pinnacle of coaching. Ironically, at the very championships that triggered my journey toward elite coaching, Scott's athlete, Samantha Riley, won two gold medals. The risk-taking approach combined with that "anything is possible" attitude has been a centerpoint of my coaching ever since.

For the past 13 years I have worked at the Queensland Academy of Sport, a state-based sport institute that is financially supported by the Queensland government. Today the Queensland Academy of Sport supports 21 sports, including 18 Olympic sports, and employs the nation's leading coaching staff, a variety of support staff, and scientists. It is Australia's most successful sport institute, winning 66% of Australia's 2008 Olympic medals. What a great breeding ground for world-class and high-performance, sport-specific information! Through my exposure to other sports and various approaches to coaching, I have been able to adapt my own approach to swimming. In the words of André Gide, "One doesn't discover new lands without consenting to lose sight of the shore for a very long time."

The following coaching concept is based on a process-driven model that employs people-management skills. It is used to positively influence human behavior in order to get athletes to reach their true potential.

PROCESS-DRIVEN COACHING VERSUS OUTCOME-ORIENTATED TRAINING

My approach has always been process-driven coaching that focuses on the day-to-day technical steps, the things one can control, and not results that may be determined by others at the end of the season.

At the beginning of the preparation, the athlete and coach should meet to discuss their individual goals and clearly identify specific areas of improvement for the next part of their journey. After this point, the coach can design a simple process to change one specific area at a time. Training throughout the preparation should not be focused on the desired outcome, such as breaking world records. That's the athlete's dream. The coach is responsible for creating opportunities where the athlete can rehearse one specific skill, often on a weekly basis.

We as coaches must also create individual standards for these areas so we can measure improvement and celebrate little steps forward. Using these small steps will create a paradigm shift in your thinking and attitude and, like anything, will take time. The tiniest progression—a baby step—requires an adequate celebration and should excite the entire team. Seeing oneself improve creates positive energy, stimulates momentum forward, increases self-belief, and increases confidence. This process will get you where you want to be.

Break down your program into each component and keep searching for new ideas and methods in these areas. Of course, you should always aim to improve a team, whether winning or losing. Accept and acknowledge differences. The best organizations encourage difference and enthusiastic contributions to the program. Such an approach stimulates change, innovation, and experimentation.

The process-driven approach to training

- creates a belief that we can always do better;
- reveals specific and individual areas to improve on;
- emphasizes that the more areas we are able to improve, the more confident the athlete is when lining up for the next big race;
- creates a more complex, experienced athlete with higher individual standards;
- relies on the athlete's dream and attitude toward their challenging training program; and
- is adaptable (the second you think you know the game, the game will change).

Following are a few other things to consider when working with a process-driven approach.

It is derived by process. Early in my coaching career, I was educated to take nothing at face value and to not blindly copy drills or anything else used by other coaches. As a coach, you must understand the process that you are trying to achieve and develop the training plans, workouts, drills, and conditioning to allow that process to happen. If you don't have a sound reason why an athlete is doing something, then they should not have to do it!

It is based in science.   Underpin your coaching by thoroughly understanding anatomy, applied physiology, and biomechanics. I firmly believe that swimming coaching should be based on science. It should inform the process we use to develop the athletes we work with.

It is shaped by experience.   Although a comprehensive knowledge of science is important, it should be used only as a guide for training principles. Regardless of what scientists may tell us, theoretical scientific research should never be used to set limitations. As swimming coaches, we move forward and break through boundaries in training and competition! Despite having a university degree in human movement, I use experience I have built up over decades to keep learning. How can I tell if the workload is too heavy for my swimmers? I know one thing for sure: I won't find the answer in a science book! I have to learn from past experience, test my athletes, push the limits, and find possible solutions.

Although coaching is process driven and science based, it is shaped by experience. You must keep learning valuable lessons from accomplishment and from disappointment. This will help you set up your vital learning process and will allow you to better understand coaching swimming.

WORKING WITH PEOPLE

Every coach must remember that we work with human beings. Therefore, we need to attain great balance between pushing an athlete to their physical and mental limit and staying emotionally in touch with the individual. A swimmer's job is testing and demanding. Pushing beyond the comfort zone set after set and day after day is challenging. Executing each repetition to full potential is hard. I guarantee them one thing every day they see me: that is pain! I want them to have a good time, but I need their full commitment.

Find the balance between having the highest expectation from yourself and your athletes and being content and able to have a laugh. The happier people are, the better the work they can do. Great training is a balancing act between progressive overload of training (physiology) and positive emotional aspects (psychology). You need to find equilibrium between a devoted, individualized exercise regimen and a happy mood. See the excitement in finding areas to improve in an athlete.

- Understand that the athlete is always a work in progress.
- Create swimming-specific versus life-related learning opportunities.
- Shape pool-based versus land-based training to optimize performance in the water.
- Find 100 or more areas where the athlete can improve.
- Give each athlete standards and make small improvements in these areas.
- Do little things a little bit better to create belief and healthier self-esteem.

◆ Teach your athletes not to rely on beating their opposition but to rely on being the best they can be in their own office and in their own lane!

◆ Give athletes process goals for racing. The better job they do in each section of their race, the more likely they will create a great outcome for themselves.

A talented athlete learns very fast. They use experience and information from the past, whether it was a positive experience or a negative one, to create a better outcome in the future. Learn equally from both positive and negative experiences!

ELEMENTS OF PROCESS-DRIVEN COACHING

A coach has to understand the complexity of human limitations, both physical and mental. What does it take to lead athletes to their potential? Where do you find the key for their ability to break world records, to win world championships, or to reach the pinnacle of sport—an Olympic gold medal?

As a coach you have to keep strong because no one will push you. If you aren't strong, then your swimmers won't be strong. If you lower your standards, your swimmers will lower their standards. It's a big challenge and a lonely job! Throughout a preparation swimmers often have different thoughts and opinions about their coach—and it's not always praise. You sometimes hurt your athletes to push them to their limits. You must help them to find the best performance that they are capable of on that day and ensure they perform to their capacity during every training session.

Coaches' Expectations of Athletes

As coaches, we always put great expectations on our athletes. And that is nothing but fair! I demand from my swimmers a very high level of multifaceted professionalism and a positive mindset toward learning for a long and prosperous athletic career.

All athletes should have a positive attitude toward reaching their true potential on a daily basis. This includes willingness to

◆ work hard consistently,

◆ be committed and stay committed,

◆ be unconditionally dedicated to learning,

◆ do things the right way at all times,

◆ perform with a high level of effort no matter what, and

◆ handle setbacks without exception.

Coaches' Expectations of Themselves

I make certain that I put higher professional expectations on myself than on my athletes. I was taught to ask myself the hard questions first and not point the finger at anyone else. What can I change in my applied coaching and teaching methods to allow my team members to grow in an efficient way and at a very fast rate? How can I set up a training environment and culture that ensures a more positive outcome for each athlete involved? This entire process has to start with me.

- If athletes don't perform to their potential at a championship event, I have to examine my own coaching performance with foremost importance.
- If my athletes underperform in the weekly main training sessions, I have to analyze my own contribution.
- If the technique of an athlete constantly falls apart under fatigue and stress, I have to reflect on my training regimen and the exercise load that I give my swimmers (volume × intensity).

My coaching expectation list includes the following:

Attitude

- Be honest with my athletes, my staff, and myself at all times.
- Have and show respect for my athletes and support and value their individuality.
- Expect perfection—starting with myself.
- Lead by example and expect more from myself than from my swimmers. There is no substitute for hard work.

Action

- Don't try to do things. Just do them!
- Be constantly innovative in my coaching methods.
- Create real, race-specific training loads.
- Consider what needs to change based on performance in training and racing. Don't introduce change without a purpose in mind.
- New isn't necessarily better. The main goal is always improvement, no matter what new developments arise.
- Create an expectation and culture in swimmers so that they perform and act in the exact way I want them to!
- Teach my swimmers that every set is a test set on its own.
- Embrace innovative technology and any progress it might bring.

Learning

- Make the difference today for a better tomorrow and prepare now for potential opportunities in the future.
- Embrace competition on all levels and adapt as progress is made.
- Spend time on self-analysis.
- Continue to learn about myself. What triggers me in a positive or negative way? How can I use my personality to more positively influence my swimmers?

A Competitive Nature

I have always had a strong desire to be the best I could be. It started in my childhood when I competed in many sports, and this desire is still one of my most important assets as a coach.

One particular coach stated to me that his vision is similar to mine, but he is not as hungry for success as I am. This is in itself a big discrepancy. You need to be passionate and enthusiastic about your coaching and about your swimmers' performances. I still highly respect that coach as a person. The only thing I mentioned to him was that I hope he communicates his belief to his swimmers and his club!

Learning Progression Through Baby Steps

The practical principle I use to improve my world-class swimmers can be successfully used to advance any area of coaching. Every improvement starts with a small change—a little baby step forward!

From the first day of its existence, a baby is confronted with amazing challenges and a very steep learning curve. Luckily, the newborn doesn't comprehend how hard and long the journey ahead actually is. The baby would probably never start this stumbling road if he or she was aware of the frequent difficulties—such as learning to walk—ahead.

Why do babies want to walk? In my opinion, it is definitely not easy and is potentially a painful experience, but they see other people doing it and therefore they know it is possible. Kids don't understand some of the potential risks of learning. They just have a real go at it.

Do you believe that the one thing you would like to change, in your coaching or in your swimmers, is harder than learning to walk? Toddlers practice very often, have a lot of learning opportunities, and handle setbacks exceptionally well. A baby doesn't give up after the first fall. They simply get up and try again.

Often, babies improve rapidly because they are profoundly supported and constantly encouraged by their loved ones to overcome their hurdles and fears. Similarly, in elite sport, the way to improve performance is to take baby steps forward, and when athletes reach a setback they can pick themselves up with support from their coaches and support staff.

By doing the following, you can teach your athletes that little steps forward are the only way to success.

- Create your own picture of what you want your future to look like.
- Create learning opportunities for little steps forward.
- Create an environment for change.
- Help the athlete believe that they actually can become what they'd like to grow into!
- Seeing change creates belief and develops confidence.

Eight Steps Toward Change

In order to take the next step in your coaching, you must be willing to fully commit to the process of change! Embrace the challenges, give yourself a chance to change, create a support team around you, and get excited about even the tiniest improvement. Following are eight steps to help you do this:

1. Identify and select your goal (dream).
2. Set high standards and keep on raising the bar (benchmarks).
3. Create learning opportunities (training).
4. Get someone you trust and respect to be your mentor (coaching).
5. Monitor and analyze your steps (results).
6. Evaluate with your mentor (analyzing).
7. Celebrate your progress (personal best marks and rewards).
8. Review your process by adapting new standards and goals (new benchmarks and dreams).

In my personal approach to coaching, throughout a preparation I never focus on the desired outcome, such as athletes breaking their own personal best times, setting new world records, or winning international events. I teach my athletes to focus mainly on the single repetition ahead of them and to be the best they can be for each single repetition. And the rest of the season takes care of itself the following way.

- The accumulation of a lot of great repetitions creates a great set.
- The accumulation of a lot of great sets creates a great session.
- The accumulation of a lot of great sessions creates a great week.
- The accumulation of a lot of great weeks creates a great preparation.

By following this simple (but not simplistic) pathway (see figure 8.1), you won't have to rely on a miracle to reach your desired outcome.

To change and progress toward their potential, athletes have to regularly leave their comfort zone for extended periods. The role of a coach is to support and guide swimmers out of their comfort zone as often as possible. While coaches are not able to endure the pain of each training session for their athletes, they must use their expertise and experience to guide the athletes through this necessary part of becoming world class. Learn about your athletes and discover what triggers them to change. Become skilled at successfully encouraging them to leave their comfort zone and set new, more challenging boundaries.

Coaches will face the challenge of change in every aspect of a preparation. They must be ready to adapt within a season, a week, a day, or a training session. A training program should be designed around improving little things that make the big difference! The same process can be used to approach each individual athlete's pathway to success.

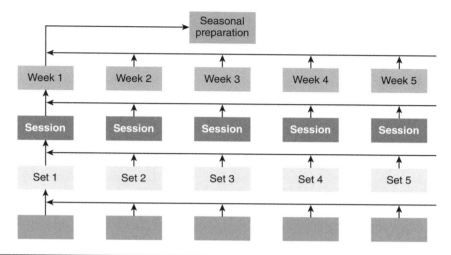

FIGURE 8.1 Seasonal preparation from beginning to end.

Plan for Change

At the beginning of every new season, I ask myself the following questions about the mindset of my athletes:

- ◆ Do they dream large enough about their short-term, seasonal goals? Or will they train without purpose for the upcoming preparation?
- ◆ Do they arrive hungry and incredibly keen for their first session? And, more vitally, are they able to maintain their enthusiasm throughout the long and extensive preparation?
- ◆ Are they satisfied and ready to rest on their laurels or eager to push their limits and discover a new level of performance?
- ◆ How badly do they want to be more skilled and better trained to become a faster swimmer by the end of the preparation?
- ◆ Do they approach my successful and slightly painful sets as opportunities that are especially created for them to improve at a faster rate than their opposition? Or will they see only obstacles on their way to the season's major competition?

When Libby Trickett (née Lenton) arrived at my program in October 2002, other swimmers warned me that she missed sessions all the time and had a dreadful attitude toward training. However, Libby was very good at recognizing what specific help and guidance she needed from her future coach. It had to be a coach with strong natural leadership, someone who set very strict boundaries and didn't accept easy options at any stage. She acknowledged this and, aware of my coaching reputation, Libby came straight to my pool. I quickly noticed that Libby was a diamond in the rough. She is a very talented athlete and it was very obvious to me why she hadn't yet performed to her potential. Within a week I decided I had to change four specific areas of my coaching in order for Libby to succeed:

1. Exactly follow the program as set up by the head coach, such as 100% attendance of training sessions.
2. Create learning opportunities for Libby to grow belief and confidence from within.
3. Develop a new race pace training regimen for her 100-meter speed.
4. Modify Libby's stroke mechanics from a catch-up model (middle-distance technique) to an advance and overlapping model (sprint-oriented technique).

Once Libby and I fully committed to my program and newly formed coaching model, things slowly started lining up so that she could realize her childhood dream.

Leisel Jones joined my program in November 2004 after the Athens Olympic Games. She had obvious talent, but at the time the general consensus was that she had a mental block associated with winning and that she sabotaged her own efforts. I never believed it. I saw only one reason that she had not won at major international championships at that time: She simply wasn't ready to win! Hearing and reading about it in the media again and again didn't help Leisel or her performances. It didn't matter whether her coach, her mother, or anyone else believed in her abilities; things were not yet in place for her to achieve what she so strongly desired.

As with Libby, I decided that I had to change four swimming-specific areas of my coaching in order for Leisel to succeed:

1. Create learning opportunities for Leisel to grow belief and confidence from within through my process-driven coaching approach.
2. Expand her kick repertoire by putting a more enhanced engine behind an already efficient kick for additional propulsion.
3. Adapt Leisel's kick–pull timing with the aims of less fluctuation with a cycle and a more consistent velocity in one stroke through a more overlapping model.
4. Steadily improve her start abilities toward world-class standards.

Leisel Jones' breakthrough came one year later at the 2005 FINA World Championships in Montreal, Canada, where she won the 100-meter and 200-meter breaststroke world titles. She proved to the swimming world and, most importantly, herself that she has both the head and the heart to perform under enormous pressure.

After winning bronze in the 100 meters at the Athens Olympics, Leisel said, "I guess I'm just not meant to win." She just forgot to add the word *yet*.

Libby and Leisel both needed change! Change allowed them to progress from being great athletes to being the greatest athletes in their events.

Look for ways to make your program better. Evaluate every part of your program to find better ways to do things. This sort of assessment should never be a matter of discarding everything or nothing but should involve a balance between retaining what is good and modifying what can be improved.

Promote change by applying some simple rules:

- Don't expect instant change or a fast progression.
- Everything worthwhile takes time!
- Make sure you recognize little steps forward and celebrate each one.
- Any positive small change should encourage you.
- The accumulation of little steps forward will lead you to forward progression.

Fueling Your Action Toward Your Dream

How often do you find yourself dreaming about specific change? Once a season, every week, or 24 hours a day and 7 days a week? We have to be—in a good way—obsessive–compulsive! I dream all the time, often at the strangest places and moments, about coaching specifics such as the following:

- A new and innovative approach to a different weekly training cycle
- A new progression of a main set
- An enhanced ability to deal with work-related stress and work more efficiently under pressure
- New ways to trigger my senior athletes

I always find myself questioning old routines or learning opportunities. How can I get to the same result faster or to a better outcome with a more efficient and innovative process? I was very fortunate throughout my schooling and coaching to have teachers and mentors that encouraged me to improve my skills in the art of great questioning. Learn to ask great questions, and you will discover the answers that will contribute to your expanding knowledge base and possibly lead to a new approach.

Is it possible to plan for success if your swimmers don't dream about their future results? Is it possible to plan for your swimmers' success without dreaming about your swimmers' future results? We can achieve our potential only by having a very strong vision about our future. You need a lot of passion if you want to achieve high standards and goals! Use this passion to actually work hard toward these goals on a daily basis. In the past I have met people who have had goals and dreams coming out of their ears but will never achieve them. There comes a time when you have to stop dreaming, roll up your sleeves, and work for it. As someone once wisely said, "Some people dream of success, while others wake up and work hard at it." You must be willing to work for your goals no matter what your dream is. Situations vary, but regardless of whether you coach Olympic champions and world record holders or age-group swimmers trying to qualify for their first state or national competition, the underpinning concepts remain the same. When planning long-term projects such as a season plan, middle-term ideas such as a weekly cycle, or short-term methods such as the progression of a main set, certain objectives should be addressed on a daily basis:

1. Setting challenging coaching values for yourself
2. Setting individual and group standards for your swimmers

3. Believing in the standards you set

4. Selling the standards to the athletes

5. Never compromising

6. Continuing to raise the bar

7. Constantly evaluating your best practice by looking for diverse ways to make progress

Ensuring that you meet these objectives each day will have a big effect on your personal and professional development and will take you a step closer to your own goals, whatever they may be. Coaches from all backgrounds and experiences have asked me how to realize their ultimate coaching dream of seeing their own swimmers give world record-breaking performances. The methods I have used in my coaching practices are as follows:

* Set realistic short-term goals. Short-term goals should lead you to a long-term goal.
* Allow for occasional setbacks along the way.
* Turn setbacks into positive learning opportunities.
* Set a training schedule and stick to it.
* Constantly challenge yourself.
* Create belief in yourself.

Characteristics of Effective Goal Setting

Throughout the years, Wendy Swift, the Queensland swimming sport psychologist, and I developed the following guidelines about the goal-setting process for our athletes and coaches:

* **Written**. Goals must be in writing to stimulate memory, which will allow you to move in that direction.
* **Positive**. You must always move toward something.
* **Present tense**. When you write a goal, it can be extremely effective to write it in the "I am" form.
* **Dated**. Goals are more effective if they include a target date for achievement.
* **Specific**. Make sure you are designing the life you want.
* **Planned**. Develop a series of action steps that lead you from where you are to where you want to be.
* **Aware**. Be aware of the changing directions you may encounter along the way.

My standards as a coach are extremely high for my athletes and even higher for myself. As a child I was very fortunate to receive great leadership and unconditional love from my parents. It wasn't until much later in life that I started to understand the great values my parents instilled in me. I grew up with the ideal that if you start something then you give it your best shot from the beginning. Life does not offer too many second chances!

Athlete Centered, Coach Driven, and Service Supported

My coaching philosophy is entirely centered on the athlete. Every coaching action has to be about the swimmers and about maximizing their individual potential. How can one develop individual learning opportunities for every season, every week, every session, every set, and every repetition? I don't believe in one massive improvement in training or at a competition but rather in the accumulation of many minuscule (1%) improvements!

In the program, the coach has to be the driving force behind actual transformation. The coach leads and manages a multidisciplinary program that is aimed at developing and delivering best-practice processes to the individuals, the training groups, and the support team. As a coach, you are the captain of the boat and entirely in charge of who gets on board and in what direction it heads! You are responsible for gaining vital experience and knowledge while developing the necessary skills and leadership abilities. Therefore, you must look very closely at yourself and your coaching performance. It's no good to blame an athlete for an unsuccessful outcome. Ensure that you keep developing and refining all the tools you need to be successful.

One thing I learned very early into my coaching career is that one cannot do all the tasks of modern coaching alone. You need support and to allow other passionate people to contribute to a central mission. Find support staff that are passionate and able to help the program maximize performances of individual athletes. The coach then has to set boundaries for the staff.

Holistic Coaching Philosophy

The process-driven approach of progression teaches young swimmers worthwhile skills not only in the arena of sport but also in life. As a coach, I hold true to a holistic coaching philosophy when preparing my swimmers. It consists of more than simply devising and supervising the technical and physiological aspects of training. I want to provide a positive environment where athletes can grow, learn, and become wise and responsible global citizens. Swimming involves so much more than winning medals and doing personal best times. Discover the many wonderful ways that swimming will help your athletes to develop physically and mentally and to acquire the many life skills they will enjoy for the rest of their lives.

Not every swimmer you coach has the talent to be victorious in the pool. But every swimmer can be victorious in life. When I try to help a swimmer improve a single skill such as stroke correction, I can succeed or I can lose. However, if I assist this same swimmer in many areas, they will improve in skills such as learning, commitment, and self-confidence that will equip them for life after sport. And that is a win for everyone.

How useful is your current approach to learning? Telling people how to stroke or swim does not lead to long-term learning, but supporting and encouraging your swimmer's journey to self-discovery does. I assume a responsibility far greater than the outcome of a single event. My desire is to provide an environment in which talent can flourish and to positively affect the leaders of tomorrow.

Aspects of the Holistic Coaching Philosophy

To coach a particular athlete is to coach a unique individual. When using a holistic philosophy, it is important to look at three aspects of an athlete's development: the performance, the socialization, and the education. Over time, these aspects must be in balance to create a stable performance platform. Both the coach and the swimmer need to ensure that each career aspect receives adequate attention and must create a long-term development plan for each area. The primary focus will vary over time, and each aspect should be allowed to develop. Be proactive about the social side and never underestimate the value of education in an athlete's development.

Performance   This aspect is a direct target zone. Allowing a swimmer to naturally develop into their niche can provide an invaluable learning experience in regards to their future ideal training program. Coaches should help athletes develop skills that prepare them for uncontrollable or challenging situations that may arise. Athletes should also be able to shift their focus over a short time frame to prepare for big events such as the Olympic Trials or Olympic Games.

Socialization   A social swimmer is a happy swimmer, and a happy swimmer is a balanced swimmer. The greater the balance and stability in an athlete's life, the more likely they will consistently reach a high level of performance. It is important to set boundaries for socialization, and the athlete should recognize the effect of their social life on their recovery. Athletes should be encouraged to surround themselves with positive people and enjoy their time with friends away from the pool.

Education   A young swimmer's education is extremely important. The recurring exam periods of a student swimmer should be valued and incorporated into training schedules. A good education encourages learning in all forums, including the training environment, and provides athletes with direction, external goals, and an opportunity to excel past their athletic ambitions.

Mentor Coach Program

The life balance we coaches preach to our athletes should also apply to ourselves. Surround yourself with people you trust and believe in and allow them to guide you toward faster learning and greater success at the pool and in life.

Being the head coach at the club level is a complex task that requires many skills and specific, relevant knowledge. Many of these proficiencies are naturally developed through experience, which is a natural teacher. Learning how to be an effective coach is not a destination, it is a journey. Grow and develop in the role by adapting to changing conditions, adopting new approaches, and seeking forums in which to help make that happen. Training programs can enhance your development of new skills and retention of new knowledge, especially if they give you ideas and structure that apply to your everyday experience.

A mentor coach program is designed to enhance the development of aspiring coaches. In effect, the learning experience involves partnership shared by a mentor and a mentee. Together, you identify what skills and knowledge you need in the job, which of those skills you most need to develop, and what resources are available to make that happen. This needs to be assessed by coaches who either are pursuing or currently occupy some level of program leadership in partnership with their managers (e.g., mentors, club president, school principal) who can create change. Following the guidelines of this program results in a development plan that, when properly executed, creates a path toward more effective management. It will also give you information that will be useful for preparing or revising personal development plans.

PRACTICAL PLANNING

Mastering planning for an entire year, the upcoming season, one single training week, or the main session is most crucial if we want our athletes to be competitive at an international level. No books discuss the complexity of training and its direct or indirect response on each individual swimmer in your training group. The true art of coaching is understanding what precise effect your detailed planning has on each of your athletes. You must adapt your coaching to a swimmer's talent and physiological and psychological makeup. Any planning process should be performed and implemented as an effort that involves your entire support staff and possibly some of your most experienced athletes. More specifically, change must be made in relation to the following.

How fast to progress
- In the number of sessions per training week
- In the volume per single session and week
- In the distance of the main set in each session

Load (volume × intensity)
- Possible volume of precise training distance at specific race pace for your targeted event (100, 200, 400, 800, or 1,500 meters)
- Recovery time for specific race pace sets

Energy system usage at different swimming speeds and its recovery processes (aerobic, anaerobic threshold, anaerobic lactic, or anaerobic alactic)

Planning is the most critical aspect of being a successful coach. As Harvey Mackay, author of two New York Times best-sellers and a nationally syndicated columnist, once said, "If you fail to plan, you plan to fail." Following are suggestions regarding every aspect of planning that are essential for your coaching. I incorporate training plans of my own that I have used to coach world record holders and still use to this day.

Annual Plan

This stage of planning gives you a great overview of the year as a whole and fragments it into two to three seasons; each season ends with a main competition. A coach has to be particular about this planning process. The better you plan for this stage, the more you and your team will benefit in the next stages of your planning procedure. Consider details such as the following.

Induction

- Communicating to your team the emphasis of the next year
- Outlining major and minor competitions for the year
- Conducting technical meetings with your support staff (group and individual)

Physiotherapy

- Swimming-specific musculoskeletal screenings
- Planning massage and physiotherapy sessions for swimmers

Sport science

- Nutritional education (balanced diet, recovery food)
- Planning skinfold sessions with set intervals between measurements
- Biomechanical testing (filming and so on)
- Physiological considerations

Psychology

- Debriefing of last season
- Individual plan for new season

Table 8.1 depicts weekly training cycles within a yearly training plan. Table 8.2 (page 102) depicts an example of an annual plan. Yearly training plans, such as the one for the 2003 season here, are designed to reach a peak performance at the time of the trials to select a team for international competition—in this case, the Australian national team. A complete plan permits covering all training zones necessary in preparation and incorporating the other competitions into the master plan.

TABLE 8.1 Weekly Training Schedule

Basic endurance phase (4 to 6 weeks)

	Monday	Tuesday	Wednesday	Thursday	Friday	Saturday	Sunday
a.m. Energy system	Pool Anaerobic threshold	Pool and gym Aerobic and kick	Off	Pool and gym Aerobic and kick	Pool Aerobic fin drills	Pool and gym Short rest/ speed	Off
p.m. Energy system	Pool Sort rest/ speed	Pool Over distance	Pool Heart rate (mod.)	Pool Threshold/ speed	Pool Aerobic and relays	Off	Off

General preparation phase (4 to 6 weeks)

	Monday	Tuesday	Wednesday	Thursday	Friday	Saturday	Sunday
a.m. Energy system	Pool Anaerobic threshold	Gym and pool Pull and kick quality	Off	Pool and gym Pull and kick quality	Pool Aerobic fin drills	Pool and gym Lactate removal	Off
p.m. Energy system	Pool Lactate removal	Pool Aerobic and pace	Pool Quality	Pool Aerobic and pace	Pool Aerobic and relays	Off	Off

Specific competition phase (4 to 8 weeks)

	Monday	Tuesday	Wednesday	Thursday	Friday	Saturday	Sunday
a.m. Energy system	Pool Anaerobic threshold	Gym and pool Pull and kick quality	Off	Pool Pull and kick quality	Pool Aerobic fin drills	Pool and gym Quality	Off
p.m. Energy system	Pool Heart rate	Pool Quality	Pool Aerobic	Pool Heart rate	Pool Aerobic and relays	Off	Off

TABLE 8.2 Yearly Training Plan

Focus	Qualification for the Australian swim team, performance at international level																								
Month	Dec. 02	Jan. 03				Feb. 03				Mar. 03					Apr. 03				May 03				June 03		
Monday	30	06	13	20	27	03	10	17	24	03	10	17	24	31	07	14	21	28	05	12	19	26	02	09	16
Major competitions	AYO Staging Camp, Canberra (4–8)	Australian Youth Olympic Festival, Sydney (9–12)	QLD State Championships, Chandler (12–17)	QAS Target Squad Assembly, Southport (19–20)						Brisbane Age and Open, Chandler (2–3)			AUS Championships, Sydney (22–29)	Training Break Open (31–6); 2 sessions		Short Course Meet, Valley Pool (12)	AUS Age Championship, Brisbane (26–30)	Training Break Age (1–18); 2 sessions per week	ASCTA Coaches Convention, Gold Coast (4–8)			Grand Prix Meet, Cairns (25–28)			
Induction			I				I																		
Technical meetings		TM						TM							TM									TM	
Professional development																	PD								
Musculoskeletal screening				MS																MS					
2,000 m time trial				TT				TT							TT						TT				TT
Efficiency test 4 × 50				ET				ET							ET						ET				ET
Skinfolds				S				S				S			S						S				S
Psychology				P																	P				
Training break															TB		(TB)	(TB)							
Holidays																				H					

Reporting mechanism
- Regular meetings convened by senior program manager (SPM)
- Written report to SPM within 7 days after major competition
- Provide SPM with month-in-advance plan by middle of previous month
- Participate in biannual sub-committee meetings with entire support network

Evaluation procedures
- 2 × sub-com meetings
- Athlete survey
- Operational plan outcomes
- Budget control
- Coach self-appraisal

Qualification for the Australian Swim Team, performance at international level

June 03		July 03				Aug. 03				Sept. 03					Oct. 03				Nov. 03				Dec. 03				
23	30	07	14	21	28	04	11	18	25	01	08	15	22	29	06	13	20	27	03	10	17	24	01	08	15	22	29
	Grand Prix Meet 2, TBA (20–22)			World Championships, Barcelona (ESP/20–27)		AUS SC Championships, Hobart (2–5)	Training Break Open (6–17), 3 Sessions per week	World University Games, Daegu (KOR/22–28)	World University Games,,Daegu (KOR/22–28)													World Cup, Melbourne (28–30)	NEC, TBA (1–6)/Metropolitan Chams (4–7)				
							I																				
		TM									TM				TM				TM				TM				
										MS																	
										TT				TT				TT					TT				
			ET							ET				ET				ET					ET				
			S							S				S				S					S				
										P																	
							TB	TB																			
							H	H	H																	H	

Season Plan

The season plan goes further into preparation details and is broken down into mesocycles (3 to 6 weeks) and single weeks. This plan can be very thought provoking and stimulating for the coach and support staff; one starts to feel the excitement of the approaching season and to clearly visualize very specific aspects of the training system. Consider the following for the season plan.

- Induction: Communicate to your team the emphasis of the upcoming season.
- Set dates for training breaks and holidays for swimmers according to major competitions.
- Plan professional development for coaches and support staff.
- Define seasonal goals.
- Re-evaluate your weekly training schedule.
- Choose a main meet and calculate the length of the season.
- Determine total volume of swimming in each energy system based on progression model and make adjustments based on previously accomplished volumes.
- Determine workload for each week based on your experience.
- Determine peak weekly volumes for each energy system.
- Prepare to adapt sessions based on evaluation of the progress of main sets in training.
- Decide on taper length (3 days drop taper or 3 or more weeks taper).

Table 8.3 (page 106) depicts a seasonal plan for the sprint group that lists the final 18 weeks of planning leading into the 2008 Olympic Games. The plan includes the swim training emphasis and dryland emphasis along with the weekly mileage and intensity level.

To refer to the weekly mileage and intensity levels only, see figure 8.2.

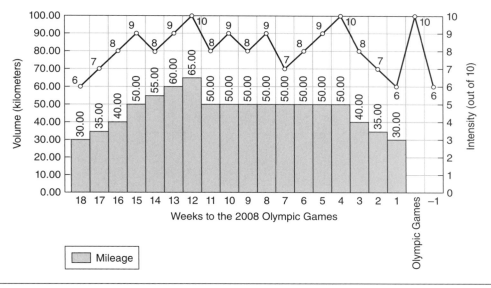

FIGURE 8.2 Sprint group volume and intensity levels in the 18 weeks leading up to the 2008 Olympic Games.

Weekly Plan

The weekly plan involves very specific parts of a training program and outlines exact details about programming and session writing and creating progressions of main sets. I believe in repeating a similar weekly structure of training and maintaining similar main sets for a period of 3 weeks. This mini periodization allows swimmers to adapt to the next level of physical conditioning. Consider the following for this level of planning:

- ◆ Define the goals for the week.
- ◆ Determine the total volume of swimming in each energy system based on your seasonal plan and make adjustments based on training results from the previous week.
- ◆ Distribute the workload for each week according to the athletes' adaptive abilities and recovery.
- ◆ Ensure that test and training protocols exist to evaluate progress in training.

Table 8.4 (page 108) is a weekly plan for the Queensland State Swimming Center. The plan lists the daily main training sets and the energy systems to be trained. It outlines both the morning and afternoon sessions and lists the mileage goals.

TABLE 8.3 Season Plan for the 2008 Olympic Games in Beijing, China (Sprinters)

Countdown Week	Date Monday–Sunday	Events	Swim training emphasis				Dryland emphasis (gym)	Body maintenance
			Type	Specials	Mileage	Intensity		
19	March 31–April 6	Training break with 3 individual sessions; head coach's holiday	Maintenance	Break with training	9 km	3	Reintroduction	1 physio treatment
18	April 7–April 13	Season start: Monday p.m. session/ AUS Age Championships (9–13)	Speed and power		30 km	6	Reintroduction/ test	1 massage treatment
17	April 14–April 20	Assistant coach's holiday (14–25)	Speed and power		35 km	7	Reintroduction/ test	1 physio treatment
16	April 21–April 27	Olympic team orientation (20–25), Grand Prix I, Canberra (25–27)	Speed and power	Camp and meet	40 km	8	Test Strength development	1 massage treatment
15	April 28–May 4	ASCTA Convention Gold Coast (29–4)	Threshold		50 km	9	Strength development	1 physio and 1 massage treatment
14	May 5–May 11	AUS male sprint camp (4–8)	Threshold		55 km	8	Strength development	1 physio and 1 massage treatment
13	May 12–May 18		Threshold		60 km	9	Strength max	1 physio and 1 massage treatment
12	May 19–May 25		Heart rate		65 km	10	Test Strength max	1 physio and 1 massage treatment
11	May 26–June 1	QLD Development Tour, Shanghai, China (23–1)	Heart rate	Kick quality and volume	50 km	8	Strength development	1 physio and 1 massage treatment
10	June 2–June 8	Oceania Championships, Christchurch, New Zealand (5–8)	Heart rate	Kick quality and volume	50 km	9	Strength development	1 physio and 1 massage treatment

Week	Dates	Event/location		Focus	Distance	Sessions	Strength	Other
9	June 9–June 15		Heart rate	Kick quality and volume	50 km	8	Strength development	1 physio and 1 massage treatment
8	June 16–June 22	QSSC Camp, Cairns (18–2)	Heart rate		50 km	9	Power development Strength max	1 physio and 1 massage treatment
7	June 23–June 29	QSSC Camp, Cairns (18–2)	Heart rate		50 km	7	Power development Strength max	1 physio and 1 massage treatment
6	June 30–July 6	Olympic team camp (2–4), Grand Prix II, Sydney (4–6)	Heart rate	Racing and training	50 km	8	Unload, competition	1 physio and 1 massage treatment
5	July 7–July 13	Trans Tasman Series, Woy Woy, Wagga, Canberra (7–12)	Heart rate	Quality and heart rate/harness	50 km	9	Strength development	1 physio and 1 massage treatment
4	July 14–July 20		Heart rate	Quality and heart rate/harness	50 km	10	Strength development	1 physio and 1 massage treatment
3	July 21–July 27	Olympic staging camp, Kuala Lumpur, Malaysia (26–3)	Taper	Quality and heart rate/harness	40 km	8	Strength development	1 physio and 1 massage treatment
2	July 28–August 3	Olympic staging camp, Kuala Lumpur, Malaysia (26–3)	Taper	Quality and heart rate/harness	35 km	7	Strength max	On Australian team
1	August 4–August 10	Olympic camp, Beijing, China (3–8)	Taper	Quality and heart rate/harness	30 km	6	Test Strength max	On Australian team
0	August 11–August 17	Olympic Games, Beijing, China (Swimming: 9–17)	Competition	Racing		10	Unload, competition	Competition
-1	August 18–August 24	Olympic Games, Beijing, China (8–24)	Speed and power	Training (SC only)		6	Strength development	
				Season total	**840 km**			
				Average	**46.7 km**	**8.10**		

TABLE 8.4 Weekly Plan and Training Times

Day		Training times	Training
Monday	a.m.	5:45–6:45 6:45–8:45	Cycle Swim
	p.m.	3:30–3:45 3:45–6:00	Dryland: shoulder control Swim
Tuesday	a.m.	5:45–8:15	Swim
	p.m.	3:30–3:45 3:45–6:00	Swim Dryland: body core
Wednesday	a.m.	6:00–8:15 8:30–10:30	Swim at the Queensland Academy of Sport (QAS)
	p.m.		Off
Thursday	a.m.	5:45–8:15	Swim
	p.m.	3:30–3:45 3:45–6:00	Dryland: shoulder control Swim
Friday	a.m.	5:45–6:45 6:45–8:45	Cycle Swim
	p.m.	3:30–3:45 3:45–6:00	Dryland: body core Swim
Saturday	a.m.	5:45–8:15 8:30–10:30	Swim Gym at the QAS
	p.m.		Off
Sunday	a.m.		Off
	p.m.		Off

Swimmers arrive on pool deck 15 minutes before training starts. A 15-minute group stretching session is conducted at the end of each p.m. session.

Creating Learning Opportunities

A good program focuses on skill development and should incorporate learning opportunities for swimmers, staff, and coaches at least once or twice per week. This means that specific elements are repeated on a frequent basis. This allows for more efficient and accelerated learning progress.

Try not to teach a specific stroke model; rather, teach swimmers to explore options and come up with their own solutions for more proficient stroking. Drills should steer the talented athlete toward their own very efficient and smart technique solutions. These solutions may not be the most time effective at that moment; however, they provide a better result in the long term. In using this approach, changing technique and learning a new stroke model or changing the current technique in the future will be easier for the swimmer and the coach.

Table 8.5 includes six race-specific parts and their components. Find numerous new learning opportunities for each and periodize them throughout a week.

This creates accurate specificity and a great diversity of training.

TABLE 8.5   Race Parts and Components

Start	State of readiness Connected and well-balanced position Hip action Push-off angle Entry in the water Start and turn times
Underwater	Streamlined position Underwater speed (start) Breakout timing (first stroke) Break surfacing skill and angle Maintaining streamlined position
Surface swimming	Racing analysis and model Specific distance per stroke Specific stroke count Specific stroke rate Race pace (sprint to distance) Front and back end speed
Turn	Approach and maintenance of velocity Rotation skill (technique and position) Anticipation of push-off Push-off and streamline posture Underwater speed (turn) Break surfacing skill and angle
Finish	Approach to wall Speed maintenance Anticipation to wall Timing of last stroke Maintaining streamlined position
Self-management	Recovery skills Mentally entering the race zone Race resilience Learning from past performances

Learning From Your Past

Every performance in training or in competition provides a valuable opportunity to learn. It is important to take all the knowledge you can from both positive and negative learning experiences! A positive outcome is a very optimistic scenario that is encouraging and easy to apply. However, learning from a negative experience is a fundamental skill that will benefit your athletes' future and your own. Developing this ability will give you the capacity to persevere, persist, and continue to fight hard no matter what obstacles you face.

Preparing for the 2008 Australian Olympic Trials in Sydney

This exercise is designed to assist in your preparation for the 2008 Olympic Trials. It has been developed to help increase your awareness of how you prepare for, execute, and recover from competition. At this competition a great deal of responsibility for your racing will be in your hands. It will be an opportunity to learn much about your current preparation and an opportunity to learn from your potential mistakes.

Most important, this exercise gives you a chance to learn from your own experience and recognize what works for you and what doesn't. It is also an opportunity for coaches to observe how you go about this process so that we can learn more about you. Our observation combined with your experiences will establish a clear direction for the approach each individual will take leading into trials.

The design of your race warm-up and swim down is up to you, as is your race analysis and the assessment of how you did. You will be given your race splits and stroke rates, and most of your racing footage will be available at the Queensland Academy kiosk. This is an excellent opportunity for you to demonstrate the nature of your commitment to the preparation.

As we near the Olympic Trials, there is still much work to do, many tough sets to conquer, and many opportunities to test the strength of your character. While success is not guaranteed, each session you train and the decisions that you make will directly affect how well you are prepared for this test.

Every day you make choices that take you either in the direction of your dreams or away from them. The more responsibility you take for your destiny, the more chance you give yourself to succeed. It is all about improving your chances, choosing the tougher path, finding the next level, and giving yourself every opportunity. That one breath, that extra kick, that last ounce of effort when you thought you had no more. That is what makes the difference. What makes the difference for you?

It is a choice to give that bit extra; it's what separates you from the person who declines that choice, who blames someone else, who says, "No, not today," or "Maybe next time." Give yourself every chance. Be proud that you could have done nothing more; know that you gave everything you had in the pool. Allow that pride to lift you, to inspire you, to make you fight back, especially when times are tough. There is no next time. Produce your best now, again and again, until that bit extra is no longer extra and it just becomes who you are.

Become someone who takes the tough path, who declines easy choices. Allow nothing to get in your way. What sort of person do you want to be standing on those blocks? Someone who has done everything they can to succeed or someone who has continuously tried to avoid the challenge? Make that decision now and act upon it.

- What path are you on?
- What do you stand for?
- Where are your choices taking you?
- What choices will make a difference for you?

TRAINING FOR RACE-SPECIFIC SPEED

Training for race-specific speed requires attention to all sections of the speed event. Top end speed, front end speed, and back end speed should all be considered when training speed.

Basic Requirements of Planning to Train Speed

I have always had a passion for stroke mechanics and technical aspects of starts, turns, and finishes and a natural curiosity for speed and race-specific training. In my earlier coaching days, I was intrigued by the 100-meter and 200-meter events. I would analyze my swimmers' final competition performances and their splits. I wanted to understand the specific speed they travelled at in each section of the race in order to work toward specific race targets. Later in my career, I was involved with a group in Brisbane that came up with a more precise race pace target model. One of the driving forces behind this approach was former sport scientist Tim Kerrison. One of the greatest attributes of this model is that it provides very clear and accurate information on each race pace zone. Years of experience in training my swimmers with this method has allowed me to gain a more complex understanding of race pace training and apply my own interpretation to create an effective training tool. My application of this model involves the following.

TES (top end speed): maximum velocity for 15 meters

- Requires high level of will and desire and some freshness
- Training distances: 15, 20 meters at TES
- Total training volume: 300 meters
- Apply close to 50-meter race-specific stroke rates.
- Practice peak surface swimming speed: Carry speed from push off straight to the surface.

FES(100) (front end speed for 100-meter racing): first 50 meters pace of 100 meters goal time

- Requires some freshness
- When: most likely early in the week
- Training distances: 15, 20, 25, 30, 35 meters at FES(100)
- Total training volume: 400 meters
- Practice race start and individualized underwater skill (precise kick count and underwater distance) for 100-meter race.
- Perform individualized specific swim stroke rates for the first 50 meters of 100-meter race using past experience (100-meter racing analysis) and future plans (100-meter racing model).
- Put into practice individualized breathing patterns required for the first 50 meters of 100 meters.

BES(100) (back end speed for 100-meter racing): second 50 meters pace of 100 meters goal time

- Requires less freshness than FES(100)
- When: possibly early week
- Training distances: 30, 35, 40, 45, 50 meters at BES(100)
- Total training volume: 600 meters
- Possibly practice race turn and individualized underwater skill (precise kick count and underwater distance) for 100-meter race.
- Perform individualized specific swim stroke rates for the second 50 meters of 100-meter race using past experience (100-meter racing analysis) and future plans (100-meter racing model).
- Put into practice individualized breathing patterns required for the second 50 meters of 100 meters.
- Rehearse race-specific finish.

FES(200) (front end speed for 200-meter racing): first 100 meters pace of 200 meters goal time

- Requires less freshness than FES(100) or BES(100)
- When: any time throughout the week
- Training distances: 35, 50, 65, 75 meters at FES(200)
- Total training volume: 800 meters
- Practice race start and individualized underwater skill (precise kick count and underwater distance) for 200-meter race.
- Perform individualized specific swim stroke rates for the first 100 meters of 200-meter race using past experience (200-meter racing analysis) and future plans (200-meter racing model).
- Put into practice individualized breathing patterns required for the first 100 meters of 200 meters.
- Rehearse race-specific turn.

BES(200) (back end speed for 200-meter racing): second 100 meters pace of 200 meters goal time

- Of the training zones, requires least amount of freshness
- When: any time throughout the week
- Training distances: 50, 65, 75, 100 meters at BES(200)
- Total training volume: 1,200 meters
- Perform individualized specific swim stroke rates for the second 100 meters of 200-meter race using past experience (200-meter racing analysis) and future plans (200-meter racing model).
- Practice race turn and individualized underwater skill (precise kick count and underwater distance) for 200-meter race.

- Put into practice individualized breathing patterns required for the second 100 meters of 200 meters.
- Rehearse race-specific finish.

Thoughts on Race Pace Training

Better performances result from continuously trying to find new ways to improve an athlete's abilities. A tiny improvement in each aspect of the race will result in a greater chance for the athlete to perform at an enhanced level in the near future. Training and racing can be broken down into components, and a slight progression in any one component will lead to improvement in future performance. Some of these components include the following:

- Speed zones (TES, FES, BES; distance and volume)
- State of readiness to train at race speed throughout the entire season and its natural progression (weekly planning)
- High skill level during fast execution of precise movements
- Development of new biofeedback systems (timing and standards)
- Effect of physical, mental, and neuromuscular fatigue on weekly training cycles
- Effect of increase in, maintenance of, or loss of will power (believing in the dream or losing the vision) on training performance
- Level of concentration in training (desire)
- Elements of race pace training (volume and frequency) and effect on weekly training cycles
- Weekly periodization of start, turn, and finish; underwater speed; relay change-over; race pace; race-specific stroke rates; and breathing habits
- Intensity of speed sessions and effect on swimmer's physiology and psychology
- Acceleration of recovery from race pace training
- Adaptation or change of swimming techniques at different race pace speeds or speed zones
- What type of "animal" (e.g., drop-dead sprinter, distance swimmer) the swimmer is
- Psychological influence of swimmer–coach relationships
- Improving your swimmer's top speed (TES) and actively seeking to do so
- Learning from your swimmer's racing history (collection of data on times, splits, stroke rate, stroke count) for a faster future
- Designing a pathway for the future (own race model and models of world-class performers)
- Planning for speed. Plan your recovery to allow speed to happen in training. (Train speed into your athlete, not out of them!)
- Recovering from speed training (neuromuscular adaptation or fatigue of the nervous system)

- How far in a session to push athletes' training volume of specific race pace sets [TES, FES(100), BES(100), FES(200), BES(200), and so on]
- Speed requirements: technique, freshness, and readiness
- Using other race analysis information (stroke rates, stroke counts, breathing habits) to further improve the specificity of race speed training
- Setting target times for 100-meter and 200-meter training based on target race time. Actual race speed should be achievable in training and not tapered.

Accurate Timing for Real Race Speed

Coaches around the world have developed many ways to time their squads. One of the most important factors in coaching is consistency and accuracy in timing technique. Swimmers will know if their coach makes up times, and I see no point of comprise in this area. It is simply not worth it! Athletes' training performances provide information that is critical in adapting and monitoring a successful training program and in their performance in future competition. To rely on relationships between training times in race pace sets and competition times, you must consistently use a precise timing method and system. One such method involves the following:

- Determining projected target times
- Calculating target times from past performances and future goal times
- Always using additional race analysis information (stroke rates, stroke counts, and breathing habits) to further improve the specificity of race speed training
- Setting target times for sprint training based on the target race time. Actual race speed should be achievable in training and not tapered.
- Continuously evaluating progress in regards to repetition distance versus target times and number of repetitions and resting times (interval times)

Timing the parts of the starts and turns is an effective way to determine what parts need improvement. Measuring the distance covered is also helpful (see table 8.6).

A race pace set development (table 8.7) recommends the number of repeat cycles and the send-off times for each cycle, the total mileage, and the intensity level of the swims.

The turn drill development (table 8.8) flows from dryland exercises to pool drills through the athlete breaking the turn down into parts and working with a partner for feedback.

TABLE 8.6 Measuring the Efficiency of Starts and Turns

Timing area	Method
Dive	Time from gun to head past the target distance
Push-off	Time from feet off the wall to head past the target distance
Second lap push	Time from feet off the wall to head past the target distance
Butterfly and breaststroke turn	Calculate times to account for turn by a factor of 1.2 s
Freestyle and backstroke turn	Calculate times to account for turn by a factor of 0.4 s

When the target distance is 50 m (or a multiple of), base times off the hand touch.

TABLE 8.7 Race Pace Set Development

	Reps	Cycle	Mileage
8 ×	200 m freestyle @ A2 50 m main stroke @ BES(100)	3:30 1:30	2,000 m
8 ×	200 m freestyle @ A2 50 m main stroke @ BES(100) 50 m main stroke @ PB + 10 s with low SC	3:30 1:30 1:00	2,400 m
4 ×	200 m freestyle @ AT 50 m main stroke @ BES(100) 50 m main stroke @ PB + 10 s with low SC 200 m freestyle @ A2 50 m main stroke @ BES(100) 50 m main stroke @ PB + 10 s with low SC	3:30 1:30 1:00 3:30 1:30 1:00	2,400 m
4 × 2 ×	200 m freestyle @ AT 50 m main stroke @ BES(100) 50 m main stroke @ PB + 10 s with low SC200 m freestyle @ A2 50 m main stroke @ BES(100) 50 m main stroke @ PB + 10 s with low SC 20 m turn sprint with key word rehearsal	3:30 1:30 1:00 3:30 1:30 1:00 1:00	2,430 m

PB: personal best; AT: anaerobic threshold swimming at 25 to 30 beats below individual maximum heart rate; BES(100): back end speed for 100 m; SC: lowest possible stroke count per 50-m lap at required pace; A2: aerobic swimming at 40 beats below individual maximum heart rate; 20 m turn sprint: race pace turn, 10 min in and 10 m out off the wall.

TABLE 8.8 Turn Drill Development

Dry land	Vertical push-off on ground Vertical push-off with partner feedback Vertical push-off with closed eyes Vertical push-off with vertical jump
Pool	Vertical jump Vertical jump with partner feedback Vertical jump with fly kick Vertical push-off with tumble turn Horizontal turn drill
Off the wall	Push-off and glide Push-off with fly kick Dead start turn push-off and glide Dead start turn push-off with fly kick
Turn	Turn with partner feedback Paced turn Turn sprint
Special	Turn spring at end of quality set (lactate) Turn with blind breakout Entire turn from flags blind

THE SUCCESSFUL TRAINING ENVIRONMENT

Surround yourself with other highly ambitious people with great vision. Success breeds success! First and most important in building a successful training environment is to ensure that your support staff possesses core values that are similar to yours. I like to have positive people around me. We have only one dance on this planet, and I want it to be positive and enjoyable! Be very careful when selecting your support staff because you will spend a lot of time together on your emotional rollercoaster journey as a coach. You will need this team to help you create the training culture that is necessary to accomplish your vision. One of the hardest things to do is change cultural aspects of individuals and groups. People prefer the known to the unknown and the old to the new!

Add to this environment healthy competition with other coaches, clubs in your town, states, or nations. This is vital to keeping yourself and your program honest through both good and bad times.

Never forget that we as coaches have to make the difference and our own vision has to become the fuel for the hard and testing journey we are on. The elite coach has to live in a very diverse and demanding environment that involves

- intense pressure to win;
- dealing with extreme highs and lows;
- long and unconventional working hours;
- earning less money than in the learn-to-swim industry;
- mixing hobby, passion, and profession;
- extended periods away from home;
- constant media confrontation;
- being a servant leader; and
- thinking at all times about making the difference to the athletes.

To perform up to personal expectations and maintain a high level of athlete performance, coaches must be able to manage their own health, life balance, and happiness from within and maintain this over a long period of time. Athletes often notice if their coach is struggling through life, and this can have a dramatic effect on coaching performance and therefore on an athlete's performance. Long hours do not always equal productivity.

Rumors circle around the world that all Australian swimming programs have perfect training conditions. My understanding is that this is true for only one location down under: the Australian Institute of Sport. All other Australian programs struggle with issues that are similar to those of the rest of the world. It is always easy to focus on the other side of the fence, where the grass is greener. But does it help you achieve your next benchmark?

2009 Queensland State Swimming Center Teamship Rules

Attitude Toward Reaching Your True Potential

As your coaching staff, we strongly believe in each of you as a person and as an athlete and we see in you the great potential for improvement of your future performance. Do you believe in this as well and how badly do you want to make it happen?

Training within a squad environment provides us with a lot of positive experience and brings, in addition to training, hard work, and fun, many challenges. Looking after you and your teammates is vital to our success in the international arena. Here are some rules for maintaining good energy, managing the workload and fatigue, communicating and cooperating well, and making the most of our time together.

Let us build a resilient confidence through excellent habits! Are you willing to change little things that will make a big difference in your future swims? Are you willing to improve your attitude toward reaching your true potential?

Respect

- Act Like A Champion program
- Teammates and staff
- Honor our sport and its people
- Language
- Gesture

Training appearance

- Attend all sessions (it is not a choice)
- Health and injury management (communication to coaches: Does it prevent you from your entire training?)
- Contact and inform your head coach (prior occasion)

Punctuality

- Arrive 15 minutes before a.m. sessions and 30 minutes before p.m. sessions
- Get mind, body, and soul ready before the session starts (gymnastics)

The holy ground

- By entering the training areas I will…
- What I can contribute to the success of every aspect of training (each rep/set/session)
- No mobile phone policy for swimmers

(continued)

2009 Queensland State Swimming Center Teamship Rules *(continued)*

Ownership

- Control of emotional state
- Be constructive
- No tolerance toward negativity (outspoken or body language)
- Mental and physical readiness for training
- Technique
- Team bonding activities (team, boys and girls)

Communication

- Greetings (no matter how you feel in the morning)
- Communicate issues at the appropriate time to coaching staff
- Communicate sickness to coaching staff and teammates (apply an appropriate and professional action plan)

Create an Environment With a Winning Culture

Coaches and athletes spend a lot of time together in and around the pool, gym, or dryland facility. This environment is where future competition results are created. This environment must be a positive, supportive, and nurturing place to excel and perform. The following is an example of the team rules that were created for my program to ensure that the training environment benefits the athletes.

Building Confidence

How would you like your athletes to feel on the biggest day of their swimming career? How would you like your athletes to think in the morning of their main swim at the Olympic Games? Some coaches and athletes believe that they can perform only on a day on which everything goes exactly according to plan. This could not be further from the truth! Feelings and performance should not have anything to do with each other. Some confidence myths are as follows.

1. You must win to be confident.
   - Many sources of confidence exist.
   - Rookies make it every year.
2. To be successful, you must have unshakeable belief you can win.
   - Winning is uncontrollable.
   - Define success because that is what builds confidence.
3. Mistakes destroy confidence.
   - Confident athletes are not afraid to make mistakes.
   - Mistakes don't hold athletes back; the fear of making mistakes does.
   - Acknowledge defeat. It is part of sport and shouldn't be scary.

4. Successful athletes have unshakeable confidence.
- High expectations
- Strive for a perfect stroke 100% of the time.
- No athlete is immune from lapses in confidence. What is your job?

Set up a process to increase the confidence of the individuals on your team. Athletes are individuals and must be treated accordingly. Find the triggers for each individual and create very specific learning opportunities accordingly to make certain they grow in the following three areas:

1. Physical execution
2. Mental skills to focus and concentrate on
3. Resilience to recover emotionally from setbacks

Micromanagement of the Human Mind

Growing in belief doesn't come from one big motivational speech each season. The human mind has to be trained the same way as the human body—on a day-to-day basis! Learn to get in the head of your athletes. It's not about what you think is possible, it's about what your athlete believes is possible. Continuously increase your understanding of their world and their thought processes. Each session should contain an element of focus dedicated to understanding the athlete a little better. Once you understand what makes them tick, consistently increase your ability to change behavior. Coaches should also apply this process to themselves. Finding the answers to the following questions can create a deeper understanding.

- What is the behavior that allows world-class performances?
- What can happen before training to prime the athlete for learning?
- What can happen after training to continue the learning and reflection?
- What triggers a change in my own behavior from bad to better on an appalling day at the office?

One of my mottos is "Fake it until you make it!" Faking a smile before you enter the pool often makes you feel better and encourages endorphins to stimulate positive feelings. Laughing and skipping around as if you were in the schoolyard will set off a good feeling through your entire body, which can only help your approach to the upcoming session.

Estrogen Versus Testosterone

Swimming is a sport in which girls and boys traditionally start out training together. The coaching staff is predominantly male and they approach coaching issues from a male perspective. This instantly prompts a few specific questions. Do coaches approach coaching boys the same way as coaching girls? Do girls and boys both respond the same way to training? Consider topics such as the following.

Coaching girls

- Learn about the challenges of puberty (physical and physiological change of the female body).
- Build a coach–swimmer relationship.
- Create opportunities for the girls to develop leadership.
- Set up a process to deal with emotional response (don't tell me what you feel; tell me what you do about it).
- Monitor the dynamic among girls (mental bullying).

Coaching boys

- Create opportunities for team bonding among boys.
- Watch behavior and manners in boys-only groups.
- Arrange competition in training and get them to race against each other.

Coaching a mixed group

- Require respect for each other (language, gestures, behavior).
- Don't allow boys to use negative comments that discriminate against girls.

Coaching Generation Y (1980 to 1994) and Preparing for the Newest Generation (1995 and Beyond)

Generation Y is better described as generation why? They always want to know the relevance of what they are about to do. They often approach leaning in a very outcome-focused manner. They want to know why they have to do things and want instant gratification once they have done them. They get bored easily but will work hard if the work is stimulating, fun, and engaging.

In contrast to the "I want it now, and I want it to be fun" attitude of generation Y, my generation believes that you have to earn the right to do things and always respects authority. Because of its different values and attitudes, generation Y is changing the makeup of the world, including the world of swimming. To accommodate this change, coaching has to change across the board. Remember: Change is good!

Generation Y will not accept that the coach always knows best, so make sure you do know best or be ready to learn from your athletes. They are not easily convinced that established methods are superior, and they have been taught to ask questions. A coach telling an athlete what to do isn't good enough. Members of generation Y need to know the purpose of what they are doing. Although they like to be in control of their own direction, they still want leadership and structure, particularly now that a lot of structure has gone from society. Build in more short-term goals so the athletes know they are succeeding. To accommodate this change, my program is very structured but very much linked to the athlete's final goal, which is extremely race and purpose specific.

I don't believe that those born in generation Y have a shorter attention span than their elders, but they do lose interest quickly if they are not immediately interested. I recognize that times have changed. I remember my parents saying how different my generation was compared with their generation, and the same is true now. However, this does not mean that we have to throw overboard everything we know and have learned about managing people. I am prepared to change, but I'm not going to change my attitude toward discipline and commitment. I'm not going to compromise my standards and I will not use generation Y as an excuse. I will simply modify my approach to find the best way for them to remain engaged and reach their potential.

CONCLUSION

Don't expect to change instantly or with rapid progression. Everything worthwhile takes time! Make sure you recognize little steps forward and celebrate them accordingly. The journey ahead of a coach is exciting. Any small change should encourage you, your swimmers, and your team. The accumulation of 100 little steps forward will lead you to the improvement you are looking for on your new chosen path. Live your passion.

9

Making Your Program Fun for Swimmers

Bob Steele

Aprogram should be fun because competitive swimming—training to be the best you can be—requires commitment, work ethic, and concentration. After the swimmer, the coach is the main motivator who determines what activities foster those requirements for success. An engaged swimmer is more likely to stick it out, have fun, leave practice smiling, and want to come back for more. Challenging practices are necessary for improvement, but challenges can also be fun and help to maintain motivation.

CREATING AND USING FUN ACTIVITIES

When creating and using fun activities, the coach must consider age, ability, and commitment. Fun activities don't just promote smiles; they also elicit a sense of pride in fulfilling challenges. Following are factors to consider when developing or implementing activities:

- **Creative.** Develop enjoyable, challenging ways to achieve goals.
- **Motivating.** Do swimmers buy into the purpose of the activity?
- **Simple.** Is it easy for the age group to understand and implement?
- **Challenging.** Does it elicit a performance that is a step above present ability?
- **Distracting.** Is the outcome more important than the pain required for success?
- **Engaging.** Are involved participants excited about winning or achieving?
- **Attendance.** Do swimmers attend practice for challenging and fun activities?
- **Fun.** Does the activity produce smiles or is it satisfying when completed?

Here are important factors in developing and using such activities.

- **Name.** Name your creation so that swimmers know what to do when it's revisited.
- **Winners and losers.** Not everyone wins; low-skilled swimmers should sometimes win.
- **Teams.** Use different methods to structure competitive teams:
    - Assign swimmers by seeding them into lanes in waves by time.
    - Assign by height, eye color, boys versus girls, year in school, total age and so on.
- **Rewards.** Reward the winners with anything from a treat to a handshake.
- **Quiet.** Give instructions when everyone is listening so that everyone understands the instructions.
- **Outcome.** Recognize the winning person(s) or team.
- **Understanding.** Swimmers that don't understand the activity should not lead.
- **Redos.** If swimmers are doing the activity incorrectly, stop and start over or redo when completed! Let teammates help the clueless rather than jumping in with your corrections; this helps build teamsmanship, leadership, and trust.

Let's get to some activities. The activities in this chapter are categorized by focus and work for both age-group and senior swimmers.

Relays

Relays help develop teamsmanship; teach racing; and improve bonding, focus, and use of racing skills under the fire and eyes of teammates. They also force swimmers to extend themselves in an effort to win for the team.

Lane Etiquette

When circle swimming, never let a swimmer stop without touching the wall because someone ahead of them in the circle is blocking them. This is quite easy to administer if you insist that it be done. When the lead swimmer finishes the swim, they move up the lane line to their left about 4 feet (1.2 m) and successive swimmers follow. Ask swimmers to not jump in front of others coming into the wall and to stay off the target so followers are accustomed to touching the target, not the gutter, with their fingertips. When the last swimmer in a circle has touched, everyone slides back into place in a horseshoe pattern and gets ready for the next repeat.

T-Shirt Relay

The ever-popular T-shirt relay requires swimmers to switch T-shirts at the end of each relay leg before continuing the relay. Swimmers need to know the technique for switching: keep elbows straight, head down, and hands clasped with those of the switching teammate. Two fellow team members stand on each side of the swimmers who are switching and pull the waist of the shirt up and over one swimmer and down onto the next. The relay is complete when everyone has swum a relay leg wearing the T-shirt.

Run-Down

A slow swimmer pairs up with a fast swimmer in each lane. Both swimmers stay on their own sides of the line and sprint a 25. The slow swimmer pushes off on the first "go!" and the fast swimmer leaves either when it's fair or on the second "go!" The winner gets five cents from the loser. In this relay, the swimmers practice holding someone off or catching someone just as they would in a relay in a meet.

Catch-Up

Set up three-person relays. Team one has two swimmers at the starting end of the pool and one swimmer at the turning end. Team two, in lane two, has the opposite setup: one swimmer at the starting end and two swimmers at the turning end. The end that has two people starts on "go!" The swimmers swim a continuous relay until one team makes up 25 yards and out-touches the other team on the same end of the pool. Teams that are evenly matched teams may go for a very long time. While some swimmers perform this drill, have similar teams race each other by pairs in the remaining lanes.

Shortening Relays

Each team has four swimmers, two at each end of the pool. The first relay is a 100. For the second relay, the turning-end swimmers move to under the pennants and swim the shorter distance, tagging hands at completion. For the third relay, the turning-end swimmers move to midpool and swim the shorter distance, tagging hands again. For the fourth relay, the midpool swimmers move to the pennants closest to the blocks and swim the shorter distance, tagging hands again. For safety, swimmers should start the fourth relay from push-offs, not dives. Each of these relays is quick and exciting.

Call It

This relay may be either a 100 or 200. To begin the relay, call out the stroke that the first swimmer in all lanes must do. When the lead swimmer reaches the pennants, the next swimmer to go on the leading team calls the next stroke and everyone leaving must do the stroke that is called. The lead swimmer continues to call the strokes (without repeating the stroke called by the incoming swimmer) throughout the relay.

Call 'n' Hold

This relay is the same as the Call It Relay. However, no swimmer exchange takes place until the swimmer on the last-place team touches.

Crazy Strokes

Four swimmers get in each lane for a 100-yard relay. To start the relay, yell out a pull for one stroke and a kick for a different stroke. Continue yelling out combinations as the relay progresses so that each swimmer does two skills simultaneously. Finish with the ever-popular corkscrew, wherein the last swimmer rotates from free to back to free to back as they do their 25.

Rock, Paper, Scissors

This relay works best in a 50-meter pool. Split the swimmers into two teams and place the teams at opposite ends of the same lane. If the squad is big, divide the swimmers into more than two teams. The first swimmer on each team starts from their end of the pool and races until they meet the person from the other end midpool; there, they play rock, paper, scissors (RPS) in the water. The winner sprints to the opposite end and the loser moves to the back of his or her team's line. The second swimmer on the losing team sprints to meet the winner midpool and plays RPS. As before, the winner stays in the middle and the loser moves back to the end of the line. The activity continues until all swimmers from one relay team win RPS and reach the opposite end of the pool. When one team wins, start another RPS and play until it's time to stop. Note that this activity may take a while to finish.

Kickboard Relay

Set up relays with seven or more swimmers per team. Every swimmer holds a kickboard. Each swimmer pushes off and kicks a 25. People with long arms should kick last in each lane. Kick 100 relays in which at every exchange the next kicker takes all the kickboards used by the relay to that point and kicks with them.

Demolition Derby

Divide the team into four squads and place one squad at each corner of the pool, or, if the pool is large, place two squads at midpool. The swimmers start 5 seconds apart on "go!" The objective is for an entire team to get across the pool and seated at the opposite corner. The first team out and seated wins. Anything goes in the middle, except swimmers cannot hold other swimmers underwater. Supervise for safety!

Favorite Challenge Sets

These training sets encourage swimmers to challenge themselves on routines performed by many fine swimmers, some of which are Olympians. These challenge sets help young swimmers to prove to themselves that they can step up to another level. In doing so, the swimmers develop greater pain tolerance, concentration under the stress of being fatigued and having to stay with or pass an opponent, and proper mechanics, turns, streamlining, and breakouts, all of which are essentials of racing. We often focus on training and not enough on racing, which is really what we are teaching.

Writing Training Sets

Teach swimmers to read your practices. It's debatable whether one should post the routine on a whiteboard (visual) or verbalize it (auditory). However, a swimmer should know how you want their energy spread over the practice, and when to swim fast and not sandbag, so that they don't save themselves for something hard and all of a sudden the practice is over. If a swimmer doesn't know what the coach wants, maladaptation occurs and the swimmer trains the wrong energy system for a specific event or distance. Some coaches think that posting the practice causes swimmers to not listen or pay attention; however, without a visual reference, the swimmers will usually be clueless or ask a teammate. A combination of the two methods is perhaps best.

Set Design Symbols

F = free

F = fly

(54) = desired pace

L25 = last 25 hard or stroke

@ = on send-off or rest

RI 25 = Rhode Island 25
   (15 yards no breath)

P = pull

K = kick

t = scooter tubes

b = bands

ss = straight set

C = control

e3f = every third 25 fly

R = reverse

LB = lung busters

lc = long course

B = back

d = drag suit

T = long tube

TO = turn over

arrow down = ascend

N/S = negative split

100/3 = breathing every 3

D = dive

NR = no rest

sr = seconds rest

MR = minutes rest

A4 = 4 swimmers alternating

BO = brains out

BC7 = breath control

p = paddles

sc = short course

b = breast

(B+3) = (best + 3 seconds)

HR = heart rate

T 25 = Texas 25
   (35 yards no breath)

arrow up = descend

BU = build-up

TT = time trial

Z = fins

SO = send-off

B = base

CH = choice

R = race

* = hard-record times

3331 = breaths/25

broken = (5/50)

Beat the Clock (2:01 Set)

The swimmers start their first 100 swim when the second hand on the clock hits 45 seconds. They must finish the 100 before the hand hits 60 for the second time (which means they have 1:15 to swim the first 100). They then start again 2:01 after starting the first swim (46) and must again finish the 100 before the 60 (which means they have 1:14 for the second swim). The set continues on a 2:01 send-off; however, the swims get faster (1 less second of swimming time) throughout the set. The athlete must always finish the 100 before the 60 or their 5-second-later send-off per wave (i.e., 5, 10, 15, 20, and so on). If a swimmer cannot hear, yell time or a lanemate can tell them they have failed. Swimmers who fail are done; they rest one swim and continue to do 100s until four swimmers are left in the contest. The end of this activity is a killer for everyone really trying to stay in the contest. For motivation in the future, record the number of swims completed or the last time made. Our team record was to make 47 and miss on 46.

Following are some objectives of this drill.

1. Credit for the number of 100s made before missing 60 seconds.
2. When a swimmer misses the 60 they skip one swim and then resume 100s, although they cannot rejoin the contest.
3. When four swimmers are still making the 60, everyone gets out and cheers the remaining four from the side of the pool.
4. Record the number of swims made, not where the swimmers failed. Swimmers may fail only while swimming. They cannot quit hanging on the wall.
5. The following chart indicates the number of swims, the time the clock is on when the swimmers leave, and the time they need to achieve to stay in the game.

Number	Clock	Time	Number	Clock	Time	Number	Clock	Time
1	45	1:15	11	55	1:05	21	1:05	55
2	46	1:14	12	56	1:04	22	1:06	54
3	47	1:13	13	57	1:03	23	1:07	53
4	48	1:12	14	58	1:02	24	1:08	52
5	49	1:11	15	59	1:01	25	1:09	51
6	50	1:10	16	60	1:00	26	1:10	50
7	51	1:09	17	1:01	59	27	1:11	49
8	52	1:08	18	1:02	58	28	1:12	48
9	53	1:07	19	1:03	57	29	1:13	47
10	54	1:06	20	1:04	56	30	1:14	46

Wave

Before and during the taper period, when it's time for a long rest set, assign the swimmers to full (race) distance heats of their specialty. Have a set send-off time for each heat in each round so swimmers may cool down between swims and know when to be up on the blocks for their heat. Record times on your whiteboard and tell your swimmers to have pride in what's posted. Tailor the send-offs and distances to the available time and time of season. This is a great activity for pretapers.

Each swimmer swims their specialty once per round; sprinters perhaps swim twice per round because their efforts are shorter. If you want the sprinters to do more, give them a second swim between heats 2 and 4.

	Round	1	2	3	4	5
Heat 1	Distance 500	@ 0	12:30	25:00	37:30	50:00
Heat 2	Mid-dist 200	@ 5:00				
Heat 3	Fly/back 200	@ 7:15				
Heat 4	Breast 200	@ 9:45				
Heat 5	Sprint 100	@ 11:30				

Race the American Record

Write the American record for the 200 of each event, men and women, on the whiteboard. Each swimmer swims 4 × 50 @ 1 and adds up their 50s for a 200 time and then a 400. Following the 400, point to every swimmer and announce times to see who is closest to the record.

Ding-a-Ling IMs

Write out a series of sets that don't include the number of swims. A swimmer picks a page in the phone book and chooses a name or business on that page. Use the seven-digit phone number of the name or business as the number of reps, or use the last four digits of the phone number as the number of swims per stroke in the set.

Fast-Feet Descending

A sample set in this drill would include a 1,650 (66 × 25), followed by an easy 300 pull; then a 1,000 (40 × 25) and an easy 300 pull; then a 500 (20 × 25) and an easy 300 pull; then a 200 (8 × 25) and an easy 300 pull; and finally, a 100 (4 × 25). All 25s are on a 20-second send-off time.

Give the times to the first wave through this whole set by yelling out the 25-yard pace at every stop and the 100 time on every 100. Have other coaches or managers time the next few waves. Stop the watch every 25 seconds and reset it at the end of the 100 after giving the swimmers their pace per 100. This activity must fit your personnel and their abilities. However, this is a great set to get a swimmer ready to race distance events, especially if they don't like distance training. Swimmers who are training poorly can prove to themselves that they can stay with the best swimmers, get more fit, and maybe race the 1,650 or 1,000. Start with distances where they can handle holding desired race pace and gradually move them up. They must get faster as the set progresses. An alternative might be 10 × 300 @ 5 or whatever your swimmers need to improve.

Race the Olympian

A variation of the American Record set is done by age-group swimmers capable of swimming 25s using the four strokes. Swimmers pull 1 ×100 (with pull buoy) @ 1:30 (or about 10 to 15 seconds rest to set up an oxygen debt) and then go immediately into 4 × (2 × 50 @ 1) with 2 or 3 minutes rest between rounds. The swimmer does 2 × 50 by stroke in individual medley (IM) order, the first 25 really fast and the second 25 fast with overkicking. If capable, the swimmers add their times on their fast 25s for a 100 IM time. Senior swimmers do these by 50s @ 1 for a 200 IM time. Ryan Lochte's time long course @ 50 seconds totaled 1:51; see just how close everyone can get to that time. During the 2 minutes rest between rounds, ask each swimmer how many seconds they were over or under Lochte's 1:51. Swimmers simply add 9 seconds to the number of seconds they were over 2 minutes (2:32 becomes 32 + 9), so they would say, for example, "plus 41."

Kicking Sets

Kicking sets should always adhere to the following criteria: Swimmers must make the send-off on kicking sets or move to a slower lane when they fail. The next time the set is done, they should try to get in more 25s or 50s on the same send-off.

Using a Pace Clock

The swimmer's feet must leave the wall on the correct second because

- leaving early cheats teammates because the time is incorrect (faster) and
- leaving late cheats the swimmer because the time is incorrect (slower).

If you record times incorrectly, the athlete will know something is wrong or teammates will complain about cheating. Training time averages must be accurate in order to meaningfully predict goal time efforts. Leaving on time requires the swimmer to know the second on which to leave and then remember it when they finish and compute their time.

Generally, team members leave five seconds apart in practice. Therefore, the feet of every swimmer will leave the wall on either zero or five as the hand sweeps around the clock or digits pass. For accurate times swimmers must have accurate push-offs, which require them to drop underwater or jump overwater 1 second ahead of the time the feet should leave the wall. Therefore, the swimmer should let go of the wall and duck under or jump on either a nine if leaving on zero or four if leaving on five. If the swimmer is standing with the shoulders out of the water, they will surface about 3 feet (0.9 m) behind others. Every swimmer's time will be accurate and comparable if everyone follows this routine. To help the clock-challenged swimmers, have the next wave or entire team yell out either nine or four about 4 seconds before that number. Swimmers with poor eyesight or who are clueless about the clock should not lead, and the leader can give them their time or figure averages. This helps the swimmers predict goal times for that time of the season, based on the day's training.

Phelps 50s

This kicking set is demanding because swimmers must extend themselves when they are really tired toward the end of the set. Swimmers use a board and pick three send-offs 5 seconds apart. The first send-off is easy, the second is moderate, and the last is hard to make (see the table below). They should start with what they can make on the fastest send-off possible for 5 × 50. Different swimmers have different send-offs; put them in lanes together by ability for motivation and encouragement. Swimmers move down one lane when they fail to make the send-off. The total set is 25 × 50 and may be done by 100s.

Easy	Moderate	Fast
1	1	1
1	1	2
1	1	3
1	1	4
1	1	5

Bucket o' Blood

Swimmers kick a 25 on the kickboard while holding a pull buoy. At the 25 they drop the kickboard and use the pull buoy. At the next 25 they drop the pull buoy and swim. This constitutes one bucket o' blood. Assign three to six buckets o' blood for the warm-up. This drill is a kick, pull, swim series that age-groupers enjoy; they may use any stroke. It's a great way to improve weak stroke across a team.

Kick Steelers

The goal is to kick 20 × 25 (short course) @ 20 seconds send-off. Because few swimmers can do this, they should use a specialty kick until they fail, at which point they get 20 seconds rest and then start again toward their 20 × 25. The entire squad leaves on the 0, 20, or 40 second mark. This is an individual set, so if they fail on, for example, the fourth set of 20, 16 sets remain. However, they must add 1 for the one they missed; therefore, 17 sets would remain. This continues until every swimmer on the team makes 20 × 25 @ 20 seconds send-off. Those that finish early should go to a vacant lane and work on 15-meter streamlining while experimenting with different underwater kick combinations. (You should make yourself immortal by naming a set after yourself!)

Whitewater

On a whistle everyone starts an overdistance kick with their feet underwater, making no splash and no sound. On the next whistle, the swimmers kick above the surface as hard as they can and make "whitewater." Blow the whistle as often as you wish or until the swimmers are exhausted.

Put It On

Kick 5 × 100 with 30 seconds rest (this drill can also be done pulling using pulling gear). Reset the pace clock at 2 minutes to remove rest from each swimmer's total time. Perform this with the following variations:

1. Hands behind back
2. Hands in front
3. A pull buoy
4. A kickboard vertical
5. A kickboard horizontal
6. Flippers with a board

Pulling Sets

Pulling sets are done to improve upper-body power and mechanics for whatever stroke the swimmer needs or the coach assigns. They may be done with varying breathing patterns, and the swimmer may experiment with various pull patterns or turnover (tempo) rates.

Switcheroo

Swimmers use pull buoys and do an over-distance pull (i.e., 800) as in a cool-down, warm-up, or recovery. During the 800, any time a whistle blows the swimmers drop the pull buoys and sprint until the next whistle (about 10 seconds), at which time they grab the closest pull buoy and resume an easy DPS (distance per stroke) pull.

Take It Off

The swimmers pull 6 × 300 with 20 seconds rest. They start wearing all equipment on the first 300 and remove a piece of equipment during each swim. Reset the clock to take out the rest (1:40), and swimmers get total time minus send-off. The 300s get faster as the arms get lighter.

Swim number	Tube	Drag suit	Band	Paddles	Pull buoy	Swim
1	X	X	X	X	X	X
2		X	X	X	X	X
3			X	X	X	X
4				X	X	X
5					X	X
6						X

Weakest and Strongest

Each swimmer does their weakest (pull or kick) on the first set. If pulling is weakest, swimmers do 10 × 100 @ 1:25; if kicking is weakest, swimmers do 8 × 100 @ 1:45. Swimmers finish with the strongest: pulling 400 or kicking 300. Everyone finishes together and gets the practice they need to improve their weaknesses. This works great as either a warm-up or cool-down.

Best Plus

To the swimmers best average time on the set, add 20 seconds for a pulling set. That is the person's send-off for the set. The swimmer constantly tries to improve the average.

Sample

Kick 8 × 100 @ 1:50 (best time is 1:30 + 20)

Pull 8 × 100 @ 1:10 (best time is 1:00 + 10)

Team Kicking Relays

The entire team is assigned to relay teams and is ready to kick 10 × 100 @ 2:30. The goal is for every relay to beat the goal time. The swimmers may change relays after every kick but must stay on the send-off. Switch the faster kickers to teams that are behind and switch slower kickers to teams that are leading. The watch stops when the last team has finished.

The set requires

1. everyone to kick all out every time,
2. teams to stay close at all times, and
3. team leaders to keep the teams even.

Games

The following are simply fun to perform at various times in practice: during warm-up or cool-down or even between serious sets.

Race Horse or Rock Band

When the swimmers finish the swim, yell out the name of either a rock band or race horse. Once the name has been given, say, "rock band," and the swimmers that think it's a rock band raise their hands. Then yell "race horse," and the swimmers that think it's a race horse raise their hands. Then yell the correct answer. The swimmers cheer or jeer and depending on their guess and then start their next swim on the next zero or five. It's a fun way to start or end practice and the kids really get into cheering for good guesses.

You may use the following list of rock bands and race horses as a send-off for a set of swims. You may also use a list generated from the horse racing or entertainment sections of a newspaper. Swimmers are not penalized for incorrect guesses.

Race horses

Hip Twenty-Five	Count It Up	Out Coached	Boston Blitz
Drew's Delight	Chain of Miracles	Jordan's Party	Cast No Shadow
Country Fair	Magic Berti	XYZ	Album Leaf
Mill Street Blues	Stormy Hostage	Phone First	Stray Cat Blues
Poolhall	Three Ladies Man	Shaolins Tale	Esther Egg
Colihan	Decipherance	Met'a Flew	Imamyto
Wegotta	Olympic Experience	Jazzamatassie	Champagne Now
Skeete's Bay	Amanzi	Lasting Joy	Island Delight
Formidable Gold	Luck Out	Taylor's Giggle	Harmony River
Bright Spot	Wild Axe	Mischievous Lover	Take My Word
Lil Firefly	Ainworthanickle	Black Cat Sally	Link to the Moon
Really Slick	Tricker	Country Silence	Unconfessed
Buzzard's Bay	Brother Derek	Brass Hat	Steppenwolfer
Bandini	Surf Cat	Descreet Cat	Sacred Light
Flower Alley	Sharp Humor	Bushfire	Splender Blender

Rock bands

Leftlane Cruisin'	Coal Kitchen	Green Machine	Longshot
Spazmatic	Black Mambazo	Aceyalone	Frisbe
Grazyna Auyisuk	Electric Eel Shock	Steel Train	Rose Hill Drive
Starflyer	Two Gallants	Talkdemonic	Darlyne Cain
AFI	Drowning Pool	Kill Hannah	Suffocation
Shadows Fall	Nouvelle Vague	Kid Beyond	Buzzcocks
Big Whiskey	Pugslee Atomz	Parliamont	Funkadelic
Alena	Naked Sunday	Gomez	Raised on Zenith
Jah Dan and JahLock	Faun Fables	Fuzzy Cousin	Bird Name
Time Machine	Gym Class Hero	S.T. Monroe	Moxie Motive
Two Timin' Three	Plastic Crimewave	Nyco	Nights of Fire
Beatle Stix			

Trivia

During your warm-up or on long rest work (20 × 50 – 1) select a topic, such as TV shows, candy bars, cereals, birds, or cars. Each time the swimmers finish a swim in the set, walk along the edge of the pool and point to each swimmer. They have 5 seconds to name an object in the selected category. If an item is repeated, the swimmer finishes the set and is out of the game. The swimmer's goal is to be the last person in the game.

Underwater Hockey

Each swimmer makes a wooden hockey stick 1 foot (30.4 cm) long or uses a wooden ruler. Draw a goal on the pool bottom with a magic marker and place a hockey puck in the middle of shallow end of the pool. The swimmers line up on each side of the shallow end. To score, players advance the puck to the goal on the opponents' side of the pool. Snorkels are optional. Players who show unsafe or unsportsmanlike conduct are sent to a penalty box.

Shark and Minnow

Swimmers line up on one side of the pool. One swimmer (the "it" person) stands in the middle of the width of the pool. On a whistle, everyone pushes off and swims underwater to the opposite side. Anyone brought to the surface by the it person is caught and joins the it person in the middle of the pool. The it person and those caught move to the other side of the pool. On the second whistle, the swimmers again push off and swim to the opposite side. The it person and those who were previously caught tag more swimmers. The game continues until everyone has been caught. The person who was caught first is it at the start of the next game.

Surfs Up

All swimmers but one stand on the pool bottom and hold a kickboard. The remaining swimmer kicks, pulls, or swims a 50 for time while at the same time teammates push water across the lane with the kickboards. It's great, challenging fun. Instead of using kickboards, teammates can pull their bodies into and off of the wall in unison to create big waves.

Baseball

Create a baseball diamond within the pool area. Mark the pitcher's mound with a cone and mark bases on the gutter or with pull buoys attached to a lane line. The batting team uses a stiff kickboard and the pitching team uses a tennis ball. The pitcher throws the ball and the team at bat hits the ball with the kickboard and swims to the bases. Younger swimmers play the infield and older swimmers play the outfield. You can designate the deck as foul territory and the outfield areas as home runs, singles, doubles, and triples.

Volleyball

Play a game of volleyball over the backstroke pennants using volleyball rules or improvised rules based on the age and ability of the players.

Football

Swimmers play football in the shallow end of the pool using a rubber ball. Use improvised rules. The ball is dead when a swimmer takes it underwater.

Pigeon

At the end of practice, the swimmers line up on the side of the pool. Tell the swimmers that the key word is "pigeon," and then tell a story. Every time you say "pigeon," the swimmers jump into the first lane, swim around the first lane line, and push up out of the pool. The last one out of the lane or anyone that jumps in without "pigeon" being said is out of the game. The winner gets a high five.

Special Events

These activities are generally related to holidays or celebrations of some kind. However, they may be done any time and are designed to challenge the swimmers and let them have fun!

New Years Special (January 1)

Swim 2,011 × 25 @ 25 based on the year 2011, or 20 × 11 yards.

Firecracker 400 (July 4)

Write the 200 IM time of each swimmer on a chalkboard and double it (e.g., 2:10 = 4:20). The fastest swimmer subtracts 0 seconds. Everyone else is handicapped by the number of seconds they are from that time (e.g., fastest time is 4:20 and their time is 5:00, so they subtract 40 seconds from each swim). Divide the team into two groups. Groups alternate through a 400 fly, 400 back, 400 breast, 400 free, and 400 IM. A swimmer subtracts the handicap from each time and totals all five swims. The swimmer with the lowest total is the winner and receives a prize.

Indy 500 (Memorial Day)

Handicap the team by kicking ability starting at the center of the pool. The two slowest kickers start, swimmers continue 5 to 10 seconds apart, and the fastest two swimmers start last. Kickers must touch each corner as they kick around the pool. They swim around the circumference of the pool—as many times as designated (depending on time available). The winners receive prizes.

Bubble, Bubble, Toil, and Trouble (Halloween)

Dump the biggest apples you can buy into the diving well. The swimmers bob for apples from underwater. No hands!

Halloween Football

Grease a watermelon with petroleum jelly or baby oil. Divide the team into two groups and station each team at opposite sides of the pool. Place the watermelon in the center of the pool and blow a whistle. The teams move the melon to the opposite side to score a point. The team with the most points at the end of the game eats the watermelon.

Christmas Party

All swimmers buy a three-dollar gift at a thrift store for a teammate in their training group (squad). At the Christmas party, each squad sits in a circle on the deck. Swimmers exchange gifts and go around the circle opening them. Once all gifts are opened, each swimmer in the circle rolls two dice when it's their turn. If a swimmer rolls a pair, 7, or 11, they get to give their gift to someone else in the circle and take the gift that person received. The interchange and exchange is amusing. Go around the circle in this manner three times. At the end of the game swimmers may trade for any gift they'd like to have. After the exchange, have fun festivities such as Santa, relays, and handicap swims (age-groupers versus seniors, kids versus parents, and so on).

Animal Ball

Divide the team in half and place the teams at opposite ends of the pool. Throw a water polo ball high in the air so that it lands at midpool. When it hits the water, swimmers sprint from both ends and work in an anything-goes environment to advance the ball to the other team's gutter. To score one point, a team must hold the ball in the gutter for three seconds.

Black Versus Red Intrasquad Meet

Kick off the season with an annual intrasquad meet; it will become a big, competitive hit with all families. Each swimmer on the team is assigned to either the red team or the black team. Two coaches draft swimmers by age group onto their squads to create two even teams. Limit the number of swims per swimmer and have seniors help create the lineup. Invite local media people to serve as honorary coaches to hype the event and create buy-in. Have a picnic following the meet; the winning team gets hamburgers and the losing team gets hot dogs. The honorary coach whose team wins understands that he or she will get thrown into the pool (great on local TV). Create other motivational ideas for everyone involved. For example, kids can paint their faces in their squad color.

Pentathlon

Every swimmer swims all of the following events and tallies their points for a total. Swimmers may also total their times in the five swims.

1. 50 fly
2. 50 back
3. 50 breast
4. 50 free
5. 100 IM

Points are awarded for each of five swims from a table designed for your team. Perhaps a 50 fly in 25.0 is worth 100 points and then scaled down to zero points. Two groups alternate, and each swimmer totals their points.

Octathlon

As in the pentathlon, the swimmers total points or times as the game progresses. Every swimmer swims all of the following events:

1. 50 free
2. 100 back
3. 200 free
4. 100 breast
5. 100 fly
6. 100 free
7. 200 IM
8. 500 free

Dual or Championship Order

Every swimmer on the team swims all of the events in the standard program for high school or college dual or championship meet. This is done nonstop and in meet order. Swimmers get their total time for all swims.

Roulette Meet

Divide the team into two to eight small teams of equal ability. Write down about 10 events, including diving, on slips of paper and place the slips in a hat. Diving is a front dive, a back dive, and a somersault. A swimmer from each team stands on the block ready to go. Draw an event out of the hat and shoot the gun. Keep score and award a prize to the winners. The scoring system depends upon the coach. For example, first place may equal five points, second four points, third three points, fourth two points, and fifth one point. Often you will find some "off event" stars.

Roll 'Em

Write a series of swims on the whiteboard, leaving a blank where the swimmer will insert a number (e.g., ___ 00, ___ × 50 @ 10 sr, K ___ × 25 @ 30, P ___ 00) and a space for breathing pattern. A swimmer throws one or two dice off a kickboard and inserts the number to be done. This swim can be done by either the entire lane or just the one swimmer.

Whiteboard

Although not the most scientific way to design a practice, this activity certainly is fun for early-season yardage training. Design four workouts that achieve the same yardage but that have entirely different methods (perhaps sprints, kicking/pulling, speed play, and distance). Draw two crossed lines on the chalkboard and write a workout in each quadrant. The swimmer throws a knotted towel from about 10 feet (3 m) away, and they perform the set that the towel hits! If they miss the board they do the hardest set; this speeds things up considerably.

Lanes 1–2	P32 × 25 @ 20	P16 × 50 @ 40	Lanes 3–4
	32 × 125 @ 1:30	16 × 250 @ 3	
	K16 × 25 @ 30	K8 × 50 @ 1	
Lanes 5–6	P8 × 100 @ 1:20	P16 × 200 @ 2:40	Lanes 7–8
	8 × 500 @ 6	4 × 1,000 @ 12	
	K4 × 100 @ 2	K2 × 200 @ 4	

Dartboard

Create a dartboard on plywood. Write hard, long sets on the outside, short sprint sets on the inside, and "go home" on the bulls-eye. (Place the bulls-eye on a knot in the wood so that the darts won't stick.) The swimmers throw for their whole workout from about 10 feet (3 m) away.

Skill Drills That Force Change

Forced change is more effective than verbal instructions. Swimmers must fail on everything they do in order to improve. Improvement comes only through correction; these drills, along with coach evaluations, can elicit change. These drills also force the swimmer to build athleticism in that they involve a variety of experiences and movements.

Gear Head Circuit

Use all the equipment you have to create a station circuit, with gear that forces change or skill development. Develop two stations per lane, and create up to 20 stations. Have equipment for five swimmers per lane. Swimmers spend about 6 minutes at each station. The swimmers switch stations by going under the lane line; one swimmer stays behind to tell the next group of swimmers what to do and how. The send-off is "tail wags the dog," which means because it is crowded, each line of five swimmers stays on their own side of the lane, and when the last swimmer touches after every 25, the first swimmer goes again. Each swimmer leaves when the preceding swimmer's feet are under the pennants. If age-group coaches use this activity twice a week, the swimmers will experience a training effect, skill development, teamsmanship, and *fun* and will never miss practice! Just keep which 2 days to yourself to surprise them! Check out the gear at www.gamesgimmickschallenges.com.

Imitations

At the end of practice, the swimmers stand on the deck and observe one swimmer who is imitating a teammate. The first swimmer to guess who is being imitated gets to do the next imitation.

Peer Stroke Check

Swimmers buddy up and are responsible for improving each other's strokes. Three swimmers work together. Two swimmers (1 and 2) are at one end of the pool and one swimmer (3) is at the other end. The activity consists of three swims: A, B, and C.

> A: 1 swims to 3; 3 views stroke from above and below and comments.
>
> B: 3 swims to 2; 2 views stroke from above and below and comments.
>
> C: 2 swims to 1; 1 views stroke from above and below and comments.

Each set of two swimmers is responsible for the improvement of the others. Stress that the team is only as strong as its slowest swimmer because if the slowest gets faster they push swimmers that may be ahead of them, therefore making the team better.

Directions

Swimmers must do exactly as they are told. Give them a routine verbally. For example, start off the block in lane three, sprint fly to the other end, get out and walk around the pool while flapping your arms like a chicken, jump in, swim backstroke in lane five, get out, and shake the coach's hand. Say you'll give the swimmers $1,000 (play money works). The swimmers do three push-ups for every mistake they make. If they are perfect, you do 25 push-ups.

Pull-Buoy Starts

If a swimmer is not using the arms as a pendulum or lifting the head up hard, take them off the block. The swimmer holds a pull buoy, throws it out in front of them, and enters the water at a 30-degree angle.

Racin' Rates

The swimmers do sprint 15s, 20s, or 25s. With two stopwatches, time the turnover rate of two swimmers and give the rate time during their rest. On the next sprint, time two others. This makes for fun competition. Time two complete arm strokes (three entries) for backstroke and freestyle or time two lifts of the chin for fly and breaststroke.

Six-Second Breakouts

At some point in every practice, start swimmers from every block and then blow a whistle at 6 seconds. Swimmers stop on the whistle and see how far they traveled. World-class swimmers get to 15 meters in 7 seconds from a start and in under 10 seconds for a push-off; therefore, swimmers need to work toward the goal of 15 meters in 7 seconds. Swimmers should try different fly kick combinations: big/fast, small/fast, on side/fast, and start big/fast and finish small/fast. Swimmers should also determine the number of kicks that are optimal and then use that number of kicks during every practice training set. Note: Misty Hyman used 11 kicks throughout her career but switched to 8 at the Olympic Games to have more air and energy for the last 50.

15-Meter Starting Contest

This activity stresses importance of great streamlining on starts and push-offs. Set up teams in lanes. Each lane should have boys first so that boys race boys and the girls follow so that girls race girls. (For etiquette reasons, the boys do not stand behind starting girls.) Start each wave and see who gets to the 15-meter mark first. The first person to 15 meters scores a point for their lane. The swimmers will work hard on streamlining to score for their lane. Have the winners of each heat start to see which individual swimmer wins the starting contest.

Lane Starting Contest

Swimmers line up, about eight per lane, and are seeded by starting ability (best to beginner). The swimmers start and the first swimmer to 15 meters scores a point for their lane. See which lane wins the contest. The swimmers keep score, and every swimmer will figure out what they need to do to be better.

Starter of the Day

The eight winners of each heat from the Lane Starting Contest (page 141) start. The first swimmer to 15 meters is named starter of the day.

Working the Walls

This activity helps every swimmer to be streamline on push-offs. Stand at the backstroke pennants pole and count the number of swimmers that start their kick and stroke before the feet pass the pennants. Before the next send-off, tell the swimmers the number that started kicking before the pennants and encourage them to work as a team to reduce the number. If too many are incorrect, use squad do-overs to force change. Don't count the swim in the set if too many are not streamlining. They'll get the word out quickly.

Tempo Trainer 25s

The swimmer sets a tempo trainer at 1.3 and swims a 25, entering the water on every beep. The swimmer rests 10 seconds and does the next 25 with a full stroke, entering the water with the left hand on every beep. The swimmer tries to have the same number of strokes going both ways, feeling DPS and tempo going slow (2.6) and fast (1.3).

Motivational Systems

Swimmers need motivation to stay focused and on task. Since not everyone is motivated by the same systems or to the same degree, it is important to involve the entire team in many different systems. Following are a few to try.

Tour de Championship

Buy a an inexpensive yellow jersey. Using iron-on fabric, put an appropriate logo on the front and on the back place Lance Armstrong's favorite sayings: carpe diem (seize the day; at top), grande seigneur (the big man; in the middle) and vente (follow me; at the bottom). After each practice, the coach selects the swimmer that had the best practice. That swimmer dries off, stands on a block, and puts on the jersey to the applause of teammates treading water. The swimmer then leads the team to the locker room. At the next afternoon practice, that swimmer leads the team onto the deck and hangs the jersey on the whiteboard. Place the name of each winner of the yellow jersey on a team bulletin board. At the end of the season, everyone that won the jersey is recognized at an awards banquet.

Celebrations

All the swimmers line up behind the pennants along a lane line and face the finish end. One at a time, they sprint in and practice finishing. After touching the end of the pool, they do a celebration. Every celebration must be different.

Rocky Road

Swimmers line up in a straight line in time order, from fastest on the left to slowest on the right. If they don't know their times, do it by height. (This method is not very accurate, but it's fast). Walk down the line and seed the swimmers into lanes by saying 1, 2, 3, 4, 5, 6/6, 5, 4, 3, 2, 1/1, 2, 3.... This quickly divides swimmers into teams of equal ability. Once swimmers know how fast they are on the type of set to be used, they line up quickly based on their last or fastest average. They swim the training set (e.g., 5 × 100 @ 3 or 20 × 100 @ 1:30) and figure their average time to the tenth of a second. The swimmers push off on all swims; the feet should leave the wall together on zero (or five if circle swimming). Check it! Write a team name for each lane on the chalkboard and list the people on that team. When the swimmers complete the set, write their average times and then total the averages for each team. Give rocky road ice cream or some other prize to the team with the fastest total average. Because everyone is motivated differently, this gimmick motivates in a variety of ways, but depends upon you to play it up.

1. You may use the lane team average (three to six swimmers) for a prize.
2. You may also use the total team average (18 to 48 swimmers) compared with the last time this set was done.
3. Let the swimmers go home or ease the training if the whole team or a percentage (e.g., 75%) of the team is faster than the last time they did the set.
4. Post the total team and lane team records for a few standard sets so they regularly see the times.
5. Keep individual records for the sets.

    ### Sample

    5 × 100 fly @ 3, 52.4, John Smith, 1985

    20 × 100 free @ 1:30, 51.9, Joe Schmo, 1985

6. Rank the top 10 and post.
7. Stress racing people because they have similar speed but are on "another" team.
8. Swimmers catch the person ahead because they are faster because of the seed.
9. Give prizes to anyone who does the set faster than the last time.
10. Keep a master sheet for standard training sets and record times so swimmers can easily check their last or best average.

RELATING TRAINING TO GOALS

Many coaches use standardized test sets as a season progresses. I believe that two things are essential to improvement. The coach must

1. relate accurate test set results to season goals, and
2. perform the same threshold set monthly to assess physical improvement by each swimmer.

These two things encourage swimmers to buy into 30 days of training in between.

Test Sets

For test sets to work, swimmers must know how to figure their exact average time on a set. If they start to give their time by saying "about," they haven't figured their exact time and the formula will not work. Follow the routine provided to teach them how to figure their exact average. For anaerobic training, straight set training is critical. The first and last swims are done as fast as the swimmer can move on the whole set. The first and last swims are very close, if not the same, although we've always said that the last one is your best one because you know you're done, not because you've been a Sammy Save-Up. Be a hero with a fast exact average time, not with your last swim of the set. Don't descend, ascend, or negative split. When a swimmer plateaus at an average time after several attempts to improve, add four swims to the set of 50s, three to the set of 100s, and two to the set of 250s. The 500 to 1,650s are more accurate for predicting women's times than they are for predicting men's times.

After each practice, have every swimmer record on a team roster list their average and what it predicts. Place it in a loose-leaf binder after test set sessions and note improvement in averages and prediction throughout the season. Prediction sets may be done long course or short course, with a send-off appropriate to the swimmer.

100 prediction	Figure the exact average on 6 × 50 @ 2:00 send-off
	Average time ( ) × 2 = __:__.__ prediction
200 prediction	Figure the exact average on 5 × 100 @ 3:00 send-off
	Average time ( ) × 2 = __:__.__ prediction
500 prediction	Figure the exact average on 6 × 250 @ 5:00 send-off
	Average time ( ) × 2 = __:__.__ prediction
1,000/1,650/1,500 prediction	Figure the exact average on 20 × 100 @ set send-off giving 10 to 15 seconds rest
	Average time ( ) × 8 for 800, × 10 for 1,000, × 15 for 1,500, × 16.5 for 1,650

Threshold Tests

Jon Urbanchek created software to help determine training paces from threshold swims and sets. You can download detailed instructions and software for free at www.gamesgimmickschallenges.com/ppt. Motivate swimmers toward accurate training and assessment of improvements of physical and racing capacity each month using these sets and figuring total time or average per 100 on the following:

Distance

3,000 or 30-minute swim

2,000 or 10 × 400 @ 20 sr or SO

Fly (free)*

10 × 300 @ 20 sr or SO

10 × 200 @ 15 sr or SO

30 × 100 @ 1:20 (sc)

30 × 100 @ 1:30 (lc)

*An option would be a rainbow set of two white, two red, two blue, and two purple

Stroke or sprint

500, 400, 300, 200

Some coaches use swims performed at meets. Once the threshold has been completed, the coach enters the swimmer's name and time into a software program. The program then creates training pace for a 50 through a 500 in six training categories, as well as a 10-second heart rate range needed for a proper training effect. Threshold is most accurate with the longest distance the swimmers can handle. Although shorter distances are less accurate, they may be more motivating for sprinters and stroke swimmers. Assess an honest effort by a total pulse over 75 beats when taken at 0, 30, and 60 seconds after finishing the T swim. Every swimmer should learn and use these essentials for accurate training.

CONCLUSION

These activities are the author's favorites and were created over a 50-year coaching career. Coaches should implement something challenging and something fun for every swimmer every day to add variety and increase retention. Attempt to create swimmer and team outcomes, whether it is a serious training set or a fun activity. Find many other ideas from quality coaches worldwide at www.gamesgimmickschallenges.com.

PART THREE

TEACHING STROKE TECHNIQUE

10

Trends and Techniques in Freestyle

Mike Bottom

The freestyle stroke has changed significantly over the past several decades. The changes may not be as dramatic as those made to breaststroke (the head breaking the surface of the water) or butterfly (requiring the dolphin kick), but they may be much more significant. Ultimately, although fast swimming is a wonderful thing, what is remembered about a competition is who touched the wall first. We remember great champions of the 50-meter freestyle such as Matt Biondi, Alex Popov, and Gary Hall, Jr., but many can't instantly recall the times with which they brought home the Olympic gold. To be sure, they were all fast, but they weren't necessarily world record holders when they reached the pinnacle of success. However, on the biggest stage in the world, they were able to put together the race it took to win. In freestyle, that means adapting, evolving, and overcoming. All great freestyle champions of recent memory have had the ability to adjust their stroke to the needs of their body and the race they find themselves in at that moment. This is key to becoming a champion, and it requires physical and mental alertness as well as appropriately focused training.

THREE STYLES OF FREESTYLE

Today, freestyle has evolved to a point where a single style is no longer sufficient to win races. The crawl stroke, as it is traditionally known, must now be viewed in a variety of methods in order to allow swimmers to achieve the speeds they are capable of. Here we break down the three styles of freestyle.

Hip-Driven Freestyle   The hip-driven stroke is the more traditional stroke swimmers use today, particularly in training. In competition, elite athletes use this for races 200 meters and longer. It's the most efficient way to swim freestyle in terms of energy consumption and is a solid core fundamental.

Shoulder-Driven Freestyle   When more speed is needed in a sprint race or at various points of other races, the shoulder-driven stroke comes into play. This sprint-speed stroke is found in 50s and 100s and is a vital part of races up to 200 meters.

Body-Driven Freestyle   When a race is coming to a close, swimmers naturally dig deep and fire away with every last ounce of energy. The body-driven stroke is designed to take advantage of this and get an athlete's fingers to the wall as quickly as possible. It's the grand finale, so to speak, of a sprint race.

With few exceptions, these stroke techniques are not intended to be swum singularly. A body-driven stroke, for instance, cannot be used for an entire race. Even if it could, it would not be the fastest tool in a swimmer's competition arsenal. Instead, each of these stroke styles has a specific time and purpose.

The exception to this rule is the shoulder-driven freestyle in a long-course 50-meter race. Because this event is brief and requires explosiveness, well-trained athletes can maintain this stroke for the duration of the event. Before discussing when to use each stroke for maximum effectiveness, one must understand the strokes themselves.

TECHNIQUES OF THE THREE STYLES OF FREESTYLE

Each stroke (hip-, shoulder-, and body-driven) has a different drive point. The drive point is where power and, ultimately, speed are developed and put to use. This makes for a simple yet literal understanding of each stroke.

Hip-Driven Freestyle

Long swims, whether in training or in competition, create movement from the hips. The stroke takes advantage of the natural rotation of a swimmer's body and requires a minimal amount of energy to effectively propel the swimmer forward in the water. This stroke is comfortable to swim and is the most efficient of the strokes, which makes it possible to use for long durations of time.

Swimmers are generally quick to realize, even when first learning how to travel through water, that the hips are paramount in the pool. If the hips are not properly placed, body line is sacrificed and a sinking effect occurs. This applies not just to freestyle but to every stroke; the difference among strokes is in which direction the hips move.

In the hip-driven freestyle, swimmers must think in terms of side-to-side rotation, which contributes to productive movement, rather than up-and-down movement, which significantly increases drag.

Each stroke of a hip-driven freestyle begins with one arm extended, the hand out in front with the palm facing downward, and the body on its side. The hand of that extended arm slides outward slightly as the hip skates on its side. In this position, the arm is prepared to put itself into a position where it can create propulsive force. To do this, the fingertips are brought down to point toward the bottom of the pool as the elbow stays high and the shoulder rolls upward.

At the same time, the leg on that same side of the body kicks, and the strength from the kick causes the hips to move around and face the bottom of the pool. This is the beginning of the rotation the body must go through in order to position itself for the next stroke. The swimmer then repeats the process.

During the pull, the body is moved forward and ultimately beyond the hand until the hand reaches the hip, where it then releases the water and exits during the recovery phase. Refer to figure 10.1 for an overwater view of the hip-driven freestyle sequence; to view the hip-driven freestyle sequence underwater, see figure 10.2.

FIGURE 10.1 Hip-driven freestyle: overwater sequence.

FIGURE 10.2 Hip-driven freestyle: underwater sequence.

Shoulder-Driven Freestyle

The shoulder-driven stroke is key when a swimmer needs to take advantage of the highest amount of power available from the rotation of the shoulders and pull of the arms. In this style, the shoulder blades move together while the hips remain stabilized.

Starting from the ground up, so to speak, think of the kick not as a mechanism of propulsion but rather one of structure. It's the foundation on which the stroke is built. It doesn't matter how well the upper portion of a tall building is constructed if the foundation is unreliable. Swimmers use the legs, kicking powerfully, to maintain strict body alignment (see figure 10.3). At high-level competition, people are quick to notice the amount of water coming up behind sprint freestyle swimmers. Many assume that this short, fast kick is used to move the swimmers forward. The kick does produce some propulsion, but it is mainly used to secure the hips so that the shoulders can express their power based off the steadiness of the provided foundation. Imagine lifting something very heavy onto a high shelf. It is a lot easier to do so while standing on solid concrete ground than while standing on a waterbed.

FIGURE 10.3 The shallow, fast kick used in the shoulder-driven freestyle stabilizes the hips.

FIGURE 10.4 Shoulder-driven freestyle.

Once a solid foundation is established, the shoulders can provide explosive power and movement. Rather than relying on the rotation of the hips to create momentum, the shoulder-driven style of freestyle is based on the connection of upper-body musculature and structure. The fingertips have to feel their connection down the arm, to the shoulder, through the middle of the back, and up through the end of the opposite arm. For every stroke cycle, complete chemistry has to be maintained within a swimmer's entire wingspan and each muscle group involved therein.

While the kick provides balance and height in the water, the upper body rotates in unison throughout each stroke. See figure 10.4 for an underwater example of the shoulder-driven freestyle. This style of swimming requires a significant amount of strength but can provide for extremely fast movement in the water. It isn't the most aesthetically pleasing stroke technique-wise—it is more function over form—but it is designed to win sprints.

Body-Driven Freestyle

The swimmer that finishes a race is not the same swimmer that started the race. The swimmer at the end is tired and drained and unable to maintain the technique that the swimmer who dove in was able to hold onto for awhile. This fatigue is caused by the acidosis effect of major lactate buildup. However, the swimmer still needs to get their hand on the wall first. In order to do so, the body-driven freestyle can be used to finish a race strong.

In the grand scheme of swimming, the body-driven freestyle is considered very inefficient compared with other strokes. Its value stems from taking advantage of muscles that haven't been used and fatigued to the point of failure.

The easiest way to understand what the body-driven freestyle looks like is to think back to swimming lessons. When a child begins swimming, the child's stroke looks strikingly similar to a body-driven stroke. Because the child doesn't understand technique or body mechanics, they move their body side to side, unknowingly rotating left to right as they press their head down in the water and throw their arms forward and pull them back. The general consensus is that the stroke needs a lot of work. However, it underlines a valuable trait that more advanced swimmers can take advantage of: tying the motion of the arms to the rotation of the body. This is the key element of body-driven freestyle.

Rather than skating the hips, as is done during hip-driven swimming, or singularly rotating the upper body, as is done during shoulder-driven swimming, the full rotation of the body is called upon during body-driven race finishing. The core muscles of the body, from the toes through the end of the fingertips, rotate as one whole being rather than operating separately. The swimmer places the head down, doesn't alter the body alignment with breathing, and just finishes.

Refer to figure 10.5 for underwater views of the body-driven freestyle. This stroke uses a lot of muscle, which is one reason it can't be maintained for long. However, it gives swimmers the potential to stay out in front of a race just long enough to finish.

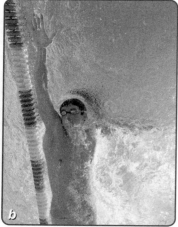

FIGURE 10.5   Body-driven freestyle: *(a)* frontal view and *(b)* bottom view.

RECOVERY STYLES

The recovery phase takes place no matter which type of freestyle an athlete swims. Two types of recovery can be used: the lift and shift recovery and the straight-arm recovery.

The recovery is, of course, a vital part of efficient and safe swimming. An improperly conducted recovery done hundreds of thousands of times over a swimmer's career can lead to significant injury. On the flip side, depending on how it is conducted and the style selected, a well-done recovery can aid the power portion of each stroke.

Lift and Shift Recovery

Essentially the standard recovery seen in swimming pools across the world, the lift and shift recovery (figure 10.6) is a simple and safe way to return the hand back in front of the swimmer. This recovery is most notable by its high elbow placement, in which the elbow first exits the water at the completion of each stroke and then stays high as the shoulder moves and rotates forward to begin the next stroke.

FIGURE 10.6 Lift and shift recovery.

Done properly, a swimmer finishes a stroke and, with the arm extended underwater, bends at the elbow, breaking the surface of the water, and continues to bring the arm out of the water entirely until the hand clears the surface. At that point, the shoulder rolls forward while the body rotates to the position in which the pull of the opposite arm commences and follows through. Once fully rotated into position, the hand is placed back out in front where the initial pull began.

Straight-Arm Recovery

The straight-arm recovery (figure 10.7) is easily identifiable; the name is a literal description. The arm maintains an extended position from the beginning to the end of the recovery, further described as from the exit point to the entry point.

Once an arm finishes a stroke underwater, rather than bending at the elbow, a swimmer simply rotates the hand so that the palm faces inward toward the body, leaving the hand in a position in which the small pinky finger faces up. That finger leads the arm upward and is the first to break the surface of the water, and the arm—like a windmill—maintains its straight position as it comes over the top to return to its starting point.

FIGURE 10.7 Straight-arm recovery.

TIME AND PLACE

As mentioned earlier, each type of freestyle has its time and place. Each swimmer must determine the exact point of a swim at which they should change their drive point. However, some general rules apply.

50 Meters A perfect example of shoulder-driven freestyle can be seen in the finals of the 50-meter freestyle of the 2008 Beijing Olympics. Every single swimmer used this type of stroke in that race, and every single swimmer in the finals of major international competitions since then has used this style of stroke. We can also presume with relative certainty that every athlete going forward in major finals will use this stroke because, simply put, this stroke develops the speed to get there. The 50s—whether yards or meters, short course or long course—are shoulder-driven races.

100 Meters An athlete who currently transitions between the three styles of freestyle better than probably anyone in the world is Olympian Nathan Adrian. His breakout swim, the race that launched him on the international scene, is a perfect example of how effective the ability to change drive points really is. At the 2008 Short Course World Championships in Manchester, England, Nathan was a newcomer against an all-star field that included veterans and record holders alike. He was up against Italy's Filippo Magnini, a former world champion, as well as others like Duje Draganja, who already had an Olympic medal to his credit.

Right off the blocks after his breakout, Nathan set his pace with a shoulder-driven stroke for a few cycles, switched to a couple cycles of the longer hip-driven stroke, and, before going into his turn, switched back to shoulder-driven strokes to build and maintain his speed. Again, off his turn breakout, Nathan built his pace with shoulder-driven swimming, used hip-driven swimming in the middle of the pool, and repeated the process. Coming off the last wall, Nathan went with a shoulder-driven stroke, and 10 meters out put his head down, used a body-driven stroke, and won the gold medal. As a result of using body-driven strokes at the end, he managed to out-split some of the fastest second-half swimmers in the world. His strategy in that race illustrates the perfect way to swim a 100.

200 Meters Swimmers still use all three styles of freestyle in the 200, but they take advantage of the hip-driven stroke for longer to maintain cadence near the end of the race. Each swimmer must figure out how far out from turns and how long after they can maintain a shoulder-driven stroke before switching back to a hip drive in order to hold onto their pace. Even though the 200 is a longer swim, one must never forget the value of the body-driven stroke to finish. Athletes around the world, including some I have trained, have led entire races only to be touched out by hundredths of a second because they thought they could hold a shoulder-driven stroke into the finish.

General rules can apply to changing styles during a 200. One rule is that, if swum properly, a shoulder-driven stroke cannot be maintained all the way through the finish. Thinking it is possible is a mistake. Another rule is that if you wait until you feel yourself slowing down before changing over, it is too late. An athlete must trust the training so that when it comes time to race, the switch is simply flipped and the body does what it knows it has to do and what will get it to the wall first.

PRACTICING TRANSITION FOR SUCCESS

Grouping different styles into sets of swims is one of the best training methods for increasing a swimmer's ability to transition into different freestyle techniques. One example of a set we do at Michigan to work on the three styles of freestyle is 10 150s on about a 2:30 send-off. During this set, swimmers work their hip-driven strokes for a full 100 and focus on taking as few strokes per length as possible. This 100 is about working on efficiency and reducing total stroke volume.

After the 100 of hip-driven swimming, the last 50 is broken down into two portions. Right off the turn the swimmers go into shoulder-driven swimming for 35 meters and focus on the stable body and coordinated shoulder movement that the stroke requires. During the last 15 meters, the swimmers use a body-driven stroke and focus on putting their heads down, holding their breath, and getting their hands on the wall.

UNDERSTANDING SPEED

The definition of speed is often misunderstood, even among high-level swimming coaches. Speed is generally defined as "fast," or, more accurately, the fastest someone or something can travel. But looking at the term in that context is basic at best and lacks truth.

Speed should not be defined simply as the fastest someone can swim. It's not a finite number. The true meaning of speed is ever changing, ever evolving, and almost never the same on two separate occasions. Speed, then, is not how fast something can go; it is how fast something—or someone—can go at that very moment.

Think of it this way. If you have an efficient, productive, full season of training followed by a perfectly timed taper where you meet all of your resting, training, and nutritional needs, your ability to swim fast in a race is significantly higher than if you tried to swim that same race after a grueling workout of 20,000 meters. Speed always varies based on what the body is capable of, and that includes factors that come up during a race itself.

While training a national team member who would later make the 2008 Beijing Olympic team, one of the most respected coaches in the world came to me to discuss the swimmer's training and my method of teaching the athlete to swim with the three styles of freestyle. Even though this athlete was swimming faster than ever before, this coach did not agree with finishing the race with the body-driven stroke. "It's not efficient," he told me. "It's not a very fast stroke." And I didn't disagree with him, but he was missing the point.

If two similar swimmers who are physically fresh are put in a one-length race heads up, and one athlete uses a shoulder-driven stroke and the other uses a body-driven stroke, the swimmer using the shoulder-driven stroke will win every time. But if both swim hip- or shoulder-driven freestyle until their bodies reached acidosis, and one swimmer switches to a body-driven stroke whereas the other maintains his stroke, the body-driven swimmer will win every time.

The point and subsequent value of switching to a body-driven stroke is that it allows a swimmer to tap relatively fresh muscle fibers. For example, in a 100-meter race the muscles of the upper body are literally exhausted after 80 or 90 meters. Acid will have built up in the blood, muscular glycogen will be depleted, energy stores in surrounding tissue will be gone, and, as a result, the chance of maintaining the same speed at 90 meters as one had at 60 meters is zero. By changing to a body-driven stroke and thus changing the drive point, new strength is discovered. No, those muscles and that technique are not superior to other stroke options at the onset of a race, but the relatively fresh muscles available the last 10 meters of a race are certainly better, and in turn faster, than continuing to punish muscles that have nothing left to give.

TECHNICAL DRILLS FOR FREESTYLE

Many drills can be used to improve the freestyle stroke. Following are my personal favorites related to the hip-driven freestyle, shoulder-driven freestyle, and body-driven freestyle.

Hip-Driven Freestyle

One drill we use to improve the hip-driven freestyle involves performing the stroke with a forearm and hand paddle on one arm and a fin on the opposite-side leg. The forearm paddle helps to bring the elbow up and the fingertips down upon entry. The fin helps to drive the opposite arm (the one with the paddle on it) down into the water upon entry.

Shoulder-Driven Freestyle

The drill we currently use when working on the shoulder-driven freestyle involves paddles on both hands, a snorkel, and fins on both feet. The stroking arm drops the fingers and wrist just slightly to build tension in the hand and wrist. Once that tension is built up, the arm recovers over the water and out to the front again. The opposite arm then does the same. Perform the process twice with each hand, and then swim several full-power strokes before repeating the sequence.

Body-Driven Freestyle

The body-driven freestyle drill that we use is done with fins on both legs as well. We start with an underwater butterfly kick (once) on each side and alternating sides after each butterfly kick. This movement helps the swimmer to recognize the water pressure that exists on the full body. Follow up these kicks with full-body sprinting and no breath.

CONCLUSION

Freestyle will continue to be an adaptive stroke, and more and more swimmers of all levels will fine-tune their abilities to switch between drive points. As this happens, athletes will get faster and their races will become more exciting.

Some question whether it is possible for athletes in the 100-meter freestyle to maintain a shoulder-driven stroke for an entire race without relying on a body-driven stroke to keep their speed into the finish. In general, this is highly unlikely unless one has a very specific genetic and physiological structure. The French have been blessed with swimmers such as Alain Bernard and Fred Bousquet, who can swim nearly an entire 100 with a shoulder-driven stroke. These athletes have a unique blend of height and muscularity and their bodies have an affinity to clearing or staving off acidosis in a way that, for most people, training alone cannot replicate.

As much as evolution plays a part in the improvement of swimming, adapting to what one's body can do is even more important. There is value in taking clues and tips from the techniques of the world's best swimmers. However, unless one is of the exact same physical stature, the real value is in finding how the intricacies discovered through watching others can be applied to one's self.

11

Trends and Techniques in Backstroke

Teri McKeever

During my years at Cal we have coached some talented backstrokers, including two Olympians—one of whom, Natalie Coughlin, has competed in two Olympic Games. We have also had individual champions in backstroke events at the Women's Division I NCAA Championships.

My approach to backstroke technique has developed from my own opinions, the work of Milt Nelms (former coach and a leading technical consultant on stroke mechanics), and the influence of the athletes I have coached at Cal and Fresno State. As a coach, I take up the challenge that I issue to my athletes, which is to use a combination of imagination and common sense. Because of this, my view of the stroke is in constant progress. However, the principles I present in this chapter will not become dated because they are fundamental to how human beings function. In "History of Stroke Images," I list the technical aspects of the backstroke that have been considered essential during various time periods. In "The New Backstroke," I list the technical aspects that, in my opinion, are currently essential to success.

A GENERAL OVERVIEW

Backstroke technique has three parts. I discuss in detail each of these three parts later in the chapter.

The Start   The start provides the greatest speed attained during any swimming race. When done efficiently, the start should enable the swimmer to break out swimming at a speed that is faster than normal.

The Stroke   The technical aspects of swimming backstroke play a large part in determining the success of the swimmer in competition. Keeping the arms connected to the body in a natural pathway during the arm stroke helps to stabilize and control the water. This chapter examines the technical aspects that maximize success.

The Turn   Turns allow the swimmer to come off the wall at a swimming speed that is faster than normal. The skill of swimmers in this transition phase contributes greatly to the speed of the competitive swim.

HISTORY OF STROKE IMAGES

Throughout my career as a swimmer and a coach, many phrases have been used to convey the traditional fundamentals of backstroke (see figure 11.1 on page 160):

Look up (or back)	Reach to make a long stroke
Chin up	Reach for length on the finish
Chest up	Deep catch
Hips up	Deep pull
Arch back	Down–up–down pull
Shrug the shoulder	Finish downward
Little finger in first, thumb out first	Throw the water toward the feet
	Keep the knees below the surface
Thumb-down finish	Elbow pointed at the bottom, fingers pointed
Get on the side	at the sky during the pull
Reach for the sky	

This is a lot to keep track of! I prefer to limit thoughts about the stroke. I believe that a coach should get a swimmer into the right position and give him or her a chance to respond with athletic instincts. Over time, this approach will help the athlete develop the stroke around a solid foundation. Giving a swimmer a lot of directive details will confuse a less-talented or less-confident athlete and will distract a talented swimmer from the more important basics of the stroke. Therefore, stick with the essences of the stroke, not the details.

THE "NEW" BACKSTROKE

The label of "new" backstroke may sound pretentious. However, enough differences exist between the model that I use and the old model to make old and new an appropriate distinction.

At Cal, we have added our own ideas, adjustments, and refinements, but following are the three basic concepts we use. Milt Nelms introduced with persistence these basic stroke principles to the swimming community in the late 1990s.

- ◆ Shape the body into a slight curve.
- ◆ Make the body into a springy unit.
- ◆ Use the arms within natural human pathways, as part of the body, to create a walking stroke.

FIGURE 11.1 Traditional backstroke images: *(a)* little finger in first, thumb out first; *(b)* reaching for the sky; *(c)* knees below the surface; and *(d)* elbow pointed at the bottom, fingers pointed at the sky during the pull.

These three concepts cover a lot. If the swimmer uses these concepts, much of the need for attention to detail vanishes and many of the directive, unnatural details in the list of common traditional backstroke ideas no longer fit into the stroke. This is advantageous because it keeps clutter and chatter out of the brain and allows the athlete to pay attention to the most important things: mental energy to establish rhythm, and the confidence needed to go fast!

Shape the Body Into a Slight Curve

This shape is more body language or gesture than an actual shape. If standing upright, the shape produces a slightly downward gaze. When in the water, this shape produces a gaze that is slightly toward the feet. The shape is created through the entire body, not just the neck.

The slightly curved shape, as opposed to the older, more traditional style of holding the chest up and head back, makes the body lighter in the water and tends to keep the legs higher (see figure 11.2), which tends to cut down on drag and add distance per cycle to the stroke. This posture also helps the athlete breathe more fully.

Because the gaze is slightly toward the feet rather than upward or backward, the swimmer also picks up more information in the peripheral vision; this gives the athlete a sense of "where they are," which helps improve overall physical confidence.

Many of the traditional stroke cues—the "chest high" and "look back" cues and all of the "reach" concepts—interfere with the slightly curved shape. These concepts tend to break the body into segments. A segmented body makes the stroke awkward and adds a stop and start that is slower and takes more energy.

FIGURE 11.2 Shaping the body into a slight curve.

Make the Body Into a Springy Unit

Racing is a very dynamic activity, and the body needs to be alert and engaged. The entire slightly curved body should feel springy and awake. Most attention should be given to the middle part of the body, from the head to the tops of the thighs, because this part of the body fatigues first. Once the middle part of the body loses springiness, the arms and legs have to take the load and achieving any kind of speed is tough. The arms and the rest of the legs should be part of this system and should approximately match the springiness of the body.

My experience with many incoming freshmen in our program is that they are turned off in the body, which leads to tension in parts of the arms and legs. Our swimming culture promotes training that, because of long durations of the same slow speeds, makes athletes naturally conserve energy by relaxing the axial unit. The axial unit refers to the rotating of the hips, trunk, and shoulders in a straight, long axis line around the core while swimming backstroke. When a swimmer relaxes the axial unit, the demand for control goes to the extremities rather than the axial part of the body. Keeping the body springy helps develop more efficient and rhythmic strokes that originate in the torso and pelvic part of the body.

Many traditional stroke cues interfere with the concept of springiness. Any cues that force the body into unnatural postures tend to cause kinks in the nervous system and body structures. You can get an idea of this by making your body springy, with a slight gesture of curve, and walking around. Then introduce some of the cues that are on the list of traditional backstroke concepts, such as looking upward, sticking the chin out, sticking the chest out, arching the back, and trying to walk around. Ask yourself which style of walking feels more efficient and more athletic; the difference between the two styles will be obvious. This interference is the same thing that happens when a swimmer introduces these postural distortions in the water.

Use the Arms Within Natural Human Pathways as Part of the Body

The arms should move within the most stable pathways possible. These are the natural pathways of the arms that keep them connected and prevent them from overextending within a pulling action. Many arm shapes (some of which are listed earlier) in traditional swimming strokes can put the shoulder into weak positions that disconnect the arm from the body. These positions are less functional and less effective in stabilizing and controlling the water as the athlete swims. I also suspect that these common traditional movements put the joints into compromising and less-functional positions, which might lead to injury. (I make this statement only from my experiences as a coach; I do not have medical expertise.)

Many of the stroke cues from the long list that I provided put the shoulder into positions that could be less functional. The concept of the scapular plane was introduced to swimming in the 1990s by Milt Nelms and former Cal swimmer Kipp Dye, a Boston physical therapist. According to this concept, if a movement puts the arm behind the normal scapular plane, the joint will not move in its natural gliding pathway as the arm goes up over the head and back down to the waist. This is particularly true if the arms are under load, as they are during the underwater phase of the stroke. Cues such as "deep catch" tend to put the shoulder out of the scapular plane.

Swimmers do many strokes in training. Each stroke should promote health and robustness in the whole body, and the shoulder should be one of the healthiest parts of a swimmer's body. Literature shows a high percentage of shoulder pain and injury in swimmers. When swimmers come to Cal with shoulder problems, the problems tend to disappear unless a lot of damage has already been done; new problems rarely appear in our program. We insist that the swimmer learn natural movements and integrate them into the stroke (see figure 11.3). I believe that this has made a lot of

FIGURE 11.3 Examples of natural arm movements in the backstroke.

difference in almost eliminating existing shoulder issues and keeping instances of new shoulder issues at close to zero.

Harmful movement patterns do not disappear overnight, and it sometimes takes most of the athlete's collegiate career to alter them. I hope that the stroke methodologies in age-group swimming are changed to avoid these injury patterns.

STARTS AND TURNS

Starts and turns differ from actual swimming in an important way. Milt Nelms pointed out the fundamental difference to me when we first met in 2000, and in the years since we have had many discussions about the importance of this difference. Swimming strokes are repeated movements—rhythmic repeated patterns that are basically cyclic, as in walking, running, or rowing. Starts and turns, however, are sequences of separate movements that need to be linked together.

To somewhat oversimplify, swimming is cyclic and the start and turns are serial. According to Nelms, many of the same brain mechanisms probably organize these two types of movement; however, different parts of the brain are likely more active in cyclic movement and less active in serial movements and vice versa. This would explain why a sharp change should occur from swimming to turning movements and from turning movements back to swimming. Swimmers commonly make the mistake of trying to retain some aspects of cyclic swimming rhythms and sensations when turning. A backstroker often swims into a turn, rolls over, and adds a bounce or body dolphin in the same rhythm as the swimming stroke, which dulls the activity within the turn. Traditional training patterns tend to promote this error. Many swimmers could benefit from learning to feel like they are throwing a switch when they make the change from swimming to turning. Swimmers should use the rhythms and sensations of turns exclusively when turning and the rhythms and sensations of swimming exclusively when swimming. The two activities are fundamentally different and should not be blended but rather treated almost as separate sports, and swimmers should be taught and trained accordingly.

The links between each of these serial events are called transitions. One transition links swimming and the start of a turn, and one transition links the end of the turn (or the start) and the beginning of swimming. Swimmers lose velocity during transitions; sharper transitions ensure that less velocity is lost.

The Start

The start has a number of variations; any variation can be successful depending upon the swimmer. Both the swimmer and the coach should learn and experiment with variations because these physical experiences go into the swimmer's overall inventory and help make the athlete's chosen start style more athletic and effective. The following fundamental principles apply to all styles.

Keep the feet as high on the wall as possible. The backstroke start should be viewed as a dive. Therefore, more advantage can be gained from placing the starting platform as high as the rules allow.

Keep the body springy throughout the start. A jumping or pouncing animal stores springiness in its body when it is preparing to jump or pounce. The backstroker should take on this concept when preparing for the horn, and then maintain that springiness throughout the whole start process of uncoiling and into the first swimming strokes.

Use the whole body to dive. The swimmer should use the whole body to create the start. The "take your mark" position introduces a lot of closed angles throughout the body, and a swimmer can produce much acceleration when opening those angles to create the dive. Many swimmers who come into our program do the backstroke start by accelerating the head, arms, and legs out of sync with the body and therefore lose a lot of potential acceleration. Virtually all jumping movements in sport are dominated by the legs. A jumping sequence is instinctive and physically logical. However, the backstroke start is less effective if these same jumping instincts are used. In the backstroke start, the body is coiled and stabilized partially by the arms and then needs to uncoil and travel upside-down perpendicular to the line of gravity. A normal jumping sequence is not applicable. The body is bigger and slower than any of the extremities and the neck, so another way of looking at it is to emphasize the body and let the arms, legs, and head fit into the whole-body movement.

Make as small a hole as possible when going into the water. No matter which start style is used, the object is to slide into the water through as small a hole as possible. The water is heavy, and the less that needs to be moved out of the way the better.

A very good start (see figure 11.4) usually includes a hole that ends up being almost round and the same size as a cross-section of the widest part of the body. You can see the footprint of a good dive after the swimmer has disappeared under the water. If the disturbed water is circular, then the body slid into the water cleanly and efficiently. If the disturbed water is elliptical or oval, then the swimmer created drag as the body went into the water, which means that some of the acceleration from the dive was unnecessarily lost.

When starting, most swimmers find better success by making sure that the heel of the hand, rather than the palm of the hand or the base of the knuckles, is on the starting bar. Also, if an athlete has problems with the feet sliding down the starting surface, two things may help.

1. The athlete can set up with an image of the pelvis moving backward (toward the turning end of the pool) as he or she pulls towards the starting block. This set-up makes the angle of leg pressure into the wall less acute and more oblique. The force of the push from the legs goes into the wall rather than down the wall toward the bottom. This strategy makes slippage less likely.

2. The athlete can think of the arms as legs in the first part of the start. The arms leap away from the block and the legs push into the wall after the arms have propelled the torso, head and neck, and arms somewhat toward the other end of the pool. This strategy helps prevent slippage and assembles the body into an accelerating unit.

FIGURE 11.4 Backstroke start sequence.

Moving Under the Water

Like many things in swimming, underwater work (kind of kicking, rate of kick, number of kicks, distance traveled, and so on) has two patterns: the ideal pattern and the practical pattern. The ideal pattern is a model for a fully accomplished athlete whose nervous system and movement patterns are 100% functional. The practical pattern is whatever has the best influence on the outcome of the athlete's race at the present moment.

Assuming that the swimmer does an effective dive, they leave the wall at a speed that is faster than their swimming speed. In a good start, the athlete should be moving slightly faster than their midpool swimming speed when they arrive at the surface. An art in coaching is to find the best strategy for an individual athlete to get to the surface without losing this speed. A pattern may suit one athlete but not another.

Many athletes come to Cal with a prescribed pattern—doing a certain number of dolphin kicks or going most of the full 15 meters underwater permitted by the rules. Some of these athletes come to the surface moving slower than their swimming speed, which means that they lose time and energy while accelerating to swimming speed.

For this part of the start, each athlete should have their own strategy and personal combination of distance, number of kicks, rate, and character of the kick itself. The individual strategy depends upon the individual's personal skill set. Underwater travel should be continually improved. However, while the athlete improves it, a coach needs to help the athlete use what they have. In reality, some athletes slow down so abruptly when they begin trying to dolphin kick that they would be better off doing a sharp flutter kick and getting to the surface as fast as possible. Or, for some swimmers, doing one or two quick body kicks, converting to a flutter kick, and then getting to the surface might be their best option for getting to the surface at slightly faster than swimming speed. A coach's job is to help the athlete sort out what works best today and continually push evolution toward the ideal model.

Suggestions for Underwater Travel

Swimmers should develop a whole-body, wave-like movement for underwater travel. Using only the legs promotes a stop–start action in most swimmers. Very few (very talented) swimmers can do well under the water using only their legs and hips.

Swimmers should also learn different frequencies of body dolphins, reflected in larger continual up and down pulses in the feet. (I call body dolphins *harmonics*, a term introduced by Bill Boomer, former collegiate head coach who has been the technical consultant to Stanford University and to the 2000 U.S. Olympic team, and Milt Nelms.) In my experience, the more even and harmonic this movement, the speedier and less fatiguing the higher frequencies. A goal is to eventually do this harmonic movement without punching the head or feet to initiate movement. The head should be part of the movement, and the kick should act as part of the overall wave. The feet should flick both upward and downward like the end of a fly fishing pole (see figure 11.5).

The swimmer should arrive at the surface in as horizontal a position as possible. Many athletes make the error of arriving at the surface at an angle, which causes deceleration as they scramble to balance and begin the swimming stroke at the same time. The ideal is to get into the neutral layer (see description later) in a balanced and horizontal position at slightly faster than swimming speed.

FIGURE 11.5 Body dolphin.

The First Strokes

For both the backstroke start and turn, we use the CVS layer concept to help athletes understand what to do in relation to the surface. This concept gives the coach and the athlete a common language of sensory descriptions that helps shape the best transition from underwater to surface swimming.

The C layer is where the athlete feels that the body is being lifted toward the surface; the V layer is the neutral, or free, layer; and the S layer is where the athlete feels he or she is above the V layer and is affected by gravity.

If the swimmer is horizontal and in the V layer and is moving faster than swimming speed, then the first two strokes will feel very light and each stroke will move the swimmer a significant distance. This establishes a pattern that automatically carries into the remaining swimming strokes. Following are some common mistakes that occur during the transition from underwater travel into swimming.

> **Mistake:** Starting to swim in the C layer, which causes an immediate deceleration
>
> **Solution:** The swimmer should be entirely in the V layer before beginning to swim.
>
> **Mistake:** Coming to the surface at an angle
>
> **Solution:** The swimmer should arrive at the surface in a horizontal position and the whole body should come into the V layer level and balanced. If the swimmer arrives at the surface at an angle, like an airplane taking off, two problems can occur: deceleration as the swimmer goes up into the S layer and falls back into the water, and two or three stacked short and frenetic strokes while the swimmer is trying to gain control. These strokes create a negative effect on the swimmer's rhythms and sense of contact with the water that will be reflected in the swimming stroke for the rest of the length.

The Turn

The turn, as well as the start, has a number of variations. All styles of turns share the following common principles.

Stay in the V layer when rolling over (avoid lifting or plunging). As the swimmer rolls from the back to the front to begin the somersault, two things should happen. First, the swimmer must stay balanced throughout the rollover. Second, the swimmer must maintain springiness during the roll and keep the springiness as they start to shape a ball with the body.

As mentioned earlier, in this part of the turn swimmers instinctively introduce rhythmic bounces and relaxation as they roll from the back onto the front; this action slows the swimmer down almost immediately. Many age-group swimmers insert a glide after the rollover. Backstrokers must develop the knowledge of their distance from the wall so that they roll over in a place where they can begin the tumble almost immediately. Part of this skill involves developing the agility to come out of the rollover with control and organize the turn immediately.

Make a round, springy ball (rather than a crimped or tight body) when executing the tumble. When doing the tumble, the body should be small and uniformly alive and springy. Human instinct is to crimp the body and turn parts of the body off when making this shape. A crimped and turned-off body is less athletic and less controlled in the push-off stage of the turn, which follows the tumble. Performing simple children's somersaults on land, from standing to standing, walking to walking, or running to running, provides the pattern and instinct for the springy form needed in the water.

Start making a ball from the V layer (not by lifting up out of the water to initiate the turn). A swimmer should stay on the swimming level or neutral plane through this movement.

Guide the body off the wall with control (rather than using frantic explosiveness). This concept is not an instruction to push away from the wall slowly. Rather, the athlete should be organized and controlled within this movement instead of frenetic and tense. In this part of the turn, the athlete's goal is to make a body shape that will slide through the water and be ready to do the harmonic parts of the turn, then guide the body into the V layer and begin swimming a proper, athletic backstroke. This phase should be viewed as a set-up because the push away from the wall affects the rest of the turn and the rest of the length of swimming. Combined with practice, athleticism and control in this part of the turn eventually produce speed. Forced speed and low quality adversely affect the rest of the turn.

Backstrokers have a tendency to fracture the body when they push off, resulting in an arched back or a Z shape in the body. This tendency to fracture happens when the athlete puts the arms over the head. Swimmers should pay attention to body form when the arms go over the head so that neither body misalignment nor body tension occur.

Refer to figure 11.6 for an example of the turn.

FIGURE 11.6 Backstroke turn sequence.

Moving Under the Water

The pattern of underwater work after the turn is very similar to the underwater work after the start. However, following the turn, the swimmer is usually going slightly slower than after the dive. Because of the dive aspect of the start and the push-off aspect of the turn, angle of travel on the way back to the surface is different in the turn than in the start; the kind of kicking, rate of kick, number of kicks, distance traveled, and so on may be slightly different as well. In the turn, as in the start, there are two patterns: the ideal pattern and the practical pattern.

If the approach to the wall, the somersault, and the push away from the wall are done effectively, the swimmer will leave the wall at a speed that is faster than their swimming speed. The athlete's goal should be to arrive at the surface going slightly faster than their midpool swimming speed without expending excess energy to get that speed.

As in the start, coaches need to help swimmers find the best strategy to get to the surface without losing the speed gained in the push away from the wall. Again, similar to the start, one pattern may suit one athlete but not another.

Underwater travel in the turns should be continually improved. While the athlete is improving this very important phase of the turn, a coach needs to help the athlete use what they have at a given moment. This is a key point in the overall priorities that an athlete should bring to their personal concept of swimming. Similar to the start, some athletes slow down so abruptly when they begin trying to dolphin kick that they would be better off doing a sharp flutter kick and getting to the surface as fast as possible. Or, for some swimmers, doing one or two quick kicks, converting to a flutter kick, and then getting to the surface might be their best option for starting swimming at a speed that is slightly faster than midpool swimming speed.

Suggestions for Underwater Travel

See the description of underwater travel on page 166. The descriptions and principles apply to turns as well.

The First Strokes

See the description of the first strokes on page 167. The descriptions and principles apply to turns as well.

TRANSITIONS IN STARTS, TURNS, AND THE STROKES

A swimmer should be acrobatic and proactive when making a transition from one move to another. Many swimmers get stuck in transitions because they do not believe that the changeover is valuable. Coaches can become drill dependent, and that dependence is reflected in athletes if they become too patterned in singular parts of turns or singular parts of a stroke and do not know how to smoothly transition from one movement to another.

Training Racing Turns in Practice

I am no longer surprised when an athlete has a disconnect between the turns that they do in training and the turn that they want to do in competition. Even on a team with very moderate training volumes, a swimmer training in a short-course pool does two to three hundred turns per day, eventually totaling tens of thousands in a year. This number is in contrast to the small handful of turns that a swimmer does in races each year. If the turns in training are of low quality, training habit will prevail the day of a race. Habitual poor qualities will show up in the race, particularly in the later turns in a race when the swimmer is fatigued and is using instinct more.

In traditional training, it is too much for the swimmer to execute a perfect, race-quality turn each time they reach the wall. A solution is for each athlete to single out one or two qualities on each turn and make sure that those selected qualities are done well, and then rotate through the different parts of the turns.

When swimmers transition poorly, they develop a mechanical look that does not look at all like efficient swimming once they get into a race. In starts and turns, pauses or lags that occur between phases of the turns while the swimmer prepares to initiate the next phase make the swimmer lose speed. Traditional training culture promotes resting in the transitions. Because most speeds are slower in training than in races and the swimmer is less engaged, lags or pauses do not create critical loss in velocity and in some cases allow a swimmer little recovery blips so that they can conserve energy and still make pace or repeat times throughout the practice. This strategy on the part of the swimmer can lead to a false-positive reward for creating lags and pauses in the transitions; these habits appear in critical phases of the races and cost speed. The coach should take care to design training that avoids introducing habits that can hurt the swimmer during races.

TECHNICAL DRILLS FOR BACKSTROKE

Following are a few drills we like to use when working on specific backstroke techniques.

Flutter Kicking

We use a fundamental flutter kicking drill with the swimmer on his back and his arms at the sides of his body. While seemingly simple, this kicking drill allows each swimmer to make body adjustments to attain his best balance and position in the water.

One Arm Stroke

In the one arm stroke drill, the swimmer starts in the same position as in the flutter kicking drill, again on his back with the arms at the sides of his body. The swimmer takes one stroke with one arm back to the side of the body, and then takes a stroke with the opposite arm, again stopping that arm at the side of the body. He continues the one arm stroke drill across the pool, alternating the arm stroke. This drill teaches the swimmer the hip and trunk rotation of the backstroke. It also assists in teaching the proper depth of entry and the line or path of the stroking arm.

Multiple Arm Strokes

We progress from this one arm stroke drill to a multiple arm stroke drill. This drill is performed in the same manner, but without switching arms. For example, the swimmer would perform three strokes with the right arm, followed by three strokes with the left arm (3/3), and continue that cycle for a given distance.

CONCLUSION

In new backstroke, the swimmer shapes the body into a slight curve that permits a free-flowing swimming motion that is less fatiguing. The curved body should feel alert, engaged, and springy. The arm strokes should be performed in the natural pathway to avoid tension in the arms and legs; this keeps the shoulders in a position of strength throughout the stroke. The axial part of the body, through the core, should maintain control during backstroke.

12

Trends and Techniques in Butterfly

Bob Bowman

The butterfly, which has captivated coaches, swimmers, and spectators alike, is perhaps the most misunderstood stroke in the current competition repertoire. Its combination of power and elegance is daunting for even the most seasoned competitor, and designing a program to maximize its potential can be quite a challenge. Over the years, athletes and coaches have attacked this problem in various ways—from megadistance regimens to power-based programs and all areas in between—with varying degrees of success. What combination of key elements will allow for the flowing, rhythmic technique of the stroke as well as produce the massive energy output needed for maximum speed? How can one achieve a proper balance between style and conditioning? This chapter examines three critical areas of effective butterfly performance: technical drills and issues, training and conditioning trends, and racing strategies.

EMERGING TECHNICAL TRENDS

Technical proficiency and efficiency are the foundation for effective swimming performance in all stroke. Athletes must be able to control the movement of the arms, torso, and legs while expending tremendous amounts of energy. Several new trends in butterfly swimming that have come forth since the late 1990s have led to incredible decreases in time and a quantum leap forward in competitive performance. Differences in head and body position have modified recovery, and catch techniques and underwater work have changed the way we teach, train, and race the butterfly.

For years and years, coaches placed a huge emphasis on undulation when teaching the butterfly. Although this method effectively helps young swimmers overcome their inherent physical weaknesses, it creates a tremendous amount of frontal resistance and drag force during the stroke. We have gradually learned that keeping the body in a nearly flat position on the surface eliminates theses negative forces and makes the stroke much more efficient. The swimmer should hold the head in a neutral position; the neck should be long and flat neck and the crown of the head should lead the movement. Lift of the chin should be minimal when taking the breath, and no downward dive of the head should occur after taking the breath. A flowing undulation of the body occurs during the stroke, but it will occur in a very narrow amplitude on the surface of the water. At the North Baltimore Aquatic Club, we look for a dry back, a body position in which a large portion of the back is visible during the stroke. This position ensures that the swimmer is moving near the surface and not performing excessive up-and-down movement (see figure 12.1). World record holder Jenny Thompson and her coach, Richard Quick, pioneered this technique, and it has been successfully used by Ian Crocker, Michael Čavić, and, to a great extent, Michael Phelps.

The world's top butterfliers now use a straight-armed, sweeping recovery (see figure 12.2) rather than a bent-arm technique that was previously popular. The reason for using a straight-arm recovery is obvious: the shortest distance between two points is a straight line. By keeping the arms low and just above the surface, the swimmer can move the arms forward with maximum efficiency and with the least disturbance to body position. A straight-arm recovery continues the forward flow of the stroke and does not introduce excessive undulation into the motion. This technique provides for quicker and more synchronized stroking action than the bent-arm technique and is more economical from an energy expenditure perspective.

FIGURE 12.1 Keeping a nearly flat body position on the surface throughout the stroke.

FIGURE 12.2 Straight-arm sweeping recovery sequence.

In an effort to maintain maximum speed during the stroke cycle, swimmers currently use a much quicker catching action as the hands enter the water (see figure 12.3). This technique allows the swimmer to begin the propulsive phase of each stroke sooner and therefore avoid a deceleration caused by gliding too much early in the stroke. Although a quick catch maximizes speed in the early phases of the butterfly stroke, it costs energy. A 200-meter swimmer must modulate this motion by slightly extending the fingertips forward before initiating the catch. This slight conservation of energy can make a huge difference in average speed over 200-meter races compared with 100- or 50-meter races. Butterfly swimming requires a constant balance of power and endurance.

The pulling action itself begins as the fingertips press downward and the armpit opens up (see figure 12.4). The elbows should be high and the forearm should be perpendicular to the bottom of the pool. Once this position is achieved the swimmer can use the large muscles of the back and scapular region to pull back and in toward midtorso. As the hands push back near the navel region, they sweep out and back to finish the stroke. As the swimmer finishes the stroke, the heel of the hand leads the motion and the fingertips point toward the bottom of the pool. Butterfly swimmers should apply constant underwater pressure during the stroke. Traditionally, swimmers strongly desired to accelerate the hands and overemphasize the final phase of the underwater stroke. This practice interferes with timing and increases drag at the end of the arm stroke. Therefore, a swimmer should deemphasize the end of the stroke and instead concentrate on continuous and steady motion of the arms and legs.

One of the by-products of a flatter stroke with less undulation is the ability to gain much more propulsion from the kicking action of the legs (see figure 12.5). Michael Phelps has taken the butterfly to a new level by using a continuous kicking action for an entire 200-meter race. He developed this feat of fitness and focus over long years of conditioning sets and rehearsal swims. In our program, we ask young swimmers to think of

FIGURE 12.3 Catching action.

FIGURE 12.4 Pulling action.

FIGURE 12.5 Kicking action.

butterfly kicking as similar to skipping a rope. The feet should always move, and the knees should bend to approximately 90° before the swimmer initiates the propulsive backward and downward motion. The swimmer holds the legs nearly straight during the recovery of the legs and must work hard to hold water on the feet. They must work to improve ankle flexibility so that the flat part of the foot is in contact with the water for as long as possible during each sweep of the kick. I believe that all kicks should have the same amplitude, contrary to the traditional thought that a big kick and a small kick exist in the butterfly. Developing a continuous kicking action requires tremendous amounts of coordination and physical stamina.

To correctly perform the butterfly stroke, timing and rhythm are critical. Perhaps the greatest hindrance to fast butterfly swimming is the timing of the breath during the stroke. The swimmer should take the breath as late as possible during the arm stroke. Just as the hands pass under the stomach to finish the propulsive phase, the chin should lift just enough for the swimmer to get a breath. The swimmer must then immediately put the head back into the neutral position. We tell young swimmers that the head should lead the hands in butterfly. The head should come out for the breath before the hands exit the water to begin the recovery, and the head should be back in line in the water before the hands enter at the front of the stroke. The hips will slightly move upward and forward before the hands enter the water on the catch. This timing is critical if the stroke is to flow in a proper fashion. A kick will help the hands start the catch motion, and another kick will finish the arm action under the body. We encourage swimmers to finish the arm pull with the heel of the hand rather than the fingertips. This allows for effective release of the water to begin the recovery phase and minimizes drag at the end of the arm stroke.

TECHNICAL DRILLS FOR BUTTERFLY

As with any of the swimming strokes, we like to break the butterfly down into components so that swimmers can focus on one thing at a time. This is particularly difficult given the double-arm action and the continuous nature of the stroke. However, several drills can effectively help swimmers grasp the feel and timing of the butterfly. Understand clearly that every drill has a cost. A technique that isolates one portion of a swimming stroke will adversely affect another aspect of the stroke. The coach must use good judgment when deciding which technical aspect receives priority at a given time. Balance of ideas is critical in developing fast swimmers.

Body Position Drills

These basic drills are designed to assist swimmers in learning the best body position and balance when performing the butterfly. The basic movements in establishing a proper flow within the water are also examined.

Flow

Swimmers move through the water with the arms at the sides of the body. The eyes look directly at the bottom of the pool, and the neck should be long and flat. The swimmers must keep the hands at the sides and propel themselves only by manipulating the chest and torso. The legs should follow naturally and should have no down kick. The swimmers begin the motion by pressing the chest and shoulders down and forward. If the swimmer needs a breath, he or she should sneak it with minimal chin lift and immediately return to the neutral position. Later, the swimmer can perform this drill with the arms extended forward and a slight sculling motion with the hands. This drill is very effective in teaching the bodily movement of the butterfly.

Best Balance and Distance

The swimmer floats on the surface in a prone position with the arms extended forward. Making a small sculling motion with the hands, the swimmer performs a chest-initiated undulating action and a very light kicking action until they feel that they are effectively balanced on the water. At this point, the swimmer takes one arm stroke and returns to the flat position on the surface. The goal is to stay on the surface of the water after the pull and to not dive down. The swimmer lightly sculls and kicks until they have regained balance, and then performs another arm stroke. The swimmer should do this drill slowly and deliberately and should decide when to take the next stroke. Perhaps the swimmer will take only three or four arm strokes per 25-yard length.

Coordination and Timing Drills

The following drills are used to establish coordination and timing. Specifically, the single-arm drills improve arm recovery, timing related to breathing, and overall timing of the stroke itself.

Single-Arm Drills

Single-arm drills effectively teach the motion of the recovery and the timing of the breath. To promote proper timing of the breath, we have swimmers breathe to the side rather than to the front on all single-arm drills. Single-arm drills may be done with the nonpulling arm either at the side or extended in front. Keeping the nonpulling arm at the side produces more undulation in the stroke, so to minimize up-and-down motion, I tend to have swimmers extend the nonpulling arm in front. The arm should be straight as it recovers forward; this will ensure that the hips are engaged in the motion. The hand should extend slightly forward as it enters the water, and the hip should be at its highest point before the hand enters the water. The kick should be light and should accompany the entry and the exit of the pulling hand. Michael Phelps uses these single-arm drills to fine tune the timing of his hips and to coordinate the arms in the stroke.

Combination Drills

Drills that combine single- and double-arms strokes can be very effective in teaching the butterfly to young swimmers and in fine tuning the stroke in advanced swimmers. At the North Baltimore Aquatic Club, one of our favorite drills is called 2–2–2. The swimmer takes two single-arm strokes with the right arm (breathing to the side), two single-arm strokes with the left arm (breathing to the side), and two full stroke cycles (breathing forward). This drill allows the swimmer to set up their timing with the single-arm movements before adding the power movement of the complete stroke. This drill is very effective when used in training sets.

We also use a drill called Single–Double. In this combination drill, the swimmer takes a single-arm stroke without a breath and then a full double-arm stroke with a breath. The pattern proceeds as follows: right arm, both arms, left arm, both arms, and so on. The Single–Double is a very effective training drill for young swimmers who are not yet strong enough to perform distances of the full butterfly stroke.

Underwater Butterfly

This drill perfects the timing of the arm stroke with the kick. The swimmer pushes off underwater and takes three or four full stroke cycles. The hands recover under the body in a manner that is similar to a breaststroke pullout. This drill emphasizes the catch phase and timing the leg action with the arms. After the swimmer has mastered the technique, they perform the drill at different speeds. This will help them develop stroke control over a range of speeds.

Kicking Drills

These kicking drills are designed to strengthen the kicking action and to help the swimmer develop a continuous kick in which all kicks are in the same range.

Vertical Kicking

This drill is popular in our program and is effective for beginners and world-class swimmers alike. Swimmers assume a position in the water where the head, shoulders, hips, and knees all line up vertically. The swimmer folds the arms across the chest and holds the elbows close to the body. The head is out of the water, the neck should be long and flat, and the eyes should look directly forward. The swimmer initiates motion in the chest, and the motion flows down the body through the torso to the feet. The amplitude of the kicking action is small and the action is continuous. The swimmer should feel water on the feet when kicking in both directions and should tighten the core muscles and drive the motion from the torso. The swimmers should maintain a vertical position and not lean forward or backward during the drill. This drill is best performed for short durations at high intensity. It reinforces the idea that the body works as a single unit in the butterfly stroke and it is invaluable in teaching swimmers how to move underwater during turns.

Side Kicking

The swimmer performs this drill on the side and extends forward the arm that is closest to the bottom of the pool. They should rest the ear on the shoulder so that they can easily take a short breath when needed. To emphasize body movement, the swimmer should minimize sculling motions with the hand. The top arm is at the side and rests on the torso. The swimmer starts movement at the chest, and the movement flows through to the feet. We often tell the swimmers that this motion is like cracking a whip. It should be continuous, and the swimmer should feel pressure of the water on both sweeps of the legs and feet. Swimmers should vary the amplitudes of the kick when performing this drill; this will give them good awareness of how the body should move in a range of speeds.

Reverse Fly Kicking

The swimmers perform dolphin kicking on the back, which allows for a greater emphasis on the down-sweep of the bottom of the feet. In actual butterfly swimming this is the up-sweep; swimmers must hold water on the feet during this motion to ensure proper timing of the stroke and gain maximum propulsion from the leg action. Swimmers can perform this drill with the arms in a streamlined position above the head (which emphasizes body line and small kick amplitude) or with the arms at the side (which emphasizes core motion and a larger kick amplitude). Both methods are effective for teaching the kicking action and for conditioning swimmers to maintain continuous kicking action while swimming butterfly.

TRAINING TECHNIQUES FOR BUTTERFLY

Designing and implementing a training program for the butterfly events presents a formidable challenge to coaches. Although some aspects of conditioning benefit both 100- and 200-meter swimmers, the energy requirements of the two events are quite different. A few of the world's top swimmers are competitive at both distances (Phelps, Meagher, Caulkins), but specialization is the norm and most swimmers excel at one event or the other (Malchow, Čavić, de Bruin). Therefore, the majority of stroke training for butterfly swimmers is geared to one of the Olympic distances, and all types of training are thrown into the mix.

The 200-Meter Butterfly

The 200 fly is a grueling mix of endurance and power that challenges any athlete. Endurance conditioning is the foundation of this event, and most often 200 flyers also are competent 400 freestylers or 400 individual medley swimmers. The general endurance work done for these events complements the more specific work done in butterfly sets. In my opinion, little benefit is gained by swimming butterfly in training with less than excellent technique. Historically, great 200 fly swimmers have been asked to complete gargantuan sets of repeat 200s, 300s, and 400s in butterfly swimming on short rest. They have also done long swims such as 1,500 or 3,000 meters for time. Although it served some of them well, it also engrained bad technical habits and virtually eliminated a continuous kicking action from the stroke in favor of a more gliding and undulating style. This limits speed potential in the 200 and is contrary to the current, horizontally oriented stroke. Over the past decade, Michael Phelps has broken the world record in the 200 butterfly five times and has seldom swum more than four or five full-stroke 200 butterflies in training per year! The reason for this is simple: He cannot use his kick effectively for long butterfly swims and must resort to a survival stroke in order to complete the distances. We have developed other methods of conditioning his butterfly stroke that challenge his physiology while allowing him to perform his stroke at levels that are near race quality.

At the North Baltimore Aquatic Club, short-course 25-yard swimming has become an important part of the training program for the 200-meter butterfly. The reasons for this are twofold:

1. The shorter distance allows the swimmer to use a stroke that is much closer to the actual racing stroke in short rest training.
2. The swimmer can maintain a higher average heart rate during conditioning sets than in 50-meter training.

For these reasons, the majority of our endurance butterfly sets are done in a 25-yard pool. We use long-course training for specific speed work and for race rehearsal training. Some examples of our short-course fly training include the following:

> 45 × 50 butterfly = 3 × (10 × 50 @ 45 seconds work on stroke control + 5 × 50 @ 35 seconds at maximum speed)

No break is given between rounds. The swimmer must immediately return to the stroke count and stroke control time assigned by the coach. Michael Phelps holds around 28 seconds on the set of 10 with 6 strokes per length. He then swims around 25 seconds on the set of 5. The pace of the 5 × 50 is at his American record speed for the 200-yard fly! Little doubt exists about why he is the best butterfly swimmer in history.

> 3 × (4 × 100 fly @ 1:10 or 1:15 hold under 60 seconds + 1 minute rest + 100 fly at maximum speed)

The goal is to swim as close as possible to the second 100 split of the 200 fly on the timed 100. There are 300 yards of recovery drilling and swimming between rounds. This is an excellent set for helping the swimmer develop a technique that will maintain speed at the end of the race. We also like to use sets of 25-yard repeats on short rest done at the best speed the swimmer can hold. Twenty to 30 or even 40 × 25 on 20 seconds is tremendously conditioning and mentally challenging. The frequent, short repetitions also allow the coach to give short feedback tips at the end of each length. This helps the swimmer stay focused on technique under the physical stress of the interval.

In addition to the short-course work that is specific to the 200, we work on longer rest intervals and higher speeds in the 50-meter pool. The swimmers perform three to four broken 200s as follows.

50 dive @ 1:30 @ going out speed of goal 200
100 push @ 2:30 @ middle 100 speed or faster
50 dive @ 1:30 @ fastest possible speed

There is up to 400 meters of active recovery swimming and drilling in between rounds. The total interval for the swim and the recovery is around 10 minutes.

8 to 24 × 50 fly @ 1:30 (odd = dive; even = push)

All are performed at maximum effort. This is a great set for working on speed endurance and offers the coach opportunities to give technical feedback at the end of each repeat. This set mimics the anaerobic stress that the swimmers feel at the end of the race and teaches them to maintain proper technique under stress.

In general, our 200 flyers spend two main sets per week on butterfly; the remaining days are devoted to distance or individual medley training. We also sprinkle small doses of butterfly sprints through the week to help the swimmers develop speed and improve technique.

The 100-Meter Butterfly

Most swimmers who excel at the 100-meter butterfly are speed oriented and also train for the 100 freestyle or possibly the short individual medley. The swimmers have a perfunctory endurance program that allows for effective recovery between speed sets in training. For these swimmers, developing power and quickness to enhance the speed of their first 50 is critical. They must also have the lactate tolerance and buffering capacities to maintain speed over the final 50 meters.

Resistance training and speed-assisted training are very effective for the 100 fly. Our swimmers do sets with parachutes, fins, and surgical tubing on a regular basis. We must ensure that technique remains intact when overloading the stroke with resistance work. The repeats should be short and the intensity should be high.

We like to do the following two sets long course (or short course) to develop the type of speed endurance that 100 butterfly swimmers need to succeed.

30 × 50 @ 1:30 (1:15 short course) (1 kick, 1 drill, 1 swim)

The swims are done at maximum speed. The kicks and drills should be done with perfect precision and at an effort that keeps the system engaged and the heart rate steady between swims. This set is tremendously effective for developing the second 50 meters of the 100 fly. Take stroke and kick counts and stroke rates to determine the maximum level of speed efficiency for each swimmer.

10 × 50 done at maximum speed (4 @ 1:30 followed by 1 each @ 1:20, 1:10, 1:00, 0:50, 0:40 and 0:30)

This set, borrowed from coach Richard Quick, mimics the final 20 meters of the 100 or 200 and teaches the body to produce and then tolerate lactic acid. We like to follow this set with 10×100 @ 1:30 freestyle holding under 1:10. This buffering set forces the body to metabolize the lactic acid that is produced during the set and makes the total physical system much more efficient.

Both of these sets simulate for the 100-meter butterfly swimmer the physical demands of the race and allow them to perform the repeats with technique that is near race level.

Some swimmers need training for both events. A careful mixture of both types of training helps the swimmer steadily reach progressive performance levels in both events while excelling at the top level of performance in his or her more natural event. Swimmers must perform these sets with proper technique at all times. This includes underwater dolphin kicking. At North Baltimore Aquatic Club, our coaching staff prescribes a number of dolphin kicks that are to be performed on each wall during each specific set. This number is calculated to achieve maximum speed and distance on the underwater work while taking into account the strokes per length the swimmer takes. This balance between power and efficiency is critical in world-class butterfly swimming.

RACE STRATEGY FOR BUTTERFLY SWIMMING

In long-course swimming, the goal is to have the fastest average pace over the entire distance of the race. To achieve this objective, swimmers must use some method of pacing or building speed so that they do not over-reach early in the race and pay for it at the end. This is particularly true in the 100-meter race, where the temptation to overswim the first 50 meters can be strong. The desire to take it out fast can backfire when the swimmers goes into a vertical body position in the final 10 meters. Remember that the fastest average speed over the distance wins the race, not the fastest first 50 meters. A cursory study of meet results at any level will show that the swimmers who consistently win 100-meter butterfly races have the fastest split times over the second 50 meters of the race. Michael Phelps is a two-time Olympic champion in the race because he can finish better than anyone else in history.

In the 200 butterfly race, pacing is even more important in order to maintain speed and stroke. North Baltimore Aquatic Club swimmers are taught to use stroke length and body control in the first 100 meters to conserve energy for the second half of the race. Swimmers should take careful count of the number of kicks and strokes that they take per length in the 200-meter fly. The number of strokes should be fairly consistent from length to length, with perhaps a single stroke increase per 50 meters split that reflects an increase in stroke rate as the race progresses. The 200 fly is won in the final 50 meters! Swimmers must have sufficient energy to hold stroke and use the legs to power into that last wall.

CONCLUSION

The butterfly is perhaps the most captivating of the swimming strokes. Its visual appeal, a combination of power and finesse, makes it a favorite of fans and swimmers alike. The stroke has moved from an endurance-dominated, undulating stroke to a power-oriented, horizontal movement pattern. Training methods have also improved to more effectively simulate the conditions of the race. The addition of underwater kicking has increased the speed potential of both butterfly races. More attention to the stroke length and stroke rate will yield even faster performances as swimmers and coaches strive to achieve the perfect balance between power output and biomechanical efficiency. The best is clearly yet to come.

13

Trends and Techniques in Breaststroke

Nort Thornton

After more than 50 years of serving as a head coach at the high school, country club, USA Swimming club, community college, and NCAA Division I levels, where I had sole responsibility of coaching the whole team on all of the four competitive strokes, I retired from the University of California at Berkeley, where I had been for the past 33 years. I decided to volunteer, and present coach David Durden was kind enough to put me to work. But it isn't really work when I love what I am doing.

For the past 3 years I have been looking after the breaststroke swimmers. When you only have one stroke to think about, you can think about it in much more detail and in different ways. I believe in the saying "When you look at something differently, the thing you look at changes." Following are my thoughts regarding a couple of laws of nature as they apply to swimming breaststroke.

HYDRODYNAMICS OF SWIMMING

Water is 800 times thicker than air. Moving through water takes concerted effort. Movement in water becomes more forceful as speed increases, and the water's resistance to this movement increases by the effort squared. If you fight, slap at, and splash around, tangling with the tension of the surface and creating counterproductive waves, the resistance increases by the effort cubed. Water not only resists one's effort to move through it; it exerts various forms of drag. Molecules of water in the form of sheets must be pushed aside to open a momentary hole through which the body can propel itself.

The quickest and most dramatic way to improve movement through water is to ensure proper technique. A 10% improvement in technique usually results in an effort that is 10% better. Speed comes from body position—the line between arm pulls. If a swimmer can create a narrow, streamlined body line so as to not push much water, they can slide through the water faster and farther on each stroke cycle. The best swimmers have the best streamline position and don't overpower the arm and leg actions.

The second most important element in fast swimming is the ability to move water quickly. This ability increases as the swimmer first gets stronger and then more powerful. The third most important element is increased conditioning. A swimmer must hold speed for the whole race distance while dealing with increasing discomfort. It would take about a 50% improvement in conditioning to produce the same 10% improvement in effort that better technique affords.

Another way to improve quickness is to become comfortable with less air while spending more time underwater. An athlete should take advantage of the walls of the pool, where a swimmer can generate the most power and speed. One can move through the water from a push-off in a streamlined position faster than one can swim on the surface. If lack of air leads a swimmer to shorten up the underwater sequence of the dive or push-off from turns, they are giving up their main advantage.

Proper technique (one that produces the least amount of drag and resistance) requires that swimmers do the following:

- ◆ Maximize the streamline off every wall (which takes breath control) and train to do this during oxygen deprivation.
- ◆ Extend the body to a maximum-reaching streamline position that is appropriate for each stroke, especially while deprived of oxygen. Developing the neuromuscular adaptations to perform under the combat of racing is key to success.
- ◆ Hold stroke length and tempo at all times and not rush the stroke just to sneak in another breath.
- ◆ Understand that less is more. Too much effort applied inappropriately during a race will not necessarily make swimmers move faster but it will assuredly make them tired faster.

Because one can obtain only a certain level of physical fitness, and because the water squares or cubes its resistance, the greatest opportunity for improvement is eliminating resistance and drag, which is accomplished by improving technique.

BUILDING THE BREASTSTROKE

When coaching, I needed to get the swimmers to understand and appreciate the laws of nature as they apply to swimming. I realized that our main goal was speed, not form, and I decided to give them speed first. On the first day of practice I warmed them up and gave them a 25-yard time trial. Here were the rules:

1. They could use any stroke that they wanted to use.
2. They had to begin from a push off the wall in the water (no diving).
3. They had to stay on their bellies.
4. They could try as often as they wished to get their fastest possible time.

The swimmers tried an average of six times, everyone got down to 10 seconds or better, and everyone evolved to a tight dolphin in a streamline body position underwater (this was even faster than sprinting crawl on the surface). Once they got their fastest possible 25-yard times, we discussed why that particular style was the fastest. This helped them appreciate that eliminating drag and resistance was more important than building power.

I then handed out printed copies of the rules for the breaststroke. I told them that I wanted them to figure out how to tweak their fastest 25-yard effort so that they would not be disqualified in a breaststroke race. I did not care what stroke they had used in the past; I just wanted them to use the fastest way of moving through the water.

Rather than teaching them a stroke and trying to build speed into it, I gave them the speed first and then built the stroke around the speed. My thinking is that a swimmer casts a body shadow (as if standing directly under a floodlight) on the deck around the feet. One must successfully squeeze that shadow down to the smallest possible circumference; this should be the racing streamline position. Anytime a swimmer moves the feet, legs, hands, elbows, or arms, these movements should occur inside the shadow. In other words, the swimmer should not increase the circumference of the drag shadow.

Avoiding Resistance and Drag

How does a swimmer avoid resistance and drag with the arm stroke? A tradeoff exists between getting more power with the arms and creating a larger drag shadow. To catch water, the swimmer needs to get the hands and forearms just outside the drag shadow of the shoulder. For most people that separation is somewhere between 12 and 18 inches (30.5 and 45.7 cm), depending on the width of the shoulders. The wider one goes, the more strength is needed and the more drag is created. Swimmers are looking for the maximum water pressure on the hands and forearms up to the elbows. They need to squeeze the arms together so as to connect with the core, hips, and heels and drag everything forward as far as possible while keeping the hips as high in the water as possible. This provides maximum distance per stroke while creating the least amount of drag. The farther a swimmer can move the hips forward on each in-sweep of the arms, the greater the distance traveled per stroke.

The heels need to be up before the arms complete the recovery in the streamline jump recovery. The maximum bend in the knee is approximately 90° so as to hide the lower legs and feet behind the body and thighs. The feet need to rotate out into a platform off of which to dive as the swimmer extends back into the streamline extended position. By recovering the heels up sooner in the inward arm sweep, the swimmer shortens the length of the back half of the body and falls back down into a quicker, longer streamline, as long as the hips remain as high as possible in the water. This action is more relaxed with a higher tempo, which can be more easily used later in a race. It saves energy and gives the swimmer the feeling of swimming downhill. Again, less is more. It is a matter of eliminating drag and resistance while maintaining the tightest possible streamline throughout as much as the whole stroke cycle as possible. The longer the swimmer can maintain the streamline, the longer the speed segment is between each arm action and kick.

Assuming that swimmers needs to produce proper body position on their own (and not by using high-tech swimsuits; see sidebar), swimmers must learn to create body tension throughout the core to maintain the body line that will maximize the

High-Tech Swimsuits

High-tech swimsuits are no longer legal, at least for now. Actually, the new rules, which allow knee-length suits, are written in such a way that swimsuit companies may still be able to produce suits that can provide some assistance. The amount of money that can be made from these suits will likely determine which direction the sport of swimming will head.

elimination of resistance and drag. To swim downhill, one must press the head and chest down; this is the most buoyant part of the body because of the lungs. When laying facedown on the surface of the water, the body is balanced somewhere near the navel. If a swimmer relaxes body tension, the chest floats up and the lower body sinks. At this point the swimmer is swimming vertically, which creates the most drag and resistance possible. The top swimmers develop enough tension in the core to keep the chest slightly lower than the hips in a tight streamline. A swimmer must not think that they need to try to swim higher in the water. Any energy devoted to staying higher in the water is energy that is taken away from forward propulsion. Speed can best be achieved by maintaining a straight line.

Manufacturing Velocity

In the water, a swimmer must manufacture velocity. One can achieve faster swimming the same way automobile companies achieve better gas mileage by designing better aerodynamically designed cars, through

1. biochemistry (the operation of muscles and expenditure and resupply of energy) and

2. biomechanics (the physical forces that govern propulsion and the generation and conservation of momentum).

Most swimmers and coaches devote the bulk of their time and attention to conditioning (biochemistry) and very little time to technique (biomechanics). Most are concerned only with producing horsepower. However, shaping and positioning the body to reduce frontal resistance (eliminating or reducing the resistance of the water to the body's passage through) it is most important because it creates or improves the properties of the stroke that produce force.

If a swimmer can be a good eliminator and just an average force producer, he or she can be a very successful competitive swimmer. The eliminating skills depend far less on pure talent than do the abilities that produce force. A swimmer can swim a great deal faster by staying out of their own way as they move through the water. (Boats, cars, planes, and swimmers are all designed for the same purpose.)

For breaststroke, a short-axis stroke, the body must align like a teeter totter (front to back) in relation to the center of gravity and flotation. A swimmer must surf the water currents with body shaping and positioning, not with hand and foot patterns.

Increasing Stroke Tempo

Stroke tempo is determined by body length, hand and foot speed, and the timing of the stroke. Stroke tempo consists of

1. distance per stroke cycle and
2. cycle rates per minute.

An athlete is usually limited by neuromuscular training rather than by conditioning. Programs that train at higher yardage create breaststroke cycling rates of around 40 to 45 cycles per minute. Swimmers in these programs will be successful at 300- to 400-yard or longer breaststroke races, but if a swimmer wants to swim a 100 yards, they need to be able to cycle at 57 to 61 cycles per minute. For the 200 yards, they need to be able to cycle at 47 to 52 cycles per minute. Swimmers need to know how to turn over at these rates and what it feels like. Cycles of distance per stroke give you quality and efficiency, but cycles per minute allow you to have this quality and efficiency. Swimmers are creating muscle memory, or learning the feel (neurally).

TRAINING FOR THE BREASTSTROKE

For the breaststroke, the three main qualities of training are

1. distance per stroke cycle,
2. cycles per minute, and
3. drag reduction or elimination (stroke technique is force production, or creation).

The trick to becoming a great swimmer is to give up less distance per stroke when increasing cycling speed. To get speed, the swimmer goes back to the core (the power plant) and the trunk (not your hands and feet) of the body.

Time is too gross a measurement because it does not provide enough ways to measure performance. To increase velocity, a swimmer can

1. increase distance per stroke and reduce cycling rate,
2. increase distance per stroke cycle and hold cycling rate the same,
3. hold distance per stroke cycle the same and increase cycling rate, and
4. slightly increase both distance per stroke cycling and cycling rate.

Think of swimming speed as a three-sided pyramid. The three sides upon which velocity may be constructed are

1. strength (conditioning),
2. stroke technique, and
3. reduced frontal resistance (vessel shaping).

Race design is based on body chemistry. Which energy systems does a swimmer use after a race begins, and when do these energy systems come into play?

Example

For the 100 yards: 25 build, 50 power, 25 finishing sprint

For the 200 yards: 75 aerobic, 50 build, 50 power, 25 finishing sprint

Key

Aerobic: relaxed effort with a heart rate below 150 beats per minute

Build: start an underwater sequence, streamline, rhythm and balance, tightened kicking action, and more hips and core action

Power: maximum distance per stroke; heart rate is 170 to 185 beats per minute

Finishing sprint: swimmer maintains stroke and gives everything they have left

CORRECTING BREASTSTROKE TECHNIQUE

The high-tech swimsuits of the 2009 season taught us all a few great lessons. The flotation from the suits allowed the swimmer to become a little lazy with leg recovery because the suit floated the legs up into a recovery position. Now, without the suits doing the work, swimmers need to be certain to get the heels up quicker to tip the body forward into the streamline earlier in the stroke cycle. The greater percentage of the total stroke cycle that a swimmer can be in a streamline position, sliding forward with a greater distance per stroke, the faster the swimmer can become. The compression that the suit provided now has to be controlled by tension in the core. The suits allowed the swimmer to bring the hips and legs along with the inward arm stroke. Now the swimmer must connect the arm pressure with the hips and core. If the swimmer cannot develop this track of tension, less distance per stroke and speed will result. The height that the hips can maintain is critical. The best way to maintain height is to drop the upper body rather than kicking the hips up, which takes away from forward propulsion. Swimmers can best achieve speed by maintaining a straight line from the head to the knees.

To implement these concepts, I begin every breaststroke session with dolphin kicking or butterfly swimming or drills. We often use a monofin to improve body dolphin technique. Then we progress from dolphin kicking to frog kicking while maintaining the body dolphin action. When performing this leg action, the swimmer does not bend much at the hips and has an approximately 90° bend at the knees. Our swimmers do a great deal of our kicking on their backs to maintain the proper body position. The hips are on the surface of the water and the knees are at or under the surface. The feet are rotated out enough to catch still water for the backward thrust, which straightens the legs and allows the feet to finish through until the soles of the feet actually touch. This is almost like clapping hands. Back in the 1980s a Hungarian coach named Jozsef Nagy (coach to world record holder Mike Barrowman) developed the wave action breaststroke technique, which is essentially what we teach today. It is more of a body dolphin flowing action, which allows less resistance and drag.

For most swimmers, the main problem of the breaststroke arm action is that they try to pull water backward immediately from the top of the stroke. They should instead slide the hands out to a catch position (hands 12 to 18 inches [30.5 and 45.7

cm] apart). Once in a Y position, they can then catch the water and begin by sculling inward. The swimmer follows the inward sweep of the arms by following through into the recovery–reach and streamline extension with a narrow, squeezed arm action into the narrow body line. No forward propulsion occurs when moving the arms outward from the center line to the catch position. The arm stroke begins from the Y position; the hands are just outside the shoulders. As the arms separate, the swimmer must press the upper body (chest) down into a connected position between the arms. Bending the neck and moving the head around pulls the body out of line because the body always follows the head. Pressing the upper body down allows the hips and legs to ride up higher in the water. I call this the cocked position. To fire the inward scull and sweeping arm action more powerfully, the swimmer must connect to the core. The swimmer catches the water by scooping the hands to hold as much water as possible while keeping the elbows as high as possible. It is important for the swim-mer to round off into a forward push and recovery with the hands, making certain that the elbows stay away from the body as they come in line behind the hands. The hands move in while the body moves forward, so the hands end up under the chin. The hands should not pause at this point but rather should drive forward while the elbows come in behind the hands and add speed to the recovery by eliminating drag and resistance on the lower arms, upper arms, shoulders, and chest. The narrower the body line, the greater the speed. In another drill that we use, swimmers recover the arms with the palms up, which really brings the elbows together into a tighter streamline.

Once the swimmer completes the kick and reaches full extension, the hands slide out to the catch position. This should be a smooth and slow separation. The swimmer should not expend any real effort during this part of the stroke because no usable propulsion is created during this period. Some propulsion can be achieved and it feels as if one is really working; however, it leaves the elbows in a position that negatively affects speed and increases fatigue.

As the swimmer sweeps inward toward the center line, an increase in propulsion occurs because of the lift force. More water slides under the body, causing a lifting effect. This is the same type of lift force that lifts airplanes or brings speed boats to a plane on the surface of the water at higher speeds. Because this force is not constant, the body returns to a lower position in the water for the kicking action between the arm sweeps. Better swimmers are able to maintain a straighter body line, which minimizes the up-and-down movement and directs the body movement into a more forward line. Because the arm in-sweep is the highest point in the body action of the stroke cycle, this is where swimmers should take their breath. Swimmers should be sure to not move the head around independently of the body line; this causes several things to happen, all of which are negative to speed.

Refer to figure 13.1 for an underwater view of the complete breaststroke sequence; to view the breaststroke sequence overwater, see figure 13.2.

FIGURE 13.1　Breaststroke underwater sequence.

FIGURE 13.2　Breaststroke overwater sequence.

Surfing

While looking for ways to eliminate more drag and resistance, I came across a way of swimming breaststroke that I call surfing. When trying to find ways to make up for the flotation and tension that was lost when FINA rules eliminated high-tech suits, I was looking for a ways to get the lower body up higher and sooner in the stroke. My first thought was to lift the feet earlier. Finally, I realized that the swimmer could best accomplish this by putting internal pressure on the upper body (chest and head together) in a downward manner. When the swimmer drops the upper body 1 or 2 inches (2.54 or 5 cm), the legs come up to the surface and slide over the water rather than drag through it. This is where the surfing comes in. By using the arms in a slightly different manner, the swimmer can use the water differently.

The swimmer lets the arms float (no effort) to a Y position that is slightly wider than the shoulders; the hands are at 11 and 1 o'clock. The swimmer then begins the stroke cycle by catching water with the hands and forearms (fingertips to elbows) and sweeping as much water as possible (a large ball or wave) in under the chest. The goal is to maintain a straight body line from the top of the skull to the knees. Once the swimmer has scooped the maximum amount of water in under the chin or chest as they move forward, the arms come together, hands to elbows, and continue without pausing back into the recovery. This sweep should be continuous, and no pause should occur at the chest. The biggest error I see is swimmers pulling the arms too far back so that the elbows are at the ribs; this blocks the arms from recovering. Now the most important part is for the swimmer to get the arms, head, and upper body ahead of the wave of water they created. If you have ever surfed (board or body), you know that the trick to getting a ride is to keep your center of gravity ahead of the crest of the wave. So all a swimmer needs to do is, using only the in-sweep of the arms (hands and elbows), get as much of the body as possible ahead of the leading edge of the largest possible wave built up under the body. More of the swimmer's body can get in front of the wave the earlier they can recover the legs.

The swimmer must not pull backward because, with forward motion of the body, one cannot recover the arms fast enough to catch the wave. Also, any motion of the head off the spine line takes a foot off the front of the surfboard, thereby changing the body's center of gravity and forcing the swimmer to slip out of the backside of the wave without a ride.

Because the upper body is a little longer than the lower, to lift the lower one can catch more water to form a larger wave, thereby getting in a better position to catch a better ride. It is faster and easier to let the water push the body ahead rather than kicking and pulling the body through the water. This is a double win. I believe this is the stroke technique of the future.

Flip Turns

Another major thing that we do differently is use only flip turns during practice. I do not want swimmers slowing down into the walls because of fatigue or crowded conditions at the wall. Using only flip turns eliminated bad habits and increased swimmers' tolerance for lack of air. At the end of all practice sessions, we allowed swimmers a minimum of fifteen minutes to work on good turning action. I broke the turn down into segments and reviewed, raced, and timed each segment. The segments are as follows:

1. Approaching the wall and timing the correct number of strokes to end up at the wall in the correct position

2. The body position in a backward somersaulting action while bringing the knees up under the body (can best be accomplished by pressing the upper body down to create a tighter ball for a faster rotation of the feet directly under the body)

3. Body and arm action with proper foot placement (feet pointed to the side of the pool, parallel to the bottom) on the wall

4. The push-off on the side while rotating onto the belly

5. The arm pull-down

6. The arm recovery within the drag shadow, and kick timing

7. The transition into the first stroke at the surface

I believe that eliminating drag and resistance is the quickest way to become faster in the water. I studied many breaststroke races to figure out where the greatest amount of drag and resistance occurs. After each wall (including the start), once a swimmer has taken the full pull-down and the hands are at the side of the legs, they encounter the most resistance upon returning the hands over the head back to a streamline position to reach the surface and begin the regular stroke cycle. It occurred to me that we could eliminate the full arm pull-down and substitute a surface-type stroke arm cycle underwater so as to recover to the surface with a regular swimming action. The steps are as follows:

1. Separate the hand to begin the breast stroke.

2. Without stopping the arm action, take a dolphin kick.

3. Take a surface-type arm stroke underwater.

4. Recover the arms while frog kicking back to the surface.

Several things happened when I implemented these steps. The swimmers surfaced a little sooner and with more speed to carry into their next stroke, and they arrived at the 12.5-yard mark 0.3 to 0.5 second faster by carrying more speed off the wall. The tradeoff is that another stroke or two is needed each length.

We have tried these steps and have cleared them with the rules committees for USA Swimming and NCAA. They are legal and faster. The only catches are that you must be willing to accept change and give up an opportunity to rest at the end of the pull-down.

Every breaststroke session was devoted entirely to breaststroke or something related to breaststroke. The swimmers never swam at the end of a freestyle lane. They did individual medley work a couple sessions per week, and the individual medley swimmers joined the group. I also learned from Jozsef Nagy a great activity that helps swimmers improve power from the walls, live with discomfort that comes from being underwater for more of the race distance, not to give up stroke count for air, and maintain a faster swimming rate for the whole duration of the swimming distance. Jozsef calls them carousel 50s, 75s, and 100s. We built portable walls out of plywood, rope, and carabineers (see figure 13.3*a*). We simply clipped the top of the vertical board on the lane lines in the desired location (usually 12.5 yards). Then we anchored the bottom of the board by running 10 feet (3 m) of rope out from each side of the corners in each direction and clipping the ends of the ropes to the lane lines to stabilize the board. This made it possible to make each lane of the pool a different length. This is illustrated in figure 13.3.

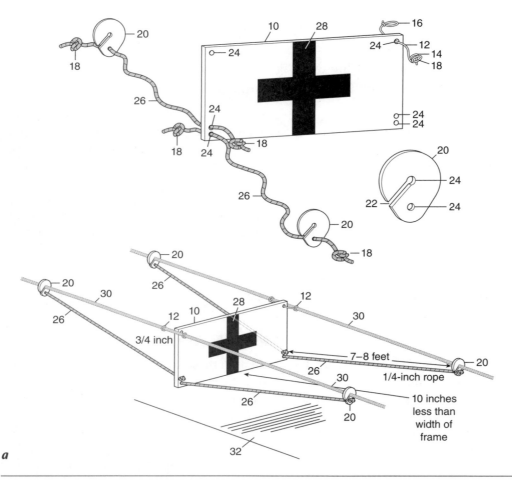

a

FIGURE 13.3 *(a)* Sheets of marine plywood with holes drilled in each corner and painted with a white waterproof, non-slip paint. A turning cross is added on both sides. (You need to be certain that the plywood is cut to fit between the width of your lanes.)

Based on an original illustration by Bob Gillett.

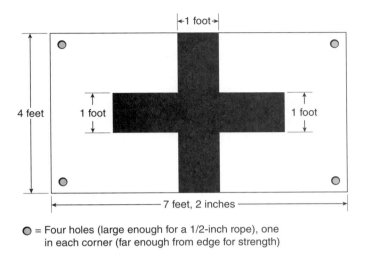

= Four holes (large enough for a 1/2-inch rope), one in each corner (far enough from edge for strength)

b

FIGURE 13.3 *(b)* The turn markings (one foot each) centered in black, non-slip paint.

Based on an original illustration by Bob Gillett.

An example of a carousel 50 might be

1. begin in lane 1;
2. swim to the 12.5-yard wall and turn;
3. return to the starting point (this is a total of 25 yards); and
4. turn again, push off going under the lane line, and sprint 25 yards (this is a total of 50 yards).

The swimmer is allowed only one stroke (with air) up on the surface before each turn. This makes for three underwater sequences, rather than the normal two sequences, in every 50-yard swim, which means that swimmers are training fast for a greater portion of the total distance on about half the amount of air. Because I am working with college-age swimmers, one stroke to the 12.5-yard wall works well. However, younger or female swimmers might need two strokes up on each segment, or the wall can be moved to 10 or 11 yards. A carousel 75 can be created by adding a turn after 50 yards, pushing off under the lane line, swimming down to the other side of the moveable wall, making a turn, and swimming back to the end opposite from the start. As you can see, you can get as creative as you wish with the number of walls and configurations.

Checklist for Breaststroke Speed

Eliminate drag and resistance while creating the proper body line.

1. Streamline front end (bow of your boat)

Tighten up the arm stroke.

Keep the catch for the in-sweep just outside the shoulder width.

Work the in-sweep while keeping the elbows away from the body and in line with the hands and forearms.

Equipment that can help: breaststroke arm paddles and fins

2. Body line from top to bottom (keeping a straight line from top of the head down through the knees)

Equipment that can help: front-mount snorkel and tick tockers

3. Body line from side to side (keeping a narrow stroke)

Keep the catch just outside the natural shoulder width.

Keep the elbows inside or behind the hands.

Keep the knees no wider than the hips.

Keep the foot catch position just outside the width of the hips.

Equipment that can help: breaststroke fins, elastic knee bands and pull buoy held between the knees

---

TECHNICAL DRILLS FOR BREASTSTROKE

If done regularly, drills effectively train the body to perform proper stroke technique and create proper muscle memory. This section presents some of our favorite drills.

Body Undulation

In this drill, the arms are at the swimmer's sides, with the hands leading. The swimmer presses the upper body (lungs) down underwater, allowing it to pop up in a forward direction. At the same time, the swimmer should perform a minimal dolphin action with the lower body. This drill works on posture, line, and balance.

Cobra

The swimmer begins by lying in the water on the belly in a streamline position and slides the hands out to a Y position. Then, the swimmer drags the body up into a vertical position; the body should be straight from the head to the knees. The knees are bent at an approximately 90° angle and the hands sweep into a prayer position in front of the chest. From here the swimmer dives forward, or strikes like a cobra, over the water as far as possible into a maximum streamlined distance per stroke.

Hesitation

Using a front-mount snorkel, a pull buoy, a tennis ball under the chin, and fins, the swimmer swims breaststroke arm stroke with a dolphin kick (a frog kick may also be used). A 3- to 5-second hesitation should occur at the catch or Y position. The spread (outward movement) of the arms must be very slow and relaxed, and the swimmer should expend as little energy as possible. The inward sweep should be constant, and hand speed should increase when rounding off into the forward extension into a recovery reach. The goal is to get as much forward body movement and as little up-and-down motion away from the body line as possible. This may vary from one swimmer to another, depending on body type and arm stroke technique. However, the goal is to travel the shortest possible distance: a straight line from one end of the pool to the other end. This will give the swimmer more time for speed between arm strokes.

Three Goggles

The swimmer should be sure to wear goggles in this drill, which consists of three strokes. In the first stroke, the swimmer's goggles should stay under the water's surface. In the second stroke, the swimmer's goggles should come just to the water's surface. In the third and final stroke, the swimmer's goggles should come just high enough to allow the swimmer to take a breath. During the drill, the swimmer should change body position without moving the head off the spine line.

CONCLUSION

The six breaststroke swimmers in my group finished the season with 100-yard times of 0:50.8 to 0:53.2 (one swimmer at 0:50.8, three at 0:52+, and two at the low 0:53s). In terms of 200-yard times, one swimmer was at 1:51.9, two were at 1:53+, one was at 1:54.0, one was at 1:55.2, and one was at 1:57.8. I am not so naïve as to think that I had a large role in their accomplishment. They are an intelligent and talented group of young men that were competitive in a very good team sense. There was great leadership and caring support for and from everyone in the group. They also used high-tech swimsuits, which played a large part. It turned out to be a positive and rewarding experience for all of us.

My present challenge is to figure out what we learned from the assistance of the speed suits and to modify our stroke technique to make up for what we lost in buoyancy and compression, which affect body position and core tension. Only time will tell how close we come to figuring this out. This time next year we will know a great deal more about proper technique. I hope this chapter gets you thinking. Good luck!

Breaststroke is the crown jewel of the four competitive strokes. You never want to abuse or hammer on it; only polish it regularly.

14

The Fifth Stroke: Underwater Kicking

Bob Gillett

Underwater kicking isn't one of the four traditional swimming strokes. However, we like to call it the fifth stroke. Underwater kicking has proven to be faster than surface strokes; it is a unique skill in itself and is examined in detail in this chapter.

A PHILOSOPHY THAT GUIDES MY COACHING

Every coach, either consciously or unconsciously, relies on some very basic beliefs that they have developed through experience or study. These beliefs influence many of the actions and teachings used in their daily work with swimmers. Two important components of my philosophy of coaching have affected my work on underwater kicking:

1. A commitment to specific techniques

2. The importance of improving performance through change

Coaches need to study, rationalize, use, and commit to specific techniques. Many skills in swimming have a lot of variations. As the coach, you eventually need to strongly commit to the best conceptual model of a specific skill that you want to teach your swimmer. If you do not make this commitment, you put your swimmer in a quandary about how to think about a skill or how to pattern or execute the skill. This is a tremendous disadvantage to your swimmer and can lead to great frustration on their part. So many times I have heard swimmers say, "I don't understand what I'm supposed to be doing or why I'm doing this skill like this!" Commit to a conceptual model and then coach it.

When you commit to a conceptual model, you are not committing for the rest of your life. Often what we thought was really great and true in the past is quite different from what we now believe in and practice with our swimmers. It is okay to change, modify, and question! You can even have different conceptual models of the same skill for different swimmers. Or, if your swimmer is capable, you may teach different conceptual models of the same skill for different situations and applications. Just remember, make the commitment to very specific conceptual models in skill development. Being right for now but wrong in the future is much better than being vague and avoiding making the commitment to specific techniques.

Also important is a passion for change. Don't change just for the sake of change, but rather continually strive for better. One of the worst traits that a coach can develop is complacency in what they are doing. They do the same thing day after day, week after week, month after month, and even year after year. Some coaches and swimmers fear change when they should embrace it! If you remain the same, you will continue to perform at approximately the same level. This is why most swimmers improve very little after they reach their ratio of adult height and weight. They keep swimming with the same tempo patterns (seconds per cycle) and cycle counts (distance per cycle), and as a result they swim the same times. If they do not change one of these variables, then they will never improve significantly. You must change to get swimmers to swim faster!

UNDERWATER KICKING: A SHORT HISTORY

Although I am given some of the credit for taking underwater kicking to new heights in recent times, I certainly am not the first to explore the speed of underwater kicking and its tremendous influence on swimming performance. Many agree that the real pioneer in work on underwater kicking in the modern period is the great backstroker David Berkoff. In 1988, he broke the world backstroke record using approximately 35 meters (30 to 31 kicks) of underwater dolphin kicking on the start and about 15 meters of kicking on the turn. He and his coach at Harvard, Joe Bernel, should be credited with this application and the success that it generated. The performances led the traditionalists of the sport to enact legislation for the 15-meter rule, which ended the long, extended breakouts that were spurring on the continuous assaults on the record books.

Many of us now wonder why we did not immediately apply the lessons of underwater kicking on backstroke to butterfly. Maybe at that time we thought that butterfly was so much faster than backstroke that we felt it would not be successful. For whatever the reason, diving the start or pushing a turn and taking two dolphin kicks into the full stroke remained the norm on butterfly.

In March of 1994, I found, quite by accident, the beginning of a new technique while I was working with one of my very young butterfliers, Misty Hyman. The speed of her starts was very poor throughout her age-group career. She finally got to the beginning level of junior national swimming by barely making the cut times in 100- and 200-yard butterfly events. Shortly before the 1994 Short Course Junior Nationals in Long Beach, California, I arranged a dive practice session with her. The objective of the session was to do something about the difficult time she had with the starts. I timed her for a 25-yard dive sprint fly at 12.4, which even during those days was going to put her way behind on the start. We talked about trying to exaggerate the streamline. As usual, Misty committed 110% to whatever I asked. She exaggerated the streamline and in the process extended the breakout with extra kicks as she strived for a better streamline position. I told her, "You will have to go back and do it again. I mistimed it: 11.8." She got back up and did it again: 11.7. Then we got excited and really went at it! I said, "Add a couple of kicks and let's see what it is." When 11.5 appeared on the stopwatch, we were off on a very exciting adventure in underwater kicking!

THE FOIL MOVEMENT

The foil movement is the term we us for an undulating, fish- or dolphin-type movement that results in forward motion in the water. As the legs move back, the knee joints stay in a fully extended position until the swimmer reaches the desired maximum range of motion (figure 14.1*a*). At this point of full backward extension, the knees push forward and flex to between 110 and 90°. At this time the feet are accelerated forward (figure 14.1*b*), which results in an arc as the knee joints between the upper and lower legs are extended to complete forward extension (figure 14.1*c*). I emphasize a very extreme and precise extension of the knees and feet at the end of the directional move of each kick. I do not want the kick to stop at the body midline or even within the body profile.

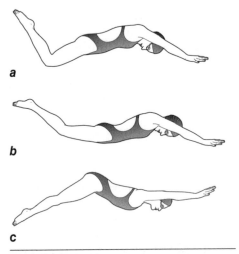

FIGURE 14.1 Range and extension of foil movement performed at race pace: *(a)* maximum knee bend, *(b)* extension, and *(c)* finish.

Dolphin Kick, Fish Kick, and Slant Kick

I began working with Misty Hyman on extended breakouts in March of 1994. In March of 1995, while walking in the airport before nationals in Minnesota, coach Don Watkins gave me a magazine and said, "You take this because it seems to be related to your work on underwater kicking." It was *Scientific American*, March 1995; the cover article, "An Efficient Swimming Machine," was written by two fluid dynamics scientists, Michael and George Triantafyllou. They studied how fish use the fins of their tails to produce counter-rotating vortices that interact to provide thrust for forward movement. In coaching terms as this relates to swimming, the kick in one direction sets up a rotating vortex, and the following kick in the other direction sets up a counter-rotating vortex. The interaction between these vortices determines the efficiency of the kicking. After I read the article, I was not sure how it might help my swimmers improve. I kept going back to it, though, trying to understand the Strouhal numbers, which relate to frequency (tempo) and spacing of the counter-rotating vortices, angle of attack of the kick, and the idea of smaller rotating vortices on the back kick and larger ones on the front kick.

In the photos that accompanied the article, the vortices were illustrated with dyed water. In November of 1995, I decided that I wanted to see the vortices of a swimmer. I taped a plastic tube down the side of Misty's body and she held the end in her hand. She laid on the deck and I filled the tube with dark blue cake coloring from a quart bottle. I told her to go underwater, push off, and turn on her side so that I could see the dye as she kicked. I was astonished to see that the arc of the vortices was huge—about 10 feet (3 m) in diameter! I realized that if we kicked in the vertical plane (dolphin kick) in pools that were only 4 to 7 feet (1.2 to 2.1 m) deep, then we destroyed the vortices as they hit the top of the water and bottom of the pool. To maintain the advantage of the counter-rotating interaction of the vortices, the swimmer would need to turn on the side and use the water of the next lanes. This is why we named this position fish kicking: Mammals kick in the vertical plane and fish kick in the horizontal plane. I videotaped our work and sent it to the authors of the *Scientific American* article. I asked them to watch it and let me know whether my interpretations were correct. The authors replied that they thought I was making the correct interpretation and that they were amazed at Misty because they "did not know that humans could do that!" Of course, I enjoyed that comment!

One other part of the article caught my attention. The scientists presented the idea that fish can capture energy from encountered vortices. After a couple of months, I began to think that it may not be so bad if vortices were created by the hands undulating over the head as a result of an increased magnitude of upper-body movement. I wondered whether, as the vortices slide down the body into the kicking zone, the foil movement of the legs could capture the energy and therefore increase distance per kick. We were thinking about letting the upper body go with more press of hands to transfer energy down the body into the kicking motion, therefore using the core body strength to a greater extent. We avoided this in the beginning in the name of streamlining! However, we wanted more distance per kick, and maybe the increased power of a more dynamic upper-body press coupled with captured energy from the resulting vortices was worth considering.

Many years later, while attending a national coaches clinic at the Olympic Training Center in Colorado, a couple of scientists presented their works on the computational fluid dynamics of swimming. I ate lunch with one of the scientists and discovered that he had studied under one of the Triantafyllou brothers. I asked him whether my interpretation—that capturing energy from the vortices created by the hands and upper-body movements was highly probable—could be correct. He thought it was entirely possible but did not know.

I think that underwater fish kicking, in the depth of water that we encounter in competitive swimming, is more efficient than dolphin kicking. Another degree of this skill exists; we call it slant kicking, which at 45° is just between the total vertical of dolphin kicking and the horizontal of fish kicking. Slant kicking takes on some of the advantages of preventing the vortices of the kick from slamming into the bottom of the pool and being destroyed by the surface of the pool.

Most swimmers feel uncomfortable when they first start doing the totally horizontal kicking of fish kick. They often say, "It seems harder to do and it makes me tired." Unfortunately, all but the most conscientious and disciplined swimmers give up on mastering the skills involved before they become comfortable and proficient at the skills. But that is why we have champions! I think this discomfort is primarily due to a change in the pressure in the thoracic cavity. The pressure is a sideways push rather than a front–back push. As with many skills, it feels perfectly normal after the skills are mastered. As I like to say, "You won't have any problems with this after a few thousand repeats of it!" A newspaper reporter once asked Misty, "Why do you kick on your side?" Her answer was great: "Because it is faster!"

Distance Per Kick, Tempo, and Interaction of Fish Kick

Traditionally, most coaches have believed that dolphin and fish kick movements should stay within the body profile for a more streamlined result. Traditionally, the swimmer has kept the upper body very straight and in alignment in an attempt to reduce resistance. With this technique, the swimmer's body movement is limited and the swimmer does the kick with a smaller range of motion and high tempo.

Here I present a much different approach that consists of a more dynamic body movement and increased magnitude of leg movement. When Misty and I really started to explore the dynamics of the fish kick in late 1995 and early 1996 before the Olympic Trials, we were faced with the quandary of whether to emphasize streamlining and smaller kicks with fast tempo or bigger kicks with a slower tempo. We committed to the traditional streamlining, smaller kicks, and fast tempo. The Olympic Trials were in March and we wanted to have our new application of fish kicking ready to go. At a grand prix meet in Seattle in January of 1996, we went with the fish kick in competition for the first time. We had to make sure it would be judged legal and not get disqualified. Misty won the 100-meter butterfly against a great field. We committed to executing the straight, stretched, streamlined body position and fast kick with reduced range of motion on all the breakouts. At 16 years of age, Misty placed third and barely missed making the U.S. Olympic team.

After the Olympic Trials, we decided, as always, to make some changes and think outside the box. We decided to challenge the traditional belief that a swimmer must stay in a tight streamline and keep the kicking motion inside the body alignment. Misty had been taking about 27 kicks on the start of the 100-meter butterfly. Our objective was to reduce the number of kicks and give up as little as possible on the tempo. For part of March, April, and May, we focused our underwater kicking on increasing the magnitude of the kick by adding more range to the front and back of the movement pattern and more knee bend. We let the upper body go and allowed for a much larger range of motion of the extended arms. Misty increased her distance down the pool with about a two-kick reduction at the same tempo. We got really excited about such an improvement. By May of 1996, Misty was much faster on that first 50 out split. The change to the bigger range of motion was a huge boost to her career. Change is good!

WHY UNDERWATER KICKING IS FASTER

Most of us associated with top-level swimming know that doing extended breakouts on starts and turns is faster for most swimmers than doing a short breakout and just starting to swim. Many swimmers and coaches do not understand why this technique is effective. Once swimmers and coaches understand exactly what they are working on and have quantified it, the practice for perfect execution will be much more precise. This will result in faster improvement and higher levels of achievement.

Races are faster with extended breakouts on starts and turns because of reduced cycle counts and the interaction with tempo. For example, in the past we would dive in and do two dolphin kicks and then start stroking. A swimmer would do two kicks and take 10 cycles at 1.10 tempo. We determined that if we could complete two kicks in about 0.90 second (0.45 kick tempo) and if we could go just as far with those two kicks as we do with one cycle, then we would be ahead in the swim by about 0.2 second. If we did it again we would be ahead another 0.2 second, and so on, and so on! In this example, if we replace three cycles at 1.10 with six additional underwater kicks at 0.45, then we would be 0.6 second faster and take seven cycles. On four lengths, we have a 2.4-second decrease in time. This is why it works!

The best is yet to come. I believe that after the swimmer gets to the very advanced stages of these skills, they can actually develop distance per kick that will allow them a little more distance with two kicks than with one stroke. Because this is applied over many kicks, they will gain enough distance to allow for one fewer cycle with only one additional kick. Now we are in for some excitement! In our example, if the swimmer can take one additional kick at 0.45 second and can reduce the cycle count by one more cycle, then they will save an additional 0.55 second. So now we save 1.15 seconds (0.2 + 0.2 + 0.2 + 0.55 = 1.15) on each length!

This magnitude is increased even more in backstroke because backstroke tempo is generally slower than butterfly tempo. For example, if a swimmer is swimming at a 1.30 tempo and replaces three cycles with six dolphin or fish kicks at 0.45 each, then they save 1.2 seconds (0.4 + 0.4 + 0.4 = 1.2) on each length. If the swimmer gets to the level of mastery and reduces the cycle count by one more cycle with only one additional kick, they save an additional 0.85 second for a whopping 2.05 seconds. This is the reason for the historical change between backstroke and butterfly times—for example, the greater improvement in backstroke compared to butterfly in NCAA short-course swimming.

Many swimmers can increase performance levels in freestyle events by using underwater kicking in extended breakouts on starts and turns. If, for example, a swimmer is swimming an intermediate split of 28.0 with three dolphin kicks on the turn breakout, the swimmer could improve performance by extending the number of kicks to five fish or dolphin kicks and replace one cycle. If it resulted in a tradeoff of 0.90 for the two additional kicks and of 1.40 for one cycle, the swimmer would improve 0.5 second per length. If the swimmer could maximize the series of five kicks on the turn breakouts, then it could even be possible to subtract two cycles per length. How fast could our top males go in the 500-yard freestyle by using five- or even seven-kick breakouts on each length? Even without a perfect correlation of efficiency, we could have performance under 4:00 from more than one of our current great freestylers. I hope this discussion will help motivate and challenge more top swimmers to maximize this skill.

Odd Number of Kicks on Breakouts

On page 203, I discuss the concept of reducing cycle counts by substituting two dolphin or fish kicks for each cycle. In relation to this, I present the technique of adding only one more kick to a series in order to take off an additional cycle, a tradeoff of one for one. This is accomplished by getting very good at the foil movement and developing more distance per kick. Very important to this goal are the pattern of movement, magnitude of the knee bend, and the increased utilization of core body strength with the magnitude of body undulation.

As with the full stroke, we face the problem of balancing distance per cycle and tempo with underwater kicking. The interaction between distance per cycle and tempo is what I humorously refer to as the essence of life. It is the essence of swimming! If they totally focus on distance per cycle and doing a slow but very precise movement pattern, most swimmers can really generate long strokes that result in very low cycle counts. However, the velocities of swimming will remain low. If a swimmer puts total focus on tempo, moving the arms as fast as they can, they will have very high tempo but short distance per cycle, which results in a high cycle count. The essence of swimming is to adjust these two variables to achieve the balance that results in the highest velocities and the best performance. It is exactly the same for underwater kicking: a swimmer must maximize distance per kick and ability to generate tempo, but within the context of interaction.

Refer back to the concept of adding one dolphin or fish kick to the breakouts with the goal of getting one more cycle off with only one more kick rather than two more kicks. I have always felt that the pursuit of this goal would have a higher probability of success if my swimmers always used an odd number of kicks in the breakouts. Therefore, I use progression of 3, 5, 7, 9, 11, or 13 kicks in my program in the hope that this approach will speed up the developmental process.

Plus Two Rule

Another important workout component is what I call the plus two rule. In my early work with Misty in 1994 to 1996, we realized that deceleration at the end of long extended breakouts was a huge problem. After working hard on this, I realized that practicing the breakouts with two more kicks than we were planning to use in meets greatly minimized this deceleration. We now ask all of our swimmers to practice using two kicks more than they plan to use in competition. For example, if a swimmer plans to do seven kicks on turns in meets, they need to do nine kicks in most of their practice sets.

Depth of Underwater Kicking on Breakouts

It is better to be too deep than to be too shallow on underwater kickouts, especially when dolphin kick is used instead of fish kick or slant kick. On dolphin kick, the vortices of the kicks are significantly disrupted when up vortices crash into the top of the water (you can easily see this trailing a shallow kickout by a swimmer) and down (forward kicking) vortices compress against the bottom of the pool. The interactions of the next kicks will not be as effective. If you are swimming in a pool that is 7 feet (2.1 m) deep and you set up the majority of the kicks at 3.5 feet (1 m), on dolphin kick about 24 inches (0.6 m) will exist between the end of your kick and the top of the water or bottom of the pool! This situation can be reduced with slant or fish kick.

Breakout Trajectory of Extended Underwater Breakouts

Breakout trajectory of extended underwater breakouts is very important. How many times have you seen developing swimmers try to keep kicking too shallow on a break-out and break the water too soon with the feet? Their velocity just falls off the cliff! I teach the swimmer to stay away from the surface of the water for as many kicks as possible and then to do a slightly sharper angle up into the surge stroke of the breakout. For example, on a nine-kick fish kick breakout on butterfly, the swimmer would be on the side for eight kicks and then transition to the front on the one last kick before the surge stroke, ascending during the last three kicks. On backstroke, the swimmer would do all nine kicks on the side and then initiate the bottom-arm breakout with flutter kick, ascending the last three cycles.

Counting Kicks

Swimmers absolutely must count their kicks on extended breakouts. It is the only way to have consistent, high-level performances that challenge the 15-meter mark, which is presently the limiting rule for underwater kicking distance. A few years ago, I was associated with a coach whose swimmer was swimming very fast on backstroke in our program. I asked the coach how many kicks his swimmer was doing on the start, and the coach replied, "I don't know; he doesn't count. But he has perfect feel on this and does a great job every time." You guessed it; in the preliminary of the 200 backstroke at junior nationals, he was at least 4 yards past the mark on the start and was disqualified! Later in the meet, he went 47.63 in the 100-yard backstroke. He left a great 200-yard backstroke time on the table for that season!

For top-level swimmers, the variance is not much at this time but it can make a big difference because every hundredth of a second counts in this sport! Also, this will change over time, but most top swimmers are now taking between 9 and 11 kicks to cover the 15-meter breakout distance and have a kick tempo of approximately 0.40 to 0.50. This information is meant to provide some starting points for your evaluations and work on underwater kicking.

My age-group coaches run a progression of kickouts for our age-group program. With the little swimmers, we start with five for drop pushes (where the swimmer holds onto the side of the pool, drops down under the water, and pushes off from that point) and three for turns. We coach the intermediate competitive swimmers to go seven on drop pushes and five on turns, and we coach the advanced age-groupers to go nine from drop pushes and seven on turns. A popular combination for junior elite swimmers is 11 and 9. For the junior elite swimmer (age 18 and under, junior national and above swimmer), I would like to see the 15-meter mark challenged on starts with 9 and challenged on all turns with 11. (This has not happened for me yet, but it will happen in the future!)

BEST OF BREED: FISH KICK, SLANT KICK, DOLPHIN KICK, OR...?

For underwater kicking, I believe that the order of maximum potential is fish kick, slant kick, and then dolphin kick. Some associated with swimming have stated that fish kick has little or no advantage over dolphin kick. I have no research to defend my position; practicing swimming coaches often find themselves in this situation on such issues. However, during my work on these skills with several top swimmers over the past 15 years, I have developed enough practical experience and coach's feel to believe that I have a good grasp on the evaluation of the different kicks. I have a reasonable probability of not being wrong—but if I am, the negative consequences of being wrong are few to none!

The difference in efficiency between fish kick and dolphin kick in the competitive situation can be expressed as follows: the distance achieved on 9 or 11 fish kicks at 0.45 tempo will be approximately the same as that achieved on 10 or 12 dolphin kicks at 0.45 tempo. Most individuals would say the difference between 11 and 12 is not very large; however, at 0.45 second per kick it is very significant number. The quantified difference is one kick!

This said, the type of kick is not really the most important variable in the effectiveness of underwater kicking. The most important variable is the number of kicks. I am amazed at how few swimmers actually challenge the 15-meter mark on starts and turns in today's swimming world. I am aware that all swimmers cannot execute this skill successfully. However, a large number of swimmers would be much better than they are now if they would develop and use better underwater kick techniques.

Measuring Kick Tempo

Measuring kick tempo on underwater kicking is very simple. Start the stopwatch at the end of a forward kick and count the kick, zero, one, two, and so on. Then split after 3 or 5 or 10 kicks. The more kicks you use in the calculation, the more valid the measurement will be. For examples, 5 kicks at 2.25 would be 0.45 tempo, 10 kicks at 4.50 would be 0.45 tempo, and 3 kicks at 1.35 would be 0.45 tempo. After you do it a few thousand times, you just know at a glance. (Works for coaches too!)

TECHNICAL DRILLS FOR UNDERWATER KICKING

Following are some drills that I have used over the years to help swimmers have a great start at underwater kicking. Using the following methods will help all levels of swimmers quickly master the underwater kick.

Fin Kicking

Start with very short distances (10 to 15 meters) with fins. The swimmers practice fish kick, slant kick, and dolphin kick and count their kicks. Immediately incorporate the concepts of distance per kick (DPK) and tempo into the kicking. It is important to do both; I like to alternate doing three on DPK and then three repeats on tempo. Insist on very precise movements on the DPK repeats. Emphasize kicking with maximum speed of movement on the tempo repeats. If you wish to skew the number of repeats, the general procedure should be to emphasize precision, big range of motion, and big magnitude of movement. Do lots of kick counting; the fewer the better!

Flex-Lane Bulkheads

Use flex-lane bulkheads to set up 15-meter lanes. Swimmers do massive numbers of quick repeats; for example: 6 (10 × 15 meters @ 0:20) 0:20 rest between subsets. If you have a movable bulkhead, set the bulkhead at 15 meters for an underwater day: fish, slant, dolphin, fins, no fins, DPK, tempo, underwater races, games of elimination by heats, relays, times, records, and so on.

Monofins

Monofins are a great tool for developing the correct foil movement involved in fish, slant, and dolphin kick. I think swimmers develop best with a monofin rather than with two individual foot fins. This has to do with the way the swimmers learn the movement—keeping the feet together while on the side, readying for the drop push, maneuvering to get out of the way of another swimmer, and the like. The swimmer should become one with the fin. The monofin should be selected for teaching the foil movement first and training second. The monofin should be of the proper size for the swimmer to handle, be made of safe material, and be the right shape and have the right flexibility. I believe that small (cut off) fins are not good for young, developing swimmers because they do not promote fin-like range of motion and emphasis at the end of each foil movement. The scientists in fish hydrodynamics say that the end, or flip, at the end of foil movement is extremely important; hard, short, inflexible fins do not develop this movement as well as flexible, longer, pliable fins.

Dive With Fish Kicks

With all age groups, I dive a lot of repeats with fish kicks based on distance in relation to number of kicks. An example for junior elite girls could be as follows: "dive; do 11 kicks and try to hit the 15-meter mark right on the button—10 kicks on your side and then 1 kick in transition; then take 5 cycles on butterfly to the 25-yard wall. Then swim back easy in the next lane." I refer to this set as Fish/Flops (10 × 50 @ 1:00 Fish/Flops). Some days it will focus on DPK, some days it will focus on tempo, and some days it will be 3 on DPK alternated with 3 on tempo. Often we use 13 kicks (the plus two rule) going past the 15-meter mark and take 3 to 4 cycles. Many, many different combinations of Fish/Flops will improve underwater kicking!

CONCLUSION

Aside from the technical aspects of the kick, a number of elements are important in coaching underwater kicking.

- ◆ Your coaching philosophy is important.
- ◆ Have a passion for change in your coaching.
- ◆ Always question and evaluate.
- ◆ Acquire and commit to a conceptual model of stroke and skill movements.

The following technique aspects of underwater kicking will enable your swimmers to become highly skilled in underwater swimming.

- ◆ The effective foil movement in underwater kicking is a result of a coordinated movement pattern of ankle and knee extension and flexion; it is not just an undulating movement of the body. The end of the forward kick is a very important focus point. Range of motion (magnitude of kick) is important. The magnitude of knee flexion is approximately 110 to 90°.
- ◆ Upper-body movement is important in transferring energy, developed by core body strength, to the power of the leg kick. The swimmer can generate more distance per kick by making significant movements in the upper body and pressing the hands.
- ◆ Underwater kicking can be divided into three or more plane positions: dolphin kick (vertical), fish kick (horizontal), and slant kick (an angled body position).
- ◆ The effectiveness of underwater kicking with these three kicks depends on numerous variables, such as distance of the kicks from the bottom of the pool, distance of the kicks from the top of the water, frequency of kicks, magnitude of kicks, range of motion of the upper-body movements, replaced cycles tempo, and the swimmer's experience, conditioning level, and tenacity.
- ◆ The number of kicks used in underwater kicking on the starts and turns is more important than the plane of the kick.

- For many swimmers, underwater kicking is faster than swimming if cycles are replaced with kicks because the cycle count is reduced. A simple reminder: if you replace one cycle at 1.10 with two kicks at 0.45, then an improvement of 0.2 second occurs.

- The essence of swimming—cycle, tempo, and interaction—is the same for extended underwater kicking as it is for swimming on top of the water.

- Use an odd number of kicks on extended breakouts to increase the probability that one additional kick will lead to a one-cycle reduction.

- Plus two rule: Use two additional kicks on extended breakouts in workouts. This will help minimize reduction of velocity, a major problem, at the end of the extended breakouts.

- It is better to be a little too deep than too shallow on extended breakouts due to the interaction of the water surface and pool bottom with the foil movement vortices.

- Approaching the surface too soon in an extended kickout drastically reduces the effectiveness of distance per kick. On butterfly, when using fish or slant kick, the swimmer should stay on the side for all kicks and use the last kick to transition to the front for the surge stroke. On backstroke and freestyle, the swimmer should do all fish or slant kicks on the side and then execute the breakout with the bottom arm using flutter kick.

- A swimmer should always count kicks on extended breakouts. It will help them attack the breakout without reservations of being disqualified for going past the 15-meter mark. It will also help maximize the number of kicks by not starting the breakout of the arms too soon. Kick counting takes out the guesswork and allows for total consistency in performance.

- The fish kick is theoretically more effective than the dolphin kick. After years of empirical evaluation and observation of performances, I think that the increased effectiveness in the competitive environment has the magnitude of 9.10 to 11.13. Is this really worth the effort? If 0.45 seconds on each length of the pool is important to you, yes!

- For a quick start in underwater kicking, follow these tips: Use it from the beginning with all age groups; fins are good, and monofins are better; balance practice of distance per kick, tempo, and interaction, skewing toward distance per kick; teach fish, slant, and dolphin kicks from the start; count kicks over short distances; and do a lot of Fish/Flop sets.

15

Better Starts, Turns, and Finishes

Dick Hannula

Streamlining is one skill that needs constant attention throughout the season. Every swimmer needs to continue to improve streamlining skills off each wall. On too many teams, streamlining is one of the most neglected skills and an area that offers the most potential for improving swimming times through faster turns. Streamlining skill is fundamental and needs to be established early in the season and then continually practiced throughout the season. Coaches should sometimes stand over the lanes during practice and emphatically remind swimmers of the importance of streamlining when they see swimmers ease back on this necessary skill. Tired swimmers will sometimes ease back on the streamline position off the walls when doing multiple repeat swims in a practice set. Having an excellent streamline position off every wall in competition comes from making it a habit in every practice session. When necessary, a coach should pull a swimmer from the water and go back to the fundamental drills of streamlining on the pool deck. Brian Goodell, the 1976 Olympic champion and world record holder in the 400- and 1,500-meter freestyle events, used to play Olympics in practice sessions leading into the Olympic Games. Going into and off his turns, he would attempt to beat and pass swimmers in the other lanes. Brian was noted for his great turning ability in competition.

This chapter helps coaches and swimmers make starts, turns, and finishes as fast and efficient as possible. Streamlining off the wall in a tight line is the first essential. The second is adding the underwater butterfly kick to this streamlined position. The other important component of great turns is the swimmer's ability to get his or her feet on the wall quickly.

FUNDAMENTAL SKILLS

The key to great starts, turns, and finishes is preparation and practice. Preparation involves the most fundamental skills necessary for better starts and turns. I can't overstate that the streamlined position off the wall and the underwater butterfly kick are critical for great starts and turns.

Streamlined Body Position

Every year at the start of a new swim season, I taught and practiced the streamlined torpedo body position. In this position, the body makes as tight a direct, streamlined line as possible from the back of the head through the spine.

We started by demonstrating the correct torpedo position on the deck of the pool. The swimmer would lie on his or her back and assume the extended streamline position. In this position the toes are pointed back, the legs are closed, and the small of the lower back is flattened and touches the ground. I would try to insert my foot, leading with the toes, under the small of the back of each swimmer; that area had to be closed off so that I could not insert the front of my foot. This position ensured the straight line from the back of the head through the spine and legs.

I would then stand over the swimmer, facing the swimmer's head, with my feet placed so that my heels were just above the swimmer's elbows. In that position, I would squeeze the swimmer's arms in tight on the back side of their ears. This inward pressure from my feet brought the swimmer into the desired tight, extended position. In this position, the swimmer's hands are placed so that the back of one hand is on the palm of the other hand and the thumb of that hand is wrapped tightly around the outside corner of the other hand.

I applied that same position and pressure to every swimmer and they applied it to each other until all were highly skilled in assuming the streamlined underwater position (see figure 15.1). Next, the swimmers would stand with their backs to a wall and assume the same position. The final dryland drill was to stand away from the wall and maintain that extended streamline position.

Once this position was excellent on dry land, we incorporated water drills. Our diving pool was 35 feet (10.6 m) across and provided an ideal distance for underwater streamlining practice. On each day of the early season, the swimmers would repeat underwater streamlined push-offs in that diving pool. If you want improvement, measure the skill. In this drill, we noted the distance that each swimmer attained from just pushing off the wall and maintaining the streamlined position without kicking or stroking. The objective was for everyone to be able to make the 35 feet (10.6 m) with some momentum and without kicking. This drill ensured that every athlete had great streamlining and push-offs going into the competitive season.

FIGURE 15.1 Streamlined underwater position: *(a)* lateral view and *(b)* frontal view.

Butterfly Kick

We added the butterfly kick to this underwater drill once the athletes attained tight torpedo and momentum in the streamlined position. The underwater butterfly kick is presented by Bob Gillett in chapter 14. The butterfly kick is often referred to as the dolphin kick. Swimmers must visualize correct technique to move toward perfect technique. Refer to chapter 14 for visual references. Coaches should time swimmers' cross-pool underwater butterfly kick torpedo swims. To measure is to accelerate improvement.

The next step was to progress to underwater butterfly kicking with swim fins or monofins and progress the streamlined torpedo position over the 25-yard or meter distance. The most improvement comes from timing this drill periodically or on special days. Swimmers recognize quickly that for these underwater butterfly kicking repeats, the fastest time comes from the tightest streamlined position. As I mentioned previously, timing accelerates learning.

STARTS

A swimmer's fastest moments within competition are experienced at the start, specifically with the momentum of the dive into the water. With proper attention, coaches can assure that a good start places the swimmer in a positive position early in the race.

Forward Start

Fast starts depend on quick reaction to the starting signal and a clean, streamlined entry and underwater butterfly kick. The breakout should always be forward and have very little upward motion. The goal is to achieve as much momentum and speed as possible in the first swimming strokes. This is efficient and allows the swimmer to ride the start into racing speed rather than tire from overstroking in the early portion of the race. The athlete has more left for the finish of the race when this start is executed effectively. Start practice must be done in deep water.

The swimmer and the coach should decide together the type of start that each swimmer uses. A number of hand positions are possible. The track start position is the current favorite for most swimmers; it permits greater velocity and has less vertical thrust than other positions. In the track start, one leg is back on the blocks or both legs are forward at the front of the blocks. At the starting signal the head leads, the hands follow, and the body finishes. In the forward start (see figure 15.2), the athlete flexes the arms, pulls toward the water, and thrusts the arms to a 90° angle with the head just above the shoulders. The athlete attempts to get out, not up, as far as possible by driving off the blocks with the entire body through the legs. Before entering the water the athlete drops the head between the shoulders, and the hyperextends to a full torpedo position on entry. The athlete attempts to make the body into a needle at both ends by entering through a small hole with the hands and getting the legs through the same hole. The athlete should point the toes on entry and add the butterfly kick to maintain the advantage of the momentum created in the start.

FIGURE 15.2 Forward start sequence.

The steps that the coach uses to increase the efficiency of the racing start are often self-learned through success and failure. At the start of the season, I would ask the swimmers to practice vertical jumps from the side of the pool and enter the water feet first. This exercise was designed to increase the height of the jump. Next, to provide incentive to increase the height of the jump, I held an aluminum pole at a challenging height and the athletes jumped over the pole and entered the water feet first. Next, we practiced jumps from the 1-meter diving board. After increasing the height of the jumps, we introduced diving over the pole using a head-first entry. We then introduced an advanced drill that consisted of diving through a large tire innertube or a hula hoop; in this drill, the athlete attempted to get the body through the same hole that the hands made in the water. After these drills, we incorporated diving starts from both the starting blocks and the 1-meter diving board. The 1-meter diving board starts provided the athletes the opportunity to get some spring from the diving board to get the feel of the legs upon entry. The diving board starts placed the swimmer well out and over the water, which gave the swimmer confidence when using the starting blocks.

Coaches should also train swimmers to react to starting signals by incorporating reaction drills in which the swimmer responds to a whistle, metal pipes, or other signal. Athletes can perform reaction drills on the deck of the pool simply by moving the arms on the signal. Reaction drills lead to a faster starting response. One of the great athletes of the past century was the horse Seabiscuit. Normally, in a horse race, horses start from a starting gate. The match race between Seabiscuit and War Admiral to prove which horse was the world's best was to have a walk-up start. War Admiral was noted for its speed out of the gate; this was an advantage for the horse. Tom Smith, the trainer of Seabiscuit, began to secretly train Seabiscuit on walk-up starts. He constructed a starting bell that was similar to the real thing. On the starting signal, he used the whip on the horse. After only a few practice starts in this manner, and Seabiscuit was off to the races on the bell alone. In the match race, Seabiscuit started fast and beat War Admiral soundly. I'm not advocating that coaches use this procedure on swim team members to get them to react to the starting signal. However, coach Bill Sweetenham has used a similar but less physical approach in which a swimmer would stand behind the starting block swimmer and hold a kickboard on the starting block swimmer's buttocks. At the start signal, the swimmer holding the kickboard would push the starting swimmer forward. That action helped to focus the swimmer's attention on the starting signal and to get off the blocks before too much pressure was applied from behind.

Backstroke Start

The backstroke start requires a position in the water (refer to figure 11.4 on page 165). The athlete should place the feet on the wall about armpit width apart. The toes should turn to the inside slightly after placing the feet, and the heels should stay away from the hips. The athlete should keep the toes just below the water surface and force them into the wall, not down it. The heels are not quite on the wall. The athlete should pull up as high as comfortably possible and in control when called to take the mark. On leaving the wall, the athlete pushes off with the hands and arms first, and then gets some snap from the head and throws backward with the entire upper body. The arms are slightly ahead of the legs. The athlete explodes from the legs, get the hips up over the water, dives through the entry with the upper body, and lifts the legs on entry to get through the same hole with added momentum. The athlete should then get to the tight streamlined position as soon as possible.

TURNS

Nothing is more obvious to spectators and coaches than the effect of poorly executed turns in competition. Winning the swimming race between the walls and losing that margin and more at the turns is frustrating and counterproductive. A successful swimmer must execute fast turns. Great turns start with establishing great basic skills and are refined by adding advanced skills later.

Freestyle and Backstroke Turns

Technique tips are the same for both the freestyle turn (see figure 15.3) and backstroke turn (refer to figure 11.6 on page 169). Swimmers should feel that the tuck into the turn is similar to diving into and through a large waterfall. The water hitting the head and shoulders should throw the swimmer into the turn position. The swimmer should tuck tight with nose to knees, chin to chest, and heels to hips. If the swimmer sees the turning T going into the turn, then he or she is lifting the head before the tuck and start of the turn. This is to be avoided so as to get in and out on the wall with full momentum. The swimmer should keep the eyes on the feet until they contact the wall and keep the arms tucked in for a faster spin. The hands, hip joints, and heels should be aligned for maximum push-off distance. The swimmer should then push off the walls on the balls of the feet and kick the wall as they make contact. The feet should be about armpit width apart on wall contact and push-off. The swimmer should kick off the wall using a fast underwater butterfly kick up to 15 meters and switch to flutter kick on the breakout. In freestyle, the breakout arm should be the lower arm.

The head of backstroke swimmers should break out during the second arm stroke; this provides added momentum on the backstroke breakout. This is best accomplished

FIGURE 15.3   Freestyle turn sequence.

by the backstroke swimmer starting the second arm from the extended arm position sooner than when swimming on the surface. The second arm starts the pull just before the finish of the pull on the first arm. Freestyle swimmers should not breathe on the first arm pull in the breakout and should avoid breathing going into the wall. Swimmers should practice turns with both a left and a right arm lead.

Practicing fast turns at goal race pace is a requirement and can be accomplished in a number of ways. Racing starts from the starting blocks or the 1-meter diving board result in speeds that are faster than race pace for short distances. Swims for 10 to 15 meters from a launching pad and with a fast turn without the wall can be effective practice. Cross-pool or diving pool starts from blocks also provide practice opportunities to do fast turns on the wall at fast, race pace speeds. Sprinters on my teams had a runway laid on the pool deck leading into our 35-foot (10.6 m) diving tank. The sprinters would practice race pace turns by running about 10 yards (9.1 m) on the runway and hurdling into the air at the pool edge to provide speed into the turning wall. Supervision and safety stipulations are necessary for this runway drill.

Towing surgical tubing while swimming faster than race pace can bring the swimmer into the wall for a fast placement of feet and streamlined push-off and breakout before meeting too much resistance from the anchored tubing. Momentum is the key at each wall. The speed attained going into the wall is rewarded by increased speed off the wall. The momentum from the push-off is greater than the speed that can be reached swimming. The momentum speed is critical in the swimmer's ability to cruise into and maintain race pace more efficiently.

Measurement is the key to improvement. The coach and swimmer should break down the parts of each turn and then practice each part in isolation, adding each part gradually until all individual parts are combined into the complete turn. The coach and swimmer should measure with a stopwatch the parts of the turn that can be objectively measured: the start of the head duck into the turn and the placement of the feet on the wall, the push-off through the breakout point, and the combination of the head duck into the wall and the breakout point. The final step in measuring is to time the entire turn from point to point (e.g., backstroke flags to backstroke flags); a marker at a point outside of the backstroke flag zone can be added to create another measuring point. Another point-to-point distance that is easy to measure is cross-pool turns from one of the two walls.

I started my new swimmers out with progressive turning drills. First, we did drop push-offs from the wall partially on the back, just streamlined and without kicking. Next we added the butterfly kick, and then we added the breakout strokes, all from only a push-off at first. We next added the approach, which started from a couple of running steps in the water and a jump into the wall to ensure momentum. The next drill involved swimming into the turn to the position of the feet on the wall. To the swimming approach, we then added the turn and push-off using only the streamlined position and with no kick or stroke applied (this can be measured for distance). In the final step of this swimming sequence, we added the butterfly kick and breakout strokes. Finally, we timed the entire turn from designated point to point.

The use of the underwater butterfly kick has had a tremendous effect on the underwater speed and subsequent breakout speed off every wall. Daily practice of the underwater butterfly kick is essential. When I started each session of a particular stroke, my first drill was the underwater streamlined kick, which led into the other stroke drills. Every practice included a 10- to 15-minute session on turns, and I frequently incorporated starts and finishes.

Some additional free and backstroke turning drills can include the following. In lane line jumps, the athlete holds the lane line about chest depth while standing, places the thumbs under the line, and goes over it, ending in a squat position. Standing jumps can be performed without a lane line by somersaulting and landing on the feet in the same spot. The athlete can time consecutive repeats to emphasize speed and try to execute a series of jumps faster. In one-arm hand paddle turns, the athlete places the paddle on the strongest arm and strokes into and turns with the paddle arm. This drill builds stroking speed into and off the walls and can be done with two paddles instead of just one. Turning drills should include underwater turns. The swimmer dives underwater at the backstroke flags approaching the wall and then executes a tight somersault turn under the water. This turn assists the swimmer in feeling the resistance created at the wall and encourages a tighter turning position. Athletes can also practice fast turns by switching to full swimming strokes as they approach the wall when doing drills and kicking without the kickboard.

Josh Davis always had great freestyle turns as a college and Olympic swimmer. He stated that his high school coach used to have him streamline off the walls with the hands rotated so that they faced each other palm to palm. This position forced a very tight streamline at the upper body and placed the arms on the backs of the ears. This drill was emphasized in many of his high school practices.

The following drill strengthens the legs for a strong push-off and is an effective streamlining drill. The drill requires a very short section of surgical tubing with a belt for the swimmer to attach to the waist. The tubing should be heavy duty so that it provides major resistance to the push-off effort. The tubing is anchored to the base of the starting blocks or the wall and is short enough to keep the swimmer close to the wall. The swimmer practices repeat push-offs and is pulled back quickly for the next repeat.

Breaststroke and Butterfly Turns

The breaststroke and butterfly turns are essentially the same turn (see figure 15.4 on page 218). The difference is in what the swimmer does on the push-off and breakout strokes to accommodate the regulating rules. The swimmer must learn to judge the walls and know when wall contact will be made. Both hands should touch the wall just short of full extension. The eyes should keep looking down even after the hands touch the wall. The swimmer should get the feet on the wall as quickly as possible. The lead hand releases the wall quickly on contact and the knees drive toward the chest as quickly as possible. The athlete stays on line by going into and out of the same hole at the wall, and then pushes off the wall in the extended streamline position and breaks out into the stroke according to the rules governing these two strokes. The swimmer uses a strong first stroke to break out with momentum and then gets into the stroking rhythm.

FIGURE 15.4 Breaststroke and butterfly turn sequence.

The butterfly turn should include up to 15 meters of underwater streamline butterfly kicking before the breakout. The breaststroke turn allows a full underwater arm stroke and one underwater butterfly kick. The swimmer should set the elbows high on this full pullout (the hands should come in under the stomach) and shrug or tuck the shoulders close to the ears at the end of the underwater pullout. One butterfly kick is permitted after the full arm pull has begun. The swimmer should streamline with the stomach and buttocks tucked in tight, the legs and feet together, and the toes pointed back and should recover the hands close to the body with the elbows in at the side. This recovery may vary from swimmer to swimmer but must offer as little negative water resistance as possible. A breaststroke kick is completed upon the forward extension of the arms into position for the first surface breaststroke. This arm stroke starts with the head still slightly under the surface; the head breaks clear on that first arm stroke.

Turn drills relating to the butterfly and breaststroke can be broken down in the same way as freestyle and backstroke drills (see page 217). Hand paddles can be used in butterfly and breaststroke turning drills to emphasize speed in the approach and breakout strokes. The quickness necessary in placing the feet on the wall can be improved by timing from the hand touch at the wall to the placement of the feet on the wall.

FINISHES

A strong finish that uses proper technique is a small but important part of any swimming race (see figure 15.5). At the time of this writing, I had just returned from the NCAA Division I Men's Championship meet, and many of the races were extremely close. The 500 free was determined by a margin of 0.01 or a touch-out, and places beyond first were frequently determined by the finish. My own coaching experience in Australia, where I first saw the combined start, turn, and finish drills, taught me the importance of providing practice time for these skills. I learned to emphasize a complete finish to the wall in every race. I would constantly remind the swimmers to finish through the touch on the wall. This meant to continue the kick all the way into the wall and to keep the head down to it. Raising the head and ceasing to kick into the wall at the finish are common age-group mistakes that I have seen in events in the Olympic Games; these mistakes resulted in the silver and not the gold medal.

FIGURE 15.5 Proper finish technique.

Freestyle swimmers have a longer reach into the wall when they go to their side on the finish stroke. The swimmer who goes to their side brings the wall almost a foot closer at the finish than the swimmer who remains on the stomach. The first year that I incorporated finish drills into our practice sessions, I watched one of our club swimmers win the 100-yard freestyle in the state high school meet with a technique-perfect finish. He was behind the leader going into the final stroke but won the touch on the wall. That same season our high school-age club swimmers won an 800-yard free relay against Division I college teams in a regional meet when our fourth swimmer held on to edge the college team swimmer with a technique-perfect finish.

I interviewed the top butterfly swimmers at the Olympic Trials in 1992 for an American Swim Coaches' Association World Clinic. One of the athletes I interviewed, Pablo Morales, was second in both the 100-meter butterfly and 200-meter individual medley at the 1984 Olympic Games in Los Angeles. He also placed fourth in the 200-meter butterfly in that meet. In 1988, he failed to make the U.S. Olympic team by a narrow margin. He had been the world record holder but had never won an individual event at the Olympic Games. He retired for several years after 1988, and then came out of retirement about 1 year before the 1992 Olympic Trials. He qualified for the 100-meter butterfly in the Olympic Games of that year. I asked Pablo how he planned to swim that race in Barcelona given that he wasn't in the same condition as he had been previously. He said that he would have to have great butterfly technique through the race. He believed that he would have to be focused on the finish when he might begin to tire and wanted to shut out the thoughts of where his competition might be at that stage of the race. He wanted to be able to focus on where the finish wall would be and hold his head down in the best streamlined position for the final stroke and touch of the wall. He won the gold medal by 0.03 second over the second-place swimmer with a technique-perfect finish. All the swimmers were bunched up approaching the finish and less than 1 second separated all eight. I watched Pablo on television in that race and thought back to the interview and how he accomplished that win exactly as he had rehearsed it mentally in that interview.

One of the best start, turn, and finish practice sessions I have witnessed was conducted by Bill Sweetenham at the Australian Institute of Sport. The swimmers were lined up behind the starting blocks as deep as necessary to include all swimmers in the group. Each wave of swimmers started on a starting signal, sprinted 12 meters, and made a fast turn midpool with no wall. When all groups had started and reached the same point in the pool, each wave then made a 25-meter sprint and a fast wall turn. Finally, each wave swam into a fast finish before getting back on the blocks for several more rounds. Key points to focus on were given verbally at each of the three stages. Depending on the pool and the number of swimmers, a coach can run a similar pattern from both ends of the pool for the wall turn section of 25 yards or meters. Swimming in both directions for that segment can make better use of time.

CONCLUSION

Improvement depends in large part on the ability to measure. Coaches and swimmers must time turns, components, and start components. Practice follows the fundamentals of preparation, and much practice takes place in the steps that I have outlined. Every training session and every wall presents a practice opportunity. All of a swimmer's starts, turns, and finishes should be videotaped in practice and in competition. Seeing is believing, and constant attention to the basic skills used in each start, turn, and finish will help every swimmer achieve success.

PART FOUR

TRAINING FOR OPTIMAL PERFORMANCE

16

The Art of Training Sprinters

David Marsh and Bill Pilczuk

Over the past couple decades, training sprinters has become an art form. Unlike art, however, speed will never be subjective. You won't find it in the eye of the beholder; rather, it is proven in the hand of the coach holding a stopwatch. The swim coaches holding the fastest times blend ideas from other sports and incorporate strength and conditioning to create a powerful hybrid of sprinters. In this chapter, we discuss techniques that have been developed over the past 20 years and are used today to enhance the training of sprint swimmers. Specifically, we share how these ideas shaped the sprint team at Auburn University and empowered them to win 12 NCAA championships. Aside from developing numerous champions at all levels, these methods prove that creative training keeps the sport of swimming fresh and exciting for sprinters and empowers them to perform their best.

HARNESSING THE SPRINTER'S DRIVE

The secret of taking any swimmer to the next level often comes down to the relationship between coach and swimmer, especially when training true sprinters. Coaching them can be taxing. The sprint swimmer is often hot headed and questions a coach's technique and even the system. However, like working with a thoroughbred racehorse, it's critical to harness that feisty personality, not suppress it. It's what gives sprinters the edge in competition.

A great case in point is a group of young sprinters that was at Auburn University in 1990. They shared this fiery mentality but struggled to channel it into speed while they trained with middle-distance methods. Coach Marsh recognized that this group needed something different and assigned Mike Bottom to the challenge of harnessing this group's personality and drive as fuel for speed. Bottom achieved this by using methods that, at that time, couldn't be used with the entire team. Bottom used the methods with the sprinters only; using them with the middle-distance and distance groups would have produced negative results. The sprinters turned around in a single season by establishing pride in details: They maximized power, competed in practice and in the weight room, and demonstrated overall raw speed. With this mix of training, the unknown swimmers (coined by *Swimming World* as "no names to know names") went from obscurity to the NCAA championship finals and the national championships in 6 months.

CREATIVE COACHING

When Auburn University moved into a new 50-meter pool in 1994, the coaches used movable bulkheads to create different shorter, measurable distances, which allowed them to keep sprint training fresh and exciting. The smaller pool created an atmosphere of more concentrated practice, and the QuickStart from Colorado Time Systems and timing pads gave immediate feedback. The QuickStart system is capable of providing timing feedback on starts, turns, and relay exchanges. This pool was used for workouts that honed turns, promoted head-to-head racing, and highlighted details that in some cases needed complete overhauls.

For starts, the coaches established a 15-meter record board for all strokes, and swimmers with the best starts would try to demonstrate their ability by breaking the record in all strokes. The design of the pool allowed the coaches to set up this smaller pool quickly, and it became a cornerstone for making great sprinters. A freestyler held the breaststroke record for a time, which annoyed the breaststroke swimmers so much that they in turn worked on their start for days until they were able to reclaim the title.

An example set in this pool is as follows: 5 × 45 meters under 50-yard personal bests @ 6:00 with active recovery, usually a 200-meter swim–kick for lactate uptake. This set allowed for three turns and highlighted three crucial areas—start, turns and waves off turns (avoiding the surface turbulence being created), and finishes—all while promoting racing. The athletes were able to compartmentalize details, feel the errors, and fix them in a way that is not possible in a full-sized pool.

FULL-RECOVERY SWIMMING

Throughout the 1990s, as detail-oriented swimming (such as in the 15-meter pool described and group power swimming) was beginning to take form, another facet of swimming began to show results. Coaches were using full-recovery swimming to help clear the lactate in the body and allow the swimmers to have bouts of true goal speeds in workouts. In these sessions, a 3,000-yard workout could take as long as 3 hours to complete. This is still a mainstay in the sprint training programs of the former Auburn coaches and other coaches around the country.

Sprint swimming and sprint coaching offer some of the most exciting moments of our sport. However, if taken out of context and allowed to dominate the sport from the age-group level, it can significantly limit an athlete's career (see page 224). Several of the best sprinters in the world, such as Dara Torres, Ryk Neethling, and George Bovell, come from middle to distance training. It's easier to go down to sprinting from these distance foundations than up to distance at a mature age. This also holds true in the race training plan, where one trains up to the next event to swim down to the primary event.

IDENTIFYING AND TRAINING SPRINTERS

Too much focus on sprint training at a young age can hamper long-term opportunities for younger athletes. Kids see the 50 and 100 distances as exciting and glamorous and want to do what the popular athletes are doing. The swimmers then rarely want to swim the distance events, 400 individual medley (IM), or even the 200 IM, and potentially never truly find their best event.

How do you identify and train sprinters generically from a young age? The short answer: Give all the swimmers the skills and tools to develop into athletes. Ultimately, getting them in a position to do the sets that fully developed sprinters can complete is paramount to their success. Some of these skills include a balanced stroke (breathing and rotation), minimal resistance swimming, and a high catch position. At SwimMAC (my club in Charlotte, North Carolina), this philosophy applies to young swimmers. Age groups are trained with a middle-distance or IM mindset, and sprint-like qualities are developed through dryland training and occasional speed sets.

Age-group swimmers should perform more rotation in long-axis stroke technique to make it easier for them to feel, develop, and establish a total connection with their body and the sense of balance that is highly associated with learning an equal rotation. Going to flatter swimming earlier in a career (like many advanced sprinters) causes a younger athlete to rely more on isolated muscle groups and shoulder firing sequences that are less than ideal. The sooner you allow a flatter stroke that is one sided, the more you potentially limit career development because these swimmers become sprint oriented and lack the proprioceptive development of the whole body.

Most athletes in age-group programs are therefore correctly trained as middle-distance or distance swimmers, even if they ultimately become sprinters. This is beneficial for future training, but swimmers must take care to avoid habits that are not technically efficient as they sacrifice form for interval. Developing athletes with a stroke that can develop in the future is difficult. But spending time honing the flowing stroke and high-elbow catch of sprinters is essential during the early years.

Once an athlete has matured but is still training in an age-group or team dynamic, you may consider altering the individual's main set so that the swimmer can achieve more specified training markers while inside the larger group. This is a good way to help gear a middle-distance set toward the potential sprinter. For example, a set of 30 × 100 meters freestyle best average could be a sprint set if the athlete holds 35 strokes on the first 50 and uses legs and reduces stroke count on the second 50 while focusing on breathing and reducing time on odd 100s. They could then descend 1 to 5 on the even 100s to a prescribed time (such as 1:03, 1:01, 0:59, 0:57, 0:55 × 3 for an elite male).

TRAINING FOR GOAL RACE SPEED

A swimmer can achieve goal race speed in workouts by reducing the distances raced and increasing them over a season, or even by using full-body suits. The lift and streamlined effect that body suits produce can still help sprinters in workouts, even if the use of the suits is limited in competition. The suits can be useful in sessions of training at goal race speed and race feel. For example, Nick Brunelli and Cullen Jones at SwimMAC would wear the suits and attempt to break 20 seconds in the 50-yard freestyle from a push as many times as possible. (Repeating this speed would be near impossible without the suits because they allow the race feel to create the race speed on the repeated bouts.)

Example set: speed + lactate actual goal speed set with reduced distances

2 × (8 × 75; 1. Push 15 meters! 2. Push 20 meters! 3. Dive 20 meters! 4. Dive 25 meters! 5. Dive fins 25 meters! 6. Dive 35 meters! 7. Dive fins 35 meters! 8. Dive 25 meters!)

(2 × 100; 1. Dive 50 meters @ target speed 2. Easy)

Can alternate fins–no fins to increase lactate production; ! = race target speed

A Strong Kick Is Key

In the most effective sprint-type stroke, the pivot point is at the middle section of the body. Whether initiated from the arms or torso, a great stroke is locked in by a strong kick. The kick essentially becomes the platform of power for the whole stroke to obtain and generate the most torque possible on the catch. This pivot point of power enables the athlete to set up their high-elbow catch, keeps their balance pressed forward, and allows a relaxed narrow hallway recovery (one that is near the body line) in the freestyle.

Some sprinters are very inefficient kickers due to flexibility issues or training gaps. To be a good kicker, a swimmer must diligently and appropriately stretch the ankles and hip region. One of the best ways to improve the kick is to encourage the athlete to do extra sessions on their own. Often, injured swimmers that can only kick, such as Simon Burnett in 2004, come back to have great seasons due to the enhanced power of their kick. Simon broke his arm and kicked during the entire healing process. Upon returning to full training, he crushed the 200-yard freestyle record by having an amazing platform of power.

Swimmers who need help in kicking can do extra sessions of 2,000-yard kicking only. The first 1,000 meters would be a warm-up and the last 1,000 meters would include variable intensities. Additionally, swimmers need to spend time streamlining in body dolphin, which hones the techniques of the fifth stroke. Kicking can be done with snorkels or fins or in a 15-meter pool. Faster kicking makes faster swimmers.

When sprint kicking, the athlete needs to develop force from the abdominal muscles through the hip region by using the lower abs as the center of balance. This allows the foot to become the exit point of the whip kick rather than the initiation point. Kicking on the sides with body tension helps the athlete learn body line and makes it easier to stay extended and straight. The athlete should fully use both sides of the body to become comfortable on either side; equal body tension is key. Kickboards tend to arch the back and disconnect the pivot point from the legs. If a swimmer uses a kickboard, the head should be placed in the water to allow a natural spinal line and the connection of the pivot point.

For breaststroke, piston kicking helps the swimmer work on foot speed. It is a modified egg beater kick that involves pushing straight back on a wall or board to improve the catch of the water, with speed, on the breaststrokers foot. This movement is like sprinting on a bike.

We routinely give a reducing set of 100s (or sometimes modified to 200s) kick into championship meets as a way to ensure through measured testing that an athlete's kick is constantly at its best. The set is 8 × 100 meters @ 3:00 (or 4 × 200 @ 6:00) and is repeated weekly until 9 weeks out from the meet. Starting at 9 weeks out, one 100-meter length is removed weekly down to 1 × 100 1 to 2 weeks out from the meet. This reducing set allows sprinters to see weekly improvement and diminishing numbers and motivates them to improve their times as the championship meet approaches.

Adjusting the Stroke

Once the athlete develops a strong kick, a coach may need to change a sprinter's stroke to increase speed. Making changes to a stroke can be one of the hardest things a coach can do with an athlete. The athlete must believe in the coach before they are likely to change what they have done for most of their career. On our teams, we focus on changing a stroke to tie to a kick, opening the swimmer's stroke, increasing the catch, and finding a strong rotational balance. In short-axis strokes, we generally flatten the stroke to, in essence, skim along the surface.

Following are some trends in sprint swimming for all strokes today.

- In backstroke, a shallower catch that gets depth through the stroke
- In breaststroke, a flat stroke that produces undulation through the legs
- In fly, a straighter pull-through and flat back that replaces the hourglass pattern
- The use of kick sets following main sets for lactate uptake or buffering
- On long-axis strokes, submerged turns into the walls
- On short-axis turns, knees toward the chest and the chin down

In sprinting the current trend is toward a flatter stroke in all four strokes while increasing acceleration and strengthening the body line. In freestyle, opening the sprint swimmer's stroke helps eliminate the drag forces of the water rather than increase lift. Opening a freestyle stroke does not necessarily increase rotation, but by developing an open narrow hallway stroke the swimmer can obtain a better positional catch. This stroke type, such as straight-arm recovery or rainbow recovery (a rounded arm recovery in which the arm is almost straight and not fully bent), positions a swimmer to drive the shoulder and hand into a catch position, which allows the body to vault for the attack position and uses the advantage of momentum. This stroke was popularized in sprinting by Michael Klim, and many top sprinters use the new variation today.

Open Narrow Hallway

When viewing a freestyle swimmer from the front or rear, one can see that their recovery occurs in a narrow path (or a small corridor); this is in contrast to the traditional high-elbow stroke, in which the recovery sweeps around and outside the body line. A lateral recovery wastes less energy and helps set up a more over-the-top position. To practice a recovery in a narrow path, the swimmer can swim along the wall lane and recover the arms over the body; this forces the swimmer to recover the arm over the body to avoid arm contact with the wall.

Adjusting strokes for increased sprint speed can help get a swimmer to the next level. Fred Bousquet, Cullen Jones, and Josh Schneider are sprint athletes that made changes from a traditional high-elbow sweep recovery to the open sprint stroke. They learned the stroke within about 5 weeks of work and drills and perfected it over the course of a couple training cycles. Using the open narrow hallway stroke, Cullen set an American record in the 50-meter freestyle and Josh won the 2010 NCAA 50-yard freestyle title. In 2005, Fred won the NCAA 50-yard free swimming for Auburn University; he was the first swimmer under 19 seconds for the 50-yard free and under 21 seconds for the 50 meters. In 2009, Bousquet broke the world record for 50 meters while swimming for France.

Swimmer César Cielo, with help from coach Brett Hawke, has used this narrow and aggressive stroke to become a dominant sprinter freestyle. In addition, as seen on his underwater video from the 2008 Olympics, his head position was key to his body alignment and was better than anyone in the field. When César came to Auburn, his head position was well out of line. Like a majority of sprinters in free, fly, and breaststroke, the head position, especially when breathing, must stay on the spinal axis.

Some drills to help develop the sprint stroke are as follows.

- Straight arm over the top 3/4 delayed catch-up: This narrows the hallway and incorporates the shoulder roll into the catch.
- Free kick with fly arms and chin out sprinting for 12.5 to 15 meters: This helps the swimmer dig the blades in aggressively as the hands and forearms dig.
- Fly body dolphin: vertical fly off the bottom with power stroke at the top of the water.
- Snake drill: underwater fly recovery. The swimmer emphasizes the pull-through.
- Backstroke spin drill: This increases the tempo of backstroke and reduces the time setting the catch.
- Piston kicking: modified eggbeater kick, pushing straight back on a wall or on a board, increasing foot speed for breaststroke.

Enhancing a Sprinter's Talent

When training for sprint swimming, a coach must develop a pathway that enhances the swimmer's talent, emphasizes the feel of the stroke, and includes sessions that create a deep, concentrated practice of details and skill. This pathway can be divided into several levels including structure (the team, discipline, and organization), training (set structures, strength training, and competitive atmosphere), and coaching (goal setting, belief, and lifestyle allowances). Taking all of this into consideration allows a coach to understand when and how much to push the athletes to get the most out of the sessions. A good rule of thumb for increasing training with sprint swimmers is 1 day on, 1 day off, depending on the athlete and the energy system being trained in the workout.

The actual macrocycle and microcycle set up during the year depends on the coach's overall goal for the swimmer. The coach can place the key sets of the week anywhere in the schedule as long as enough recovery time is allotted so that the next session doesn't empty the bank. Table 16.1 gives an example of a general midseason sprint training microcycle.

Main sets for midseason microcycle

1. 2 × (2 × 50 @ 0:60 200 pace, 1 × 50 kilometers! @ 1:30, 2 × 50 pace, 1 × 100 kilometers!, 2 × 50 pace, 1 × 200 kilometers!); rd2 only 1 × 50 pace

2. Power session, 4 × 15 meters @ 35, 4 × 25, 2 × 25, 1 × 15, 1 × 25, 4 × 15 meters mix strokes

3. 8 × 100 25-kilometer 75s, kick is cycled through positions in the 100; goal: ~10 seconds of personal bests 100

4. 3 × 100 kilometers @ 3:00, 3 × 50 kilometers @ 1:30, 2 × 100 kilometers, 2 × 50 kilometers, 1 × 100 kilometers, 1 × 50 kilometers

5. Descending interval 50s starting at 0:55 reducing by 1 second. Start with kick, on miss, swim backstroke, on miss finish as far as possible freestyle.

TABLE 16.1   Example of Midseason Microcycle

Monday	Tuesday	Wednesday	Thursday	Friday	Saturday	Sunday
Mix kick pull swim	Power morning Set 2	Off	IM aerobic and speed kick Set 4 Kick	Power morning Set 2 variation	Mixed $\dot{V}O_2$ and speed set Set 6	Off
Technique Mix Set 1	Speed and kick Set 3	Active recovery	Aerobic and flow Set 5	45 min team stretch and 1 hour swim	Off	Off Massage Stretch

6. 4 × 75 push sprint @ 3:00, easy swim, 10 × 100 @ 2:00 fins under 0:50 DPS, easy swim, 6 × 50 cords

    1. eliminate resistance

    2. faster than cord

    3. technical speed, easy swim

    4. 4 × runner

! = race target speed; DPS = distance per stroke

Dryland and Strength Training

A sprint program is only as good as its dryland and weights components. An athlete can start weight training when it will not interfere with the athlete's development and growth, but dryland training can start at almost any age. A dryland program should create a solid, rigid core that is purposefully elongated at all times; this is necessary in sprint swimming. Movements outside the body line cost the most in the sprint events, and up to four times resistance can be seen as speeds in the water increase. Therefore, a strong core and rigid line are fundamental to speed.

At Auburn University, the strength program designed by Brian "PK" Karkoska has been instrumental in getting the sprint program to its highest level. A good strength coach that can incorporate new ideas while finding challenging ways to motivate the swimmers is a bonus to any team. Karkoska is always at the cutting edge of performance, from the gym to the water. The workouts tend to change season by season as things are updated and made more swimming specific. In the past, a typical sprinter's power morning involved 60 minutes of strength, power, or endurance work administered by the strength coaches; a 5-minute transition period; a 5-minute water warm-up; and a 20-minute power water session that often involved Karkoska. These water power session included power racks, RocketTowers, T-shirts, fins, paddles, or cords. The RocketTower is a new tool that is similar to the power rack but offers resistance and towing capabilities; the buckets on the end of the RocketTower can be filled with up to 500 pounds (226.8 kg) of water. All the workouts are designed to provide bouts of speed or power for 5 to 10 seconds for a total of about 24 efforts.

Example Power Session 1

    1. 4 × 20m! @ 35 r:60 (wear all equipment)

    2. 4 × 15m! change direction midpool @ 35 r:60 (no paddles)

    3. 3 × power rack at protocol time/tempo @ 0:60 (no fins)

    4. 4 × scrunch scull 12.5 yards (no paddles; knees tucked to vertical; chest and shins parallel to surface [Dr. Salo])

    5. 4 × 25 yards no breath! @ 0:40 r:60 (only fins and paddles)

    6. 4 × 15m! @ 0:40 (no equipment)

Example Power Session 2

1. 4 × broken 50 meters: swim through 15 meters timed r:20 while backing up to 10 meters, full speed through 15 meters through 25 meters r:20 while backing up to 20 meters, full speed through 25 meters through 35 meters, r:20 while backing up to 30 meters, full speed through 35 meters to finish (fins, paddles, T-shirts)
2. Overall time given (T-shirts)
3. 3 × 50 meters @ 1:30 in between even rounds breathing 2, 1, 0 × 50 (fins and paddles)
4. 3 × 25 yards @ 1:30 tubing (odd rounds: no equipment) against/with
   1. eliminate resistance
   2. full-over speed
   3. ideal race efficiency

In the power sessions that are incorporated with the weight room, all efforts are race or race feel and each effort is performed at goal pace or faster than goal pace speed; the athlete always holds form. If done properly, the power session will have some physical or emotional transfer from the weight room to the water. Incorporating races and challenges into the session also builds teams and bolsters individuals.

Dryland and strength training can also help develop or increase the athleticism, or fight, in a swimmer. If a swimmer appears too awkward or has poor body awareness, teaching them the basics of other sports such as gymnastics, ballet, or basketball as part of dryland can help them learn coordination, improve jumping, or improve a weakness in their swimming technique. If a swimmer appears to be timid, learning sports that require discipline and confrontation such as tae kwon do, wrestling, or judo can help increase their toughness in workouts or races. At Auburn, the system of the strength coach creates individual strength and empowers the athlete through teamwork and discipline. In Charlotte, we assess the needs of individual athletes and build each athlete's personal program around those needs.

Short-Distance Racing

Regardless of the type of training session in the water, a top-level sprinter does some sort of short-race speed during every session, usually over a distance of approximately 12.5 yards or 15 meters or sometimes just three to four cycles of the stroke. At this distance, swimmers can hold race speed or faster than race speed with technical form. This is an important feel that sprinters should never lose at any time in a cycle. A good mix of fin work, paddles, cords, and three-man drafting sets (two swimmers with fins on either side of a swimmer without fins in the same lane) can also produce desired goal speeds. If done properly, these bouts of speed should not deplete significant glycogen stores while giving that sense of speed and feel.

Hypoxic Training

Another type of training typically done for our sprinters is hypoxic training. Hypoxic is a term that coaches and athletes use to denote holding one's breath to mimic the effects felt off walls and toward the end of a race. It is a bit of a misnomer, but using extended breathing patterns and swimming distances without breathing reminds athletes how to maintain a disciplined stroke at crucial times in a race. A hypoxic set may also create an increased heart rate in sets by limiting the amount of available oxygen to muscles. An example set of 8 × 100 yards @ 1:40, allowing breathing of 1, 2, 2, 1 × 25 or 1, 2, 2, 0 × 25 teaches the advanced sprinter how to time breaths and manage breathing and how much oxygen they can still function without instead of relying on the feel of demand.

> *Caution*   Many athletes use this process as an area for competition and try to outdo one another. Swimmers can pass out while attempting no-breath distances due to the increased carbon dioxide in the blood. Always practice this training with caution.

USING CHALLENGES TO DEVELOP A MENTAL EDGE

Challenging sprinters against one another or against their own abilities throughout the season gives them a mental edge in competition. Running an elimination or round robin tournament with the sprinters at various distances and disciplines (including kicking) allows swimmers with different abilities or specialties to shine. A series could include the following:

7 × 15 meters sprint with 8 swimmers, 1 eliminated each round @ 2:00

6 × 50 meters sprint best average, add up for all 6 efforts

5 × (2 × 25 r:15) @ full recovery, kicking—match-ups race each round of 25s kick

10 × 100 yards @ 2:00 (25 under 10.0 seconds male, 11.0 female; 50 easy, 25 no breath perfect finish—best average first 25 for overall winner)

Often, a coach can create challenges from what is available around the pool. For example, to overcome leg dropping and lackluster jumps in starts, we challenged sprinters at Auburn to start off a 1-meter dry diving board. This board was located about 4 feet (1.2 m) from the ledge of the pool and was the perfect height for diving with a proper angle into the water. A swimmer using a perfect start with good form and a solid jump would clear the concrete and execute a perfect dive. This was mentally challenging and scary for the weaker jumpers and leg droppers. For safety, we placed a mat on top of the concrete.

Details Matter

In both freestyle and butterfly, the highest point of resistance is created when a swimmer takes a breath outside the body line. This creates increased drag either at the head or by repositioning the hips. Many sprinters reduce this potential problem by limiting their breaths to every three in butterfly or to no breath in the 50-meter events. However, an efficient breather tends to catch a breath inside the body line and does not interrupt speed progression. To take an efficient breath, the swimmer breathes low to the water and the head remains on the spinal axis.

In a finish, the speed created throughout the race needs to be maximized into the wall. As the swimmer approaches the wall, they will tend to raise the head, lower the hips, or both due to the approaching wall or fatigue. For an accelerated finish, swimmers should remain swimming downhill into the wall while touching a point 6 inches (15.2 cm) beyond the wall. Swimmers should learn to spot the wall about 5 meters out by using either the 5-meter mark or flags for making adjustments or the 2-meter mark or cross T as they approach. A swimmer should practice any adjustments at these points to always finish on a full-extension stroke with high velocity. During the final stroke the swimmer should maintain maximum pressure through the entire stroke, maintain a streamlined body position or dolphin kick, and allow for full extension of the finishing arm and hand.

The hydroline goggle is an excellent tool for helping swimmers make this adjustment. The goggle allows the head to remain low while the swimmer looks forward. A good way to practice finishes is to set up imaginary walls at midpool using cones as markers and a rubber cord extended across the ropes as a wall. A swimmer can see and feel any deviation in speed more easily if a wall is not present to stop them.

Quick Starts

In 1994, during the first sessions in the 15-meter pool at Auburn University, Dean Hutchinson (1994 Goodwill Games and Auburn University captain) and I (Bill Pilczuk, 1998 world champion) honed our starts by racing against each other for hours on the timing system. We decided that this was the best way to become fast because during the start a swimmer achieves the fastest speed of an entire race while using the least effort. We realized that reaction time and entry time were important, but being able to produce and hold the most velocity possible in the air and then holding this through the breakout gave us our advantage. Using the track start, we were able to pull on the blocks so hard that our toes would bleed with the force and need to be taped.

In order to develop this fast track start, an athlete needs to hone three crucial areas:

1. flexibility,
2. line of attack, and
3. first-stroke speed.

The track start has the distinct advantage of being able to throw the center of gravity forward; a swimmer can increase their total velocity by pulling on the front of the blocks and driving against the back leg. This pull–push motion helps the athlete's hips to stay low and allows the athlete to have minimal vertical direction on the start and to jump straight off the front of the blocks. Hutchinson and others were known to pull so hard against the back foot that blocks that were not properly bolted down would rip off the hinges. Today, with the wedge block (a start platform raised on the back side that allows swimmers using the track start to get more thrust out of their back leg), the swimmer should quickly be able to create directional power right into their straight-line entry.

To position on the blocks for maximum speed with minimal effort, a swimmer must consider increasing the flexibility of the hips, legs, and back. A loose muscle tends to react faster and stronger than a tight muscle. An athlete will not be able to develop power or velocity if bending over causes undue tension on the body. In order for an athlete to pull with maximal force through the hips and remain on a low trajectory off the block, these muscles must work together without tightness changing an ideal position.

A large amount of energy is lost in vertical directions when an athlete enters the water at an angle that continually changes or is too deep. A good angle of attack is one that allows the speed of entry to continue horizontally and lifts the athlete toward or along the surface at close to entry speed. One can visualize this horizontal speed by throwing a stick into the pool at different angles and watching as it accelerates or stalls.

Holding the Speed Off the Blocks and Walls

Holding the speed created off the blocks and walls, and travelling at a faster than swimming speed at the breakout, is crucial. Holding this speed does not require more energy from the athlete, but it does require spatial awareness. One can achieve this awareness for breaking out by diving underwater, flykicking to the surface into a breakout, and feeling for the best depth to begin the first stroke. An athlete can get about five breakouts by repeating the sequence as many times as possible in a 25-yard course. This drill helps the athlete develop the feel for when and how deep to break out.

Athletes can also develop speed through walking or running the side of the pool and using a competition dive that has a higher rate of speed than a starting block. Any subtle variation in entry position, being outside streamline, or beginning a breakout too soon or late will cause an immediate decrease in acceleration that the athlete can sense. Generally, the athlete holds the dive through the breakout into three cycles of sprint swimming without decelerating.

AVOIDING INJURIES

Sprinting imposes a great deal of stress on the body, especially the shoulders, lower back, and hip flexors. One of the most common injuries is to the rotator cuff because the rotator cuff controls movement of the arms over the shoulders. This position is one of vulnerability because the humerus is virtually freefloating and generally controlled by these small muscles in this position. In order to help prevent imbalances that occur in training, which may lead to injuries, swimmers should use a regimen of prehabilitation at the beginning and end of each session. These exercises incorporate tubing or very light weights and strengthen internal and external rotators. An athlete with a swimming-related injury should seek a program recommended by a physical therapist.

CONCLUSION

Sprinting uses the best of an athlete's total ability and combines hard work with God-given talent, learned technique, and unwavering passion to win. What separates sprinters from other swimmers? Raw power, strength, explosiveness, and flexibility blended with proper stroke technique, outstanding starts, quick turns, and smart finishes. Add creative coaching methods and the skill to harness sprinters' unique personalities and you'll separate the champions from those who are just sprinters.

Middle-Distance Training for All Strokes

Jon Urbanchek

In swimming, middle distance refers to events lasting from about 2 to 4 minutes in duration. These events are 200 yards or 200 meters to 400 meters or 500 yards and most often include the 200 to 400 freestyle events, the individual medleys, and the 200 backstroke and butterfly.

This tendency to lean toward middle-distance events is the most common in the adult population. Physiologically speaking, middle-distance swimmers possess a combination of fast-twitch muscle fibers (anaerobic) for speed and slow-twitch muscle fibers (aerobic) for the endurance components for these events. Two types of mid-distance swimmers exist. One group comprises the anaerobic type—with more speed—who move up to the 200 to 400 (e.g., Ian Thorpe and Michael Phelps). The other group comprises aerobic distance swimmers who move down to the shorter distance events (e.g., Grant Hackett, Peter Vanderkaay, Ous Mellouli, and Erik Vendt). Those swimmers who move up from the 100 distance increase the aerobic level of their training, and those who move down from the distance events experience more anaerobic levels than before.

TRAINING SYSTEMS USED AT THE UNIVERSITY OF MICHIGAN

Training is broken into the usage of two energy systems: anaerobic and aerobic. The anaerobic energy system is characterized by lack of air, and the buildup of lactic acid is a concern. The aerobic energy system is characterized with air. Training of the anaerobic energy system is limited by the swimmer's ability to withstand the lactate buildup, whereas in low-level aerobic training the swimmer meets his or her oxygen requirements by breathing.

The anaerobic threshold is the transition point between aerobic and anaerobic work. This threshold is not well defined and is difficult to pinpoint accurately in swimming velocity. When setting up the program at the University of Michigan, we spent valuable time finding the anaerobic threshold for each swimmer. A coach should make the threshold pace as accurate as possible because the use of the energy system is based on the anaerobic threshold. To determine anaerobic threshold we used a noninvasive, no-blood method that included various swimming distances. In the past, one would determine lactate levels by drawing blood and using a lactate analyzer. This was time consuming, presented a risk of infection, and required specialization because the results had to be read and analyzed. The methods that we used at Michigan were much simpler and accurate. For this purpose, the following lists the various tests that one can use to determine threshold paces.

Threshold Test Sets

1. **Continuous steady-state swim, 20 to 30 minutes:** This test is the most optimal for middle-distance swimmers.
2. **Blood lactate test/step test:** This test is optimal for anaerobic swimmers (50 to 100 distances).
3. **Interval test sets, 2,000 to 3,000 meters:** 10×200 or 10×300 average, with 20- to 30-second rest intervals.
4. **All-out 400-meter or 500-yard effort:** The 90% effort should result in a heart rate of 160 to 175 beats per minute and the training paces determined from the average 100 time during the swim.

The aerobic training zones are separated by degree of intensity. The following categories of aerobic training progress from basic, low intensity to aerobic threshold and beyond to $\dot{V}O_2$max. I use a chart to indicate the level of intensity, moving from EN-1 and 1+ to EN-2 and 2+ to EN-3. This helps the swimmers understand the changes in their body that may occur in progressive intensities.

EN-1 (basic aerobic training): This training is about 5% below the anaerobic threshold pace. It is low intensity and the heart rate is approximately 120 to 140. The rest interval is short (10 to 20 seconds).

EN-1+: This is subthreshold training that is a little more intense than the EN-1 training pace. The heart rates should be between 140 and 150. The rest interval is short (10 to 15 seconds).

EN-2 (anaerobic threshold training): The heart rate should be between 150 and 170. The rest interval is short (10 to 15 seconds) and the training set should be 40 to 60 minutes long. This is the optimal intensity for improvement.

EN-2+: This is a little faster than the EN-2 training pace. The heart rate should be between 160 and 180. The rest interval is 15 to 30 seconds and the training set should be 20 to 40 minutes long.

EN-3 (maximum $\dot{V}O_2$max training): This is well above threshold. The heart rate should be between 180 and 190. The rest interval can be 30 seconds to 1 minute 30 seconds. This is high intensity, and lactate tolerance and lactate buffering take place. Training sets should be 1,500 to 2,000.

We found that the most accurate threshold paces were the results of a 3,000-yard or meter swim (what I call a "real T-30"). Table 17.1 shows the real T-30 test results.

From the results of the 3,000 test shown in table 17.1, we created the aerobic training categories. The intensity level increases as one moves from low-aerobic work toward high-aerobic work. Along with the swimming speed, we established a heart rate zone that corresponds with the intensity of the effort. These increasing efforts are reflected in increased heart rates from EN-1 through EN-3.

Aerobic and Threshold Energy Systems

Tables 17.2 through 17.4 (starting on page 238) list average 100-yard times of the T-30 test. The T-30 test is a continuous 30-minute swim at the fastest steady pace that the swimmer can maintain throughout the entire swim. The swimmer or coach then determines the average time for each 100 yards or meters; this is the T-30 result. The T-30 result for each 100 is then determined. The 3,000 continuous swim above is more preferred, but both are similar in the method used to determine the average 100 time throughout the test swim.

TABLE 17.1 3,000 Test (Real T-30)*

Name	Stroke	3,000 time	T-30 pace	Paces	50	100	150	200	300	400	500
XYZ	Freestyle	28:22.0	0:56.7	EN-1	0:26.5	0:57.2	1:26.5	1:55.9	2:54.9	3:54.0	4:53.2
				EN-1+	0:25.6	0:55.3	1:24.8	1:54.4	2:52.7	3:51.7	4:52.6
				EN-2	0:25.2	0:54.4	1:22.2	1:50.2	2:46.2	3:42.4	4:38.6
				EN-2+	0:24.3	0:52.5	1:20.6	1:48.7	2:44.0	3:40.1	4:36.0
				EN-3	0:23.4	0:50.7	1:17.7	1:44.8	2:38.2	3:32.2	4:28.1
ABC	Freestyle	28:45.0	0:57.5	EN-1	0:26.9	0:57.9	1:27.7	1:57.5	2:57.3	3:57.2	4:57.2
				EN-1+	0:25.9	0:56.1	1:26.0	1:56.0	2:55.0	3:54.8	4:56.6
				EN-2	0:25.5	0:55.1	1:23.3	1:51.7	2:48.4	3:45.4	4:42.3
				EN-2+	0:24.6	0:53.2	1:21.7	1:50.1	2:46.2	3:43.1	4:39.7
				EN-3	0:23.8	0:51.4	1:18.8	1:46.2	2:40.4	3:35.1	4:31.7
PQR	Freestyle	28:50.0	0:57.7	EN-1	0:26.9	0:58.1	1:27.9	1:57.8	2:57.8	3:57.9	4:58.0
				EN-1+	0:26.0	0:56.2	1:26.2	1:56.3	2:55.5	3:55.5	4:57.5
				EN-2	0:25.6	0:55.3	1:23.6	1:52.0	2:48.9	3:46.1	4:43.1
				EN-2+	0:24.7	0:53.4	1:21.9	1:50.5	2:46.7	3:43.7	4:40.5
				EN-3	0:23.8	0:51.5	1:19.0	1:46.6	2:40.8	3:35.7	4:32.5

* A straight 30-minute swim can be substituted, averaging by 100s.

Basic Aerobic Training: EN-1   Table 17.2 lists the suggested training paces to attain EN-1 and 1+ for various repeat distances based on the T-30 test.

TABLE 17.2   Endurance Training Paces Based on T-30 Test and Suggested Training Paces to Attain EN-1 and 1+

Subthreshold training paces: EN-1 to EN-1+ and a heart rate of 120 to 150; 0:10 to 0:15 rest interval

T-30 average pace/100	50s	75s	100s	125s	150s	175s	200s	250s	300s	400s	500s	550s
0:55.0	0:25.7	0:40.4	0:55.5	1:09.7	1:23.9	1:38.1	1:52.4	2:21.0	2:49.6	3:46.9	4:44.3	5:13.0
0:56.0	0:26.2	0:41.1	0:56.5	1:10.9	1:25.4	1:39.9	1:54.4	2:23.5	2:52.7	3:51.0	4:49.4	5:18.7
0:57.0	0:26.6	0:41.9	0:57.5	1:12.2	1:26.9	1:41.7	1:56.5	2:26.1	2:55.7	3:55.2	4:54.5	5:24.3
0:58.0	0:27.1	0:42.6	0:58.5	1:13.5	1:28.5	1:43.5	1:58.5	2:28.7	2:58.8	3:59.3	4:59.8	5:30.0
0:59.0	0:27.6	0:43.3	0:59.5	1:14.7	1:30.0	1:45.3	2:00.5	2:31.2	3:01.9	4:03.4	5:04.9	5:35.7
1:00.0	0:28.0	0:44.1	1:00.5	1:16.0	1:31.5	1:47.1	2:02.6	2:33.8	3:05.0	4:07.5	5:10.1	5:41.4
1:01.0	0:28.5	0:44.8	1:01.5	1:17.2	1:33.0	1:48.8	2:04.6	2:36.4	3:08.1	4:11.7	5:15.3	4:47.1
1:02.0	0:29.0	0:45.5	1:02.5	1:18.5	1:34.6	1:50.6	2:06.7	2:38.9	3:11.2	4:15.8	5:20.4	5:52.8
1:03.0	0:29.4	0:46.3	1:03.5	1:19.8	1:36.1	1:52.4	2:08.7	2:41.5	3:14.2	4:19.9	5:25.6	5:58.5
1:04.0	0:29.9	0:47.0	1:04.5	1:21.0	1:37.6	1:54.2	2:10.8	2:44.0	3:17.3	4:24.0	5:30.8	6:04.2
1:05.0	0:30.4	0:47.7	1:05.5	1:22.3	1:39.1	1:56.0	2:12.8	2:46.6	3:20.4	4:28.2	5:35.9	6:09.9
1:06.0	0:30.8	0:48.5	1:06.5	1:23.6	1:40.7	1:57.8	2:14.8	2:49.2	3:23.5	4:32.3	5:41.1	6:15.6
1:07.0	0:31.3	0:49.2	1:07.6	1:24.8	1:42.2	1:59.5	2:16.9	2:51.7	3:26.6	4:36.4	5:46.3	6:21.3
1:08.0	0:31.8	0:49.9	1:08.6	1:26.1	1:43.7	2:01.3	2:18.9	2:54.3	3:29.7	4:40.5	5:51.4	6:26.9
1:09.0	0:32.2	0:50.7	1:09.6	1:27.4	1:45.2	2:03.1	2:21.0	2:56.9	3:32.7	4:44.7	5:56.6	6:32.6
1:10.0	0:32.7	0:51.4	1:10.6	1:28.6	1:46.8	2:04.9	2:23.0	2:59.4	3:35.8	4:48.8	6:01.8	6:38.3
1:11.0	0:33.2	0:52.1	1:11.6	1:29.9	1:48.3	2:06.7	2:25.1	3:02.0	3:38.9	4:52.9	6:07.0	6:44.0

Anaerobic Threshold Training: EN-2 Table 17.3 lists the suggested training paces to attain anaerobic threshold, EN-2 and 2+, for various repeat distances based on the T-30 test.

TABLE 17.3 Endurance Training Paces Based on T-30 Test and Suggested Training Paces to Attain EN-2 and 2+

Anaerobic threshold training paces: EN-2 to EN-2+ and a heart rate of 150 to 180; 0:10 to 0:15 rest interval

T-30 average pace/100	50s	75s	100s	125s	150s	175s	200s	250s	300s	400s	500s	550s
0:55.0	0:24.4	0:38.4	0:52.7	1:06.2	1:19.7	1:33.2	1:46.8	2:13.9	2:41.1	3:35.6	4:30.0	4:57.3
0:56.0	0:24.9	0:39.1	0:53.6	1:07.4	1:21.1	1:34.9	1:48.7	2:16.4	2:44.0	3:39.5	4:35.0	5:02.7
0:57.0	0:25.3	0:39.8	0:54.6	1:08.6	1:22.6	1:36.6	1:50.6	2:18.8	2:47.0	3:43.4	4:39.9	5:08.1
0:58.0	0:25.7	0:40.5	0:55.6	1:09.8	1:24.0	1:38.3	1:52.6	2:21.2	2:49.9	3:47.3	4:44.8	5:13.5
0:59.0	0:26.2	0:41.2	0:56.5	1:11.0	1:25.5	1:40.0	1:54.5	2:23.7	2:52.8	3:51.2	4:49.7	5:18.9
1:00.0	0:26.6	0:41.9	0:57.5	1:12.2	1:26.9	1:41.7	1:56.5	2:26.1	2:55.7	3:55.2	4:54.6	5:24.3
1:01.0	0:27.1	0:42.5	0:58.4	1:13.4	1:28.4	1:43.4	1:58.4	2:28.5	2:58.7	3:59.1	4:59.5	5:29.8
1:02.0	0:27.5	0:43.2	0:59.4	1:14.6	1:29.8	1:45.1	2:00.3	2:31.0	3:01.6	4:03.0	5:04.4	5:35.2
1:03.0	0:28.0	0:43.9	1:00.3	1:15.8	1:31.3	1:46.8	2:02.3	2:33.4	3:04.5	4:06.9	5:09.3	5:40.6
1:04.0	0:28.4	0:44.6	1:01.3	1:17.0	1:32.7	1:48.5	2:04.2	2:35.8	3:07.5	4:10.8	5:14.2	5:46.0
1:05.0	0:28.9	0:45.3	1:02.3	1:18.2	1:34.2	1:50.2	2:06.2	2:38.3	3:10.4	4:14.7	5:19.1	5:51.4
1:06.0	0:29.3	0:46.0	1:03.2	1:19.4	1:35.6	1:51.9	2:08.1	2:40.7	3:13.3	4:18.7	5:24.1	5:56.8
1:07.0	0:29.7	0:46.7	1:04.2	1:20.6	1:37.1	1:53.6	2:10.0	2:43.1	3:16.3	4:22.6	5:29.0	6:02.2
1:08.0	0:30.2	0:47.4	1:05.1	1:21.8	1:38.5	1:55.3	2:12.0	2:45.6	3:19.2	4:26.5	5:33.9	6:07.6
1:09.0	0:30.6	0:48.1	1:06.1	1:23.0	1:40.0	1:57.0	2:13.9	2:48.0	3:22.1	4:30.4	5:38.8	6:13.0
1:10.0	0:31.1	0:48.8	1:07.1	1:24.2	1:41.4	1:58.7	2:15.9	2:50.5	3:25.0	4:34.3	5:43.7	6:18.4

Maximum V̇O₂max Training: EN-3 Table 17.4 lists the suggested training paces to attain maximum V̇O₂max, EN-3, for various repeat distances based on the T-30 test. The heart rate should be between 180 and 190, and the pace should be 7% faster than the threshold pace. Once the aerobic base and threshold levels are well established, this V̇O₂max training should become the most important part of race preparation. For the 200 to 400 events, rest intervals should be 30 seconds to 1 minute 30 seconds—enough rest to enable the swimmer to hold race pace or faster. Lactate levels are near maximum, and tolerance and buffering take place. A swimmer should do this type of training twice per week in distances of 50 to 200 yards or meters.

TABLE 17.4 Endurance Training Paces Based on T-30 Test and Suggested Training Paces to Attain V̇O₂max

V̇O₂max training paces: EN-3 and a heart rate of 180 to 190; 0:30 to 1:30 rest interval

T-30 average pace/100	50s	75s	100s	125s	150s	175s	200s	250s	300s	400s	500s	550s
0:55.0	0:22.7	0:36.1	0:49.1	1:02.2	1:15.3	1:28.5	1:41.6	2:07.4	2:33.4	3:25.8	4:19.9	4:46.3
0:56.0	0:23.1	0:36.7	0:50.0	1:03.4	1:16.7	1:30.1	1:43.4	2:09.7	2:36.1	3:29.5	4:24.6	4:51.5
0:57.0	0:23.5	0:37.4	0:50.9	1:04.5	1:18.1	1:31.7	1:45.3	2:12.0	2:38.9	3:33.2	4:29.3	4:56.7
0:58.0	0:23.9	0:38.1	0:51.8	1:05.6	1:19.4	1:33.3	1:47.1	2:14.4	2:41.7	3:37.0	4:34.1	5:01.9
0:59.0	0:24.4	0:38.7	0:52.7	1:06.7	1:20.8	1:34.9	1:49.0	2:16.7	2:44.5	3:40.7	4:38.8	5:07.1
1:00.0	0:24.8	0:39.4	0:53.6	1:07.9	1:22.2	1:36.5	1:50.8	2:19.0	2:47.3	3:44.5	4:43.5	5:12.3
1:01.0	0:25.2	0:40.0	0:54.5	1:09.0	1:23.6	1:38.1	1:52.7	2:21.3	2:50.1	3:48.2	4:48.2	5:17.5
1:02.0	0:25.6	0:40.7	0:55.4	1:10.1	1:24.9	1:39.7	1:54.5	2:23.6	2:52.9	3:52.0	4:53.0	5:22.7
1:03.0	0:26.0	0:41.3	0:56.3	1:11.3	1:26.3	1:41.3	1:56.4	2:25.9	2:55.7	3:55.7	4:57.7	5:28.0
1:04.0	0:26.4	0:42.0	0:57.2	1:12.4	1:27.7	1:43.0	1:58.2	2:28.3	2:58.5	3:59.4	5:02.4	5:33.2
1:05.0	0:26.8	0:42.6	0:58.1	1:13.5	1:29.0	1:44.6	2:00.1	2:30.6	3:01.2	4:03.2	5:07.1	5:38.4
1:06.0	0:27.3	0:43.3	0:59.0	1:14.7	1:30.4	1:46.2	2:01.9	2:32.9	3:04.0	4:06.9	5:11.9	5:43.6
1:07.0	0:27.7	0:44.0	0:59.9	1:15.8	1:31.8	1:47.8	2:03.8	2:35.2	3:06.8	4:10.7	5:16.6	5:48.8
1:08.0	0:28.1	0:44.6	1:00.8	1:16.9	1:33.1	1:49.4	2:05.6	2:37.5	3:09.6	4:14.4	5:21.3	5:54.0
1:09.0	0:28.5	0:45.3	1:01.7	1:18.1	1:34.5	1:51.0	2:07.5	2:39.8	3:12.4	4:18.1	5:26.0	5:59.2
1:10.0	0:28.9	0:45.9	1:02.5	1:19.2	1:35.9	1:52.6	2:09.3	2:42.2	3:15.2	4:21.9	5:30.8	6:04.4

See table 17.5 for a test that serves as an alternative to the 3,000 continuous swim test. This test is for a suggested number of repeat swims of a shorter distance, in this case 10 × 300 with a rest interval of 20 to 30 seconds.

To administer this test, record all times and take the average time of all 10 efforts. In this sample the average time is 2:45.00. Place this 300 time of 2:45.00 in the 300 column and it yields 56.3 for a T-30 pace for athlete XYZ. The interval set is ideal for those swimmers who cannot sustain a continuous 3,000 swim. The correlation coefficient between the two tests is .98.

TABLE 17.5 300 Average Interval Test

10 × 300; 0:20 to 0:30 rest intervals

Name	Stroke	300 time	T-30 pace	Paces	50	100	150	200	300	400	500
XYZ	Freestyle	2:45.0	0:56.3	EN-1	0:26.3	0:56.8	1:25.9	1:55.1	2:53.7	3:52.4	4:51.1
				EN-1+	0:25.4	0:54.9	1:24.2	1:53.6	2:51.5	3:50.0	4:50.6
				EN-2	0:25.0	0:54.0	1:21.6	1:49.4	2:45.0	3:40.8	4:36.6
				EN-2+	0:24.1	0:52.2	1:20.0	1:47.9	2:42.8	3:38.6	4:34.1
				EN-3	0:23.3	0:50.3	1:17.2	1:44.1	2:37.1	3:30.7	4:26.2
ABC	Freestyle	2:47.0	0:57.0	EN-1	0:26.6	0:57.5	1:26.9	1:56.5	2:55.8	3:55.2	4:54.7
				EN-1+	0:25.7	0:55.6	1:25.2	1:55.0	2:53.6	3:52.8	3:54.1
				EN-2	0:25.3	0:54.6	1:22.6	1:50.7	2:47.0	3:43.5	4:39.9
				EN-2+	0:24.4	0:52.8	1:21.0	1:49.2	2:44.8	3:41.2	4:37.4
				EN-3	0:23.6	0:50.9	1:18.1	1:45.3	2:39.0	3:33.3	4:29.4
PQR	Freestyle	2:47.5	0:57.2	EN-1	0:26.7	0:57.6	1:27.2	1:56.8	2:56.3	3:55.9	4:55.6
				EN-1+	0:25.8	0:55.8	1:25.5	1:55.3	2:54.1	3:53.5	4:55.0
				EN-2	0:25.4	0:54.8	1:22.9	1:51.0	2:47.5	3:44.2	4:40.8
				EN-2+	0:24.5	0:53.0	1:21.2	1:49.5	2:45.3	3:41.9	4:38.2
				EN-3	0:23.6	0:51.1	1:18.3	1:45.7	2:39.5	3:33.9	4:30.2

Anaerobic Energy Systems

This training improves speed over a 100 race. It also subjects the swimmer to higher lactate levels in training that can carry over to more sustained speed in the 200s and 400 or 500s. This training is used less often than the previous endurance training paces because of the intensity levels involved. During this type of training, we use the percentage of best times, and rest intervals are 4 to 6 minutes of active rest recovery between swims.

Training for 100 yards or meters	6 × 50 at 8:00; 92% of best time
Training for 200 yards or meters	6 × 100 at 8:00; 92% of best time
Training for 400 meters or 500 yards	6 × 200 at 8:00; 95% of best time

The percentage of best times training has a great correlation to goal times. Three to 4 minutes of active rest should occur between the intense swims. Maximum lactate production and lactate buffering are involved in these sets, and maximum heart rates are attained. Swimmers should hold 92% for 200 training and 90% for 400 or 500 training.

Table 17.6 provides the desired time one would attain in 50 swims to reach 92% of the goal time. This training is excellent for 200 swimmers.

Table 17.7 (page 244) provides the desired 92% training times based on the goal time of 200 swimmers as well as the 90% of goal time for 400-meter or 500-yard swimmers.

The training pace in table 17.8 (page 245) is designed for 400-meter or 500-yard swimmers (race preparation is 95% of training pace) and 1,000-meter or 1,500-yard swimmers (race preparation is 92% of training pace).

Another example training set includes a broken 4 × 500 free on 12:00. The swimmer dives a 200 on 3:00 @ going-out 500 pace, pushes a 150 on 2:30 @ $\dot{V}O_2$max pace (EN-3), dives a 100 on 2:00 @ $\dot{V}O_2$max pace (EN-3), and pushes a 50 on 1:00 at best effort. The coach or swimmer then adds up each segment time. The goal is to attain a 500 time that is 4 to 6 seconds under goal time.

TABLE 17.6 Desired Times Attained in 50 Swims to Reach 92% of Goal Time

6 × 50 @ 8 minutes; 92% of best time

Goal time	94%	93%	92%	91%	90%	89%	88%	87%
0:21.00	0:22.34	0:22.58	0:22.83	0:23.08	0:23.33	0:23.60	0:23.86	0:24.14
0:21.25	0:22.61	0:22.85	0:23.10	0:23.35	0:23.61	0:23.88	0:24.15	0:24.43
0:21.50	0:22.87	0:23.12	0:23.37	0:23.63	0:23.89	0:24.16	0:24.43	0:24.71
0:21.75	0:23.14	0:23.39	0:23.64	0:23.90	0:24.17	0:24.44	0:24.72	0:25.00
0:22.00	0:23.40	0:23.66	0:23.91	0:24.18	0:24.44	0:24.72	0:25.00	0:25.29
0:22.25	0:23.67	0:23.92	0:24.18	0:24.45	0:24.72	0:25.00	0:25.28	0:25.57
0:22.50	0:23.94	0:24.19	0:24.46	0:24.73	0:25.00	0:25.28	0:25.57	0:25.86
0:22.75	0:24.20	0:24.46	0:24.73	0:25.00	0:25.28	0:25.56	0:25.85	0:26.15
0:23.00	0:24.47	0:24.73	0:25.00	0:25.27	0:25.56	0:25.84	0:26.14	0:26.44
0:23.25	0:24.73	0:25.00	0:25.27	0:25.55	0:25.83	0:26.12	0:26.42	0:26.72
0:23.50	0:25.00	0:25.27	0:25.54	0:25.82	0:26.11	0:26.40	0:26.70	0:27.01
0:23.75	0:25.27	0:25.54	0:25.82	0:26.10	0:26.39	0:26.69	0:26.99	0:27.30
0:24.00	0:25.53	0:25.81	0:26.09	0:26.37	0:26.67	0:26.97	0:27.27	0:27.59
0:24.25	0:25.80	0:26.08	0:26.36	0:26.65	0:26.94	0:27.25	0:27.56	0:27.87
0:24.50	0:26.06	0:26.34	0:26.63	0:26.92	0:27.22	0:27.53	0:27.84	0:28.16
0:24.75	0:26.33	0:26.61	0:26.90	0:27.20	0:27.50	0:27.81	0:28.13	0:28.45
0:25.00	0:26.60	0:26.88	0:27.17	0:27.47	0:27.78	0:28.09	0:28.41	0:28.74
0:25.25	0:26.86	0:27.15	0:27.45	0:27.75	0:28.06	0:28.37	0:28.69	0:29.02
0:25.50	0:27.13	0:27.42	0:27.72	0:28.02	0:28.33	0:28.65	0:28.98	0:29.31
0:25.75	0:27.39	0:27.69	0:27.99	0:28.30	0:28.61	0:28.93	0:29.26	0:29.60
0:26.00	0:27.66	0:27.96	0:28.26	0:28.57	0:28.89	0:29.21	0:29.55	0:29.89

TABLE 17.7 Desired Training Times Based on Goal Time (92% for 200 Swimmers and 90% for 400-Meter or 500-Yard Swimmers)

6 × 100 @ 8 minutes; 92% of best time

Goal time	94%	93%	92% (200)	91%	90% (400)	89%	88%	87%
0:46.00	0:48.94	0:49.46	0:50.00	0:50.55	0:51.11	0:51.69	0:52.27	0:52.87
0:47.00	0:50.00	0:50.54	0:51.09	0:51.65	0:52.22	0:52.81	0:53.41	0:54.02
0:48.00	0:51.06	0:51.61	0:52.17	0:52.75	0:53.33	0:53.93	0:54.55	0:55.17
0:49.00	0:52.13	0:52.69	0:53.26	0:53.85	0:54.44	0:55.06	0:55.68	0:56.32
0:50.00	0:53.19	0:53.76	0:54.35	0:54.95	0:55.56	0:56.18	0:56.82	0:57.47
0:51.00	0:54.26	0:54.84	0:55.43	0:56.04	0:56.67	0:57.30	0:57.95	0:58.62
0:52.00	0:55.32	0:55.91	0:56.52	0:57.14	0:57.78	0:58.43	0:59.09	0:59.77
0:53.00	0:56.38	0:56.99	0:57.61	0:58.24	0:58.89	0:59.55	1:00.23	1:00.92
0:54.00	0:57.45	0:58.06	0:58.70	0:59.34	1:00.00	1:00.67	1:01.36	1:02.07
0:55.00	0:58.51	0:59.14	0:59.78	1:00.44	1:01.11	1:01.80	1:02.50	1:03.22
0:56.00	0:59.57	1:00.22	1:00.87	1:01.54	1:02.22	1:02.92	1:03.64	1:04.37
0:57.00	1:00.64	1:01.29	1:01.96	1:02.64	1:03.33	1:04.04	1:04.77	1:05.52
0:58.00	1:01.70	1:02.37	1:03.04	1:03.74	1:04.44	1:05.17	1:05.91	1:06.67
0:59.00	1:02.77	1:03.44	1:04.13	1:04.84	1:05.56	1:06.29	1:07.05	1:07.82
1:00.00	1:03.83	1:04.52	1:05.22	1:05.93	1:06.67	1:07.42	1:08.18	1:08.97

TABLE 17.8 Training Paces for 400-Meter or 500-Yard Swimmers (95%) and 1,000-Meter or 1,500-Yard Swimmers (92%)

6 × 200 @ 8 minutes; 95% of goal time and 92% of goal time

Goal time	96%	95%	94%	93%	92%	91%	90%	89%
1:30.00	1:33.75	1:34.74	1:35.74	1:36.77	1:37.83	1:38.90	1:40.00	1:41.12
1:31.00	1:34.79	1:35.79	1:36.81	1:37.85	1:38.91	1:40.00	1:41.11	1:42.25
1:32.00	1:35.83	1:36.84	1:37.87	1:38.92	1:40.00	1:41.10	1:42.22	1:43.37
1:33.00	1:36.88	1:37.89	1:38.94	1:40.00	1:41.09	1:42.20	1:43.33	1:44.49
1:34.00	1:37.92	1:38.94	1:40.00	1:41.08	1:42.17	1:43.30	1:44.44	1:45.62
1:35.00	1:38.96	1:40.00	1:41.05	1:42.15	1:43.26	1:44.40	1:45.56	1:46.74
1:36.00	1:40.00	1:41.05	1:42.13	1:43.23	1:44.35	1:45.49	1:46.67	1:47.87
1:37.00	1:41.04	1:42.11	1:43.19	1:44.30	1:45.43	1:46.59	1:47.78	1:48.99
1:38.00	1:42.08	1:43.16	1:44.26	1:45.38	1:46.52	1:47.69	1:48.89	1:50.11
1:39.00	1:43.13	1:44.21	1:45.32	1:46.45	1:47.61	1:48.79	1:50.00	1:51.24
1:40.00	1:44.17	1:45.26	1:46.38	1:47.53	1:48.70	1:49.89	1:51.11	1:52.36
1:41:00	1:45.21	1:46.32	1:47.45	1:48.60	1:49.78	1:50.99	1:52.22	1:53.48
1:42.00	1:46.25	1:47.37	1:48.51	1:49.68	1:50.87	1:52.09	1:53.33	1:54.61
1:43.00	1:47.29	1:48.42	1:49.57	1:50.75	1:51.96	1:53.19	1:54.44	1:55.73
1:44.00	1:48.33	1:49.47	1:50.64	1:51.83	1:53.04	1:54.29	1:55.56	1:56.85
1:45.00	1:49.38	1:50.53	1:51.70	1:52.90	1:54.13	1:55.38	1:56.67	1:57.98
1:46.00	1:50.42	1:51.58	1:52.77	1:53.98	1:55.22	1:56.48	1:57.78	1:59.10
1:47.00	1:51.46	1:52.63	1:53.83	1:55.05	1:56.30	1:57.58	1:58.89	2:00.22
1:48.00	1:52.50	1:53.68	1:54.89	1:56.13	1:57.39	1:58.68	2:00.00	2:01.35
1:49.00	1:53.54	1:54.74	1:55.96	1:57.20	1:58.48	1:59.78	2:01.11	2:02.47
1:50.00	1:54.58	1:55.79	1:57.02	1:58.28	1:59.57	2:00.88	2:02.22	2:03.60
1:51.00	1:55.63	1:56.84	1:58.09	1:59.35	2:00.65	2:01.98	2:03.33	2:04.72
1:52.00	1:56.67	1:57.89	1:59.15	2:00.43	2:01.74	2:03.08	2:04.44	2:05.84
1:53.00	1:57.71	1:58.95	2:00.21	2:01.51	2:02.83	2:04.18	2:05.56	2:06.97

PERIODIZATION

Adjust the training schedule for the periodization effect in order to provide your swimmers the best opportunity to attain goal times at the championship meet and the major competitions along the way to the championship.

Annual Training Plan at the University of Michigan

The training plan that follows indicates the number of weeks and the training zones most emphasized in each macrocycle.

First Macrocycle: Collegiate Season September to November (12 Weeks)

- 6 weeks aerobic training and skill development; heart rate < 150; EN1 and EN-1+
- 6 weeks aerobic, threshold, $\dot{V}O_2$max, and lactate; EN-1, EN-1+, EN-2, EN-2+, and EN-3 and above
- Major competition (1-week taper)

Second Macrocycle: Collegiate Season December to February (15 Weeks)

- 3 weeks aerobic endurance training; EN-1 through EN-3
- 10 weeks all training zones and energy systems; more emphasis on $\dot{V}O_2$max and lactate production. This period includes three to four dual meets per month (short course).

Third Macrocycle: Collegiate Season March

- 3-week taper period
- Dryland reduced to maintenance and dropped 10 days out
- Training distance gradually reduced from 70,000 meters per week to 30,000 to 20,000 meters per week

Middle-Distance 3-Week Taper to Championship Meet

Taper phase: As the physical preparation of yards or meters is gradually reduced, the athlete should spend more time on mental preparation, attitude, and visualization. The swimmer should picture him or herself going through races from start to finish with the splits needed for goal time.

Refer to figure 17.1. The yardage and amount of intensity is gradually reduced over 3 weeks. Begin with day 20. The shaded section of each bar indicates the proportion of race-pace and intensity swimming (EN-1+, EN-2, EN-2+, and EN-3) that is done. The nonshaded portion is the low-intensity swimming (EN-1) done that day. The height of the bar indicates the number of yards swum on that day. The yardage and amount of intensity are gradually reduced over 3 weeks.

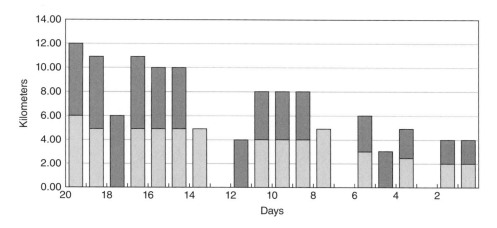

FIGURE 17.1   The three-week taper for a championship meet.

The following instructions are designed for swimmers throughout the training preparation.

1. **Mental attitude and visualization instructions.** Picture yourself doing your races from start to finish with all the splits you need for your goal time.

   1. Start: Alert and explosive
   2. Turns: Accelerate into and streamline out. Breast and fly: Set up for turn rather than glide in.
   3. Pace: Split well, swim well! Study old splits and look at experts in your event. Example: For a 200-meter free goal time of 1:50.00, 50 splits 26, 28, 28, 28 = 1:50.00
   4. Control: Level off the splits and pick up the pace if needed.
   5. Technique: Head and hand positions are the two most important indicators of technique. In freestyle, the head should align with the spine and the hands should catch with the elbow positioned above the hand.
   6. Breathing patterns: Races longer than 20 seconds require oxygen.

      50 freestyle: no breather (19.99 or one breath)

      100 freestyle: four to six strokes per breath

      200 and up freestyle: normal breathing from the start. Do not hold breath and do not overkick at the start.

      200 fly: one breath for every two strokes or one breath each stroke
   7. Kick: Continuous, relaxed, must have it at the end ("white water dome coming home").
   8. Finish: Drive hard into the pad and then look up and watch your opponents come in. Champ finish: Raise your arm to salute the crowd and teammates.
   9. Relay take-offs: Total concentration and timing.

2. **Rest.** You must control your rest or sleep. You need a minimum of 8 to 10 hours of sleep per night during the taper and championship period. You spend less time at the pool; use that additional time for rest and relaxation.

3. **Weights and dryland.** You can continue select weight training exercises on an individual basis. Continue dryland training three times per week. Spend more time more on core work (e.g., sit-ups, pull-ups, and stretching).

Middle-Distance Training Week at a Glance

Table 17.9 provides an example of a three-day microcycle during midseason.

TABLE 17.9 3-Day Microcycle (5 Workouts)

Monday a.m.: general	Monday p.m.: threshold training
Tuesday a.m.: general	Tuesday p.m.: active rest; EN-1 and EN-3
Wednesday a.m.: off	Wednesday p.m.: $\dot{V}O_2$max or lactate work

General = nonspecific training

Tables 17.10 through 7.12 provide specific examples of training on each of these three days (Monday, Tuesday, and Wednesday).

TABLE 17.10 Day 1 Microcycle (Midseason)

Monday a.m.	Monday p.m.
Aerobic technique	Dryland, stretching
Pull set/free: 2,000–3,000	1 hour general work
Kick/endurance: 800–1,200	Main set:
Hypoxic swim free	• Threshold work: 2,000–3,000*
Fin swim/individual medley	• Energy system: EN-2
7,000 meters	7,000 meters

* Specific Sets for Monday Threshold Work (2,000–3,000):

4 × 200 at 2:30 (EN-1)

6 × 150 at 2:00 (EN-1+)

0:30 extra rest

8 × 100 at 1:20 (EN-2)

10 × 50 at 0:45 (EN-2+)

TABLE 17.11 Day 2 Microcycle (Midseason)

Tuesday a.m. (aerobic/recovery)	Tuesday p.m.
Skill and drill work	Strength training, stretching
Kick and speed power	1 hour general work
Swim-specific power	Main set:
Parachutes	• Active rest work*
	• Continuous easy race pace: 2,000–3,000
Stretch cords and tethered swim; negative work and positive speed assistance sprints	• Alternating energy systems: EN-1 and EN-3
7,000 meters	7,000 meters

* Tuesday Active Rest Work:

3 × (300 free + 100 casual on 1:30)

Descend 300s 1 thru 3

3 × (200 free + 100 casual on 1:30)

Descend 200s 1 through 3

3 × (100 free + 100 casual on 1:30)

Descend 100s 1 through 3

3 × [4 × (50 casual + 50 free pace)]

First round at +1.0 second per 50 0:27s

Second round at pace 0:26s

Third round at −1.0 second per 50 0:25s

Total distance = 3,900

TABLE 17.12 Day 3 Microcycle (Midseason)

Wednesday a.m.	Wednesday p.m.
Off	Main set:
	• $\dot{V}O_2$max work, rainbow set (all intensities), lactate work, or broken swims or test sets; 6,000 meters
	• Example: 4 × 200 on 8:00 broken swim
	• 50 dive on 1:30 (going-out 200 pace 0:24.5)
	• 100 push on 2:30 (middle 100 of the 200 pace 0:52.5)
	• 50 push on 1:30 (best you can come home 0:25.5)
	• Add up for 200 meters 1:42.5
	• Active rest recovery 200 between rounds

CONCLUSION

Most swimmers will fall into the middle-distance group. The combination of speed and endurance training provides a variety of options. Middle-distance swimmers come from both ends of the spectrum and give equal attention to the energy requirements in training. Identifying each swimmer's threshold will enhance proper training in the energy systems. The swimmer and coach should recognize that the swimmer must develop a broad aerobic base in order to support anaerobic endurance training at race pace. Middle-distance races are neither sprint nor endurance; the ability to learn pace is important. A swimmer should learn to control his or her race and try to negative or even split the 400-meter or 500-yard races. The first part of the season is 90% physical preparation and only 10% mental preparation; the last part of the season is only 10% physical preparation and 90% mental preparation.

18

Freestyle Distance Training

Bill Rose With Mike Lewis

Distance training has noticeably evolved over the years. Are today's distance swimmers different from those of the past? Are they less willing to train long distances and work as hard? Should we treat them differently? Should we cushion the training in any way? What shall we do in the future? To find out whether today's distance swimmers are different, we need to look at the past. And in looking at the past I contend that today's swimmers aren't inherently different, but the climate in which we develop distance swimmers has changed.

Like in all sports, in competitive swimming the climate is often dictated by the heroes of the day, and that greatly affects what kind of overall swimmers we are going to have. Some great heroes existed back in the late 1960s and early 1970s. If at that time you asked your team, "Who do you emulate? Who do you want to be like? Who is your hero?" the name Mike Burton would inevitably come up. Everyone wanted to be like Mike Burton. He was a distance swimmer, an Olympic gold medalist, and a world record holder. He practiced farther and faster than anyone else. A few years later your team might answer, "Gee, I want to be like John Kinsella." Everyone wanted to be like John Kinsella, another American and world record holder in the distance freestyle. As time went on in the 1970s, the team's answer would be, "Boy, would I like to be like Brian Goodell." Brian held the world record in the 1,500, and his American record in the 1,500 freestyle was not broken for 24 years. If you were to ask any one of those swimmers who held the 1,500-meter American record the same question, they would answer the name of the one who preceded them. Everybody was working off each other, and it was the thing to do. Was it cool to be a distance swimmer? It was very cool to be a distance swimmer!

A BRIEF HISTORY OF DISTANCE SWIMMING

In the 1970s coaches and swimmers constantly looked for ways to one up the competition. Coaches were commonly on the phone with one another espousing the impossible set their swimmers had accomplished that day in workout. The following day a new was standard shared, and the day after that, another. The mindset was that if the athlete could do something no one else had done in workout, no one could beat them in a race.

As we moved through the 1980s, things were a little different. We asked ourselves, "Is all this overdistance training really worth it? Isn't there a better way? Is more really better?" As we Americans started to embrace sport science, a lot of research was conducted on the concept of overload. Universities throughout the nation started researching energy systems, lactic acid levels, and $\dot{V}O_2$max more deeply, and generalizations were extended into the swimming community. The results—some shown inconclusive years later upon further review—stated that swimmers could indeed achieve the same results by swimming smarter rather than swimming more yardage.

The adage of "smarter, not harder" may be partially true but, in my opinion, some coaches took the information to a level that was destructive for the distance swimmer. The whole idea of distance training during the 1970s was work ethic. The harder you worked, the more you got out of it. The more work you did, the more someone else would outdo you. If you shared a monster set, someone else would do even a bigger set. Again, people starting thinking, "We can't continue to work the 100,000-meter weeks." They wondered where it would all end, whether less was best, and whether an easier way existed.

That is not to say that during the 1980s and 1990s other events (sprint and stroke) did not improve immensely; they did! In fact, they did so well that the heroes of swimming changed. With the exception of the great Janet Evans, the answer to the question, "Who is your swimming hero and who do you want to emulate?" changed. No longer was it the distance swimmer of the past. In the United States, it became swimmers like Tom Jager and Matt Biondi and, in the 1990s, Gary Hall. All of these swimmers are truly great heroes and earned their position in swimming, but they are fantastic sprinters, not distance swimmers. Times and mindsets changed and it was no longer cool to be a distance swimmer. In fact, if in the early 1990s you asked the swimmer on the street whether they wanted to be a distance swimmer, the answer would be something like, "Are you kidding? Those guys are nuts!"

Fortunately, distance swimming has somewhat come full circle over the past decade or so. Thanks to the Australians and many other countries throughout the world, it is once again okay to be a distance swimmer. An example of the recent excitement for distance swimming is the great 1,500 match-up at the 2000 Sydney Olympics. Australians love swimming. Actually, Australians are nuts about swimming. The buzz that emanated from the natatorium at the 2000 games was extraordinary. The races throughout the initial days of competition were amazing. Much of the hype surrounded the Aussie phenom, Ian Thorpe, who opened up the first night with a world record and gold medal in the 400 free. There also was the showdown between the Americans and the Australians in the 400 free relay (strumming guitars by Michael Klim and his teammates as they knocked off the Americans and their flamboyant rock star, Gary Hall, Jr.). But the really big race came on the final night as Aussie legend Kieren Perkins went head to head with fellow distance great Grant Hackett. Perkins was a sentimental favorite of the Australians. He became a national hero after winning the gold at the 1992 and 1996 Olympics, and many of his fans dreamed that he would win the third consecutive gold in this event on his home soil at the 2000 games. Hackett had taken the mantle from Perkins at the 1998 world championships;

however, he was overcome with a viral infection at the 2000 games and his dominance in the 1,500 was in question—he had qualified third behind Perkins. The Australian media had a field day speculating on the big Aussie Olympic showdown. The crowd was in a frenzy that night at the Sydney Aquatic Center. Never have I seen a crowd on their feet, screaming, cheering, and waving signs at a swim meet—maybe at a World Cup soccer match, but at a swim meet? Despite his illness, Hackett assumed the lead from the start and never let up. It was one of the greatest days for men's distance swimming. I'm sure that night every young Aussie swimmer set their sights on becoming the next Grant Hackett.

WHAT MAKES A DISTANCE SWIMMER?

What kind of person does it take to be a distance swimmer? The answer is not that complex: It takes a person who really loves swimming and is willing to pay the price of admission. One is not necessarily born to be a distance swimmer. One must not have any specific body type (mesomorph, a muscular, athletic body; ectomorph, a slender, angular body; or endomorph, a heavy, rounded body) to excel. Usually, the best distance swimmers are those that cover the five Ds of being a distance swimmer. Those Ds are

1. discipline,
2. desire,
3. devotion,
4. determination, and
5. dedication.

These characteristics don't have too much to do with innate talent. That is not to say that talent doesn't help. Many of the great distance swimmers will tell you that they became a distance swimmer by default, meaning that they did not necessarily excel in the other areas of swimming, such as sprinting or specialty events. But they did love to swim and were willing to do whatever it took to be the best they could be at the sport. Whether swimmers gravitate to distance events by default or simply because they have a proclivity for long-distance swimming, they are intrinsically the same in their ability to commit and their desire.

A great example is the true story of a young boy who was on a team simply because his sister swam and his parents wanted to keep them in the same activity. He was never going to be a quality swimmer in any skill event. In fact, at 12 years of age, he was constantly teased for being a "physical moron." He had a physical problem that allowed him to walk on only his toes. His coach could not find a compatible group for him because he could only swim freestyle. When he kicked, not only did he stay in the same spot, but eventually he would go backward! When others swam strokes, he would go freestyle. Individual medley? Forget it! His coach became frustrated and finally said, "I give up. You just continue to swim freestyle and keep moving."

He did what his coach said and ended up swimming freestyle longer than the others as they did stroke and specialty training. He steadily got better and better despite any handicap attributed to him. He ended up making junior nationals, then senior nationals, then getting a scholarship to attend University of Cincinnati, then got eighth place at the NCAA championships, and finally competed in the Olympic Trials. He had a good career and continued in open-water competition. This story is proof that anybody who is perceived to be a nonathlete can actually make it to one of the highest places in competitive swimming. The same cannot be said in relation to the sprint or skilled events in swimming.

WHEN TO START DISTANCE TRAINING

The age at which to start pure distance training varies based on several factors. First of all, the younger age groups (8 to 11 years) should be taught to swim correctly in all strokes! Distance training during this time of the swimmer's career should be only an afterthought. As the young swimmer starts to show efficiency of movement in the different strokes, the next step may be for the swimmer to go a little farther while showing the same efficiency. When the stroke is no longer efficient, more teaching should take place. The distances may continue to increase, but not at the expense of technique, which must continue to be at the forefront.

Additionally, as one of the great coaches with whom I work reminds me, training must be fun. Young swimmers can learn the proper technique and they can begin to learn the strategic aspects of racing, but if it's not fun you'll lose them. Too often coaches will identify a young boy or girl with special talent and begin to cultivate them like miniature national-team swimmers. The first problem with this is that you cannot necessarily predict a mature swimmer's performance based on what you see in their youth. More importantly, too much (of anything) too soon is an ideal recipe for burnout.

We all know that children develop physically at different rates. We also know that girls are usually 1 to 2 years ahead of boys in physical development. As coaches, we must understand and observe the maturation cycles. The age at which distance training starts can and should vary by as much as 2 to 3 years for different individuals. As a norm, 12-year-old girls and 13-year-old boys can begin a distance-training regimen on a gradual basis.

Throughout the age-group period, the coach must convey to their swimmers that it is okay to be a distance swimmer. Swimmers must learn to go against the flow of the fast-paced concept of the modern day. If the coach is passionate about the rewards, both intrinsic and extrinsic, of swimming distance, the swimmers will follow suit. Be sure to give as much, if not more, praise to those doing the distance sets as is given to the other swimmers doing normal training. Remember that at this age swimmers are very receptive to what the coach says to them and what others think of them. Also, peers will hear a coach's praise of the distance swimmers and will in turn accept them more readily as one of the whole group.

PRINCIPLES OF DISTANCE SWIMMING

Coaches have taken broad and diverse positions on training for distance. Some coaches have gone back to the concept of overdistance whereas others have found good fortune in the concept of distance specificity. At one time it was all about more, more, more. In the overdistance tradition, overload, reduce, and race was often the skeleton of the swim coach's season plan. Swimmers were training insane sets such as 8,000 individual medley, 5 × 1,000 fly, and 10,000 for time. We learned a lot from those days of long, long swimming—some good lessons and some bad. Some athletes adapted phenomenally and set world records, others were injured, and some quit. In many cases today's distance swim training is somewhat of a hybrid between the ultradistance training of the 1970s and the science-driven, "less is more" concept that followed. This is the distance specificity method. We now know that it's important to adequately condition our distance swimmers at distances equal to and beyond those they'll encounter in a race, yet we also know that it's important to train specifically for these distances. Great distance swimmers develop a keen awareness of pace and speed at all distances greater than 400 meters.

Pace work is the foundation of all my workouts. Developing a sense of pace takes lots and lots of practice. Swimmers must continually develop an understanding of what it means to swim at a particular pace regardless of where they are in the training cycle. In other words, swimming 1:00 100-meter repeats midseason may not feel the same as it feels at the end of the season, but the important thing is understanding the feel for hitting the 1:00 time and time again.

One of my former swimmers, Larsen Jensen, did an amazing job in developing a sense of pace. In March preceding the 2004 Olympic Trials, we were at a training camp at the Olympic Training Center in Colorado Springs. I explained to Larsen the importance of truly getting to know his body. I challenged him to develop a sense of awareness that would allow him to do something truly amazing. That night Larsen retreated to his room and proceeded to record all the splits for his ideal 1,500 meters. The next morning he showed these to me, and I asked him to come up with a way to keep those times in his head. When we returned to the club in Mission Viejo, California, Larsen came to work out with his kickboard, which looked like an ancient stone tablet that had each of those splits written in large calligraphy. Whenever Larsen kicked, the kickboard reminded him what the pace he needed to hold for his ideal 1,500. When we did countless pace 100s, he knew what he needed to do and he did it. By the time the race came around in Athens, Larsen was optimally prepared and he was within 0.3 second of his goal time in winning the silver medal and breaking his own American record, set a month earlier at the Olympic Trials. The most impressive part of this to me is that he was never more than 0.3 off his 100 pace at any point in the race. In fact, for the majority of the race he was within 0.2 second.

Numerous ways exist to develop a sense of pace. Start by having swimmers do longer interval sets of 50s, 100s, or 200s, and shorten the interval as the swimmers get better at pace precision. One of my favorite ways to work on pace is a ±0.5 game.

I give the swimmers a set such as 5 × 100 and challenge them to go a particular pace. If they go outside the boundaries of ±0.5, we add a 100. Later, you can use countless variations of broken 400s, 800s, and 1,500s to help your athletes develop pace and race awareness.

SEASON PLANNING FOR THE DISTANCE SWIMMER

The adage "failing to plan is planning to fail" is true for every coach. A season plan should start gradually to ensure that the swimmer adapts to increasing stress levels. This will result in fewer injuries and prepare the swimmer for the intense swimming sets to come.

Early Season

Assuming that a yearly season plan is in effect, the early season lasts approximately 12 weeks. During this time, the athlete gradually builds up in several areas. The first 3 to 4 weeks usually consist of once-daily workouts. The starting distance may be as short as 3,000 meters per workout and increase approximately 10,000 meters per week until the normal workout distance is achieved. The workouts consist of technique work and aerobic repeats.

During this time, the coach and swimmer discuss and practice over and over the little things such as turn technique, streamlines, breakouts, and distance per stroke. Proper execution of all aspects of freestyle is emphasized. At this point, the swimmers must understand how much the final outcome of a distance race can be affected by such things as streamlining 3 inches (7.6 cm) further each 50 or making the turn just 0.1 second faster. During this time, speed is secondary to developing the ability to do the proper things without having to consciously think about them along the way. This is not something to take lightly. I compare this to compounding interest. If an athlete can increase their efficiency, the payout is huge at the end of the race. Great efficiency means increased speed and reduced effort. When it comes down to the end of the race, compounding the benefits of increased efficiency can mean winning or setting a specific time standard. It's the most important foundational aspect of everything you will do as a distance coach.

The early season is also when the swimmers meet with the coach for goal sessions. These sessions need to be one on one and should last for at least 30 minutes. This is your opportunity to really get to know your athlete. The knowledge gained through these early-season meetings will enable you to gauge the swimmer's training, affect their motivation, and set agreeable standards to reach the desired outcomes. The swimmer should come in with his or her goals in writing for each event that will be swum that year in the championship season. They should include the splits for every 100. The coach and athlete should discuss what it will take to achieve each goal. That discussion should include training both in and out of the water as well as nutrition, proper rest, and time management. The coach must stress what the swimmer must do in practice along the way in order to achieve the goal at the end of the season. Intermediate goals should also be addressed. All too often swimmers simply write what they think the coach wants to hear and turn in unrealistic expectations. The coach must help the swimmer understand what achieving each goal will require on a day-to-day basis! So much of any practice is the continued attempt to swim goal pace for whatever the season goal is. It doesn't matter whether the race pace may be 25 or 50 meters in one repeat and then rest. The pace to achieve must be ingrained in the swimmer's mind and body.

After 3 to 4 weeks of single-practice days, introduce morning practices. In the average year, you may offer one practice the first week, two the second week, three the third week, and so on. The number of morning practices offered varies with the age of the swimmer and factors such as school commitments, ability to secure water time, and experience of the swimmers. Many of the top programs include a morning off in the middle of the week for recovery. The coach must read the needs of each swimmer to determine how many practices each week the swimmer can handle. You should probably not expect a younger swimmer in high school to attend five and six morning practices. This is not a rule, but it is something to consider. During the school year, some of the top teams have gone to a regimen of one 3- to 4-hour practice per day instead of two practices per day. It is up to the coach to decide whether this schedule is better for the school-age swimmer.

Average weekly mileage is often a debatable subject. This is where the overdistance and the distance-specific philosophies meet head to head. In the early-season phase, the swimmer should achieve full weekly average mileage around the eighth week of training. The coach must find and believe in what works for his or her own philosophy, water time, and swimmer experience. Each year may differ from the previous year. For example, in 2004, my club, the Mission Viejo Nadadores, averaged approximately 90,000 meters per week once the full mileage was attained. That year, the morning practices averaged 6,000 to 8,000 meters and the evening practices averaged 8,000 to 11,000 meters. In 2008, the mileage was 80,000 meters per week, but each workout equaled very close to 8,000 meters. Some clubs went substantially more and some much less. What is right? The answer is up to the coach, who must have confidence in his or her philosophy of what is right!

Midseason

Midseason is when you nurture the foundational work of early-season training. Throughout the early season the swimmer worked on technique (keep this up) and developed a strong aerobic base. Midseason training sets the stage for the extreme intensity of prolonged racing. At this point in the season, both the length and intensity of workouts increase. It's the time to look for the mental threshold of each athlete and guide them through it. I challenge my swimmers to get comfortable with being uncomfortable. Without a doubt, tolerance plays a huge role in distance swimming. I constantly work to build this tolerance, both physiologically and psychologically, through increased duration and intensity.

Let me take a moment here to recount a lesson I learned early in my coaching career: adaptation. We humans have an amazing ability to adapt in a multitude of situations. I am often struck by stories of people managing and persevering through seemingly impossible situations. As a species we've adapted to hostile environments and to physical and mental hardships. In essence, we are programmed to adapt. Yet too often we have a very strong tendency to gravitate toward the comfortable and familiar—the paths of least resistance. Biologists refer to reaching this comfort zone as stasis; I think of it as a waiting area for pushing to the next and higher level. As I coach I use this knowledge to train my athletes to move step by step in adapting to the stresses of training. Once they've adapted to a particular level of discomfort, it's time to up the ante. Using my understanding of the natural desire to be comfortable and my understanding of the human ability to adapt to stress, I steer my swimmers toward a greater ability to tolerate the stresses of competition.

At this point in the season, competition becomes very important. I try to have my athletes compete every 4 to 6 weeks. Not only do we seek adaptation in training, we look to apply these adaptations to our racing—we're after breakthrough swims. But here lies a challenge: It's not easy for a swimmer to swim a distance race several times over the course of the season. Swimmers are a very motivated group, and early on they are taught the rewards of achieving their best time. However, as swimmers get older (I'm talking over 15) and faster, it's more difficult to set those best times over and over throughout the season. But I'm ardent in my belief that the best way to practice racing is by racing. So how do you keep the swimmer motivated to go out and give a level of intensity over a long period of time that often won't yield that best time? I took a tip from the great coach Peter Daland, who preached moving away from success. In other words, if a swimmer has a breakthrough swim, we're likely to not swim that race at the next meet during the midseason. I want to nurture their confidence as they continue to adapt. We may also create goals within a particular race in order to break up the races and create small challenges within the in-season competition. I may have my swimmer compete in a 1,500-meter event and complete a smooth 1,000 followed by 5 × 100 descend, or I may have the same swimmer hit goal pace between 800 to 1,200. The important takeaway here is that I give the swimmer the same level of praise that I would if they hit their overall best time. You have to keep swimmers motivated and confident as they walk this challenging path of adaptation. Countless variations of this strategy exist, and I encourage you to explore ways that work on an individual basis for each of your swimmers.

Tapering and Main Competition

A detailed explanation of tapering is beyond the scope of this writing and I encourage you to study this as a coach. Detailed scientific explanations for a successful taper are available, and I've spent a great deal of time studying them, but to me tapering is an art. In my program, we methodically reduce yardage but I keep the same percentages of the key components of my workouts (warm-up, pace work, kicking, and so on). The most important thing is that we build the confidence and true belief that the swimmers need in order to be successful. This is not the time to introduce unnecessary changes; I don't change strokes and I don't encourage nutritional changes (aside from encouraging my athletes to monitor caloric intake). I want swimmers to cultivate the sense that their success is imminent based on their efforts throughout the season. I remind them, "The more you put in the bank, the more you can take out."

I remember hearing the legendary coach George Haines say, "I'm not a great swim coach; I just convinced swimmers to swim fast." Of course Haines was one of the greatest coaches, but his statement illustrates the importance of developing confidence in your swimmers.

THE IMPORTANCE OF READING YOUR ATHLETES

I was recently talking coaching philosophies with a colleague whose background is steeped in formal sport science. I told him, "I'm not a scientist; I'm a trainer." "Wrong," he replied. "All coaches are scientists. They just may not follow the text-book example of the scientific method: observe, question, hypothesize, analyze, and report. All good coaches are watching their athletes and looking for better ways to help them get faster."

What this colleague meant was that we all are like scientists. Akin to an old-school boxing trainer, although I possess a firm understanding of the physiological and biomechanical aspects of swimming, my strength lies in training my athletes. I spend a great deal of time reading my athletes and developing training protocol to maximize their adaptation in the formal scientific areas. I look to their mood, their performance, and any other indicators that can help me improve their conditioning. This approach is especially effective with my distance swimmers. Over the years I have learned when to push them and when to ease off. I've learned the importance of introducing humor into the training process. The fact that distance training can be long, arduous, and, at times, boring is not lost on me. Through the process of reading my athletes I can help them stay on track and focus on their long-term goals.

One of my current athletes is one of the top female distance swimmers in the world. Before joining us at the Nadadores, she worked with several coaches and had good success. She came here to settle down and reach her goal of making an Olympic team. Motivating her isn't hard—she's one of the most committed young women I've had the pleasure to coach. Every day she arrives to practice 30 minutes early, walks into my office, and asks to see the workout. She first goes to the end—total yardage—and then methodically analyzes the workout to mentally prepare herself for each set. I carefully read her physical and emotional state as we collaborate in reaching her goals.

Others in my current distance group take different approaches. Some look for loopholes, some try to bargain, and some decide to take it easy and save up for the last. My job is to read all of the swimmers in the group and motivate each of them to attack the challenges ahead.

Get to know your athletes both formally and informally. You can have structured meetings to go over specific aspects of goals, technique, or other factors related to swimming. You also can get a very good handle by observing them as they prepare for workout. By getting a good read on your athletes, you increase your ability to show them you care. When you care, they care!

THE FUTURE OF DISTANCE SWIMMING

Where are we headed in distance swimming? No doubt exists that we have a phenomenal base of athletes in the United States who can be great distance swimmers. I believe it's up to coaches to determine the success of our distance program. A program doesn't have to be either sprint based or exclusively distance oriented. You have to look at each of your swimmers and help set them on the best path for success. The appeal of distance swimming is different than that of shorter races. Much of the success of distance swimming is culturally bound. In other words, does the culture of swimming embrace the determination and fortitude of long-distance swimming, and do our young swimmers have distance heroes to emulate? We have to view our distance swimmers as equals to their counterparts who swim the seemingly more exciting races. It's somewhat analogous to our ability to understand the excitement of the Tour de France once Americans started winning the multistage marathon bike classic. Now that open-water swimming is included in the Olympic program, our athletes certainly have more opportunities. In fact, the tactical aspects of this extreme-distance racing are very exciting and many of the races come down to fractions of a second. I hope I've been able to share with you that distance swimming can be very exciting and that it is a worthy pursuit for both coach and athlete.

SAMPLE WORKOUTS

The following sample workouts indicate the type of training and the yardage involved at different parts of the season. The training involved is challenging, and kicking and pulling sets are included. Each coach should design training sessions based on the level of swimmers on his or her team. These workouts were designed for my Olympic training group.

Early Season

This is the time to gradually establish a solid aerobic base for the later, more intensive training.

Example A

Very early in the early season

1. Abdominal circuit: 16 minutes
2. Warm-up: swim 400, 300, 200, 100 @ base 1:30, the last 100 of each in individual medley
3. Swim 2,000, every fourth 50 pace time
4. Kick 900 with partner, 100 together pace, 50 fast, join together at end of each 50
5. Pull or swim 3 rounds (6 × 100 @ 1:25, 1:20, and 1:15 by the round, each round more intense)
6. Cool-down: swim 200 easy

Total: 5,900 meters

Example B

A couple of weeks into the early season

1. Warm-up: swim 800 mixed, then 10 × 100 @ 1:30 with numbers 4, 7, 9, and 10 in individual medley @ 1:35
2. Swim 2,000 done @ 130 heart rate, except every fourth 100 is at threshold+ (160+ heart rate)
3. Kick 4 × 250 @ 4:00, descending 1 to 4
4. Swim 100 easy
5. Pull 8 × 150 @ 2:10 with the last 50 with no more than 4 breaths
6. Swim 4 rounds: 100 set up @ 1:30, 300 negative split starting at threshold @ 4:10
7. Cool-down: swim 200 easy

Total: 7,900 meters

Example C

Late in the early season

1. Warm-up: swim 4 × 400 @ 6:00 and build reverse individual medleys
2. Pull/swim/pull 1,500 @ 20:00; pull/swim 1,000 @ 13:00; swim 500 @ 6:30; descend by the 500 on each repeat, with the last 500 the fastest
3. Kick 4 rounds, 4 × 50: round 1 with board @ 1:00, round 2 with board and snorkel @ 1:00, round 3 streamline with fins @ 1:00, round 4 streamline with snorkel and fins @ 1:00
4. Swim 100 easy
5. Swim 5 × 500 @ 7:00
6. Cool-down: swim 200 moderate

Total: 8,200 meters

Midseason

In midseason, we build on the aerobic base established throughout the early season. We add more intensity to the training sessions and introduce more race specifics.

Example A

Early in midseason

1. Warm-up: swim 5 × 200 @ 3:00, build an individual medley by the 50s on a base 0:50 for each 50 within the individual medley
2. Kick 6 × 150 @ 3:00; descend each 50, and descend total time 1 to 3 and 4 to 6
3. Swim 100 easy
4. Pull 6 × 200 @ 3:00, lung busters (or less breathing)
5. Swim 4 × 1,200 @ 15:00, negative split and descend 1 to 4
6. Cool-down: swim 200 moderate to easy

Total: 8,100 meters

Example B

Late in midseason

1. Warm-up: swim 800 mixed, then swim 400, 200, and 100; divide and descend from aerobic to aerobic+ @ 10 to 15 seconds rest interval
2. Swim 2 × 300 @ 10:45, 2 × 400 @ 5:30, 2 × 200 @ 2:40, and 2 × 100 @ 1:30; descend within each and descend in each set of two
3. Pull/kick choice/swim 1,500 with snorkel by 500s
4. Swim 10 × 50 butterfly with fins @ 0:45
5. Pull/swim 4 × 400 @ 5:30; odd repeats pull solid, even repeats swim fast
6. Cool-down: swim 200 moderate or easy

Total: 8,100 meters

Late Season (Tapering and Main Competition)

Training in the late season, or tapering period, is designed to provide recovery and to help the distance swimmer hold a strong aerobic capacity. The swimmer does less yardage, and the rest intervals provide a bit more rest.

Example

8 days before the Olympic Trials

1. Warm-up: 4 rounds; swim 200 @ 3:00, kick 150 @ 3:10, swim 100 (50 free, 50 nonfree) @ 1:40; descend by rounds
2. Swim 3 × 300 @ 4:30 (snorkels, paddles, and fins), then 1 × 300 @ 4:30 negative split
3. Kick 200 @ 4:10 @ varying speeds; kick 4 × 50 @ 1:10 fast
4. Pull 300 @ 4:40, then 4 × 50 @ 1:10 with 2 to 3 breaths only
5. Swim 800 (700 aerobic subthreshold, 100 fast)
6. Cool-down: swim 200

Total: 4,900 meters

CONCLUSION

In distance training, the early season provides a gradual ascent to total yardage and creates the aerobic base necessary to successfully incorporate the coming training intensities. Midseason is a period of full and intense training. The late season, or taper, should put the frosting on the cake and help the swimmer to recover. Swimmers need to understand that they may not feel great every day throughout the taper. This is normal. Full-season training is designed for the swimmer to swim their best on championship race day. Swimmers must understand that, at this stage of the season, the physical preparation has been completed, and it is time to believe and focus on positive thoughts.

19

Training for Open Water

Sid Cassidy

Open-water swimming could stake a claim as both the oldest and youngest recognized aquatic discipline. Stone Age drawings found in "the cave of swimmers" near Wadi Sora in the southwestern part of Egypt depict ancient swimmers in the local river. Many more depictions of swimming from the Middle East region date back 3,000 to 6,000 thousand years. China, Japan, and India all boast similar ancient drawings, and written references to swimming can be found in such historical texts as *The Iliad*, *The Odyssey*, and the Bible. The great Greek philosopher Plato once stated that anyone who could not swim lacked a proper education. The history of open-water swimming is certainly rich in both tradition and cultural importance.

The most celebrated open-water venue in modern Western civilization is, without question, the English Channel. When Captain Matthew Webb made the first successful crossing in August of 1875, marathon swimming entered an incredible new era. Open-water swimmers were held in the highest regard; some even affected society as a whole. Gertrude Ederle stood as an icon for the suffragette movement by becoming the first woman to make a successful crossing in 1928. She crushed the men's record by more than 2 hours and destroyed the myth that women were somehow incapable of exerting athletic prowess. In turn, that single act of mastering the Channel empowered women worldwide to achieve new heights of success in all walks of life.

OPEN-WATER SWIMMING TODAY

Today, competitive open-water swimming is undergoing a global resurgence at every level, and the modern swim coach would be foolish to ignore the benefits that this extraordinary aquatic discipline provides. Training and competing way outside of one's comfort zone provides an outstanding opportunity for athletes to grow, not just as swimmers but as young students of life. Interest in this newest of Olympic swimming events has skyrocketed since August of 2008, when the very first Olympic marathon swim was contested in the Beijing Olympic Games. It is somewhat startling that simply gaining recognition as an Olympic event has done so much to validate what many of us have known for so long: Open-water swimming is truly an awesome experience.

Yet the reality of the dangers inherent in this emerging sport was never made more clear than on October 23, 2010, when we tragically lost one of our greatest brothers and heroes, Fran Crippen. Fran died while competing in a FINA World Cup event in the United Arab Emirates, and the fallout from that tragedy will continue to affect the aquatic world for a long, long time. The responsibility of organizers and the safety requirements of hosting sanctioned events have been under intense scrutiny since Fran's passing, and numerous new rules and regulations are now being set in place. I count myself among those who refuse to believe that his death will be in vain. In his memory, his sister Maddy, his family, his long-time coach Dick Shoulberg, and some of his closest friends have established the Fran Crippen Elevation Foundation to "advocate for safety and aid athletes as they journey to elevate themselves." Fran would have to be proud to see the efforts of so many to improve this great sport. Shortly before he passed away, he eagerly responded to my request for input in constructing this chapter. His comments are listed in the Conclusion section at the end of the chapter.

I am humbled to be able to share with any interested parties my thoughts and beliefs on this discipline. I believe I have been supposedly labeled an expert in the field primarily because I have been promoting the joys of swimming in nature for so long. I was blessed as a young child to have a father who insisted on vacations at the shore and taught me the magic of riding waves. That sheer thrill of bodysurfing led to learning and respecting the many nuances of nature's open-water venues, and I became a rabid fan of swimming in any lake, reservoir, river, bay, or ocean. Just before I started high school, I was lucky enough to move to Delaware and join the legendary Wilmington Aquatic Club. This team had no 50-meter pool; instead, we trained in a quarry hole in Avondale, Pennsylvania, to get our long-course experience. It was under Bob Mattson's tutelage in that 220-meter × 60-meter swimming hole that I really came to learn the great advantages of drafting and swimming a straight course. I remember the magic of being able to beat much faster pool swimmers by simply applying good tactics, keeping on line, and opening up my mind to the wonderment of open water. Those experiences certainly led to my love for lifeguard races and eventually a marathon swim career, where I earned some lofty world rankings.

When it became apparent that a career in swimming was my calling, I found myself attending the earliest of the United States Aquatic Sports conventions as a young coach eager to contribute to this new entity of USA Swimming. The long-distance committee seemed like a natural place to get started. Yet in those fledgling days of the early meetings of our undeveloped national governing body, my pleas for consideration and support were often dismissed as little more than fool's fodder. Nevertheless, in fashion similar to that of a determined channel swimmer, a core of believers bought into the quest and stayed the course. Because of these people both in the United States and beyond, this exciting discipline is now becoming acknowledged worldwide as the incredible aquatic opportunity that it has always been.

PREPARING FOR OPEN-WATER SWIMMING

One faces so many variables in open-water swimming that it could become overwhelming for a swimmer—or a coach—who does not embrace the thrill and excitement of facing the unknown. As the coach, you must prepare for this appropriately, impart good advice, and exude confidence in your students. In order to do this, you need to follow some very basic steps of preparation.

1. **Identify the goal.** Why do you want your swimmers to train and race in open water?

   ◆ Be honest and open with them and be ready to explain why you want this new challenge for them. You should also understand that some swimmers—and parents—will have significant fear. Although I strongly encourage all of our swimmers to participate, I never require it; I do prefer to increase the enticement for those who unite for the challenge.

   ◆ Hold a classroom for them to openly discuss this new challenge. Show them some footage of open-water racing. USA Swimming offers an outstanding video called *Out of the Box: Open-Water Swimming* that you could be shown in segments to help your swimmers visually and mentally prepare for the challenges ahead.

   ◆ Look within your area for an interesting event to prepare for and attend as a team. Really make it an adventure—perhaps even some type of reward trip. If no organized event is offered, create one! Resources are available, and people in our sport are always willing to help.

2. **Prepare swimmers in your own pool.** POW stands for pool open water, and numerous swim teams hold POW training and competitive events with great success. It is the easiest way to get your athletes started in open water.

   ◆ Simply remove all the lane lines and drop in a few turn buoys—homemade versions include any soft flotation device such as a ring buoy or lifeguard torpedo attached to a dumbbell or two.

   ◆ Set the athletes off in heats depending on their size and ability. Be creative and feel free to do sets of swims that are appropriate for their level.

   ◆ Set up drills to specifically practice turning a crowded buoy.

   ◆ Run a sanctioned POW event complete with awards, and be sure to include officials who are ready to explain and enforce the rules.

3. **Follow a safe and logical plan for the move to actual open water.** There is no substitute for safety! We have found success in combining training swims with other local clubs to increase the competitive experience. Swimmers always seem to rise to the occasion when facing a challenge from rivals, so it adds a bit of fun to the mix. Whether it is a training swim or an actual competitive event in the open water, you should always have the following:

- Permission and advice from the local managing authorities such as Coast Guard, beach patrol, or park rangers. Water quality is an issue no matter where you swim. In addition, I find it extremely helpful to seek advice from those who regularly spend time on the water, such as local fishermen, surfers, boaters, and the like. They are a great source of information on currents, weather patterns, and marine life.

- Adequate support craft. How many is enough? In my opinion, you can never have too many human-powered support craft for any training or racing event. These are paddleboards, surf boats, kayaks, and canoes—great to get close to the swimmers as guides and support, but not always great to rescue them. A good rule of thumb is eight swimmers per escort craft, but that also depends on the venue and how far away from land the course will take the swimmers. Power boats or jet skis are mandatory if the swim takes swimmers more than 200 meters from land and for sanctioned events, and emergency medical technician personnel should always be on hand.

- Emergency plan. If you need to evacuate, everyone must know how to do so and what signal will be used to announce it.

- Communication tools. Waterproof or bagged radios and cell phones are a must for keeping all of your support crew aware of what is going on.

WHAT MAKES AN OPEN-WATER SWIMMER?

As a coach, you may have already identified talent in your swimmers that could translate into success in the open water. The first and most important quality any open-water swimmer must develop to sustain success is a true love of the challenge itself. You know the type of student I am describing. Many times it may not be the most talented athlete but rather the most relentless participant who will really develop a love for open-water racing.

A good swimming coach knows that experience is the greatest teacher. Coach Mattson even boiled it down to one simple statement: "Life has but one thing to offer: experience." No matter how many classroom sessions and practices in the pool you conduct, eventually getting out there in true open-water events is what allows your swimmers to develop their open-water racing skills. The more time one spends in the open water, the more comfortable one becomes. Veteran marathoners from Matthew Webb to Maarten van der Weijden (the 2008 Olympic marathon swim champion) have been known to find a comfortable place amidst the persistent pain commonly associated with endurance sports and the challenge of being in extremely close quarters with their fiercest competitors. When identifying talent within a group of swimmers, we naturally look first for athletes with distance skill, but the ability to relax in uncomfortable situations is essential to success in open water. Never underestimate the capability of an athlete who rolls with the punches; that flexible personality trait is a common to all the greats.

For the past two decades, one of the world's greatest marathon swimmers has been Britta Kamrau from Germany. On this topic, Britta said

> *For open-water swimming you need above all endurance, a strong willpower, the ability to assert yourself, and love for the water in any condition that might confront you. You should never fight against the water but with the water; you need to make it your friend no matter how big the waves are or how cold the temperature might be.*

Britta eloquently describes the essence of the cerebral calm that elite marathoners master while their bodies are churning endlessly at the task at hand. Common among many of the world's best open-water swimmers is the notion that one should strive to find tranquility and peace in the water even though a highly competitive race may be raging all around. Britta further explained

> *What you also need to consider is that there are numerous other swimmers with you fighting for the same good position and course of the race itself. You definitely need to be prepared for that because it can cost you a lot of concentration and energy, but you need to be able to fight for your position as well. That's why crowded lanes at the pool shouldn't be seen as something disturbing while training, but as a chance to practice some open-water race conditions. Coaches could even let a few swimmers start at the same time in one lane and let them race, but obviously you should never hurt anybody or be unfair.*

For more than a decade, Erica Rose has been considered the queen of American marathon swimmers. Her breakthrough into the elite open-water scene was a magnificent victory in the inaugural FINA Five-Kilometer World Championship in Perth, Australia in January of 1998. She swam to the 2,500-meter mark as a part of the lead pack and then sharply increased her stroke rate to quickly pull away and win in a most convincing negative-split manner. Through the ensuing years, Erica won 10 national titles and 5 titles in Pan American and Pan Pacific competitions ranging from the 5-kilometer to the 25-kilometer distance. She grew up in Cleveland swimming for Rick Stacy and Jerry Holtrey and the Lake Erie Silver Dolphins, where she noted that she "grew accustomed to very long sets that included very little rest." She was an elite pool swimmer before making the transition to open water and explained to me that she always preferred using the pool as her primary training venue.

> *Training for open-water swims—even those that are extremely long open-water swims—can most definitely be done in a pool. Throughout my open-water swimming career, I did about 95% (if not more) of my training in the pool. The only time I trained in open water was right before a competition when I was at the venue and had a chance to be on the course. The rest of the time, I focused on doing high-volume, high-intensity, low-rest sets in the pool to simulate the long distances I would be swimming in an open-water race.*

When I asked her how she managed to avoid becoming bored or burned out with all that pool training, she responded

Training for open-water races in the pool can—and should—be fun for athletes. When I was training at Northwestern University with Bob Groseth, he found a new and different way to simulate open-water conditions every Saturday morning. He asked other swimmers to use their kickboards in the pool to make waves for me. He filled up a cooler with ice-cold water and dumped it on me, simulating a cold patch in an open-water race. He tangled stretch cords and put them on top of me, challenging me to swim my way out of 'seaweed.' He asked other swimmers to swim on either side of me, shoving their elbows into my sides and kicking me every now and then so that I wouldn't be shocked when jostled by competitors in a race. If coaches are creative and have fun coming up with ideas to help prepare their athletes for open-water swims, the athletes will look forward to the races and will learn to enjoy the sport as well.

One of the most successful open-water coaches in the United States is Rick Walker, who is also the longtime head coach of the men's team at Southern Illinois University. Rick served as this nation's National Open Water Team head coach for more than a decade until the national governing body restructured their committee system to bring more programs under staff control. Yet to this day, Rick is still annually called upon to conduct the highly successful USA Swimming Open-Water Camp that he helped structure. Aside from placing his own athletes on numerous national teams, Rick has served as a guru to dozens of our very best open-water competitors. He is lauded as an outstanding mentor whose specialty has been getting the nation's best pool swimmers to bridge the gap and experience success in the world of open-water swimming. In preparing this chapter I called on Rick to lend his expertise, and I am proud to share some of his thoughts as follows.

When you are looking for new athletes to challenge the rigors of open-water competition, three prominent characteristics will greatly increase their chance for success:

1. *The first trait to look for is whether the swimmer can handle the heavy workload and never really break down. These swimmers may not be the fastest but can handle a decent pace and hold it over a very long period of time, and often will win the longer training swims simply by attrition.*

2. *The swimmer who finds a way to gut it out has an increased chance to succeed. This athlete finds a way to handle whatever task (set) you give them. They seem to have a feel or sense of what it takes and simply gets it done.*

3. *The third trait is whether the swimmer goes with the flow. By this, we look for the swimmer who takes every situation as it comes. They do not get rattled easily, nor do the conditions have to be perfect in order for them to perform at high levels. Swimmers who do not have this trait can have difficulty overcoming the changes that happen before, during, and even after an open-water swim.*

If you can find a swimmer that has at least two of these three traits, then you may well have a potential open-water swimmer on your hands.

OPEN-WATER TRAINING

After finding athletes in your program that might be suited for open water-swimming events, it is time to train them for the event. I have always found it beneficial to give them 2 days a week of straight swims to get their bodies ready for the length of the swim. The other days I try to train them on the longer end of distances (800s, 1,000s, and 2,000s) and multiple repeats. After a cycle of this I then take those 3 days and train pace and speed at shorter distances (200s, 300s, 400s, and 500s). I continue to train at least 2 days of the longer distances. In the third cycle you can do a mix of 100s pace or speed with various mixed sets of middle-distance sets. This would conclude a three-cycle training plan. After recovery, you begin the cycle again. I try to increase the yardage as I go and move through the cycles with a "train up to swim down" attitude. While you cannot repeat 10,000-meter swims, every once in a while you want to throw in swims that come close to or exceed the 10 kilometers. This will assure the athlete that they can do it and give them a sense of how they want to approach a strategy for the event.

The benefits of training for open water and of racing open-water events are numerous. If you have ever had a swimmer that you know can go out faster or that simply starts out too slow in pool distance events, open water may be the way to teach them how to better approach their pool events. I have never had an open-water swimmer who did not view the 1,650 as a sprint compared with some of the open-water swims they had done. They approached the 1,650 from a different point of view. It has always been for the better.

I share a great deal of Rick Walker's philosophy of preparing athletes for races of 10,000 meters and beyond. It is critical to cycle these swimmers appropriately and include what I call race simulators weekly. Usually I build two 3-day microcycles into a week and finish the sixth day with one of these simulators. I like to build into day 1 good aerobic distance sets that include lots of ladders, or mind-grinders, the term I've inherited from the Sea Tigers. (The sea tiger was the mascot of the Wilmington Aquatic Club, my swim team, coached by Bob Mattson.) It describes an aerobic set that may follow a pattern for anywhere from 40 minutes to 2 hours or more. Such a set should be designed to challenge the athlete with a solid interval that will allow them to maintain some good threshold swimming.

Day 2 generally involves a bit more leg work and some strong speed work, something that is very critical for today's elite-level open-water swimmer. The United States' Andrew Gemmell, who captured the 10-kilometer silver medal in the 2009 Rome world championships, shared with me the following comments to illustrate this point.

> *Open-water swimming takes two types of training. First, you have to be able to swim 10,000 yards at a pretty high aerobic rate. That's the easy part. The second part is being able to race with speed the closing 500 even when you're dead tired. The second part is the most important because it is what makes the difference between a gold medal and a tenth-place finish. That's also the best part of open-water swimming. It comes down to just a pure race at the end—a 2-hour race decided by mere seconds!*

Day 3 in my microcycle is the longer swim in the pool and often includes a bit of paddle training, or pulling, or both. The second half of the week I repeat the same 3-day cycle and finish with the race simulator on Saturday, and follow that up with a day off Sunday, our recovery day. If done in a pool, the simulator can be done traditionally or without lane lines and walls by swimming in a circular pattern complete with marker buoys. I prefer this method when training a small team of athletes so that we can even replicate some of the bumping and drafting and getting around the buoys quickly. I have them take very short feeding breaks and imitate the race feed where they get 8 to 12 ounces (236.6 to 354.9 ml) of fluid replacement every 20 to 25 minutes. I communicate with them by using a whiteboard to indicate their stroke rate or other relevant information.

If you are in proximity to good open water for training purposes, it is even more desirable to get out of the chlorine and into open water, provided the athlete's primary focus is the upcoming open-water event. I like to build a 12-week training cycle where our simulators on Saturday increase percentage-wise for 3 weeks before decreasing slightly to start the next 3-week cycle. For instance, if the swim is 10,000 meters, I build the 12 week-ending simulators as follows. The first 3 weeks we go 5,000, 6,000, and 7,000; the second 3 weeks we go 6,500, 7,500, 8,500; and then we plan to peak training in week 9 and go 8,000, 9,000, and 10,000 as our Saturday swims. The 10-kilometer simulator is done at the end of the ninth week, which is also our peak training week. We then follow up with simulators of 7,500 2 weeks before and 5,000 1 week before the big race. I tend to follow a similar build–rest cycle with the overall yardage. I have found that the older males can certainly handle a bit more rest than younger swimmers, and true distance-oriented female swimmers of any age seem to get stale if they are given too much rest, so you must get to know what best works for your own athletes.

OPEN-WATER TACTICS

The tactics and strategies of open-water racing are evolving rapidly, and the modern coach should wisely consider how best to prepare athletes for the mind games that await. Mark Warkentin became the first American in history to qualify for an Olympic marathon swim and performed admirably in Beijing, where he snared an eighth-place finish a mere 22 seconds behind van der Weijden's gold-medal performance. A consistently successful pool swimmer at the national level, Mark turned to open water and gained more opportunities to compete internationally for his country. He shared with me some thoughts on the importance of using mental abilities in elite open-water racing.

> *Strategy, awareness, patience, and the ability to make split-second decisions are more important than talent or training regimen. This makes open-water swimming the thinking man's water sport.*

Mark went on to explain how he learned some valuable lessons racing against the best marathon swimmers in the world.

> *Early in my career when I tried to win races on talent and training, I found that I was competitive early in the race, then faded toward the end. I needlessly used energy because I fell into the trap of trying to win from the front when I should have played the mental chess game that others were playing. I consistently made poor decisions with race strategy, always thinking that I could dominate the field if I was the leader of the pack. I made the decision to play the game in the summer of 2007 at a race in London. There was no pressure on the race and I was not expected to be successful, so I tried to be as cautious and controlled as possible until the absolute moment necessary. I swam 9,500 meters of controlled swimming followed by a 500 sprint and placed second in a very close finish. It was then that I realized that my strategy dictated my finish more than anything else. Five months later at the U.S. world championship trials (selection for Olympics) I swam 7,500 meters of very cautious swimming. I was purposefully in last place after the first 2,500 meters of the most important race of my life. I was in sixth place for most of the time between the 2,500 and 7,500, and didn't start to challenge myself until the 8,500-meter mark. I ended up winning because my first 7,500 was completely controlled. I knew my competitors and I knew their personalities. I spent time researching the other athletes in the race, and I knew what they would and would not do in particular circumstances. I studied the other athletes as if it were a boxing match rather than a swim race. The research and time spent analyzing my competitors proved more valuable than any training regimen.*

One of the leading authorities on open-water racing strategy and technique is coach Gerry Rodriguez, who exemplifies excellence in his craft by practicing what he preaches. Gerry is a veteran of more than 400 open-water swimming events, and he consistently finishes at the top of the field not only in his age group but in the overall categories as well. He is also an enlightened student and teacher of the sport, and recently we discussed the high stroke rate count of today's elite marathon swimmers. Most men who earn podium spots at FINA events swim 70 to 80% of a 10-kilometer race well over 70 strokes per minute, only to crank it up into the high 80s or 90s with a six-beat kick for the last couple kilometers as they sprint to the finish. More often than not, the women have an even higher RPM (rate [stroke] per minute). Gerry shared the following observations on stroke rate, heart rate, and the need for speed in contemporary open-water racing.

> *Stroke rates are critical to very fast swimming in open water no matter what the age or level of competition. Train to get to those rates if you want to be competitive. I'd also be pretty hard pressed to believe any of the athletes that raced the Brazil 10-kilometer [FINA World Cup event in December of 2009] had heart rates of 110 at any point during their race. There is no substitute for hard work and deliberate, effective, specific training. These modern 10-kilometer events call for just that, and it is equally true for all the 1- and 2-mile (1.6 and 3.2 km) races and triathlon swim legs around the world. These athletes have to be able to accelerate and slow down, position themselves, and create boxed-in positions on*

others, thus requiring various stroke rate capabilities and heart rate changes. This is the Tour de France in the aquatic world. They need to practice all of this, and they do—at least the ones who win consistently.

OPEN-WATER EVENTS

The open-water events in the senior program include the 5,000-, 10,000-, and 25,000-meter events. But the creative coach should realize that open-water swimming does not necessarily mean long-distance swimming. I am aware of numerous novice races of 100 to 400 yards in rivers, lakes, and oceans that often award medals to all who participate. We sponsored a fun bay swim for years in Atlantic City that measured a mere 200 yards and in which our club swimmers partnered with local Special Olympians to earn the prestigious "I swam across the bay" T-shirts. Elite sprinters participate in the Sea Sprints at the Pacific Open-Water Challenge in Long Beach, California. This imaginative addition from Steve Munatones features a beach finish following a straightaway sprint and different stroke categories. Steve is quite the aquatic visionary and has put an incredible amount of time into exploring new ways to promote all aspects of our sport. His Long Beach event also featured this continent's first Open-Water Pursuit event, a 4-kilometer race in which teams of three or four athletes begin together as a team in staggered starts and finish together. Like cyclists, the Open-Water Pursuit event requires teammates to form an aquatic peloton and use all the requisite drafting, positioning, navigating, and pacing skills of open-water swimming. This is actually the newest of approved FINA World Championship events. Steve currently serves as the nation's representative to the FINA Technical Open-Water Swimming Committee and put together the inaugural Global Open-Water Swimming Conference during the same week of the Pacific Open-Water events in 2010. He makes himself available to all open-water enthusiasts via his expansive website, www.openwatersource.com. The site regularly receives more than 10,000 individual visitors per day and is an incredible resource for coaches and the entire open-water community. I strongly encourage you to use it.

CONCLUSION

From the earliest of times to the modern day, the passion for open-water swimming has rolled along like a mighty river. Even with the many changes that continue to come down the line, the words spoken from today's heroes echo with reverence in tones eerily similar to those who went before. Six-time U.S. champion, 2009 World Championship medalist, and 2010 Pan American champion Fran Crippen once stated

The most important factor in adding open-water swimming to an athlete's event list is having an open mind and an enthusiasm for trying new things in our sport. Open-water swimming takes the aspects of strategy and tactics to a whole new level. This causes every race to have its own identity, which can be very intriguing to a young athlete. Personally, I find open-water swimming to be racing in its purest form. It is endurance athletes battling from start to finish, with the victor being the swimmer who combines strategy, smarts, and speed.

Another of America's national champions (in both pool and open-water events) and the United States' first female Olympic marathon swimmer, Chloe Sutton, also invoked the theme of purity when she summed it quite simply.

Open-water swimming is swimming at its purest. When you have to battle elements as well as other swimmers, it adds a whole new level of excitement to competition. I love every minute of it!

20

Individual Medley Training

Gregg Troy

To many the individual medley (IM) appears to be the four competitive strokes swum in order. In reality, it is an event in itself. Many athletes can swim all four strokes well but are not able to excel in the medley. At the same time, some athletes with average or even weak strokes can develop into very good or even outstanding medley swimmers.

Training for the IM event is much more diverse than training for any one stroke and is possibly more demanding. The athlete must develop and refine all four strokes, pay close attention to stroke transitions, and develop the endurance to swim all strokes at high rates of speed. The medley events combine all the elements of speed (the 100 and 200 IM) and power with the aerobic capacity and endurance (400 IM) of distance events.

ADVANTAGES OF AN IM TRAINING PLATFORM

Many of the best programs in the world have used the IM as the platform for their team training. Using the medley as a foundation for developing athletes is especially useful at the age-group and junior levels because it provides good overall fitness and a tremendous aerobic background and develops all four strokes. When age-group athletes are developed in this manner, they develop a base for future versatility and the ability to change and add events as the body matures and changes. Very often, athletes developed in this type of environment can change priority strokes and events throughout their careers.

Another advantage of an IM platform is that athletes develop an increased awareness of all aspects of the sport. Practices are more varied, and younger and maturing athletes are much more able to find an area of success. The ultimate result is a group that is fresh, happy, and well rounded. The use of all four strokes creates greater overall strength and a wider range of physical skills and provides the necessary platform for more focuses and individual training at advanced levels.

IM TRAINING BLOCKS

As athletes show promise and interest in the medley, the coach can identify what areas need to be addressed for future and more elite levels of success. To address weaknesses and to develop the medley, the athlete and coach must spend extended periods working on each area of the medley. Many times, weak strokes or areas are identified but not addressed properly. For the athlete to truly develop, significant amounts of time need to be devoted to each stroke. Drills and attention to stroke development are good, but many times the athlete needs to train the stroke with athletes who specialize in that event.

For example, a medley athlete who desires to improve a weak backstroke leg needs to do more than just drill and swim the stroke more. The drills and swims are keys for improvement, but true improvement comes from an extended period of time training as a backstroke athlete. This is equally true for all of the strokes.

In the past, I have used sessions of 4 to 12 weeks that focused on the weakest stroke. The athlete improving a weak backstroke leg would be a backstroker for this entire period of time and would train on challenging intervals with backstroke specialists. Little if any compensation would be made for intervals; the key is to train the stroke, not just swim it.

Over the course of a year of training, the development of a medley should include blocks of training that focus on each of the four strokes in the same manner. Attention is given to all four strokes during all training phases, but emphasis of one stroke for an extended period of time is the key to optimal performance and improvement in the IM. Many times, the results from these training blocks are not immediately apparent but rather follow after the athlete has recovered from the fatigue associated with focusing on one stroke.

As the athlete comes closer to major competition, all four strokes should be trained more equally. Though the athlete may need to change the emphasis or amount of training in each area due to individual needs and preferences, total confidence in all four strokes can be developed over several years of this type of evaluation of needs and weaknesses.

One of the greatest challenges in developing a medley athlete is the amount of time and patience required. The individual's ability to adapt and change may vary greatly by stroke and distance, and true improvement in a weak area may be apparent long before time is improved. This seems to especially be true as an athlete becomes older and more experienced.

When developing all four strokes, the weak stroke can quite often change. The athlete and coach must continually pay attention to improvements and challenges in each discipline. Many times, the weak stroke is not the key stroke to eventual success in the medley. This is most apparent in the breaststroke. In our program, many athletes who had more than adequate breast legs of the IM continued to view the breaststroke as their weak stroke. Many times, they were outstanding fly athletes who were overswimming or undertraining that stroke, which showed in the breast leg when they were fatigued.

In evaluating the individual athlete and his or her development of the medley, these problems make training, development, and identifying areas of focus more complex. Both coach and athlete need to spend time addressing interrelated effects of strokes and race strategy. The challenge of where to place both racing and training is much more complex in the IM than in any individual stroke. Communication and exchange between athlete and coach is a major component of medley development at the highest levels.

200 IM

The short IM are sprint events in nature. This is especially true in the short-course version. In training for the 200 IM, the emphasis is much less on stroke improvement (though it is a key component) and more on power and speed.

The 200 IM short course is very much about the athlete's ability to sprint and turn. Athletes with some obvious stroke flaws can be very successful in the short-course 200 IM, but they need good speed and must be able to turn with the very best in each stroke. Outstanding underwater work and great legs can hide butterfly and backstroke weaknesses in the 200 IM short course. Breaststroke weaknesses must be addressed but can be negated by tremendous underwater pullouts, breakouts, and quick turns.

In the long-course version of the 200 IM, a greater need exists for good stroke mechanics because the athlete spends less time underwater. Speed is again a key component, but the athlete must be able to build each stroke. Many athletes who are successful short course never master the long-course event because race strategy does not allow an all-out approach that is sometimes successful in the short-course version. In both short-course and long-course 200 IM, the athlete must focus on transition turns.

When evaluating the 200 IM, attention should be given to building and maintaining speed through the transition. In the short-course version, we evaluate the splits from the first 25 and the second 25 of each stroke; little or no difference should exist between the two. We constantly strive to have the fly and freestyle splits as close as possible. If the two are more than 0.5 second apart, then the fly leg is overswum, the athlete is not conditioned for the event, or the freestyle is the dramatically weaker stroke for the athlete.

These same principles are true in the long-course event. An even greater stress is placed on comparing the fly and freestyle splits. It is amazing that athletes and coaches look for faster and faster fly splits even though the freestyle is dramatically slower. This should happen only in athletes who are exceptional in the butterfly and very weak in the free.

In pace and premeet warm-up work for the IM, we look for things other than than pace for other 200 events. In short course, we recommend 2 to 3 × 50 @ 20 seconds rest. These 50s always include the transition turn. One option is 3 × 50s: the second 25 of the fly and the first 25 of the back; the second 25 of the back and the first 25 of the breast; and the second 25 of the breast and the first 25 of the free. If two 50s are used, we go 1 fly/back, 1 back/breast, 1 back/breast, or 1 breast/free.

We then follow through with a 25 free push and a dive 25 fly where the two times are the same or very close.

These 50 times are worked out well in advance to the end of the season and are used as training paces for transition sets in practice. By the time the athlete is at the key meets at the season's end, these times are the pace work in warm-up. Traditionally, we would do three of these in the morning and only two in the evening. It creates a bit of a nightmare in warm-up, but the preference is to do them so that the transition turn is at the transition end in the meet.

In the long-course IM, we have used as a warm-up set 3×50, one of each stroke, or 2×50 (1 back, 1 breast) followed by a push 25 free and a dive 25 fly. I prefer 2×50 and then trying to match the push free and dive fly times as in the 200 IM. This seems to give the athlete a feel for all four strokes and ends with a dive fly that sets up the race.

400 IM

The same general philosophy of developing all four strokes and the ability to transition is still key in the longer medleys, but stroke refinement and increased training time are even more essential. The 400 IM is truly a distance event. It may in fact be the most demanding of all swimming events because the athlete needs speed, versatility, and timing as well as a true distance-based approach. Stroke deficiencies can be hidden in the 200 IM by outstanding turns and underwater work, but the 400 requires proficiency in these areas as well as a good, sound stroke foundation in all strokes.

The general work for the long IM events must be coupled with work in the distance free, which is a key component for success. Many of the best 400 IM athletes were distance freestyle swimmers early in their careers. Quite often, the 400 IM athlete will not have success in the 200 due to an inability to combine both the speed and distance work required to succeed at both.

In training for the 400, it is essential to train large blocks of time in each stroke area. At the same time, attention should be given to an aerobic emphasis on freestyle and medley transitions. The early-season volumes and time commitments for the long IM are very similar to those required of distance athletes.

Race splits in the 400 IM are similar to those in the 200 in that we still prefer the butterfly and freestyle splits to be the same. In fact, this is key in evaluating how quickly the event should be swum up front. Except in cases where the athlete is a dramatically better butterfly swimmer, the athlete does not need to be faster on the fly leg if the freestyle is slower.

When evaluating the race, the second 50 of each stroke should be faster than the first, with the exception of butterfly. In the butterfly, the difference between the first and second 50 should be no more than 2 seconds. The backstroke and breaststroke second 50 of each should be very similar; the second should be a bit better. If the second 50 is more than 1 second faster than the first, the athlete is underswimming the first 50. The athlete may have a larger improvement on the second 50 of the freestyle leg due to the touch of the hand.

The 400 IM requires a conscious effort by the athlete to not overswim the first part of any of the 100s. This is especially true for the first 50 fly. The athlete should build effort and speed through each 100 and focus on smoothly transitioning to the next stroke.

Warm-up paces for the longer IM can be done in either 50s or 100s but must be accurate because overswimming any part of the race (especially the first 200) can dramatically and negatively affect total performance. In the short-course 400 IM, I prefer 4×75 in warm-up with a 25 free swim at a moderate rate for increased heart rate followed by a 50 swim at the pace of the first 50 of each stroke (the exception is the butterfly, where it is the second 50). The up-tempo freestyle before the 50 allows for a greater feel of the race and true pace work. In each 75, the transition from free to the stroke is made relative to the race by adjusting the last few strokes to provide for a true transition turn. These can be followed by a dive 50 fly in which the athlete works on how controlled the first 50 should be. The first 50 of the 400 IM is essential; it sets up the first quarter of the race and must be controlled.

The warm-up for the long-course version of the 400 IM is similar, but I prefer 3×100. I have had success at the three 100s, the first 50 fly/50 back, the second 50 breast/50 breast, and the third 50 breast/50 free. When done in this manner, the athlete should take great care to not overswim the first 50. We have found greater success in doing 3×100 in the same manner as the 3×75 short course; the first 50 is up-tempo freestyle and is followed by a 50 of the stroke. This seems to give the athlete a feel for the race without overstressing the system before the event.

YEARLY TRAINING PLAN

When planning an entire year of training for the medley, one must devote adequate time to developing each of the strokes to the best possible form. Devoting specific time blocks to focus on each stroke allows the athlete to emphasize each stroke as a specialist in each stroke would.

The actual amount of time each athlete devotes to each stroke may vary by length of season and specific needs. I prefer to focus on the weakest stroke during the first cycle. During this cycle, the athlete must train not just with other medley athletes but with specialists in that stroke. The athlete and coach should pay close attention to technical development and drills. Training sets should be stressful and should change little from normal intervals. The athlete must train and develop the stroke, not merely swim it more often.

As the season progresses, the athlete rotates through each of the strokes through each training cycle. During each of these focus periods, attention is still given to all strokes and to total IM development. Rotation of focus can be performed in large blocks or can be broken into smaller blocks that are repeated throughout the season or year. As each stroke develops, the order and the amount of time devoted to each focus cycle may change.

This type of approach to building an IM creates a well-rounded athlete who is confident in all four strokes. It also provides for a greater variety in race strategy and options for swimming the race. The 400 IM specialists may want to devote a cycle or more to focusing on distance freestyle. The 200 IM specialists may spend some time within the sprint areas. See table 20.1 for an example of a yearly training plan (48 weeks).

Although specific strokes are emphasized during each training period, all four are trained. Distance freestyle is a key component in all early training.

TABLE 20.1   48-Week Training Module IM

Weeks 1–4	Focus on general fitness and conditioning.
Weeks 5–8	Focus on aerobic background and overtraining the weakest stroke of the IM.
Weeks 9–12	
Weeks 13–16	Continued emphasis on aerobic work. Reduced stress from a volume standpoint on weak strokes, but development of speed and race pace for the weak stroke. Emphasis on training the second stroke.
Weeks 17–20	
Weeks 21–24	Continued distance freestyle training. Development of race pace for the weakest and second-weakest strokes. Emphasis on training the best stroke.
Weeks 25–28	
Weeks 29–32	Reduced emphasis on distance free and increased training on transitional sets and speed and pace development of all four strokes.
Weeks 33–36	
Weeks 37–40	Focus on competition and race-related skills. Final development of speed and pace race strategies.
Weeks 41–48	Focus on taper and race strategy training.

WEEKLY TRAINING PLAN

Within each week, a definite plan should provide for adequate focus on training, technique, and race structure for each of the strokes and the overall race. How much focus is directed toward each stroke is relative to the individual, the time of the year, competition schedule, and actual needs.

A typical week of 9 to 10 training sessions may include the following:

One to two sessions devoted to distance free training or speed work

Three sessions devoted to the focus stroke for that cycle

One to two sessions devoted to each of the other strokes

One session focused on the total IM

DAILY TRAINING PLAN

When designing the daily workout, the coach should direct attention to skill development and technique in each session. Constant reinforcement of technical weaknesses and improvement is key to overall development and change.

Whenever possible, a workout design should provide a flow in practice that contributes to IM development. Some possible plans follow.

Workout A

1. Warm-up session focusing on skills and drills of one specific stroke
2. A moderate swim set of the next stroke of the medley
3. A major series of the next stroke of the medley
4. A kick series of either the next stroke or the weakest

Workout B

1. Warm-up session with an aerobic freestyle set that includes all four strokes in a drill manner
2. A moderate pull series of either butterfly or backstroke (possibly both of those strokes in transition)
3. A major IM series
4. Speed kick set freestyle

Workout C

1. General warm-up
2. A major series of the focus stroke for that cycle
3. A drill or kick set of the stroke in the IM that follows the focus stroke
4. A long swim of any stroke or a kick series

Workout D

1. General warm-up
2. A drill series of the stroke before the focus stroke
3. A major set of the focus stroke
4. Long swim of any stroke or weak stroke

All of these examples use the transition of sets within the practice to help the athlete develop a greater feel for each stroke and develop use of energy in a medley manner.

Three Sample Workout Days: IM Training, Midseason Summer

Following are sample training sets that can be done in the summer midseason, when the training is more intense. These are long-course training sets except when designated as short course.

Day 1

a.m.

3 × 600 IM—all with buoy

100 free/100 fly; 100 free/100 back; 100 free/100 breast*

2 × (100 free/200 IM)*

200 fly/back/100 free; 200 back/breast/100 free*

3 × (4 × 50 fly with band @ 45 seconds—keep hips up); (3 × 100 back with buoy @ 1:30—negative split); (1 × 200 breaststroke swim @ 3:30—first 50 1 stroke under race pace stroke count and second and third 50s as fast as possible); (1 × 100 free @ 1:30—perfect technique); (1 × 400 IM for time)

1,600 of power work—towers, tubing, pull working all 4 strokes

p.m.

500 free; 400 (alternate 50 back/50 free), 300 (alternate 50 breast/50 free), 200 (alternate 50 fly/50 free), 100 kick—all at 30 seconds rest

3 × (100 fly @ 1:40); (100 free @ 1:30), (100 back @ 1:40), (100 free @ 1:30), (100 breaststroke @ 1:40), (100 free @ 1:30), (400 IM fast). All 100 free swims @ butterfly time, all stroke 100s negative split, and 400 IM within 20% of best goal time.

1,500–2,000 weak stroke IM with fins and work technique

* All with 30 seconds rest and pull buoy for body position

Day 2

a.m.

One practice short course (SC) and one practice long course (LC). Men and women switch the LC and SC sessions between a.m. and p.m.

LC: 4 × 400 IM @ 6:30/7:00 (50 fly, 50 back, 150 breast, 150 free)

3 × [3 × (100 weak IM stroke, 100 transition fly/back; back/breast, breast/free); back/fly @ 1:30–1:40; back/breast @ 1:40–1:50]—first set with snorkel

3 × (8 × 100 free pull @ 1:15–1:20)—distance group

12 × 100 kick @ 2:00 (4 stroke, 4 choice, 4 free)

Distance 3,000 pull/strokes 2,000 pull

p.m.

SC: 40 × 50 (20 @ 0:45, free) 20 @ 0:50 with 4 stroke, 4 free, remainder IM order or stroke (first smooth, second kick/drill, third drill/technique, fourth build fast)

20 × 25 fly @ 0:30 (6 with band, 6 with buoy, 8 swim)

20 × 25 back @ 0:30 (1 spin, 1 double arm, 2 swim descend)

20 × 25 breast @ 0:40 (1 with 1 stroke and 5 kicks, 1 smooth, 1 pullout and kick fly, 1 form)

20 × 25 free @ 0:25 (odds: hypoxic, no breath; even: heart rates)

2,000 pull with band

Day 3

a.m.

SC: 3 × 600 @ 8:00; first 200 free, fly, back; second 200 free, back, breast; third 200 free, back, free

2 × (200 IM; 400 IM; 600 IM; 800 IM; 400 IM; 200 IM)—use a 1:20 base on the way up through the 800 IM, then a 1:15 base on the way down

p.m.

LC: 2,000 general warm-up

4 × 100 fly @ 1:40, 200 free @ 3:00 smooth (emphasize 6-beat kick on 200s)

400 IM @ 6:00, 200 free @ 3:00 smooth

4 × 100 back @ 1:40, 200 free @ 300 smooth

400 IM @ 6:00, 200 free @ 3:00 smooth

4 × 100 breast @ 1:50, 200 free @ 3:00 smooth

400 IM @ 6:00

Same set but 50s of the strokes, 200 free, then a 200 IM in place of the 400 IM

CONCLUSION

Medley training and preparation provides the athlete with greater variety and a strong platform for overall fitness. It also requires great patience and a larger amount of planning to adequately cover the many diverse areas. Drills and swimming in a weaker stroke are necessary, but the real improvement comes from an extended period of training with the specialists in that stroke.

21

Training for Relays

David Durden

Relays. Just the word evokes excitement, fun, and an anticipation that no individual swim could ever elicit. Of all the moments of swimming throughout any competitor's career, a relay swim or performance likely stands out in one's memory. As coaches and spectators, the relay moments capture our cheering and passion. Remember Jason Lezak running down Alain Bernard in Michael Phelps' quest for eight gold medals? How about Klete Keller swimming a beautiful anchor leg in Athens in the 800 free relay to hold off Olympic champion Ian Thorpe? If those two don't get you, then Bruce Hayes versus Michael Gross in the epic 800 free relay during the 1984 Olympics definitely has to send some chills up your spine.

THE IMPORTANCE OF RELAYS

As coaches, we often sell our athletes on the idea of representing something larger than themselves. We talk about the notion of team. We illustrate the ideas of racing and competing for the group standing on the side of the pool rather than the person standing on the blocks. Relays are the one tangible time in our sport that a group of athletes can stand behind the blocks and represent something larger than their individual selves. No individual performance can create the deep well of emotion that relays create.

We have all heard about that mythical relay split: the time when someone threw down an incredible performance inside or at the end of a relay that could never be repeated from a flat start. My coaching memory of such a split is from the 2003 world championships in Barcelona. At the time, I had worked with Fred Bousquet for about 8 months. He was coming off a successful NCAA short-course yard season in which he won the 50 freestyle, and it was time to translate that success over to the long-course format. Fred anchored the French 4 × 100 free relay in a blistering 47.03 to hold off Ian Thorpe's Australia team by 0.01 and to help secure the bronze medal for France. Fred's time in the final of the 100 free: 49.30. The winning time from Alexander Popov in the 100 freestyle at that year's world championships: 48.42. How does that happen?!

Just mention the word relay in the course of your practice and watch the dynamic change. Relays either start or end (or sometimes both) every organized swim meet, from neighbor swim leagues up through the collegiate ranks, because they are just plain fun and exciting.

Outside of the emotion that relays create, relays hold huge quantitative importance at the high school and collegiate levels. Relays count as double in most team point competitions. At the NCAA Division I Championships, relay points make up more than 40% of the available points of the swimming competition. During the 2010 NCAA Championships, our Cal relay teams won four of the five relays over the 3-day competition, which propelled our program to a second-place team finish. At the 2011 NCAA Championships, we won three of the five relays and won the NCAA title.

The importance of relays is inherent. Whether they create healthy competition in a practice session, generate some momentum at the start of a neighborhood swim meet, or leave a lasting Bruce Hayes-type moment, relays serve as a shocking event that everyone will remember. Now, how do we train for them?

TRAINING RELAY STARTS

At Cal I teach two types of relay starts: the single-foot step-up start and the two-foot step-up start. Even though we work with only two types of starts, our athletes have developed many variations. In this chapter we discuss both types; I hope that you will find the start that can work for you and your swimmers.

Single-Foot Step-Up Start

The single-foot step-up start is a relay start in which the athlete's front foot is at the edge of the starting block and the back foot is positioned toward the middle or the back of the block (figure 21.1). The swimmer can use either the left or right foot as the front foot; it is a matter of personal preference and trial and error.

A swimmer can determine which foot to use as the front foot in this relay start by noticing which is the lead foot when they ride a skateboard, surfboard, or snowboard. Or, in case the X Games are not their thing, a swimmer can have someone push them in

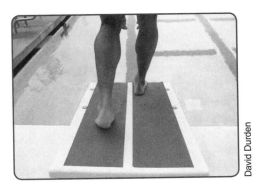

FIGURE 21.1 Correct positioning of the feet in the single-foot step-up start.

the back (gently!) while their feet are together and shoulder-width apart. Whichever foot steps forward to help with balance is usually the more dominant foot and should serve as the front foot in this type of relay start.

A swimmer should try both feet in this position. The goal is to establish the more dominant foot, which typically provides more balance. This is critical because for a short time during this start all of the weight is placed on the front foot.

The positioning of the back foot is equally important to that of the front foot. First, the left foot and right foot need to stay shoulder-width apart. If the back foot is wider or narrower than shoulder-width apart, then the ensuing relay start will typically cause the swimmer to enter at an angle off the center line (i.e., when the swimmer enters the water, they will shoot off to either the right or the left). This information is helpful when a swimmer finally puts together the final product of a single-foot step-up start. If they shoot off to one side or the other as they enter the water, a coach or another swimmer should check the position of the back foot before they begin the start.

FIGURE 21.2 Correct spacing between the feet in the single-foot step-up start.

The distance between the front foot and back foot also plays an important role in the single-foot step-up start. A teammate or coach should place a hand on the block, in a relaxed position with the fingers spread, between the heel of the swimmer's front foot and the toes of the swimmer's back foot. A swimmer is in a good position if the coach or teammate can slide the hand on the block without much space between the hand and the swimmer's heel and toes (figure 21.2). If the back foot is too close to or too far from the front foot, it can limit the amount of power that this relay start generates.

When positioning the feet on the block during this start, a general theme for the swimmer to remember is to "be athletic." As we get into the timing and rhythm of this start, the movement is very athletic. Swimmers are often characterized (unfairly, in my opinion) as being awkward and uncoordinated. This start relies on athleticism and coordination.

Now that the swimmer is on the blocks with the feet in the correct position, it's time to get the rest of the body in the right spot as well. First, the swimmer should keep the knees soft. A small bend in the knees keeps the body relaxed and ready to go. Neither knee should be locked at any time during this start. Second, the swimmer should bend at the waist so that the back and chest are about 45° from horizontal. The back must stay straight as the swimmer bends from the waist. In other words, the chest should press down in such a way that the shoulders stay back and the buttocks sticks out to keep the back in a straight position from shoulders to rump. At this point, the arms should stay relaxed and hang from the body, and the head and eyes should look forward to the incoming swimmer that is in the water (figure 21.3a).

Again, a swimmer should be very aware of posture throughout this positioning on the blocks. Remaining athletic (more of an idea than a position at this point) on the blocks will transfer to the actual movement of the relay start when the swimmer begins the actual relay exchange. One final thing to keep in mind is distribution of weight on the feet. The weight should be neither all on the heels nor all on the balls of the feet. Rather, the weight should be distributed at about 60% on the balls of the feet and 40% on the heels, which puts the swimmer in a great position to jump and react. If the swimmer has a good position and the weight is well distributed on each foot, the distribution of weight between the front foot and back foot should not matter. Once the swimmer achieves a good, athletic body posture on the blocks, everything else falls into place.

The body positioning on the block is more important than the movement of the relay start. The body has to be in a proper initial position well before movement can be added. Once the body is in position, the swimmer adds movement.

Much like in a flat start, in a relay start the swimmer first uses arm movement to create initial momentum. As shown in figure 21.3*a*, the arms are initially in a relaxed position and are essentially hanging down from the body. Without moving or changing any other body position, the swimmer begins the relay start by swinging the arms forward and up above the head (figure 21.3*b*), meaning that the arms rotate backward (think double-arm backstroke). I use the description "forward and up above the head" because, as shown figures 21.3*a* and 21.3*b*, the athlete's arms go from a hanging position to out over the pool to up above the head. The arms continue along this path and end back in front of the athlete.

The arms must begin the relay start process before the back foot even begins to move. As mentioned earlier, the arms can create a tremendous amount of momentum within the relay start. If the relay start begins with the back foot or with the back foot and arms together, it loses power. This aspect of the relay start is always the easiest to teach but the most difficult for the athlete to understand.

Also, as shown in figure 21.3*b*, the body (other than the arms) must remain in the same position. A common mistake among athletes is raising the torso when raising the arms. In effect, the athlete is in a standing position as the arms rise above the head; this creates too much of an up-and-down movement in the start. In keeping the body position consistent as the arms swing above the head, the swimmer keeps any vertical component of the start to a minimum. In this start, the swimmer should direct all the power in the horizontal plane.

David Durden

FIGURE 21.3 Single-foot step-up start sequence.

Now that the swimmer has created the initial movement, it is time to incorporate timing. This start is called the single-foot step-up start because, to oversimplify, the swimmer steps the back foot forward within the arm swing to finish in the position shown in figure 21.3c (page 287). How the swimmer gets there is the trick.

As the arms swing around the body, the swimmer must wait to step forward with the back foot until the momentum created from the arms is moving either down or forward. The goal is to combine the momentum from both the arm swing and the single step before beginning the relay dive. If the swimmer begins the step too soon (i.e., stepping at the initial arm swing movement), then the step forward with the back foot will be completed before the athlete sees any positive gain from the arm swing momentum. If the step is too late (i.e., the arms return to the original start position before the step begins), the athlete again loses the momentum created from the arm swing because they have to literally stop their arm swing and then step forward.

An easy dryland exercise that helps with this timing is called the Three-Swing Jump. To start this drill, the swimmer gets in good, athletic relay start position. The swimmer maintains good posture and lets the arms continuously swing around the body three times. On the third arm swing, the swimmer steps forward with the back foot so that it is even with the front foot and then jumps up. Rather than placing emphasis on the jump itself, the swimmer should focus on the ease with which the momentum from the arm swing transfers to the step and then to the jump. This is an exercise of rhythm more than it is an exercise of power.

As with any exercise or drill, whether on dry land or in the water, the swimmer should finish with good swimming posture. Therefore, when the swimmer finishes the three arm swings into the jump, they should get into a good, streamlined position. If you do this drill, other patrons of the pool may think you are crazy, but just tell them that you are crazy fast and continue on with your dryland exercise.

As the athlete continues to work on this dryland exercise for the single-foot step-up start, the body should remain in an athletic position. Some athletes will have bigger arm swings than others due to varying degrees of shoulder flexibility. Arm swings for this relay start should not take the body out of position, and the arm swings should fit the athlete's level of shoulder flexibility. In other words, the swimmer should let the arm swings flow naturally and not force the arms around the body. Creating momentum should be the focus of the arm swings.

If an athlete is having trouble timing the step into the jump in this dryland exercise, a second drill that helps with timing is 1/4 Swing Jump. In this exercise, the swimmer gets into a good single-foot step-up start position. Instead of swinging the arms forward around the body, the swimmer should position the arms behind the body; this puts the arms in a loaded position. To effectively feel the timing of the single-foot step-up relay start, the swimmer should swing the arms forward and up while stepping the back foot forward to complete the jump. Stepping the back foot forward in conjunction with swinging the arms forward simplifies this start movement.

Again, the 1/4 Swing Jump helps with timing, whereas the Three-Swing Jump helps perfect the rhythm of the start while maintaining good body position.

Two-Foot Step-Up Start

We first work with our athletes toward the single-foot step-up start. Once the athletes have the timing and rhythm down for this start, we make the relay start a bit more complex by adding the two-foot step-up start. Much like it sounds, the two-foot step-up relay start begins with both feet at the back of the block and ends with both feet at the edge of the block. As you can imagine, it is difficult to do a two-foot step-up start without knowing and mastering the single-foot step-up start. Body posture, timing, and rhythm are similar between the two starts; the biggest difference is initial foot position.

As in the single-foot step-up start, the body posture in this initial position is extremely important because it provides the foundation for the movement of the start. At the beginning of the two-foot step-up start, the swimmer should place both feet shoulder-width apart at the back of the block with the front toes of both the left and right foot in alignment. The shoulders are back, the back is straight, and the buttocks are pushed out. The line from the shoulders through the buttocks should be 45° from horizontal. The arms remain in a relaxed position and hang from the body and the head looks forward (figure 21.4).

FIGURE 21.4 Correct positioning of the two-foot step-up start.

David Durden

Again, distribution of weight on the feet is important for both reaction and power. The weight distribution is the same as in the single-foot step-up start: 60% of the weight should be forward on the balls of the feet and 40% of the weight should be back on the heels. As long as the body position remains athletic and in the position shown in figure 21.4, the weight distribution should take care of itself.

Like the single-foot step-up start, the two-foot step-up start begins with arm movement. Even though an athlete takes two steps in this start rather than one, creating the momentum in the start is equally important. From a good, established foundation, the swimmer begins the two-foot step-up start by swinging the arms forward and around the body. The arms should follow a path similar to that of the single-foot step-up start. Again, the arm movement should vary by athlete based on shoulder flexibility and the arms should flow naturally around the body.

Timing and rhythm play an even more important role in the two-foot step-up start than they do in the single-foot step-up start. As the arm movement initiates the start, the swimmer takes the first step of the two-foot step-up start toward the front of the blocks. The dominant foot should step forward first in order to maintain balance and generate power during the moment in the start when all of the weight is on this particular foot. As athletes become more comfortable with the timing and rhythm of this start, they can experiment with which foot takes the first step.

As the arms swing forward, the first step (or the forward foot) plants at the front of the block. Block size plays an important role in where to plant this foot, but exactness is not the key to generating the most power. Posture, rhythm, and timing win out over placing that foot in the perfect, toes-over-the-edge position. As the arms swing forward and the forward foot plants, the arms continue along a natural path up over the head. At this instant, the athlete is in the same position as in the single-foot step-up start (see figure 21.3*b* on page 287). A common mistake among athletes is to "stand up" during this phase of the start. As mentioned earlier, the swimmer must eliminate the up-and-down component of this start in order to carry forward the most momentum and, subsequently, the most power. Athletes have a tendency to allow the torso to rise up with the first step in the start (even moreso in the two-foot version of the start) and subsequently squat into the second step of the start. Too much vertical movement in relay starts hinders the power one can generate horizontally.

As the arms continue their natural path around the body, the swimmer takes the second step forward when the arm swing is generating momentum either in a downward fashion or in a direction that moves the body forward. As with the single-foot step-up start, the goal is to take into the start the momentum from both the arm swing and the back foot moving forward. If the timing is incorrect, the athlete effectively loses one component (either the arm swing or the back foot moving forward) of momentum generation. As the arm swing begins to create the forward momentum we are looking for in the start, the athlete plants the back foot shoulder-width apart from the other foot before moving into the dive of the relay start. The position finishes as shown in figure 21.3*c* on page 287.

As with the single-foot step-up start, the athlete must use dryland exercises and drills to perfect rhythm, timing, and movement. As one could imagine, the two-foot step-up start begins with perfect, athletic posture. When performing dryland exercises with the two-foot step-up start, the athlete should position both feet shoulder-width apart.

The Three-Swing Jump drill works extremely well with the two-foot step-up start. This drill allows the athlete to solidify their posture, swing the arms in a free, natural motion, and feel the momentum of the arm swings. It is important for the athlete to feel the momentum that the arm swing creates as they begin to fit the two steps within the timing of those swings. As the athlete begins the third arm swing, he or she should start the first of two steps forward into the jump. The forward, more dominant foot takes the first step. As that step is completed, the back foot begins to step forward. The back foot should plant even with and shoulder-width apart from the front foot. The athlete completes the drill with a jump up (finishing in a streamlined position), emphasizing rhythm and timing rather than the jump itself.

This drill is extremely helpful in establishing the speed of the arm swing with the timing of the two steps. The arm swings should never be labored, and the athlete should never try to speed them up. The arm swings generate and create momentum that can be taken into the start itself. Finally, when using this drill for either the single- or two-foot step-up start, the rhythm of the arm swings should be consistent throughout the three swings. Therefore, as the athlete takes a step forward (or two steps forward as in the two-foot step-up start), the speed of the arm swing on that third swing should never increase or decrease. The athlete simply times the step (or two steps) in with a natural arm swing.

TAKING THE MOVEMENT TO THE BLOCKS

Once the athlete has the movement down or has the idea of what the movement should be, it's time to take it to the blocks. The athlete should first practice a start without a swimmer coming into the wall. In fact, when practicing a start for the first time, the swimmer doesn't need to complete the movement with a dive. When learning something new or even when revisiting the start from a foundational perspective, removing some of the complexities of a traditional relay start (such as timing the takeover as a swimmer is swimming into the wall) or the dive itself allows the athlete to focus on the rhythm and timing of the movement.

Therefore, the first thing I coach is a relay jump. This basically reads as written. As an athlete steps up on the block, the athlete completes either the single-foot step-up start or the two-foot step-up start (either works for this drill) with a feet-first jump, rather than a dive, into the water. This gives the athlete the opportunity to become comfortable with the movement and timing up on the blocks.

When determining the type of relay start to use, take into account the block size and type. A pool is a pool and the race distance is consistent over the course of 25 yards, 25 meters, or 50 meters. The one inconsistent aspect of racing is the starting blocks. As a general rule of thumb, the longer the block (from front to back) or the more grip on the block, the easier it is to fit the two-foot step-up start. When a swimmer doesn't know which of the two starts to use, they should always fall back on the single-foot step-up start.

> *Caution* With doing a relay start jump, make sure that the pool is at least 8 feet (2.4 m) deep. Although some athletes can complete dives into less than 8 feet of water, fitting a jump into less than 8 feet of water is too dangerous.

Once the movement is established and the athlete becomes more and more comfortable with a relay jump (and again, it is important to finish each jump in a streamlined position), they can add power to the jump to add a level of mastery to the drill. Once the athlete has practiced every aspect (timing, rhythm, and power) of the relay jump, it is time to take that movement into a dive. When describing the movement of the relay start, I emphasize posture because it is such a key component of the start itself. (I could spend another chapter penning my thoughts on the start itself, but I digress and instead focus on the relay movement.) One inherent disadvantage of practicing the relay jump ad nauseam is that the final position that the athlete is in (feet first) is the complete opposite of where the athletes should be moving. One reason the athlete maintains good posture in the Three-Swing Jump drill is to reinforce solid posture throughout the arm movement. Ideally, throughout the entirety of the start movement the shoulders should never be higher than they are in the initial position. By the time the athlete finishes the arm swing into the step, the shoulders should be in a position that is lower than where they initially started.

At the completion of the relay movement into the dive, the hips should be in a low position so that the line discussed earlier in this chapter (the 45° line from horizontal that the swimmer creates with the back from the shoulders to the buttocks) is parallel to the water surface or effectively 0° to horizontal. If the athlete can get to that position (video is one of the only ways to effectively see this), then we know that the athlete takes into the dive every drop of power and velocity generated from the relay start. If the line of the back is at a positive angle when compared with the horizontal, then some of the power and velocity is going up or in a vertical direction. In that scenario, at some point during the dive the athlete must reposition the body for a proper entry angle. If the line of the back is at a negative angle when compared with the horizontal, then some of the power and velocity is going down directly to the water. At this point, the swimmer cannot reposition the body midair and the result is a deeper dive upon entry.

REACTION TIME: THE MOST OVERANALYZED STATISTIC

Now it is time to put everything together. It is not an official relay start until an athlete swims into the wall for a relay exchange. Up until now, we have focused on movement, rhythm, and timing. A swimmer can completely abandon that focus when adding the variable of a swimmer swimming into the wall. In fact, the only way it gets worse is when a group of athletes is swimming into the wall in a heat of relays for a relay exchange. And at its worst, a relay team is in the heart of a race in the midst of a relay exchange.

The only measurable variable in evaluating a successful exchange is reaction time, which is the time differential between the touch of the athlete completing the relay leg and the moment the foot (or feet) of the next athlete leave the block. At local club, high school, and neighborhood meets, this is evaluated by officials judging the legality of the relay start. Only two types of information are returned in this scenario: good or bad. A good relay exchange, or safe relay exchange, means only that the athlete in the water touched the wall before the athlete on the block left the block. The bad relay exchange means the relay team is disqualified because the athlete on the block left the block before the athlete in the water touched the wall.

At major national, collegiate, and international meets, reaction time is returned from an electronic timing system that is installed both on the wall (touch pads) and on the block (relay judging platform). Simply put, if the reaction time is positive, the relay exchange was safe, and (in most cases) if the reaction time is negative, the relay team is disqualified. The positive reaction time that is generated from the electronic timing system can become the most overanalyzed statistic in training relays. It is similar to using the metric of yardage throughout a practice or a year to define how good your training was over the course of that practice or season. Remember that the reaction time metric is just that: a metric. It does not measure the momentum created from the arm swing, or the position of the body leaving the block, or the timing of the step (or steps) from the relay start, all of which significantly affect the power and velocity created from the relay start. A perfect relay start in terms of power and velocity can easily and significantly overcome a slower reaction time. The next time you find yourself obsessing over the reaction time, step back to see the totality of the relay start rather than merely one metric that is generated from an electronic timing system.

What makes the timing in a relay exchange difficult is the number of variables that the swimmer on the block must take into account in knowing when to begin their relay start. Some of those variables include how fast the swimmer is coming into the finish, whether they are fatiguing at the end of their race to a point that it will change how they are moving in their stroke, whether they touch long or short, whether they will take an extra stroke, whether they will take a breath on their last stroke, and whether they are touching high or low on the touch pad. Even though the swimmer on the block takes all of these variables into account to determine when to initiate the arm swing in the relay start, responsibility is placed on the swimmer in the water to finish strong (fast) and to keep a level of consistency in the last 7 meters of swimming their leg of the relay in order to help the swimmer on the block with their timing.

While the swimmer on the block is processing all of this information (how fast the swimmer is coming into the wall, whether their movement is consistent, and so on), they start the initial arm swing before the swimmer in the water touches the wall. Ideally, the swimmer on the block will have a perfect and powerful relay movement that transitions into the dive (toes and feet still on the block) at the exact moment the swimmer in the water touches the wall. That is extremely difficult to do. In fact, in the four relays that we won at NCAAs in 2010 (200 medley relay, 200 free relay, 400 medley relay, and 400 free relay), the swimmer in the water never touched the touchpad at the exact same time that the swimmer on the block left for the start. Most of the reaction times that we generated were around 0.20.

There is no specific way to determine when to start the initial arm swing in the relay start. Some athletes use the guidance of their hands in following an incoming swimmer into the wall. As a coach, I do not have my athletes use their hands in following a swimmer into the wall because I feel they focus their posture more on what their hands are doing than on how to move athletically through the relay start. Some athletes begin their relay start when the swimmer hits a certain point in the pool, such as the T marking. Markings differ across pools, so I like for my athletes to rely on their instincts rather than become too mechanical on their start. Finally, some athletes wait for the swimmer to touch the wall before they even begin their initial arm movement. While this most certainly results in a safe relay exchange, it also guarantees that the relay exchange will be slow. How do you know when to start that initial arm movement? Practice.

Even though I write that reaction time is an overanalyzed statistic, we still use the metric of reaction time in training our relays. We have the benefit at Cal of having a relay judging platform, a touchpad, and an electronic timing system that measures reaction time. These items are not necessities in training great relays, but rather are mere luxuries that we use in our training. Coaches could argue based upon the metric of reaction time that a perfect relay exchange is 0.00 (i.e., the swimmer swimming into the wall touched at the exact same time that the swimmer left the blocks). I tell my athletes that the reaction time of a perfect relay exchange is 0.10. Throughout the course of the year when we practice relay starts, we work toward a reaction time of 0.10. Our stated goal is to hit a 0.10 reaction time three times in a row. Throughout all of the years that I have incorporated this philosophy into the programs that I have worked with, only one athlete has hit that 0.10 mark three times in a row. On the fourth time he recorded a 0.11 reaction, and I thought that was pretty darn impressive.

Common sense and wisdom would dispute the notion that 0.10 is a perfect reaction time compared with 0.00. The logic and reasoning that I use with our athletes is simple. If our timing is just a bit off, we have leeway on both sides of our 0.10 reaction time. If we establish that 0.00 is the marker that we are working toward and in competition we are just a bit off perfect and record a reaction time of –0.01, then our relay is disqualified. Having your whole relay disqualified for being just one one-hundredth off the mark is a hard pill to swallow. When we set our perfect mark of 0.10 and we happen to be just off the mark, we still have a safe exchange and get the benefit of a quick reaction time.

We practice relay starts in several ways throughout the course of the year. From a practice perspective, we change the speed of our athletes that are swimming into the wall. At times, we require the swimmer swimming into the wall to move at 70% effort. In much the same way, we have the athlete on the block slow down their time to a 70% effort so that they can focus on their technique of moving through the relay start. At times, we use bands to pull the swimmer into the wall so that they may move at or faster than their race speed in coming into the wall. We use our pool setup to have the athletes run along the deck, dive into the water, and carry that speed for 7 meters into their finish as the athlete on the block makes the adjustment on their relay start.

We will typically do no more than three relay starts and exchanges in a practice, and we incorporate this into our practice usually twice a week. We can move through our exchanges over the course of 5 to 10 minutes during a practice setting. Sometimes we video the exchanges and sometimes we don't. Sometimes we use our timing system to receive reaction times and sometimes we don't. When we practice our exchanges, we practice the full exchange and make sure that our athletes swim through the break and into the first couple of cycles of their stroke. Many times we have to educate our freshmen on this common mistake because they like to just dive into the water and then immediately know their reaction time, or they feel that the exchange is completed because they dove into the water. As mentioned earlier in this section, the power and velocity generated from the relay start many times supersedes the reaction time. Limiting how the power and velocity carried through the relay start translates into the first couple of cycles of swimming results in a lost opportunity to learn how to perfect relay starts.

In mid-January of our collegiate season, we become very systematic with our relay exchanges and, more importantly, our relay order. This gives our athletes close to 2.5 months to get their relay exchanges to our perfect reaction time of 0.10. Also, by solidifying our relay order this far in advance, our athletes learn the tendencies of the athlete swimming toward them in the water and learn when to start their initial arm movement in the relay start and how to make athletic adjustments based on their knowledge about the athlete in the water.

Most times, when we practice relay exchanges we have a group of athletes that are moving through different exchanges. It may be a group of 8 to 10 athletes that are working both freestyle relay and medley relay exchanges. When coaching these small sessions, I remind the athletes to watch, learn, and focus on the swimmer swimming into the wall even if they themselves are not physically performing the relay exchange from the blocks. The athletes that are watching rather than doing the exchange often learn the tendencies and habits of the swimmers swimming into the wall better than the athlete on the block who is physically performing the relay exchange.

By systematically training relay exchanges and relay orders in this way, our athletes develop confidence in each other. The last thing that they ever think about when a swimmer is swimming into the wall is their reaction time. This is good because that is the most overanalyzed statistic out there.

MAKING GOOD BETTER

This chapter has so far covered both of the starts I like to teach, the timing of when that start is meant to begin (which is always more instinctual than mechanical), and how we continue the practice of relay starts throughout the season. These aspects of training relays are all good, but how do you make good better?

I have mentioned several times the notion of being athletic. Whether it is described in terms of posture or in the overall context of relay start movement, a swimmer can develop athleticism to help with relay starts. Outside of practicing relay starts without an athlete swimming into the wall, one athletic movement that we develop amongst our team is running. In our facility, our athletes are able to create a lot of speed through running on the deck and diving into the water from deck level. This simple drill allows us to easily see which athlete is best in doing a start, whether it is a flat start or a relay start.

> *Caution*   Closely supervise your athletes when they are running on the deck to begin a start. Use mats to prevent injury.

With the relay start, using a single-foot step-up start or a two-foot step-up start allows the athlete to start the actual dive with a greater level of velocity than if using a flat start. Taking that idea a step further, our athletes use the runner to create an even greater velocity than that created by the relay start. In developing better relay starts, the runner can provide an overall concept of athleticism. Our athletes learn how to shape their bodies on entry at higher velocities and translate that speed into the first few cycles of their stroke.

Also, developing better athleticism creates different variations of the two relay starts we teach at Cal. As an example, when working with athletes that have mastered the timing, power, and cadence of the two-foot step-up start, we incorporate a quicker, hop-like movement through the two steps that can generate more velocity than a regular two-foot step-up start can. This movement allows athletes to get away from the idea of taking two steps into the start and allows them to feel that they are running into the start. The hop movement into the steps distributes the weight more forward on the balls of the feet and more quickly from the initial beginning of the relay start to the moment the athlete's feet leave the blocks. This allows the athlete on the blocks to evaluate the incoming swimmer just a bit longer to ensure a quicker reaction time.

The hop-like movement should not turn into a jump. I have watched other athletes use a jump-type movement from an initial position of both feet at the back of the blocks (the initial position of the two-foot step-up start). In this start, athletes jump both feet simultaneously forward, land both feet, and then transition into their relay exchange. In this type of start, momentum is stopped because the athletes have to land the first jump before transitioning into the relay start itself. A continuation of momentum, whether through the arm swings or through the steps into the start, is essential.

The final way to make good relay starts better involves technology rather than mechanics. Major international competitions have now incorporated wedge-type starting blocks that have long been used in track and field. The wedge itself is positioned toward the middle of the block and is adjustable toward the back of the block. It is one solid piece and creates an approximately 45° angle in reference to the surface of the starting block. Having had limited interaction with this type of starting block (we competed as a collegiate team in December of 2009 with this type of block), our athletes made very quick adjustments to learn how to incorporate this piece of technology into their relay start. We found that the single-foot step-up start works better with this technology. We also found that the athletes initially put the back foot on the wedge and placed a greater amount of weight on that back foot, almost rocking the hips back so that more weight was placed over the back foot. As the arms flowed around the body in the relay start, the back foot used the wedge to take a more aggressive step forward, putting a bit more initial velocity into the start.

Unfortunately, at this time, collegiate swimming does not use the wedge starting blocks. Therefore, we do not need to immediately change how we treat relay starts. We simply incorporate into our relay start training some of the nuggets that we learned in using the wedge blocks.

PSYCHOLOGICAL TRAINING

The last aspect of training relays is more psychological than mechanical. Some athletes out there just absolutely believe that they are relay swimmers. We all have them, and we all define them that way. Many times I have heard coaches describe a swimmer as a great relay swimmer. It becomes a badge of honor. It's almost as if some swimmers out there feel that, individually, they will never be a Michael Phelps or the best swimmer in the neighborhood, but if you put that swimmer on a relay, watch out!

If I could harness this, and more importantly if I could write about this, far more people out there would be reading this chapter. It is an X factor, something that most people would never be able to explain. Some 6 years later, Fred Bousquet found himself in a similar position as he dove in on the 4 × 100 free relay as the anchor man with two other teams (the United States and Russia) at the 2009 world championships in Rome. Trying to finally best his 47.0 relay split from 2003 and in a technical, shiny suit that is now banned, his 47.4 split brought home a bronze medal for France. Fortunately, a new relay swimmer was earning his badge of honor. Anchoring in a 46.79 and bringing the gold medal home to the United States was a young, up-and-coming sprinter, Nathan Adrian. Go Bears!

CONCLUSION

I hope this chapter helps reaffirm ideas you have about relays and helps you create new ideas on how to train relays. I've learned through coaching that there are no secrets out there, and 90% of what we read in chapters like these or what we hear from coaches on the pool deck we have already tried or incorporated into our coaching philosophy. And, more importantly, 50% of that 90% actually works. And 25% of the 50% we just stopped doing for some reason. So, basically, 11% of the information in this chapter you have already done, and you need to get back to it as a coach. Enjoy!

22

Dryland Training

Vern Gambetta

Dryland training is a means of creating an efficient swimmer that is injury free and fully capable of adapting to the stress of training and competition. The goal of dryland training is to better prepare the human body, essentially nonaquatic, to be efficient in the aquatic environment.

I have found it futile and in many ways counterproductive to attempt to imitate the aquatic environment on dry land. Seeking specificity by attempting to duplicate the swim strokes on dry land can add stress to stress and be counterproductive. Instead I prefer to focus on swim-appropriate movements that prepare swimmers for the demands of their respective events. The highest degree of specificity is the actual swimming workout; dryland training must both supplement and complement actual swim training. I use dryland training to create an adaptable body that can optimally thrive on the stress of training in the water. The goal is to design and implement an effective, practical dryland training program that produces measurable and visible results in the required time frame. To achieve this goal we follow a functional path to build the complete swimming athlete and rebuild them if they are injured.

THE IMPORTANCE OF DRYLAND TRAINING

Dryland training for today's swimmer can potentially address several problems that did not exist for previous generations of swimmers.

Early Specialization   Today's youngsters are encouraged to choose a sport and an event within that sport early. This has caused them to miss out on the broad foundation of athleticism and fitness that is developed through playing a variety of sports. Dryland training must fundamentally develop athleticism to address this deficiency.

Lack of Fundamental Movement Skills and a General Fitness Base   Because children get less free play and often no physical education in schools and they live a more sedentary lifestyle than in the past, they do not acquire the fundamental movement skills that are prerequisites for acquiring and perfecting sport skills. In essence, dryland training for all ages is a period of daily physical education that emphasizes fundamental skill development and remediation of basic movement deficiencies.

Extended Competitive Seasons   Less training time is available due to longer competitive seasons. Dryland must be part of the year-round preparation in order to keep the swimmer at optimal performance level and free of injury.

Injuries Related To and Potentially Caused By All of the Above   The dryland program must have an injury-prevention component that addresses each swimmer's individual needs. I have found it best that this component is transparent and blended into the training program on a regular basis.

AN EFFECTIVE DRYLAND TRAINING PROGRAM

Traditionally, dryland training has been a means to add volume to the training load of the swimmer. More was considered better. It was often medicine balls until you puked or dumbbells until you dropped. As a result, the intensity was low and the goal became to survive the workout, to grind it out, to just do more work. What we know today about the potential for improvement through a comprehensive dryland program refutes this approach. We have moved past this to a more progressive approach that allows the swimmer to thrive and make a direct connection to their swimming.

Ultimately, for dryland training to be most effective it must be completely integrated with the objectives of the water workouts. If the two are not compatible, then the net result will be negative. The two elements of training must fit together seamlessly. Dryland work is not an end unto itself; it must be swimming appropriate and completely connected to the needs of the individual swimmer and the demands of their event and race distance. The movements in dryland must be coached just as thoroughly as each swim stroke is coached and must be related to movements in the water so that the swimmer can make the connection. Linkage and connections between body parts are essential—everything possible must be done to reinforce the hip-to-shoulder relationship. The swimmer must train movements, not muscles—it is not bodybuilding. This will reinforce linkage and utilization of the whole kinetic chain. Neurologically, the body does not recognize individual muscles but rather recognizes patterns of moments. By training movements, we stress coordination and linkage in order to transfer the dryland work more effectively to the swim strokes.

An effective, comprehensive dryland program incorporates the principles of functional training. Functional training consists of full-spectrum work in multiple planes using multiple joints through a full range of motion that is proprioceptively demanding. For efficient movement, the body relies on feedback from the proprioceptors to position and reposition the limbs and the body. This is highly trainable and is an integral part of dryland training. It also incorporates a complete range of training methods that are designed to elicit optimal adaptive responses that are appropriate for the stroke and the event for which the athlete trains. No one system of the body is emphasized to the exclusion of another; rather, the emphasis is on the synergistic relationship of all systems.

Conceptually, dryland training is both a supplement and a complement to swim training. Whether it is a supplement or a complement depends on what stage the swimmer is at in their career, the time of the year, and, to a certain extent, the stroke and the distance.

The starting point of the dryland program is the swimming body. In many ways the swimming body is unique in terms of body proportions and segmental relationships. As swimmers progress to the elite level, body types and body proportions vary less. We know how the body is constructed; therefore, we must respect the structure–function relationship. Based on research and best practice, various regimens of work produce predictable adaptive responses. Synergy exists among all the systems of the body—neural, muscular, skeletal, cardiovascular, immune, and endocrine hormonal. We must respect male–female differences during and after puberty as well as growth and development considerations. No one method or physical quality becomes an end unto itself. Each athlete is a case study of one; therefore, one size does not fit all. I discuss those aspects in more depth once I get into actual implementation and programming of dryland training.

Preparing the body to perform in the aquatic environment presents some unique challenges. Unless one is swimming in open-water competition, the aquatic environment is consistent and predictable. However, it is a foreign environment for the human body. We must respect the fact that we are bipedal land animals that spend the majority of our existence on land in a gravity-enriched state. Therefore, one of the major objectives of dryland training is to help shape the body to be more efficient in the aquatic environment.

We must be clear on a couple of things. We are not training weight lifters, gymnasts, or football players, although we might borrow concepts and ideas from other sport disciplines. Our goal in dryland training is to develop the best swimming athlete possible!

PROGRAM DESIGN AND IMPLEMENTATION

Start with a clear framework for design and implementation of the program. Clearly map out progressions and decide how you want to organize your dryland program. Consider how many coaches you will have and the space, equipment, and time available. How will you separate age groups, strokes, distances, and sexes? All of these factors will provide the framework for the program and ultimately impact its effectiveness.

Training is cumulative, so the program should be designed as cycles that take advantage of the accumulation of work rather than as individual training sessions. Training effects accumulate from session to session, cycle to cycle, year to year throughout a career. Effective program design ensures that a swimmer continually adapts throughout his or her career. It is not a one-off proposition but rather a consistent, building-block approach. One workout cannot make an athlete, but one workout can break an athlete.

According to sport scientist Roger Enoka (1994), "The function of a muscle depends critically on the context in which it is activated." Consequently, if we want the swimmer's muscles to work synergistically, we must train functionally through movements that take advantage of aggregate muscle actions. Aggregate muscle actions, as defined by Logan and McKinney (1970), means that muscles work together synergistically to stabilize, reduce, and produce force all at the same time. All these actions occur within the swim stroke cycle regardless of the stroke. As stated earlier, one enhances connectivity and linkage by training movements, not muscles. Neurologically, the brain does not recognize individual muscles but rather recognizes patterns of movement. This is all an extension of the concept of the kinetic chain: training movement from toenails to fingernails to improve efficiency.

Objectives

Dryland strength training is intended to accomplish the following two primary objectives.

1. **Maximize the potential for propulsion.** Appropriate strengthening of the upper quadrant (the body from the bottom of the ribs up) enhances anchoring, which is the ability to hold water elbow to elbow in the upper quadrant. The majority of propulsion in swimming comes from the movements of this portion of the body, essentially the thoracic spine. This is not grip and rip, no pulling; it is holding water in order to optimize propulsive forces.

2. **Create greater potential to minimize resistance.** In other words, shaping the body to improve hydrodynamics or streamlining. This is an underemphasized and unexplored aspect of dryland training. It assumes even more importance with the emphasis on underwater swimming in the fifth stroke, or dolphin kick. Essentially, we can achieve the effect of shaping the body through observing good functional strength-training principles. This is not to be confused with bodybuilding, which emphasizes development of isolated muscles. Shaping takes advantage of the connections through the whole kinetic chain to achieve elongation to streamline and by enhancing the ability to "hold" water. The mantra here is lengthen while you strengthen the connections.

Dryland training is an opportunity to train readiness for speed into your swimmers during all phases of the year. Dryland training is not a time to condition; that is done in the water, although conditioning is an ancillary benefit of the accumulation of work. Because the ultimate determining factor for racing success is speed, approaching dryland with intensity provides the foundation for speed. The dryland program should be structured around speed development throughout the training year, from the first day through the taper. Recognize and train for the demands of the event, but keep in mind that it always comes down to speed. The winner in any event is the swimmer who can maintain the highest percentage of their maximum for the duration of the race.

Specificity

We need to recognize the varied demands of the different race distances and strokes. A simple rule of thumb is that as the race gets longer, power and power endurance are emphasized less and strength endurance is emphasized more. Power endurance is the ability to endure more rapid movements in a climate of fatigue. It is developed on dry land through work in the range of 20 repetitions at a rate of 1 repetition per second. Strength endurance is the ability to endure strength in a climate of fatigue. It is developed through slower, more rhythmic work done in more than 20 repetitions. Short course with more turns demands more explosive leg work, although you can't minimize the contribution of efficient turns in long course, where they contribute 20 to 25% to the final time. Both power and strength endurance are factors in swimming, and the swimmer must blend them depending on his or her race and level of development.

One must account for the demands of the stroke—long axis or short axis. In the butterfly, the major accommodation is an increase in flexion and extension movements in the core work. The breaststroke demands significantly more work on the legs, hip mobility, and knee stability as well as more flexion and extension work in the core. Swimmers of the butterfly or breaststroke need to back off the leg work approaching taper more than those who swim the other strokes.

Injury Prevention

Injury prevention is an essential element of an effective dryland program. It is most effective when it is transparent, meaning that it is incorporated into the structure of the actual program rather than a separate, identifiable component. In particular, shoulder stabilization movements, knee stability, and hip and ankle mobility should be emphasized. The areas most often injured in swimming are the shoulder, lower back, and knee. As I delineate the actual structure of the program, I identify those exercises and modes of training that are directed toward preventing injury.

Useful in injury prevention is a thorough physical competency assessment, which establishes a starting point for training by helping to determine the swimmer's training age (the number of years the swimmer has been in a formal training program). This helps to determine trainability, and it is a baseline for comparison in subsequent years. This assessment is intended to identify strengths and weaknesses so that individually prescribed exercise routines can eradicate any deficiencies and limitations that would limit the swimmer's ability to perform.

The competency tests are modified to take into consideration growth and development. A young age-group swimmer is not expected to achieve the same standards as a mature elite swimmer. Select the competency tests based on the demands of the swim strokes.

The basic physical competency assessment tests for swimming are as follows.

Flexibility

Thomas test

Seated gluteus

Wall adductor

Thigh internal rotation

Ankle range

Stability

Side (lateral) bridge (forearm)

Front bridge (arms at 45°)

Supine bridge

Squatting

Squat

Single-leg squat (static)

Shoulder

Shoulder lift-off

Protraction–retraction

Wall angel

Trunk

60° static sit-up

Back or trunk extension static

Upper body

Push-up

Lying pull-up

Go www.movementdynamics.com for information on how to administer these tests. Address any limitations that are identified in the physical competency assessment through remedial modules in the training program.

TRAINING SWIMMERS ACCORDING TO DEVELOPMENT

When training swimmers, carefully consider the development continuum. Chronological age (the swimmer's age in years based on birth date) is of secondary consideration; the primary consideration is biological age (the swimmer's physical and physiological maturation level). It is easy to lose sight of that because, at the developmental level, swimming is organized in age-group divisions. You must take into account late developers and early developers. Pay particular attention to the relative age effect. Those born early in the year have a growth and development advantage over those born late in the year; that disadvantage is not overcome until peak height velocity is achieved (and sometimes later).

Age Group

This is the foundational and fundamental period when the emphasis is on teaching, not training. The training is a logical outcome of the teaching. Above all, teach routine and good training habits. At this age, young swimmers must learn that dryland training is part of their daily preparation. This is the time when they understand the body and how all the parts connect. Dryland training serves to improve body awareness and coordination, which enhances swimmers' ability to learn and refine technique in the water.

For the male swimmer before puberty, emphasize control of the body and strength building primarily through bodyweight exercises. In this stage of development it is important to reinforce body awareness and coordination in order to minimize the awkwardness and loss of coordination that occurs during the growth spurt. The female swimmer before puberty does not need to train any differently than the male swimmer. Simple bodyweight exercises like push-ups, crawling, and climbing are very effective in teaching the young swimmer to effectively handle their body weight.

Emerging Elite

This transition period usually coincides with peak height velocity (growth spurt), which is a time of rapid growth and the accompanying awkwardness. The main goal of dryland during this phase is to reinforce good coordination and help the swimmer regain control of the body and awareness of the parts. This is sometimes called the "training to train" phase.

For the male swimmer, training during puberty should be similar to the age-group training discussed previously. The main difference is that a day of strength training should be added. For the female swimmer, strength training should be majorly emphasized. Due to the endocrine hormonal changes that occur with the onset of menarche, strength training serves to maintain a leaner body composition and build muscle mass. Because of differences in testosterone levels and less muscle mass, the female swimmer loses strength much more rapidly than the male, so a female must incorporate strength training into all phases of training, including the taper. Female athletes should strength train a minimum of 3 days a week (preferably 4 days when appropriate). At this stage, it is appropriate to add more dumbbell work and other strength-training exercises that incorporate external resistance beyond body weight.

Elite

An athlete must eradicate all physical limitations by the time they reach this level. Each swimmer should know what they need in terms of dryland training and how to correlate this with the swimming workouts. The focus here is training to win.

For male swimmers, after puberty and achievement of peak height velocity (growth spurt), the amount of external resistance can progressively increase based on the swimmer's ability to handle loading. Training frequency and loading can also increase for female swimmers. The methods can vary from bodyweight resistance to heavy external loading depending on the individual swimmer's event and their ability to handle a load.

RECOVERY AND ADAPTABILITY

We must understand the swimmer's recoverability and adaptability. If a swimmer cannot recover from the work, then the work is counterproductive. It is just work, not training. We also must determine the optimal training load and mode for each individual. Some swimmers are fast adaptors and some are slow adaptors, and they must be trained differently. The sooner this is identified, the more effective the training program will be. Slow adaptors cannot be pushed to the same degree as fast adaptors. It is also important to consider the concept of the 24-hour athlete. Essentially, this means that an athlete is an athlete during the entire day, not just during training time, and that we must look at the whole athlete and their lifestyle in order to effectively plan and implement training.

Carefully consider the development continuum described earlier. Also consider training age, which is essentially the length of time a swimmer has been in a formal training program. Generally, an older training age indicates that the swimmer is able to handle more volume and a more intense workload. Also carefully consider training readiness, which is the psychological and emotional maturity necessary to accept coaching and provide honest and clear feedback. A key part of training readiness is the ability to understand, assimilate, and execute a training program. None of these considerations can be minimized. They all must be carefully weighed in order to optimize return from the dryland and overall swimming training.

THE COMPONENTS OF DRYLAND TRAINING

A sound, comprehensive dryland program incorporates all of the following components in a systematic and sequential manner. For more information regarding the ideas and exercises found here, visit www.gambetta.com.

Development of Athleticism

This is the cornerstone of the program and is developed first and foremost. Essentially, this component consists of movement skills to enhance coordination, body control, and awareness. Up to 40% of the total program of age-group swimmers should consist of athleticism development. As the swimmer matures the proportion of this work is reduced so that eventually at the elite level it makes up approximately 5 to 10% of the total work. This type of work is best done as part of the warm-up or immediately following the warm-up. Swimmers can easily do some of the basic coordination movements on the pool deck.

To develop athleticism, use exercises that stress connection and coordination, such as the following:

Skipping
Side steps
Galloping
Jumping rope
Crawling movements

Flexibility

Flexibility is traditionally defined as range of motion around a joint. This definition does not take into account the component of dynamic stability. The term mostability is preferable to flexibility. Mostability is the correct amount of motion, at the correct joint, in the correct plane, at the correct time. It comprises mobility and stability. Emphasize joint integrity; never compromise joint integrity for mobility. Mobility at the hip is crucial for swimming success and for staying injury free. Mobility at the ankle is also very important in swimming.

The following can be used as a daily flexibility routine (before swimming):

Dynamic reach series

> Reach out
>
> Reach across
>
> Reach around

Hip flexor stretch

Dynamic lat stretch

Dynamic pec stretch

In addition, a swimmer must do extensive static stretching that is individualized to their needs based on the results of the physical competency assessment. (For example, a deficiency on the Thomas test would warrant more stretching of the psoas muscles.) This serves to aid recovery and improve flexibility. To develop flexibility the body must be warmed up, so the logical time to achieve the dual objectives of recovery and development of flexibility is after practice. The postpractice static stretching routine should be no longer than 15 minutes.

Strength Training

The following three considerations dictate the structure and content of the dryland strength training program.

1. The propulsion comes primarily from the upper quadrant.
2. The core is responsible for stabilization and alignment.
3. The legs contribute to propulsion and efficiency.

The strength-training program is organized to address each of these areas in a systematic, sequential, and progressive manner that is appropriate for the stroke and race distance.

Strength training is coordination training with appropriate resistance, and the main goal is to enhance linkage and connectivity. Rob Sleamaker, inventor of the Vasa Trainer (an exercise machine designed specifically for swimming; see page 317 of chapter 23 for more information), sums it up quite well: "Muscles must be built in, not built on." Building in muscles through movements goes a long way toward improving coordination in the water. In addition, strength training excites the nervous system, which enhances explosiveness.

The strength training program must include the following movements:

Pulling: Movements in which the resistance is moved toward the body

Pushing: Movements in which the resistance is pushed away from the body

Squatting and squat-derivative movements: Movements that require triple flexion and triple extension of the ankle, knee, and hip

Rotation: Movements in the transverse plane and diagonal rotational patterns

Bracing: Movements that require the ability to hold a position or a posture

In a good, balanced program, all of those movements should be incorporated into the selected exercises and applied in a 7-day microcycle. All of the movements must be executed through a full spectrum that incorporates the following:

Multiple planes: Movements go through the sagittal, frontal, and transverse planes of motion.

Multiple joints: Movements involve more than one joint.

Full range of motion: Movements go through as large a range of motion as the swimmer can control.

High proprioceptive demand: Movements require the body to position and reposition the limbs based on feedback from the proprioceptors.

These spectrum considerations dictate the selection of the exercises.

All dryland training, including strength training, is designed around modular training. This approach effectively manages the various elements of dryland training and addresses individual differences. Modules are combinations and sequences of exercises that are designed to be very specific and compatible. Volume and intensity are determined for each session based on a thorough analysis of the previous training sessions.

Everything must be specific to the objectives of the individual training session, the swimming workout, and the overall plan. It is not about the mode, method, or exercise; it is about how they all are applied in a systematic approach.

Core Strength and Stability

Core strength and stability is the starting point because, conceptually, we build the swimmer around and through the center. As a foundational principle, train core strength before extremity strength both in a training session and in the training cycles. The goal is to achieve a high volume of core work by the end of first training block and then hold that volume through the increase in volume of upper-body work. When the volume of upper-body work is at its peak, reduce core work proportionally.

In terms of body structure, the core consists of the hips, abdomen, back, and neck. In their landmark work, Logan and McKinney (1970) identified the serape effect (see figure 22.1 on page 308). The serape is a Mexican garment, essentially a shawl that wraps diagonally around the upper body. The concept of the serape moved us away from thinking of abdominal development just in terms of flexion and extension movements and toward the use of diagonal and rotational patterns of work that emphasize connection of all the links.

We need to go beyond that based on our understanding of fascial trains and connections through the body (fascia that overlays the muscle connects the parts of the body). Essentially, in core training we want to take advantage of what I call the X effect.

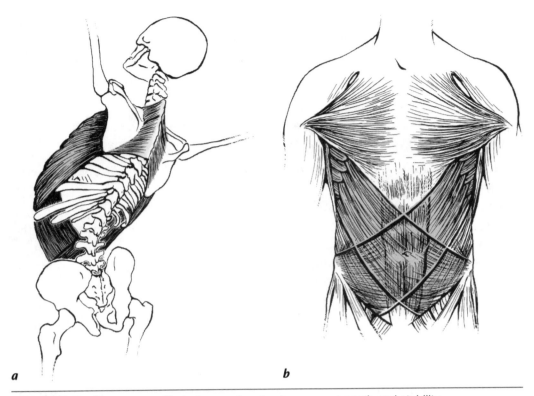

a   *b*

FIGURE 22.1 The serape effect of muscular structure core strength and stability.

Adapted from G.A. Logan and W.C. McKinney, 1977, *Anatomic kinesiology,* 2nd ed. (Dubuque: William C. Brown), 198.

The fascial trains that run through the center of the body from the tips of each of the extremities make the core the relay center of the body, the center of the action, the connector. Because of the X effect, all training is core training. We must constantly try to connect through the center to optimize the use of this segment in the water.

Core strength and stability exercises are classified as the following:

Stabilization: Exercises that enhance stabilization, the ability to control movement through the core (inherent in all core exercises)

Flexion and extension: Exercises that work in the sagittal plane

Rotation: Exercises that work in the transverse plane and diagonal rotational patterns

Throwing and catching: Exercises that involve throwing and catching

The core training exercise postures are as follows:

Prone: Body lying down with face down

Supine: Body lying down with face up

Standing: Body upright, supported by feet only

Moving: Changing position (e.g., walking and crawling)

The preferred postures are standing and moving. It has been my experience that these postures are optimal for enhancing linkage and use of the core as the relay center.

The following core module is used daily as part of warm-up:

Walking rotations (use medicine ball or weight plate)

   Walking wide rotation ($\times$ 20)

   Walking tight rotation ($\times$ 20)

   Walking over the top ($\times$ 20)

   Walking figure eight ($\times$ 20)

Total-Body Strength

Total-body strength is achieved mainly through pulling movements that involve the whole body, from toenails to fingernails. These movements are threaded throughout each of the training phases and vary in volume and intensity based on the phase of training and the adaptive capacity of the swimmer. I have found that the most effective total-body movements for swimmers are the following dumbbell exercises, performed with both one and two arms. I recommend dumbbells instead of a bar because use of dumbbells is safer and easier to teach and enables the athlete to work through multiple planes of motion.

Dumbbell jump shrug

Dumbbell high pull

Dumbbell snatch

All of these exercises require the athlete to concentrate and use the whole kinetic chain. Resistance is determined as a percentage of body weight as a starting point and progresses to traditional loading parameters in which repetitions determine load. The athlete should start with 15% of body weight in each hand and progress as they achieve technical proficiency.

Upper-Body Strength

The upper quadrant receives the most stress in daily training because it is the main source of propulsion in swimming. Consequently, the coach and swimmer must carefully control the type and volume of upper-quadrant strength training so as to not add stress to stress. The highest volume of upper-quadrant work should precede the highest volume of swimming training. There is a careful buildup to this phase. This phase is not long; it does not need to be. The upper quadrant is the main mechanism of propulsion. Therefore, if the athlete develops strength to the optimum before attempting the highest volume in the pool, then the volume work will be of higher intensity and more efficient and will pose minimal risk of overuse injuries. Upper-quadrant strength work consists primarily of pushing, pressing, and rowing movements that constantly emphasize connecting the hip to the shoulder. The primary exercises are as follows:

Ring pull-ups
Ring push-ups
Dumbbell bench press
Dumbbell curl and press
Bent-arm pullover

With the exception of the bench press and pullover, the athlete performs all overhead lifting movements while standing in order to facilitate the hip-to-shoulder connection and reinforce the X effect.

The athlete should execute the following remedial supportive strength routine with stretch cord before swimming. It helps prevent injury and warms the athlete up to swim.

Dynamic protraction–retraction with stretch cord
Dynamic scarecrow with stretch cord
Nordic row with stretch cord
Punching with stretch cord

Lower-Body Strength

Some still believe that extensive leg-strength work is either a waste of time or counterproductive for swimmers. I do not subscribe to this school of thought. The legs are very important in all strokes, and leg strength can help with kicking. If nothing else, leg-strength work prepares the swimmer for the kicking work done in the water. The highest volume of leg work precedes the highest volume of kicking. The benefits are increased capillarization, improved streamlining ability, kicking more effectively and efficiently, and the ability to start more explosively and push off the wall in turns.

The following are exercises for lower-body strength:

Squat
Lunge (in all three planes)
Step-up (low box and high box)
Leg circuit
    Squat
    Lunge
    Step-up
    Jump squat

THE PLAN

Planned performance training is the sequence and timing of applying the training stimulus. It is certainly is not about time; it is about timing. The following is an overview of the training blocks of the University of Michigan women's swim team for the 2009 to 2010 season.

Foundational Strength (September 10 to September 30)

Emphasis: Total-body and multiple-joint movements with external resistance and body weight

Means: Total body movements in a repetition range of 4 to 6; individual exercises with resistance in a repetition range of 6 to 10; bodyweight repetitions of 15 to 20 for upper body and 20 for lower body

Basic Strength (October 1 to October 20)

Emphasis: Volume loading through push–pull—squat sequence work

Means: Dumbbell complex (high pull, alternate press, squat, and row) and upper-body giant sets (three exercises sequenced into one set; e.g., ring pull-up followed by ring push-up followed by arm step-up)

Strength Endurance (October 22 to November 10)

Emphasis: Work in the range of 30 to 60 seconds in duration with recovery up to 1:1 (but more frequently 1:1/2 or 1:1/3)

Means: Bias circuits (stressing one area of the body; i.e., the core, the legs, or the upper body) and peripheral heart action circuits (moving in sequence from upper body to core to lower body, thus forcing the heart to work to circulate blood rapidly from one body part to another)

Hybrid Recovery (November 12 to December 5)

Purdue Invite: Mini peak

Strength Endurance (December 7 to December 23)

Emphasis: Component endurance (15 minutes maximum)

Means: Leg circuit (page 310), upper-body circuit (page 310), core circuit (page 309)

Power Endurance (December 28 to January 23)

Emphasis: High-intensity work 10, 30, and 60 seconds in duration with a work-to-rest ration in multiple sets of 1:1 for sprint and middle distance and 1:1/3 or 1:1/4 for distance

Means: Growth hormone work (middle distance; total-body movements that involve as much muscle mass as possible; high-intensity work from 20 to 30 seconds in duration performed for multiple sets in a 1:1 work-to-rest ratio);

circuit 2 (distance; a shorter rest interval of 1:1/3 or 1:1/4); cluster training (sprinters; as many reps of an exercise as possible in 10 seconds, with 20 seconds rest before repeating the exercise)

Recycle (January 25 to February 16)

Emphasis: Each of the previous components recycled through for short periods to reawaken those aspects

Means: Combination of selected previous methods

Hybrid (February 22 to March 16)

Emphasis: Each component touched on in a microcycle in order to stabilize strength components in peaking or tapering

Means: Combination of each of the previous methods

CONCLUSION

Effective dryland training is more than exercises and training methodology—it is the application of the principles of sport science and sound pedagogy coupled with knowledge of swimming. Following are a few of the important tips to remember as you create your dryland training program.

- Understand and respect the spectrum of strength, power, and flexibility demands in swimming.
- Always think and analyze. Ask why. Keep looking for optimal combinations based on the current group of swimmers you are working with.
- Build strength in; do not build it on.
- Train power in; do not train it out.
- Seek the optimal, not the maximum, to ensure transfer to swimming.
- Always link—sync and connect—to take advantage of coordination and muscle synergies.
- All systems work all the time. We just tune them up and get them working together better.
- Consistent application of varied stress and stressors results in continual adaptation.
- Vary the load and vary the mode in a systematic and sequential manner.

Remember, as coach Steve Myrland, an expert on swimming training, once said, "We want bodies that are adaptable rather than simply adapted."

23

Power Training in the Pool

Dick Shoulberg

Power training in the pool provides overload specificity that dryland training is unable to duplicate. Swimmers should vary their power training from the pool to the pool deck and back to the pool again within the training session; this variety is motivating and swimmers note the positive effects of the on-deck training when re-entering the pool. Power training in the pool increases the stress placed on the swimmer and enhances strength, power, and fitness to higher levels than can be achieved by just swimming. As another advantage, much of the equipment used for power training in the pool is low cost.

POWER TRAINING WATER DRILLS

The following power training water drills, including the equipment described, are used in our Germantown Academy program.

Drag Suits

Drag suits are swimsuits with added material or cups that provide resistance or drag while using them. Drag suits with a strong drag effect are very difficult to purchase because not many places carry them. A current age-group mother made 36 drag suits for me this year.

From 1991 to 1992 I coached a young swimmer, Julie Cole. In 1988 Julie was third at the Olympic Trials in the 800 freestyle. I knew she lacked strength so I designed a 24-minute drag suit set for her to do every day. This set consisted of 22 × 100 on 1:20 holding 1:01 short course.

The drag suit puts a different stress on the body than buckets. The drag suits are good correcting tools in free and backstroke, where hip rotation comes into play. Drag suit sets are done three times a week. The sprinters do long rest sets, and the distance swimmers do short rest repeat swims.

Buckets

I started using buckets in 1984. I believe that a bucket is the poor man's weight room. It is a great tool for swimmers because it 100% specific to the sport of swimming and can be used for all four strokes. A bucket is attached by a rope or surgical tubing to a belt that the swimmer wears. The size of the bucket determines how much water the swimmer tows when using it. The better athletes that use buckets can feel when they are out of alignment. For example, if the swimmer drops the elbow in the pull of the freestyle, the bucket moves out of alignment. When this happens, the swimmer is able to adjust the stroke to realign the bucket. Dr. Genadijus Sokolovas, former physiologist for USA Swimming, feels that buckets are one of the greatest pieces of equipment swimmers can use.

I prefer to use buckets up until the day we leave for a major or national meet because it guarantees that the athlete will not lose strength. When I was the head coach of the Pan Pacific team in Japan in 2000, the great swimmer Jenny Thompson told me that she needed a weight room because she had to lift heavy within 72 hours of her main race. Swimmers need some reduced resistance work to maintain strength through the taper; bucket sets can offer this resistance work.

In 1988, the coaches on the Olympic staff criticized buckets because they felt that using them was detrimental to the athlete's stroke technique. Four of my athletes—some current swimmers and some in university swimming programs—were on that Olympic team, including former world record holder Dave Wharton. Albert Stevens, the inventor of the Stroke Scope, videotaped Wharton doing all four strokes long course at the University of Texas. I showed the coaches of that Olympic team the video of Wharton in slow motion and asked what they thought of his stroke technique. All of the coaches said that his strokes were flawless. As they continued to watch the video they saw the bucket appear. I had proven my point: Buckets are incredibly important.

Bucket sets are done three times a week. Sprinters do long rest sets, and distance swimmers do short rest repeat swims.

Pipe Swimming

Pipe swimming is a low-cost exercise. It is used to build and improve the kicking power of the freestyle swimmer and to increase the length of their stroke. The swimmer holds a pipe out in front with one extended arm and swims up to it with the stroking arm, and then alternates which arm holds the pipe. Swimmers can use different kinds of pipes that provide different levels of difficulty. The younger age-group swimmers use wooden pipes (or a piece of noodle), which are less difficult to use because they float. Swimmers then progress to using an 8-inch (20.3 cm) piece of polyvinyl chloride (PVC) piping, and then to weighting the PVC pipe with sand. The PVC pipe requires that the swimmer uses a stronger kick, and the weighted pipe requires an even stronger kick to keep the pipe close to the surface. Pipe swimming is a great way to ensure proper catch-up freestyle (long overlapping of arm strokes to the front end of the stroke). Pipe swimming can also be done while wearing a snorkel, which will help a swimmer maintain proper body alignment.

We also use the pipe and snorkel rather than a kickboard to do kicking drills because it eliminates conversation among the swimmers and there is more emphasis just on the kicking. I feel that this is the best kicking drill my team does. For the more advanced swimmers, I do a variation of pipe kicking in which the swimmers take a rubber weight from a weight room—5, 10, 20, or 25 pounds (2.3, 4.6, 9, or 11.3 kg), depending on ability—and kick (fly, flutter, or breast kick) across the pool with the weight held straight out in front like in a streamline.

Rope Climbing

In 1971 I installed two 24-foot (7.3 m) climbing ropes over the surface of the water in the deep end of the pool. I installed them specifically for the sprinters to develop finger, hand, wrist, and forearm strength. However, since their installation, the ropes have benefitted every swimmer in the program. Three times a week, the swimmers climb up the rope, climb down, and immediately climb up again; they continue in this manner until failure. The rope has benefitted other students at the school besides the swimmers; for example, the wrestlers rope climb daily.

In the classes I teach, the students climb ropes as early as pre-K (always supervised) to encourage strength development. Trina Radke (1988 Olympic team) climbed the rope 13 times up and down, never taking her hands off the rope. Erika Hansen (1988 and 1992 Olympic teams) then beat that record in the early 1990s by climbing up and down the rope 14 times. In 2005, Alicia Aemisegger (Princeton Female Athlete of the Decade and All-American) set a new record and climbed up and down the rope 21 times. On the boys' side, Greg Gorniak, a Germantown Academy high school swimmer, set the record at 17 times. Each time he started climbing up the rope he would lead with his feet, so that he was upside down, until he was too tired to continue in that manner; he would then finish climbing to the top of the rope head first.

Vertical Kicking

Vertical kicking helps swimmers develop great kicking action. My swimmers perform vertical kicking three mornings a week. They go for about 28 minutes and hold between 12 and 20 pounds (5.4 and 9 kg), depending on the strength of the swimmer.

Vertical kicking can be done in two ways. In the most common way, the swimmer does vertical kicking at the surface of the water while holding the weight across the chest. If the swimmer is using a heavier weight, a snorkel can facilitate breathing. In the other way, the swimmer drops to the bottom of the pool. If the swimmer is using a weight belt, they drop to the bottom using their arms, and then put their arms in a perfect streamline and kick to the surface. Once the swimmer reaches the surface, they do three really fast kicks at the surface while in the streamline position. If the swimmer holds the weight, the drill is done the same way as with a weight belt except the swimmer does not assume the streamline position. These drills should be closely monitored by the coach.

We do vertical kicking in conjunction with the rope climb. The swimmers climb the rope and then switch with their partners and perform vertical kicking.

Power Racks

Power racks have been around for about 20 to 30 years. They are commercially available and are placed on pool decks. On a power rack, a line travels through a pulley and is attached to weights. The other end of the line is attached to a belt that the swimmer wears around the waist. The swimmer swims and tows the weight that is on the rack. I have four power racks, set up on a pulley system, suspended from the 25-foot (7.6 m) ceiling over lane 6.

A basic set on a power rack is 12 × 25 on 1:30. Four swimmers work this set at one time. The two swimmers start diagonal from each other, leaving on 0, and the other two swimmers leave on 0:45. When swimmers perform this set, I look for

1. number of stroke cycles,
2. amount of weight, and
3. speed.

My goal is to decrease the number of stroke cycles and increase speed while maintaining the weight, which is set for each individual swimmer. We do this set three times a week.

T-Shirts and Sneakers

Swimming in wet T-shirts and shoes increases resistance and is old-school training in my mind. The Eastern Europeans did a lot of this type of resistance training in the 1970s and 1980s. When I do this type of resistance training, 30 seconds after the set is complete I have the swimmers remove the T-shirts and sneakers and go 6 × 25s on 0:25 or 6 × 50s on 0:45 in an all-out race. The athletes say that it gives them the sensation of a taper. This type of resistance training guarantees the athlete's ability to maintain the proper stroke technique at high speed.

I rarely use T-shirts and sneakers in practice. I break out this equipment when things get a little stale and I need a change to maintain swimmer focus.

Paddles

Swim paddles are oversized hands made of plastic. They are manufactured in various shapes and sizes and provide more hand surface to engage more water. Our swimmers do a lot of technique work with paddles on. We do a series of drills that ends with the swimmer holding the paddle at the top; this helps the swimmer maintain proper hand position in the water. I am always cautious when using paddles because introducing paddles too early in the training year can result in injury (as can overuse of any equipment)—in this case, to the shoulder. I do not give any paddle sets during the first 4 to 5 weeks of the season because I want to be sure the athletes are at a certain level of fitness before I introduce them. We then continue with graduated use. Once paddle use is established, we do normal pulling and swim sets with them.

Paddles and Bands

I started using bands about 40 years ago when I began coaching. I purchased used car tire innertubes at the local tire shop and then cut the innertubes 1.5 inches (3.8 cm) thick. The athletes put the tubes on their ankles in a figure eight configuration. Bands decrease or eliminate the kick and consequently increase power in the arm stroke. I prefer using a band over a pull buoy because using a band also engages the core.

I introduced paddles to the band about 30 years ago. I researched different types of paddles and found that paddles increase technique and range of motion. Using the paddles simultaneously with the band helps the swimmer neurologically and builds overall strength.

Fins and Paddles

This is speed-assisted training. Putting paddles and fins on the swimmers allows the athlete to go faster than normal neurologically. Because my swimmers do a large amount of resistance training, I try to counterbalance it with such speed-assisted training.

When we use fins and paddles we do sets that try to control the swimmers' stroke count. We start with 8 × 25s @ 0:25 to get an average stroke count for the swimmers. We then follow with 1 × 300 going 100 normal stroke count, 100 – 1 stroke per lap, and 100 – 2 strokes per lap. This is followed by 3 × 100s going as fast as the swimmer can maintain – 2 strokes per lap. We also do paddles and fins with a snorkel because it helps the swimmer control body alignment. I believe that the snorkel is one of the best tools available for a swimmer to use in the water.

Ergometers and Hop Blocks

The ergometer (better known as a Vasa Trainer) is an exercise machine with an ergometer that measures the work performed. The swimmer lies on the stomach on the bench and uses the arms to pull the handles, simulating a swimming stroke. At Germantown Academy I have nine ergometers on the pool deck; next to them are nine hop blocks (plyometric blocks) of three heights ranging from 12 to 32 inches (30.5 to 81.3 cm). In my opinion, the ergometer is the greatest land tool at Germantown Academy for the money we spent on it. We do a series of exercises on the ergometer, and the swimmers rotate between an ergometer and hop blocks. We also do circuit training using the ergometer, hop blocks, and water. The swimmers perform the hop block exercises while wearing footwear to prevent slipping on the wet pool deck.

In the course of a 3-hour practice the swimmer trains both in and out of the water and has about 30 seconds to switch stations. The swimmer spends about 1 hour and 45 minutes of that 3-hour period in the water and the rest doing land work. I believe that certain land exercises build strength more quickly than water exercises. The dryland training on our pool deck is designed to improve total-body fitness, including the core through the extremities.

Stretch Cords

We use stretch cords of varying lengths to accommodate the different strokes and exercises. These cords provide tension while being stretched. One end of the cord is secured safely to an immobile attachment such as wall mounts and the other end is attached to handles or swim paddles.

About 24 stretch cords of a range of strengths hang around the perimeter of the pool deck. Another two cords hang about 15 feet (4.6 m) off the ground and are used for the top half of the stroke. The swimmers stand directly under the cords and pull down. We do sets of 50 on 10 off, then 40 on 20 off, then 30 on 30 off. The swimmers always change the exercise but always work at full intensity.

Many coaches use stretch cords in the water for power training. Unfortunately, because of space limitations I am not able to use them in the water. I am also hesitant to do so because about 15 years ago a cord snapped and hit me; I could not walk for 3 days.

Straps

Six straps that are stable hang on our three pull-up bars at the end of the pool. Three of the straps are TRX Professional trainers and the other three straps are jungle gym trainers. I purchased the straps about 4 years ago when Teresa Crippen (2011 world championship team member, silver medal in 200 butterfly) and Katie Riefenstahl (2008 U.S. Olympic trials two-time finalist) were juniors in high school. I got the idea from Vern Gambetta (author of chapter 22, Dryland Training) when he spoke at the American Swimming Coaches Association World Clinic. He has really influenced a lot of my thinking, so I always try to pick his brain for new ideas.

We do a variety of exercises that work the upper body, lower body, and core. The swimmers like to get creative and make up new exercises. The one they like the most involves placing the feet in the bottom of the TRX strap and holding the jungle gym in the hands. Once in this position, they do push-ups and abdominal work. It is a great tool because it is inexpensive and safe. I always have the kids come out of the water to use the straps. A swimmer might get pulled out of practice for 20 minutes, and I'll tell them to work on the strap then get back in the water.

Kettlebells

A kettlebell is a ball-shaped weight that has a hand attachment. We have six yellow (17.6 lb; 7.9 kg), six green (26.4 lb; 11.9 kg), and six red (35.2 lb; 15.9 kg) kettlebells. I like them because the athlete can use them while performing a wide variety of exercises. The kettlebell improves range of motion, strength, power, flexibility, and endurance. Any exercise that causes resistance and allows the athlete to go through the full range of motion is critical to the contribution and success of the athlete.

David Wharton, former world record holder in the 400-meter individual medley and 1988 Olympic team member, first broke a world record while he was still in high school.

Bart Schineder, Germantown Academy's current high school 50-yard record holder, was a 20.0 50 freestyler in the early 1980s. Both of these swimmers would perform range of motion exercises with a 5- or 10-pound (2.3 or 4.6 kg) weight at the end of the pool and would then dive back in the water and do a series of 100–200–300 at full speed. After racing that they would climb out of the water and go right back into a new exercise with the weight.

A variety of exercises can be performed with the kettlebells, including the one-arm swings and squat lifts depicted in the photo as well as straight-arm lifts, curls, and reverse curls.

Pull-Ups

One cannot do enough pull-ups because they improve total-body fitness. At the end of every practice, I make the swimmers do pull-ups before they can leave the pool deck. However, if the exercise causes the athlete any pain, they should stop immediately.

CONCLUSION

Power training in the pool permits the greatest specificity possible because the swimmer is actually swimming. More resistance work is being added to pool training. Pool deck training is designed to improve total body-fitness and flexibility, which have always led to faster and stronger swimming in the Germantown Academy program.

I hope my ideas help you. Most important, coaches are always welcome to come observe any of my practices. I do this because I know I will learn something new from any coach, old or young, that stands on my pool deck. I take any opportunity I can to learn something new because it always benefits the swimmers.

PART FIVE

FINAL TOUCHES
FOR PEAK PERFORMANCE

24

Positive Communication, Positive Results

Lanny Landtroop

Have you ever watched a fellow coach talking with a team when the athletes seem to hang on every word? Does it seem that you have trouble getting or keeping your athletes' full attention when you talk with them? Talk itself is cheap. The authentic communication we discuss in this chapter involves connecting with others. Think about the blue chip quarterback on a football team. He has a rifle arm and pinpoint accuracy. In a critical game with the outcome on the line, he calls a play to pass to his favorite receiver. He fades back after the snap, sets up, spots his receiver, and lets the ball fly. A perfect spiral goes over the heads of the defenders and right to the receiver. The ball hits the receiver right in the numbers...and bounces out. The players have failed to connect; therefore, the game is lost.

Developing a sustainable program that continually produces athletes who succeed in the pool is important. However, it is also essential to develop swimmers into productive citizens who, as a result of their team experience, understand the importance of their roles in society. This is a very complex task. The connections crucial to such development require that the coach connects with each individual athlete as well as with the team as a whole. The athletes and team must also connect with the coach. For a team to achieve the maximum effect from their experience, the members of the team must connect with one another. In addition, by connecting with his or her profession, a coach has the opportunity to learn from fellow coaches and, in turn, contribute to the sport. Finally, the coach who also connects with the board (athletic director, administration, and so on) has the best opportunity to develop and sustain a program that is the envy of those who fail to recognize the importance of such connections outside the pool area.

Finally, one of the most important connections the coach can help foster is the connection that athletes make with themselves. Young people who develop self-knowledge and reflection more readily and effectively connect with others in a wide variety of relationships. The swimmer who practices positive self-feedback becomes much more centered and productive.

As you read this chapter, be aware that a great deal of it concerns the coach–athlete connection, but all the techniques involved can be applied to the many other relationships that a coach develops.

A COACH–ATHLETE PARADIGM

As Nort Thornton once said, "Our goal is to create an atmosphere where champions are inevitable." When I first heard Thornton's statement, I thought, "Wow!" It was the most powerful observation I had heard regarding athletics. So much is involved in working to achieve this goal, but communication and connecting are essential in moving in that direction. In reaction, I immediately began to think about how my team and I could adopt this concept and bring it to fruition. What would it take to establish an atmosphere that produces even one champion, much less one in which champions are inevitable? The more I thought about it, I realized I had to improve my ability to connect with the athletes so we would all be on the same page.

Becoming a good swimmer takes time and patience; coaches must communicate this to team members so that they understand the process they are undergoing. This concept is illustrated by a story about a Chinese bamboo tree. The tree was carefully planted and watered and fertilized; it was meticulously cared for. At the end of its first year, no change occurred. The same held true for the second, third, and fourth years. Then, in the fifth year, the tree grew 40 feet (12.2 m) in just 6 weeks! Athletes readily relate to this story and understand that, in swimming, a significant payoff down the line requires meticulous training and preparation. Thornton's atmosphere is created only through patient interaction, communication, and especially inspiration.

Connecting With the Athlete

A team is made up of individuals with many different backgrounds, various needs, and a variety of levels of motivation. My next task was to find ways to connect with such a diverse group. For this task, I turned to Stephen Covey's 7 *Habits of Highly Effective People* (1989). One of these habits, "seek first to understand, then to be understood," encouraged me to be assiduously proactive in discovering the stories of each athlete. In pursuing that information, I learned much that allowed me to more effectively connect with each athlete and create a bond of trust that was necessary to realize our vision. The better I knew and understood my athletes, the more effective I became in recognizing their personal needs and gifts, and the better they understood and embraced our vision for excellence.

Developing Team Goals

To continue moving steadily in the right direction, the team and I needed to nurture a common mindset. The success of our goal required that we connect on an individual level. Some coaches say that their biggest problem is getting their athletes to practice on time. Our team determined that, to succeed, it was crucial that everyone arrive to practice on time. After thinking about this for a while, I proposed some negative

Communicating With the Athlete

In the book *The One-Minute Manager,* authors Ken Blanchard and Spencer Johnson recommend congratulating people when you find them doing something right. In coaching, it is easy to spend all of our time correcting swimmers as part of the learning process and to spend too little time celebrating all the things that the athletes are doing well.

A technique that is often useful in this regard is the sandwich technique. When using this technique, one communicates something positive to a person, then makes corrections, and follows with something else positive. This technique should not be used all the time, but it certainly is effective in some situations.

Knowing individual athletes beyond the pool deck gives a coach many opportunities to connect with the athlete in a positive way. Especially with older athletes, recognizing good academic performance or the achievement of something like the Eagle Scout award communicates to the athlete that you are truly interested in them as a person outside of the pool.

I find the following helpful to foster an atmosphere of open communication with my swimmers. All interactions can be viewed as a bank account. Someone who does something positive for someone else makes a deposit (cha-ching) to that account. On the other hand, when the interaction is negative, a withdrawal occurs. If enough deposits are made and the account builds up, a withdrawal has much less effect. In practical terms, a coach is in the habit of congratulating a swimmer when they swim a good repeat or set (cha-ching). This is an example of positive reinforcement. Each "way to go" is a deposit, and the account increases. Then, on the day the swimmer is not doing a good job and the coach points out that fact (makes a withdrawal), the interaction is more likely to be accepted as constructive criticism. The good will generated by the positive interaction creates a safe environment for the athletes to keep each other doing their best.

This device works equally well in swimmer–swimmer and coach–team relationships. We have all been around someone who is very negative and constantly points out what they don't like about an athlete's performance or habits. After some time of such behavior (withdrawals), that person creates a deficit of good will and is likely to be tuned out, or the athletes and team on the receiving end decide they would rather be somewhere else.

motivation that could have positive results. At a local scuba dive shop I purchased some nylon web belting and about a dozen 2-pound (0.9 kg) weights. Together we determined that anyone who was tardy to practice would voluntarily wear a 2-pound weight belt for that training session. Anyone who failed to pick up the 2-pound belt on their own and had to be reminded was awarded the privilege of wearing a 4-pound (1.8 kg) weight belt. Wearing the weight belt throughout that swim session was a constant reminder to the swimmer to avoid being tardy in the future.

This activity had nearly miraculous results. Within only a few days, tardiness became history. When my athletes and I forged the connection and agreed to turn the lateness problem into an accountability positive, we created a contract for personal responsibility. This contract cemented in each athlete the idea that being on time for each training session was critical to the team's success and emphasized the importance of every session.

The Importance of Nonverbal Communication

Ralph Waldo Emerson said, "What you are speaks so loudly that I can't hear what you say." As Emerson suggests, connection often occurs in a nonverbal way. This type of communication can be at least as effective, and in some instances even more effective, than the most eloquent verbal instruction. Young people have a natural tendency to really look up to their coaches. This proclivity gives a coach the serious responsibility to consciously become a good role model. Just ask yourself the following question. As an athlete who spends countless hours training under a coach, would you train better with a coach who is energetic, positive, and engaged in every aspect of the training session or with a coach who writes the practice on the board and then pays little attention to what is happening in the pool?

The answer to this question is rather obvious, isn't it? The lists of speaker qualities in Sonya Hamlin's *How to Talk So People Listen* (1988) directly relate to coaches and their communications with individual athletes and teams.

List 1	List 2
Warm	Pompous
Honest	Vague
Friendly	Flat
Exciting	Complex
Interesting	Patronizing
Knowledgeable	Nervous
Organized	Formal
Creative	Irrelevant
Confident	Stuffy
Inspiring	Monotonous
Open	Intense
Authentic	Closed
Informal	
Funny	

To gain information and insight into how your athletes feel about your tendencies as a coach, allow them to use these lists to evaluate your coaching style. You will probably find a mixed response, but it could provide valuable information that will help you to better connect with your swimmers. Such an activity can, if taken objectively without defensiveness, give you a fresh perspective from which to improve your communication with your athletes and with others. We very easily fall into ruts over time, and such periodic reflection can be invaluable.

Constant Awareness

Most young people are very perceptive and can tell you things you are not aware of—things you said or did that in your mind were unimportant but that made a gigantic impression on them. In the past, I have been amazed that something I considered a casual aside affected an athlete far beyond what I could have imagined.

One example that comes to mind is a small comment I made to several members of my team. I was talking about the value of the team and commented that we needed synergy. When they asked me to define synergy, I gave this classic example: if 10 people could each lift 100 pounds, it would seem that together they could lift 1,000 pounds, but they actually could lift much more—maybe as much as 1,500 pounds.

About a month later, we had a dual meet with our big rival. It was close, but we were able to win both the girls and boys meets. When I came out of the pool about 20 minutes after the meet, a couple of very excited swimmers asked me to follow them into the parking lot. When I arrived, the teams lifted a big car. They looked at me and said, "Look, Coach—synergy!" For the next several years, the athletes lifted a car every time we won a big meet. They demonstrated synergy both in and out of the pool.

Hopefully the positives far outweigh the negatives in your bank account in these instances.

Components of Connection

A UCLA study found that face-to-face communication has three components:

1. words,
2. tone of voice, and
3. body language (Mehrabian and Ferris, 1967).

According to John C. Maxwell, author of *Everyone Communicates, Few Connect* (2010), when we communicate we must include

- thought (something we know)
- emotion (something we feel), and
- action (something we do).

He says that all three are necessary for true connection to happen. If I try to communicate

- something I know but do not feel, my communication is dispassionate;
- something I know but do not do, my communication is theoretical;
- something I feel but do not know, my communication is unfounded;
- something I do but do not feel, my communication is hypocritical;
- something I do but do not know, my communication is presumptuous; and
- something I do but do not feel, my communication is mechanical.

Certainly coaches want to communicate passion for our sport and our athletes and to provide athletes with the best behavior and modeling we can. We want to have knowledge and grounding in our sport so that we can communicate with authenticity and honesty. Above all, we want to practice and exemplify sincerity because young people quickly recognize hypocrisy and phoniness. In other words, we want to work on our character so as to provide effective and powerful verbal and nonverbal communication. To truly connect, all these ingredients are necessary and provide much-needed credibility. Always remember that your messages are sent through words, tone of voice, and body language.

Sharpening the Communication Connection

I was talking to a new swimmer from out of state to get an idea of the kind of program he had come from and the level of work he was used to. He had come from a good program and was able to perform well enough to compete in our program. Toward the end of the conversation, he began critiquing his experience on his former team. His main complaint was that every time his former coach went to a clinic, he returned with a lot of new information and, in trying to pass his knowledge on to his athletes, discussed it endlessly. In the end, the athletes were confused and unsure of what he was really trying to say. The young man stated that he would have preferred that the information be simplified so it was easy to understand. Had the coach taken time to absorb his new knowledge and rework it to the appropriate level for his swimmers, he might have been more effective. Though information from clinics is invaluable, a coach must consider the swimmers' level of experience and knowledge and present the information accordingly. The adjustment saves time, energy, and frustration on both sides. As John C. Maxwell has stated, "In the end, people are persuaded not by what we say but by what they understand" (2010).

A well-known and valuable concept that illustrates this issue is the KISS (keep it simple, stupid) principle. Most often, a true connection is made when ideas are broken down to their simplest form. You may know the similar scientific concept of Occam's razor. To explain the concept in layman's terms, the simplest solution is usually the correct one. So, when explaining something new such as a drill or strategy, first do it in the simplest terms and then, for the individual who needs more, address it individually. The coach must understand at much greater depth whatever he or she is trying to communicate, and the athletes must fully understand the intent of the concept. That is usually accomplished by presenting the simplest explanation.

Connecting the Athlete to Confidence

I have always felt that my primary job as a coach is to help each athlete develop confidence. The first year I taught and coached, I had a young man named Edwin on the team. Toward the end of the season, a fellow teacher stopped me in the hall and asked, "What have you done to Edwin?" Unsure whether this question leaned toward the positive or negative, I was slow to answer. When I asked the motivation for the question, the teacher replied that at the beginning of the year Edwin sat in the back of the room, was very quiet, and always walked with his head down. Gradually, Edwin moved to the front of the room and began to participate in lively class discussion, and now walked with his head held high. In reflection, I didn't think that

I had done anything special, but I came to realize that Edwin's many opportunities with the swim team helped him gain confidence, not just in the pool but in himself. That was a major lesson for me at the very beginning of my career, and helping young people gain confidence has been an essential core value in my coaching career.

For most people, just being part of a team that has high goals, not just in athletic performance but in the classroom and community as well, is a great confidence builder. Team participation provides many opportunities for individuals to succeed in something other than swimming and is especially valuable for those with less swimming talent. Through the years we have given the athletes a wide variety of opportunities to experience success. For example, for several years we played water polo; a number of athletes who were not the best swimmers found that they excelled in water polo. Among the many competitions in our dryland and off-season programs were softball, Ultimate Frisbee, contests using various exercises (e.g., crunches, push-ups, pull-ups), and rope climbing. In addition to improving physical condition, team members enjoyed bonding, friendly rivalry, and building confidence.

Setting individual goals with athletes presents a tremendous opportunity to connect them with confidence. Helping them create an action plan that furnishes a comprehensive and incremental picture for success communicates support and foments trust. As athletes progress toward those goals with the coach's guidance, a special bond evolves and the athlete often gains the confidence to reset his or her original goals for even greater accomplishment. This goal-setting process is not limited to just athletics, but can be successfully applied for a lifetime in whatever areas they choose. One of the great rewards of coaching is seeing this process develop and realizing that these athletes have developed a tool that will aid them throughout their lives.

Connecting Through Listening

Really listening to athletes is a major factor in connecting. This statement may sound obvious, but it is particularly important in the busy world we live in today. Some young people seldom have an adult listen to them and understand what they are saying. Also, the many athletes who come from single-parent homes often need an additional sounding board for their thoughts and ideas. This may sound like co-opting the job of the parent, but if communication or connection is not happening in the home, the coach plays a vital role as an adult mentor. Often one must read between the lines to receive what the student really intends, but a coach develops and improves his or her ear with experience and with the growing connection with the athlete. By listening—really listening—a coach strengthens the bonds of communication and enhances the athlete's trust.

Communication with the individual athlete or the team requires attention to three basic questions they have:

1. Do you care for me?
2. Can you help me?
3. Can I trust you?

These questions need positive answers for a coach to effectively connect with the swimmers. The stronger the swimmer believes in the coach's sincere commitment to them, the stronger the connection to be made. We all have basic human needs, and as young people grow up and search for answers in their lives, they have a deep need to connect with adults who care for them, will help them, and are implicitly trustworthy.

Such a relationship can go a long way in helping young people develop other healthy personal interactions.

A COACH–TEAM PARADIGM

Several years ago I took a job with a high school team that had never moved beyond the second level of a three-level championship season. In an early team meeting, I talked to them about national ranking. I didn't find out until our banquet at the end of the season that, at the time, they all thought I was crazy. They had never even considered competing at that level, and my casual mention of it opened their minds to the possibility. They went on to win several state championships and several Swimming World national championships. It is truly amazing what raising the bar can do for your athletes. In this experience, I discovered some talented athletes that just needed their horizons broadened by the articulation of possibility.

> *When you make a commitment you create hope.*
> *When you keep a commitment, you create trust.*

Athlete-to-Athlete Connections

When beginning a new season or year, for a group to develop as a team, the athletes must get to know one another and become comfortable with one another. Rather than assuming it will happen naturally, a coach needs a proactive approach. Playing games is a great way to facilitate camaraderie. In one of my favorite "get to know you" games, each athlete writes the name of a tangible item on a sticky note. (You can imagine that they have a good time thinking of items to use.) The notes are then mixed up and each athlete places a note on his or her forehead or back. Team members are then instructed that they may ask a teammate one question, answerable only by yes or no, about the item on their sticky note. However, before they ask the question, they must introduce themselves to the other person and shake hands. The other person then follows the same process. The procedure is repeated and each athlete goes to another teammate until everyone has met. Depending on the size of the group, this activity can be repeated until all team members have interacted. Alternatively, you may set a time limit. This activity provides a controlled situation for athletes to interact with each other, especially athletes who are new to the program. This simple activity is just one of many that can be used to break the ice in a group. Remember, the important thing is not the activity itself but the connecting that takes place.

Athlete-to-Team Connection

I like to assume that every athlete sincerely wants to improve and be successful and to work with the group to achieve team success. To get the entire group in the same mindset and feel that they have ownership of the necessary principles to achieve success, they must determine those principles. Because we were in a high school environment, we went into a classroom with a whiteboard and markers. One athlete was responsible for recording on the board all the suggestions from teammates about what it takes to achieve success. No value judgments were made on any of the suggestions. In activities such as this, three dozen and sometimes as many as four dozen ideas might be recorded. The group then pared down the list to 15 or 20 principles by combining similar items and discussing which ideas were most important. All athletes then copied the list on the first page of their workout logs. The activity culminated with a discussion, led by an experienced member of the team, about the importance of each concept and how best to hold each other accountable. Such working together fosters the creation of a team creed and provides the athletes with a great opportunity to get to know each other and connect through the discussion.

To cite an example of this process, team members decided that they should support their teammates and not place limits on them. To accomplish this, the team decided to outlaw the word "can't," which they referred to as "the C word." When a team member used the C word, they were required to do 25 push-ups no matter where they were. The team members discovered an effective and fun way to purge the idea of limits to achievement. Because the team took the idea quite seriously and practiced it throughout the school day, I can recall many instances of athletes doing push-ups in cafeteria lines.

Like many swim teams, we trained at 5:30 a.m. One day I noticed the athletes were coming in, getting in the water, and going through the motions for a portion of the session and failing to maximize their opportunity. At a subsequent team meeting I proposed a new game called the greeting game. The rules we set up were that if I should greet an athlete before he or she greeted me, they became the sourpuss of the day and did the sourpuss of the day drill. This drill changed from year to year but always included athletic enhancement exercises such as push-ups or crunches. Attitude improved almost immediately: More smiling and interaction occurred, and the athletes even began voluntarily greeting one another. After a few weeks I asked if the team could accept the challenge of going to the advanced level. Always up for a challenge, they eagerly accepted. In the advanced game, I hid on those early mornings and jumped out to greet them before they could greet me. After only a couple of successes on my part, athletes started sneaking into the dressing area, looking carefully into every nook and cranny on the alert so they would not be greeted first. What a fun way to get athletes awake, engaged, and ready to maximize the morning training sessions! It worked so well that I started using a similar game in my classroom, and it was equally successful there.

Connecting to Leadership

Every person on the team has a significant role to play in making the team experience happy and successful, coaches should encourage every member to embrace the concept of team leadership. To communicate this idea in a nonverbal way, we played a game called run with the rope, which required a length of rope just long enough to allow all team members to get inside with a little room when it was stretched around them. We played the game on outdoor football practice fields. The most external members of the group held the rope at their waists. The group was then charged to run around the field while encircled by the rope. Without fail, one or more athletes would go too fast or too slow or would in some other way not realize the importance of cooperating with the group. As they pulled the rope on one side, it placed undue pressure on the opposite side and often an athlete tumbled to the ground. After the first round, I told them their time—they weren't aware I was timing them—and asked if they could improve. Accepting the challenge, they took off again. This effort was a little better, although some athletes still tumbled. By the third try (it always seemed to take three attempts), some of the stronger athletes decided to move those who were having trouble into the middle to protect the group. The emerging team leaders then organized the group so they could successfully circle the practice fields in good time with no casualties. To reinforce and better connect the effects of this experience, I gave each athlete a typed article in which all the Es had been replaced with Xs. Even though just one letter of 26 had been changed, the change made it very difficult, if not impossible, to read the page. The discussion that followed emphasized the importance of every person and the role each played in team success.

Coach-to-Team Connection

People have known for eons that telling stories is an effective way to teach. Oral histories were the only record early man had; hence, the tradition of storytelling was set in our psyche thousands of years ago. Even today, one can offer a host of facts that gradually fade from memory, but relating a story that makes the same point helps the learner retain the information much better and much longer. One of my favorite stories is about flea trainers. I used it to help athletes understand that, in many cases, they have been conditioned to limit themselves. The team recognized this concept when they accepted the team principle of the C word.

The story is based on the fact that a flea can jump many times its length. To limit the fleas' extraordinary jumping ability, a trainer places them in a Mason jar and covers the top with a piece of plate glass. As the fleas jump, they hit the plate glass. They continue to jump and hit the glass and don't understand why they can't jump the great distances they used to. After banging against the plate glass over and over, they reach a point where they jump up just short of the glass. Once they have reached this point, the glass can be removed; the fleas are trained and will not jump out of the jar. Are athletes ever conditioned in this same way? Well-meaning people often try to protect young people by placing plate glass over their heads, thereby limiting their belief in their possibilities. Through this analogy, athletes are reminded that they perhaps limit themselves just as the fleas were limited. A virtually unlimited supply of such stories exists for your use, and you'll be surprised how much students enjoy and benefit from them.

Another useful tool that communicates who is responsible for both the individual and team experiences is the accountability inventory, a questionnaire that asks four or five dozen questions, all of which start with "Who is responsible for…?" The questionnaire includes everyday activities such as brushing one's teeth as well as things such as getting to practice on time, learning something new every session, improving academic performance, and positively encouraging teammates. This exercise brings to the athletes' attention the fact that they are responsible for not only their athletic experience but also their life experience. Such coach-directed activities and narratives are just another communication technique to help swimmers discover the significance of their roles and responsibilities to their program, their teammates, and their school community.

A COACH–COMMUNITY PARADIGM

Coaches often fail to recognize the importance of communicating with their community. For our purposes, the community includes swim boards, school administrations, civic clubs, and the unique activities of local communities. To foster connections with these groups and individuals, invite them to your competitions, special water shows, or any kind of activity you use in your program. Make contact with local sportswriters and notify them of your team's activities. Civic clubs need speakers for their meetings; consider volunteering your services. Invite people outside the swimming community to be the coach of the week. Use your imagination to get your team recognized and to celebrate with you all the good things that come from participating in our sport.

CONCLUSION

Absorbing this information and implementing these concepts is not easy. But who wants it to be easy? Anything worth working for is worth the effort it takes to create something special. The long-lasting value of making these connections is immeasurable. It involves you, the coach, your athletes, and the community in a project so worthwhile that every participant enjoys enormous benefits.

I write very little in this chapter about what happens in the pool because that is discussed elsewhere in this book. The purpose of this chapter is to make you aware, or in many cases just remind you, that creating the kind of program you desire and giving your athletes the best possible opportunities involves much more than swimming. Once we connect the dots among all the participants in a program, the dots form strong lines of communication that bring all the rich and diverse elements of your swimming community together. Such cooperation and interaction provides an essential pathway for your student–athletes to achieve success not just in swimming competitions but in life itself.

25

Mind Over Body in Competition

Brett Hawke

Confidence, especially self-confidence, is the key to success in all aspects of life, including athletics. Time and time again the history of sport has shown that it is not always the physically superior athletes or the most well-trained athletes who win gold medals or break world records. Physical strength and training are not enough to make an athlete a champion. In most cases, an athlete must also possess a superior mental capacity that is as well-trained as the body. Indeed, an athlete and, for that matter, a coach will never reach the pinnacle of their sport if they do not believe in themselves and possess self-confidence.

Unlike raw physical talent and genetic giftedness, self-confidence is completely accessible to all athletes and coaches who choose to acknowledge its power and desire to capitalize on its link to success. This raises a couple questions. From where does self-confidence emanate? How can coaches help their athletes develop the kind of unwavering and unbridled belief in themselves and their abilities that will propel them to become the most elite of the elite—champions?

THREE ESSENTIAL FACTORS IN DEVELOPING SELF-CONFIDENCE

Athletes may achieve mental fortitude in many ways, but I believe that three particular factors are absolutely essential in the development of self-confidence:

1. The condition of the athlete–coach relationship
2. The coach's recognition of the difference between performance contributors and performance detractors
3. The deliberate use of opportunities to mentally and athletically train and perform at peak levels

These factors serve as the foundation of an athlete's mental preparation for the highest levels of competition. Coaches who understand the dynamic relationships that exist among these factors will be masters of preparing their athletes to win gold medals and break world records.

The Athlete–Coach Relationship

The athlete–coach relationship is one of the most fundamental dynamics in any sport at any level. It can also be an athlete's greatest source of confidence. In many cases, the confidence a coach shows in an athlete's abilities can be the deciding factor in whether the athlete believes in his or her own abilities.

To inspire athletes to achieve new competitive heights, coaches must first establish a good working rapport with their athletes. This is the best way for coaches to demonstrate their knowledge, credibility, and competence. Only after such rapport and trust are established are coaches able to open the eyes of their athletes and show them that anything is possible. It is then that athletes are able to break through whatever mental (and sometimes physical) barriers that may have prevented them from obtaining goals that once seemed beyond reach. Whether swimmers achieve their first A standard or make a national team, their success reflects the trust they've developed in their coach.

Over the years, I have noticed certain interactions, and put in place deliberate practices, that have positively contributed to the development of the trust that builds athletes' self-confidence and allows them to pursue their full potential. I try to read their body language—at workouts and in competition—to look for clues for what I should say to them and when to say it. In addition, I get to know my athletes both as competitors and as individuals. In individual meetings throughout the pre- and postseason, I listen to their concerns with the aim of understanding what their drive is and where it comes from. By knowing my athletes well and knowing their ups and downs, I am able to teach them the focus and release way of life—how to become mentally focused and stay focused at practice and in competition and then how to release their minds when they are away from the pool so that they can simply enjoy lives as individuals.

The athlete–coach relationship can often mirror that of a parent–child relationship, where in order to establish trust the parent must set boundaries and expectations for the child to live and, ultimately, succeed by. The trust that develops within this relationship can alter lifestyles and have dramatic results.

As an assistant coach here at Auburn University, I had the privilege and honor of working with the great Richard Quick, who is a legend in the coaching world. It was a period of time (albeit too short) that I am extremely grateful I experienced. Very early on Richard provided me with one of the most vivid examples of the power of trust in the athlete–coach relationship. In the fall of 2007, as Richard was taking over the Auburn program, I received a phone call from an ex-swimmer who used to compete at Auburn—the first man under nineteen seconds in the 50-yard freestyle, Frenchman Fred Bousquet. At the time, Fred was living and training in France. We were very good friends and competitors back when I was swimming, and we had a lot of mutual respect. Fred called to ask whether he could come back to Auburn to train and compete because he missed the program and truly wanted to be a part of it. He said, "I don't like the results I'm getting," and ended the call with the question, "What do I need to do differently?"

I took this information to Richard Quick, who asked my opinion on what we should do and posed the question, "Should we allow him to join us?" I was honest and said that I felt that some issues with Fred's social life were getting in the way of him performing at his best, taking it to the next level, and really having a shot at a world record and an Olympic medal. Shortly after our conversation Richard asked me to get Fred on the phone.

As they talked, Richard asked Fred what his goals were. Fred's response was quick and simple: "I want to be Olympic champion and world record holder." Richard directly stated that he understood that some aspects of Fred's social life were preventing Fred from reaching his goals. Richard wanted to make sure that Fred knew that Auburn was a place where athletes were held accountable to extremely high standards and made it clear that if he were to coach Fred, Fred was going to have to live by those high standards. Richard told Fred that he would send him back to France at the first sign of Fred breaking those rules or not living by those standards. It was a no-tolerance policy: One strike and you're out. Fred immediately agreed to live the champion lifestyle in and out of the pool and he committed to drop the things that were preventing him from being the best athlete he could be. In that instant Fred made the decision to be excellent.

When Fred came back to Auburn to train, he brought that champion lifestyle to the program. He instantly bought into Richard's high standards, and not a day passed that Fred did not live by those principles and appreciate those values. The most valuable lesson came when Fred shared and taught those standards to other athletes. In fact, Fred set a benchmark for every other athlete in the program at the time and set the foundation for what is now the professional team that swims here at Auburn.

Few feelings in sport are worse than not performing up to your own expectations. This can be frustrating and discouraging and can ultimately lead to significant decreases in confidence. When Fred re-entered the Auburn program in 2007, his confidence was at an all-time low. However, the trust between a coach and an athlete can never be underestimated and it is ultimately what allows the athlete's self-confidence to take hold. Through his dedication to excellence and his commitment to Richard's lifestyle changes and mantra "believe in belief," Fred won a silver medal at the 2008 Olympic Games. In 2009, Fred's dream of breaking a world record in the long-course pool became a reality when he became the first man under 21 seconds in the 50-meter freestyle, setting a new standard of 20.94 at the French trials.

Performance Contributors Versus Performance Detractors

Although trusting in one's self and one's abilities is fundamental to success, the ability to consistently trust in one's self is not easily achieved. Two factors determine the extent to which an athlete comes to believe in him or herself: performance contributors and performance detractors. Of the two, performance detractors are toxic to an athlete's success and always leave the athlete—and the coach—disappointed.

Performance Contributors

A performance contributor is any aspect of an athlete's attitude and disposition that contributes to his or her competitive success. Mental actions such as positive self-talk, visualization and imagery, staying focused on the goal, accepting and releasing control of the situation, and believing in one's self are examples of performance contributors. As with an athlete's physical actions, each of these mental actions can be acquired through practice and repetition so that it becomes an automatic response to any given competitive situation.

For example, every competitive athlete knows exactly where they are headed at the end of a training cycle—the competition site, or, as I like to call it, the Coliseum. Like a gladiator who has prepared for battle, athletes are thrown into the environment where they need to perform. The sounds, sights, and setting of the competition environment are not experienced every day. All the competitors that the athletes have been visualizing in practice are now in the ready room waiting for the event to start, and outside that room wait the fans and the parents with expectations of great things about to happen. How do coaches really prepare athletes for all that exists in that moment when everything they have trained for is now on the proverbial line? The practice of realistic visualization can be a great tool for mental preparation.

About 2 weeks out from the 2008 Beijing Olympics, I was preparing with the Brazilian team in Macau, China. I wanted to create a situation in which César Cielo would experience the same conditions he would at the Olympic Games—the pressure, the sounds, the noise, the people—all while simulating his race in his mind. I wanted to go through a visualization session during which he would sense and feel and hear the same things he would experience during the race. I told him that we would swim in the morning and that in the afternoon we were going to do something special. I told him to bring a pair of walking shoes and some light clothes because it was very hot, and asked him to bring U.S. $100. He asked where we were going, but I kept it a surprise.

In the afternoon we got in a taxi and I told the driver to take us to the busiest street in Macau, which is a heavily populated city in China that is renowned for its casinos. The driver took us to the busiest street in Macau, and when we jumped out of the taxi people were everywhere; it was like a street in New York City. People were charging along and bumping into each other, and there was very little room to walk.

I said to César, "Alright. For the next 20 minutes we're going to walk down this street and visualize your race at the Olympics. We're going to walk into the Olympic pool, you're going to see the people, you're going to prepare for the warm-up, you're going to go through your warm-up routine. Then you're going to get out, you're going to put your suit on, and you're going to prepare for your race. Next, you're going to walk to the ready room, you're going to sit in the ready room with your competitors, and then you're going to walk outside and you're going to perform your race. There will be cameras around. There will be people. There will be noise and cheering. I want you to get up on your block and I want you to swim your 100-meter race. Start by slowly going through your dive and breakout, through to your second 25, then flip turn through to the 75, and finally into the finish. I want you to visualize exactly how you want to swim the race."

Then I said, "We're going to do this while we walk down this busy street, and I want you to block out the noise. I want you to block out the people. I want you to block out the sounds and I want you to visualize this experience while you're walking down this street."

For the next 20 minutes we walked down the street and didn't say a word to each other. I could sense him visualizing things. People were getting out of his way. At no point did he bump into anyone or force himself into anyone's way; they were just stepping aside. And I could tell he was in a zone and really concentrating on his race.

For me it was a hands-on experience of visualization, a realistic approach to getting what we needed. After that experience I told him to find someone on the street who looked like they needed some extra money. We looked and looked for another 20 minutes but we couldn't find anyone, so I told him to forget it and that we were going to leave. Just as we hailed a taxi, we saw a man pushing his whole life up a hill. He wore no shoes and no shirt, just a ragged pair of shorts. I told César, "That's the man. Go give him the hundred dollars." César ran over and gave the man the money, and the man was in complete shock. He had only one tooth and he was very dirty, and I could tell it was like someone had just given him a winning lottery ticket. This was our way to release César from the competitive visualization and finish off the day with a relaxed and good feeling.

Performance Detractors

In contrast to performance contributors, performance detractors are any actions in which an athlete engages that impede competitive success. Performance detractors include fear of failure; negative self-talk, visualization, or imagery; loss of muscular coordination (e.g., muscle tension and increased heart rate); overanalyzing the competitive situation; becoming distracted by one's surroundings or competitors; and feeling abandoned by a coach or teammate. In essence, performance detractors involve doubt about one's ability to win. Instead of viewing the competitive situation as a challenge in which to rise and conquer, the athlete views the competitive situation as an overwhelming threat to be feared.

When such skepticism overcomes an athlete, the coach must take immediate, and sometimes creative and drastic, measures to reverse this mindset. I am not above subjecting myself to the same mental demands I place on my athletes in order to prove a point. I believe such a practice can go a long way in developing the trust that is so critical. Not only does it reinforce your personal commitment to the athlete, it gives you, the coach, an opportunity to move from an outsider to a person connected with the athlete's feelings. This enables you to attain greater understanding of and insight into your athlete's mental state. In César's case, this became evident as we moved from the training camp to the Olympic Games venue in Beijing.

About 4 days out from the beginning of competition, we arrived for the first time at the Olympic pool in Beijing for warm-ups. For a 21-year-old, it's a pretty scary environment to walk into, and I could tell César was nervous. All of the top swimmers in the world were there, finally getting a chance to see each other. I knew that César was pretty daunted by this, so we tried to stay focused on ourselves and I tried to keep him with his Brazilian team. However, almost immediately he started with the negative self-talk. He started saying things like, "I'm tired today. It's really hot outside." So I decided to get him in and out of the pool as fast as I could. When he was in the pool he started to say things like, "My stroke feels like trash. My heart rate won't go down." At one point I think he even conceded defeat to one of his competitors. Then he tried on one of his new racing suits for the first time said, "This suit sucks. I don't feel good in this suit." Everything he said was negative, negative, negative. I tried to ease his mind by giving him a simple warm up, and even that he had issue with: "This warm-up is too long. The pool's too cold. The pool feels really long. There are too many people in the lane." You name it, he had a problem with it.

I could tell that he was getting more nervous by the minute. So he wouldn't see that I was nervous as well, I wanted to put an end to it and get angry with him. I tried to shock him a little bit. I told him to shut up and said, "I am so sick of hearing you complain." At that moment our relationship was under enormous pressure. I was a first-time Olympic coach with one of the best athletes in the world. I knew I had to resolve the issue. I tried to think of a way to prevent César from thinking about how his body felt. I believe the most common mistake a swimmer can make is saying, "I missed my taper. I don't feel good."

For some reason, we in the Brazilian federation were given winter jackets to use in Beijing. I had a crazy idea of putting on this winter jacket, walking around for a couple of hours, and trying to convince my body that it was actually cold outside and that I was freezing. I wanted to see whether I could create a response inside of my own body and go from really hot to really cold just by thinking about it.

So, I did it! I put on the jacket and went outside to wait with the Brazilian team for the shuttle to the pool. The temperature outside was surely more than 100 °F. The Brazilians started laughing at me and said, "Why do you have that jacket on? It's 100° outside!" and "How can you wear that? You're gonna pass out!" I came up with a story and told them, "I feel like I'm getting sick. I feel like I'm getting the flu so I put this jacket on to get warm." And then I pretended to shiver like I was getting sick and I was freezing cold. In my mind I imagined that snow was falling from the sky. At first my body responded normally: sweating, increased heart rate, dizziness. After about 15 minutes, though, I no longer felt really overheated. My heart rate lowered and I stopped sweating, and I actually started to feel really cold. I could sense that my body was no longer producing sweat, and then I started to shiver with cold.

On the bus with the athletes going to the Olympic pool, I was stuck in this icy cold winter land (in my mind). Finally, everything disappeared from my mind and that's all I could see and focus on. My body actually stopped sweating and I felt like I was shivering for the first time without having to force my body to do it, and I could truly sense that I was in this snowy environment. I was quite amazed that I could change my mindset and change my body's physical reactions just by thinking about being cold.

When I got to the pool I told César exactly what had happened and I asked him to agree that he would stop telling himself that he felt like trash and saying all the negative things to himself. He agreed that when he was in the warm-up pool he would stop every 50 meters and say something positive 10 times while he bobbed up and down, and then as he was swimming he would repeat that same word over and over. Adjectives such as strong, powerful, fast—any kind of positive words to reinforce the good feelings and emotions he was conjuring up.

César Cielo won the gold medal in the 50-meter free in the 2008 Olympic Games and became the only swimmer from Brazil to win an Olympic gold. The most important part, however, was that César was committed to the purpose of the exercise. If the purpose has no value in the eyes of the athlete, then their performance will be significantly less than their true performance capability. In this case, César fully committed himself to the purpose and the results were extraordinary.

Training to Perform

Any matters dealing with mental capacities can be subjective, especially in the first two factors discussed. However, I believe that achieving a high level of self-confidence can come by way of practical application. With that in mind, I now pose the question of which factors affect which outcomes. In other words, is it the hard work that builds confidence, is it the confidence that creates successful competition, or does successful competition bring about confidence?

Many athletes work extremely hard only to see their hard work crumble because of low self-esteem or a negative attitude about competing, so we can safely assume that, although extremely important, hard work is only half of the equation. My athletes understand that I often structure my training sessions to replicate competition. The purpose is to prepare each athlete for the rigors of competitive racing at the highest level and to develop in each athlete a mental fortitude that ensures a higher percentage of great performances under pressure.

A foremost concern for me in the Auburn University swim program is how to transform our practice and training sessions into a competition. How do we make it challenging enough so that the athletes feel secure in a competitive environment and believe that they can perform at their best, simply from the training that they have done? My goals have shifted to make practice harder and tougher than what athletes would normally face in competition so that when they get to a particular event they feel at ease and confident that their training has enabled them to perform at the highest level.

When I recruit athletes to join my program, I look for competitors who can contribute to what we are doing in our daily workouts. I seek out certain types of personalities. I look for individuals that are hungry to take knowledge from the program, but I also want someone who is eager to give back and share ideas, thoughts, and creativity. I create a culture where the athletes may perform at their highest level, challenge each other every single day, and support each other to leap to a new level of success. By maintaining this type of attitude, this program has produced incredible results, including several world records and Olympic medals.

With the type of athletes that I have in the Auburn sprint program, such as César Cielo, Fred Bousquet, Matt Targett, George Bovell, and Bryan Lundquist, I attempt to create an environment in which they can compete against each other on a daily basis without recognizing that they are actually competing. I don't like to put the same athletes next to each other every day. I try to mix up who is swimming next to whom, even when they are swimming casually. I find that my sprinters are always competing with each other, even about who can produce the biggest gasp from their teammates by entering the water with a backward flip or belly flop.

I often put Fred Bousquet at the front of the lane and César Cielo at the back of the lane, or vice versa, each day. I try to match them up head to head only once or twice a week. This strictly limits the time during which they can compete against each other. This creates an environment that simulates a competition because the competition does not happen every day. They long for it and anticipate the next time they can contend against each other.

A major component of the Auburn sprint program is our power sessions, which we do on Monday and Friday mornings. Each athlete match-races another athlete on Monday morning and then match-races a different athlete on Friday. They do not get the chance to go head to head with the same individual again until the following week. I often extend and diversify workouts for 2 or more weeks so that their workout partners vary.

If an athlete loses a match-race on a Monday, they have to wait another 2 weeks until they can race that same person again; therefore, they lose the opportunity to gain the upper hand. This method creates an environment in which they truly strive to be the best they can be against each other every day because they know they will not get that opportunity again soon. Coaches must create competition in practice that is similar to the competition itself and give athletes only one shot at becoming the champion. This motivates the athletes to succeed, which in turn helps build mentally stronger athletes who have an edge over their competition.

CONCLUSION

When assessing an athlete's capabilities, we as coaches look for such attributes as size, strength, body type, and genetic makeup. We look at these physical attributes and, based on our coaching capabilities, evaluate the types of physical training (sets, gym workouts, dryland) that would prepare the athlete for greatness. We map out their entire season and training cycles into weekly schedules. We spend hours on the pool deck honing their skills—stroke technique, breathing rates, starts, turns, and finishes. But in most circumstances, I venture to say that we as coaches overlook the necessity of mental training within our regimens. Mental training, especially self-confidence, is an abstract concept that we are inclined to leave up to the athlete to develop based on their own interpretations of their abilities and results.

I wholeheartedly believe that, although the mind and the building of self-confidence can be subjective and complex, we as coaches can and should apply practical and deliberate techniques throughout our training to build and strengthen self-confidence in our athletes. First and foremost, I believe the condition of the athlete–coach relationship requires the most intentional effort on our part. The base of trust is established from the initial stages of laying down the law to the continual individual follow-up sessions aimed toward creating a positive and encouraging environment. Once this trust is established, the coach has wider opportunities to implement techniques that will enhance performance contributors. The coach will also have more freedom to identify an athlete's mental detractors and apply correction. Equally as important as the trust you form with your athletes are the opportunities you create for them to experience the realities of competition through their training every day.

It is paramount for us as coaches to recognize that the confidence we display in our athletes can often produce the shot in the arm they need to excel and exceed expectations. Through their words and actions, successful coaches communicate confidence to their athletes, help them see and fulfill the untapped potential inside of them, and instill a self-confidence that cannot be obtained simply from winning alone.

References

CHAPTER 2

Hill, Napoleon. 1928. *The law of success.* Repr., New York: Penguin Group, 2008.

Sweetenham, Bill, and John Atkinson. 2003. *Championship swim training.* Champaign, IL: Human Kinetics.

CHAPTER 4

Harvard Men's Health Watch. 2011. Exercising to relax. February. http://www.health.harvard.edu/newsletters/Harvard_Mens_Health_Watch/2011/February/exercising-to-relax.

Neighmond, Patti. 2011. Seniors can still bulk up on muscle by pressing iron. *NPR*, February 21, 2011. http://www.npr.org/2011/02/21/133776800/seniors-can-still-bulk-up-on-muscle-by-pressing-iron.

Peterson, Mark D., Ananda Sen, and Paul M. Gordon. 2011. Influence of Resistance Exercise on Lean Body Mass in Aging Adults: A Meta-Analysis. *Medicine & Science in Sports & Exercise* 43 (February): 249–258.

CHAPTER 6

Prins, Jan H. 2007. Swimming stroke mechanics: A biomechanical viewpoint on the role of the hips and trunk in swimming. *Journal of Swimming Research* 17(Spring): 39–44.

CHAPTER 7

Covey, Stephen R. 1989. *7 habits of highly successful people.* New York: Simon and Schuster.

Goleman, Daniel. 1996. *Emotional intelligence.* New York: Bantam Books.

Goleman, Daniel. 1998. *Working with emotional intelligence.* New York: Bantam Books.

Gwaltney, James. 2009. *20 immutable laws of leadership.* Bloomington, IN: Xlibris.

Maxwell, John C. 1998. *21 irrefutable laws of leadership.* Nashville, TN: Thomas Nelson.

Maxwell, John C. 2001. *17 indisputable laws of teamwork.* Nashville, TN: Thomas Nelson.

Maxwell, John C. 2004. *Today Matters: 12 daily practices.* New York: Time Warner Book Group.

Maxwell, John C. 2005. *25 ways to win with people.* Nashville, TN: Thomas Nelson.

CHAPTER 14

Triantafyllou, Michael S., and George S. Triantafyllou. 1995. An efficient swimming machine. *Scientific American* 272(March): 64–70.

CHAPTER 22

Enoka, Roger M. 1994. *Neuromechanical basis of kinesiology.* 2nd ed. Champaign, Illinois: Human Kinetics.

Logan, Gene A., and Wayne C. McKinney. 1970. *Kinesiology.* Dubuque, IA: Wm. C. Brown.

CHAPTER 24

Blanchard, Ken, & Spencer Johnson. 1981. *The one-minute manager.* New York: William Morrow and Company.

Covey, Stephen R. 1989. *7 habits of highly successful people.* New York: Simon and Schuster.

Hamlin, Sonya. 1988. *How to talk so people listen.* New York: Harper & Row.

Maxwell, John C. 2010. *Everyone communicates, few connect.* Nashville, TN: Thomas Nelson.

Mehrabian, Albert, and Susan R. Ferris. 1967. Inference of attitudes from nonverbal communication in two channels. *Journal of Consulting Psychology* 31: 248–252.

About the Editors

Courtesy of Dick Hannula

Dick Hannula is one of the winningest high school and club coaches in the history of swimming. Before retiring in 1993, he coached for 41 years—25 years at Wilson High School and 7 years at Lincoln High School, both in Tacoma, Washington. While at Wilson, he racked up the longest high school undefeated streak on record, winning 323 consecutive meets, including 24 consecutive boys' Washington state high school swimming championships.

Hannula founded Tacoma Swim Club and served as head coach for 42 years. He has coached four U.S. Olympic team swimmers, including Kaye Hall, Olympic- and world-record holder for the 100-meter backstroke. He has also coached numerous Olympic team members, including one Olympic gold medalist and one world record holder; World University Games swimmers; Pan American Games and World Championship swimmers; several U.S. national champions; and American record holders.

Hannula served multiple terms as president of the American Swimming Coaches Association and is a former vice president of the World Swim Coaches Association. He has been inducted into several halls of fame, including the International Swimming Hall of Fame. Hannula resides in Tacoma, Washington.

Courtesy of University of California, Berkeley; photo by GoldenBearSports.com

Nort Thornton served as head men's swimming coach at the University of California at Berkeley before retiring in 2007 after 33 years of service. His teams consistently finished in the top 10 nationally while Thornton was at the helm of Golden Bears swimming. Thornton coached Cal to two NCAA Championships and was named NCAA Coach of the Year in 1979 and 1980. An inductee into the International Swimming Hall of Fame, he has coached the U.S. national team at the Olympics and Pan American Games. Forty-eight of his athletes at Cal have gone on to compete in the Olympic Games, winning 14 gold, 10 silver, and 5 bronze medals. He has also served the swimming community as president of the American Swimming Coaches Association.

Thornton continues to remain active on the Cal pool deck as a volunteer coach. His recruits, Milorad Cavic and Nathan Adrian, both earned medals at the 2008 Beijing Olympics. Adrian took home a gold medal as part of the United States' 400-meter freestyle relay. Cavic won a silver medal in the 100-meter butterfly after being out-touched at the wall by Michael Phelps by one-hundredth of a second. Thornton resides in Moraga, California.

About the Contributors

Jack Bauerle has been the head coach of the University of Georgia men's swim team for 26 years and the women's team for 30 years. His 415 wins are the most wins in college swimming of any active coach. His women's teams have won 4 NCAA Championship team titles, and he was the USA Olympic Women's Swim Team head coach in 2008 at Beijing. He was an assistant coach at the 2000 Sydney Olympic Games and was head coach of the 2005 USA World Championship Women's Swim Team and the assistant coach in 2001 and 2003. He also served as the head coach of the USA World University Games Women's Team in 1997 and as the head coach of the 2011 USA Women's Team for the Dual in the Pool.

George Block serves as president and chief executive officer of Haven for Hope. Before that, George was the director of aquatics for the Northside School District since 1977 and assistant director of athletics since 1993. In that time, he developed the Northside Aquatic Center into an internationally recognized center for athlete development. In over three decades at Northside, Block has developed 6 Olympians in three sports (swimming, triathlon, and pentathlon); 50 UIL state gold medalists; over 285 All-Americans; Olympic Trials qualifiers in 1984, 1988, 1992, 1996, and 2000; and numerous national and junior champions. In 1987, Coach Block was awarded the Phillips 66 Performance Award. Block was the Coca-Cola Texas Coach of Honor in 1992. In 1997, the United States Water Fitness Association named the Northside Aquatics Center the Top School District/Community Facility in the nation and Block as its top aquatics director. Block served as the president of the American Swimming Coaches Association from 1997 to 1998, and in 2000 he was given the Silver Award of Excellence for 20 years of USA Swimming national finalists. He was vice president of USA Swimming from 2006 to 2010 and is currently president of the World Swimming Coaches Association. Coach Block is married to Margie, a retired nurse. They have three children.

Mike Bottom has been the head coach of Michigan swimming and diving since 2008 and is recognized as one of the finest swimming coaches in the world. Bottom has guided Michigan to a pair of Big Ten championships and was named the 2011 Big Ten Swimming Coach of the Year. Mike brings a wealth of collegiate and international coaching experience. He has coached at each of the past four Olympic Games and spent 17 years in collegiate coaching. Bottom has been with the Race Club in Tavernier, Florida, since 2003 and has served as head coach of the world team, its elite-level training group. Among his most notable protégés is 10-time Olympic medalist Gary Hall Jr. Perhaps the world's best sprint coach, Bottom coached the top two finishers in the 50-meter freestyle at the 2000 and 2004 Olympic Games. From the 1996 to 2004 Olympiads, 9 of the 18 medals awarded in the 50- and

100-meter freestyle events have been won by his swimmers. Bottom was also selected as an assistant coach at the 2009 FINA World Championship in Rome during the summer of 2009. At the NCAA level, Bottom has mentored individuals in every stroke to 19 national titles. Since 1987, Bottom has directed BottomLine Aquatics, a start-up company dedicated to promoting health and growth in people of all ages. Initiatives include afterschool care programs for children ages 4 to 11, fundraisers, and classes for beginning- to elite-level swimmers.

A member of the 1980 United States Olympic team, Bottom was a world-record holder in the 400-meter freestyle relay. A four-time U.S. national team member, he was part of three NCAA champion teams at USC and was an NCAA medley relay champion and five-time All-American. Bottom is a charter member of the American College Counseling Association, the American Counseling Association, the American Swim Coaches Association, and College Swim Coaches Association of America. He is also certified by the National Board of Certified Counselors. Bottom received his bachelor's degree in psychology from the University of Southern California in 1978. In 1993, he graduated summa cum laude with a master's degree in counseling psychology from Auburn University and has completed all course work for a PhD in sport psychology. Bottom and his wife, Lauralyn, have three daughters.

Bob Bowman is head coach and CEO of the North Baltimore Aquatic Club. Six of Bowman's swimmers competed in the Beijing Olympic Games, and three won gold medals. Michael Phelps swam to Olympic history by winning 8 gold medals and became the most successful athlete ever at the Games by amassing a career total of 14 gold medals. Bowman's swimmers have set 43 world records and over 50 American records. He has coached 12 individual swimmers to 65 U.S. national championships as well as leading Club Wolverine to 10 U.S. national team titles during his tenure. Before returning to Baltimore, Bowman was the head men's swimming coach at the University of Michigan and the head coach for Club Wolverine. He has been named National Coach of the Year by the American Swimming Coaches Association four times and USA Swimming five times. In 2002 he was USA Swimming's Developmental Coach of the Year. Bowman was inducted into the ASCA Hall of Fame in 2010.

Stephen "Sid" Cassidy is an accomplished coach in both pool and open water venues, and he currently runs the aquatic program at Saint Andrew's School in Boca Raton, Florida. He is recognized for leading USA Swimming and FINA into the Olympic era of marathon swimming. He was a world-ranked marathon swimmer in the 1970's and has served as a coach on numerous USA Swimming National Team trips dating back to 1985. In 2009, USA Swimming honored Cassidy with their highest accolade, the USA Swimming Award.

David Durden leads the University of California swim program and guided them to their first NCAA team title since 1980. Durden was selected both National and Pac-10 Coach of the Year in consecutive seasons. He was also named the College Swimming Coaches Association of America swimming coach of the championships. In his previous three years, Durden led the Bears to a runner-up finish in 2010 and two fourth-place finishes at the NCAAs. He has guided Cal to 17 NCAA titles, including seven relay crowns and 31 Pac-10 individual and relay titles.

Durden is an NCAA Division I certified coach, a member of U.S. Swimming, and a member of the American Swimming Coaches Association. For five years, he was involved with the swim camps at Auburn, serving as the camp director in 2004 and 2005. Before coaching at Auburn, Durden served as an assistant for the highly regarded Irvine Novaquatics club team under current USC coach Dave Salo. A 1998 graduate of UC Irvine, Durden earned a degree in electrical engineering. He competed on the Anteaters' swim team from 1994 to 1997 and was the 1997 Big West Conference champion in the 200 butterfly. He and his wife, Cathy, reside in Concord with their young children.

James O. Ellis is an educator, swim coach, and motivational speaker. He has taught mathematics to urban youth for over 30 years in the Chester-Upland School District and the Philadelphia School District. Jim founded the Sayre Swim Club in 1971. Sayre transformed into the PDR swim team in 1979 and eventually became nationally and internationally regarded as the best urban swim team in America. This distinction helped inspire the recent swimming movie *Pride*. As a motivational speaker for the Keppler Speakers Bureau, Jim travels the country speaking at universities, corporations, and school districts.

Jim's coaching resume includes developing swimmers who competed in Olympic Trials in 1992, 1994, 2000, 2004, and 2008 and working with swimmers who competed in the Pan American Games, Pan Pacific Swimming Championships, World University Games, U.S. junior national team, and the Olympic Festival. Jim has been a member of the USA Swimming national team coaches' list, both national and international, since 1996. In 2002, he served as U.S. junior national team coach in Australia. He was senior chairman of Middle Atlantic Swimming and a member of the Outreach Committee of United States Swimming. During his tenure on the Outreach Committee, he was a part of a team that developed an outreach camp at Olympic Training Center for promising swimmers. He has served as coach of camps at the Olympic Training Center and as clinician at the Olympic Training Center for developing coaches. In 2007, Jim received the Trumpet Award and the First Diversity Award from USA Swimming. Ellis has received the President's Award from International Swimming Hall of Fame and is a member of the Board of Directors International Swimming Hall of Fame.

Jim is currently the senior aquatics director with the Salvation Army at the Ray and Joan Kroc Corps Community Center in Philadelphia, where he implements a diverse program with an emphasis on building the largest learn-to-swim program in the country. He is a graduate of Cheyney University and holds a master's degree in secondary education from Temple University.

Vern Gambetta is currently is the director of Gambetta Sports Training Systems. As a pioneer in the field, he is considered the father of functional sports training. Having worked with world-class athletes and teams in a variety of sports, Gambetta is recognized internationally as an expert in training and conditioning for sport. Vern is a popular speaker and writer on conditioning and has lectured and conducted clinics in Canada, Japan, Australia, the United Arab Emirates, and throughout Europe.

Vern's coaching experience spans 42 years at all levels of competition. His background is track and field and he has coached at all levels of the sport. Vern served as the first director of the TAC Coaching Education Program, designed to upgrade the standard of track and field coaching in the United States. He has authored over 100 articles and 8 books on various aspects of training. Gambetta received his BA from Fresno State University and his teaching credential with a coaching minor from the University of California at Santa Barbara. Vern also attended Stanford University and obtained his MA in education with an emphasis in physical education.

Bob Gillett is recognized as a major developer of the underwater dolphin kick. His innovations in the style of the dolphin kick resulted in an Olympic gold medal for Missy Hyman who won the 200 meter butterfly at the 2000 Sydney Olympics. He has coached 11 national champions and over 50 junior national champions over his coaching career. He retired from the Golden West Swim Club in 2011. Prior to that he was the owner and coach of the Arizona Sports Ranch in the Phoenix, Arizona area where over 15,000 youngsters participated in their sports programs.

Brett Hawke is in his sixth season on the Auburn University coaching staff and his third full season as head coach. While at Auburn, he has led the Tigers to three team NCAA Championships (two men's and one women's) and extended Auburn's streak to 15 consecutive men's SEC titles. The 2009 NCAA Coach of the Year, Hawke has coached more than a dozen NCAA champions, including 2008 Olympic gold medalist and current 50 and 100 free world-record holder Cesar Cielo. On the international stage, Hawke has served as an assistant coach for both Brazil and the United States. In the pool, he was a two-time Olympian for Australia, a 17-time All-American at Auburn, and winner of nine NCAA individual titles from 1997 to 1999.

Lanny Landtroop has the most coaching wins in Texas high school swimming history. He has coached at five high schools, primarily Clear Lake and Kingwood, over his 37-year career. He has coached over 300 high school All-Americans and his teams have won 67 of a possible 71 district championships, 16 state swimming and diving championships, 2 state water polo championships, and 3 swimming national championships. His honors include 18-time TISCA State Swimming Coach of the Year, National Federation Coach of the Year, Texas High School Swimming Coach of the 20th Century, Texas Swimming and Diving Hall of Fame member, NISCA Hall of Fame member, and National Collegiate and Scholastic Award recipient. He has served as president of TISCA and NISCA and on local, state, and national committees and boards for the benefit of the sport. He has also been a sought-after clinician, having given coaching clinics in more than 20 states as well as several ASCA World Clinic presentations.

John Leonard has been the executive director of the American Swimming Coaches Association in Fort Lauderdale, Florida, since 1985. In 42 years of coaching, he has become one of the best known names in the world of swimming and has overseen a staff that has developed educational programs and services that include 26 types of coaching schools; overseen the development of a program that has certified over 12,500 coaches; organized the model learn-to-swim school in SwimAmerica, which has taught over 3.4 million American youngsters to swim; and turned the American Swimming Coaches Association into an advocacy force that is respected nationally and internationally.

John was a founder of the World Swimming Coaches Association in 1988 and still serves on the board. He received the USA Athletes Appreciation Award in 1996 for his strong antidoping actions in world sport. In 2004, he received the Paragon Award from the International Swimming Hall of Fame. In 2010, John once again received the Paragon Award, this time for competitive swimming. In 2005, he was honored with the Collegiate/Scholastic Trophy from NISCA for his contributions to swimming, and *Aquatics International* magazine named him one of the 25 most influential people in aquatics. In January 2010, *Swimming World* magazine named him one of the 10 most influential people in USA Swimming. He serves on multiple committees for USA Swimming, including the Olympic International Operations and International Relations Committees, and is a member of the FINA International Coaches Commission.

John has served on 18 U.S. national team staffs and has worked for American swimming at 7 Olympic Games. He has served as the chairman of the United States Swimming Steering Committee for the U.S. Olympic team. An accomplished writer and editor, Leonard has authored over 1,000 articles on the sport of swimming, written 4 books on swimming, and edited 3 others. John lectures internationally and has provided international leadership in swimming in 47 nations. Leonard has three children and three stepchildren and lives in Fort Lauderdale and High Springs, Florida, with his wife, Dianne. As a hobby he continues to coach with his own team, SwimFast, in the Fort Lauderdale area, working with the senior group and the stroke school introductory level for new swimmers.

Mike Lewis has nearly two decades of coaching experience. He has worked with a wide range of athletes, including Olympians and world-record holders. Mike holds a master's degree in exercise science and has published research in the area of physical activity and academic achievement. He worked as an administrator in the U.S. Olympic movement for 10 years and was a team director for the 2000 Olympic Games. Mike is an avid swimmer and has notched several top 10 rankings in U.S. masters swimming. He currently is the chief operating officer with Open Water Source—the global information hub for open water swimming—specializing in all aspects of the sport from the Olympic 10K to ultramarathon events. He lives with his wife, Cynthia, in San Clemente, California.

David Marsh is a 12-time NCAA National Champion, 8-time Coach of the Year, USA National Team staff member, mentor to 30 Olympians, and coach at every level of age group swimming. David has spent his last 30 years developing athletes to excel in the pool and out. At SwimMAC Carolina, Marsh impacts the elite level swimmers all the way through the learn-to-swim programs. A five-time All-American at Auburn, he capped his career with a 1980 SEC Backstroke title.

Regarded as one of the top swimming mentors in the United States, **Teri McKeever** is in her 20th season as head coach of California's women's swimming and diving program. Also the U.S. head coach for the 2012 Olympics, McKeever has taken Cal to new heights—including the 2009 and 2011 NCAA team championships—and is often regarded as the sport's influential innovator because of her unique training methods. Under McKeever's tutelage, the Golden Bears have produced 4 NCAA Swimmers of the Year (three-time winner Natalie Coughlin and Dana Vollmer), 5 Pac-10 Swimmers of the Year, and 15 consecutive top 10 NCAA finishes. A former USC star in her own right, McKeever has produced an impressive 153-52 dual-meet record and numerous Olympians, NCAA champions, and All-Americans at Cal.

Bob Miller has been a swim coach for over 60 years. He has been very successful with both inexperienced and elite swimmers. He was an owner of the Olympic Swim School from which the Cascade Swim Club evolved. Miller was captain of the University of Washington swim team; after graduating, he represented the United States at several world championships, two Pan American Games, and the Melbourne Olympics in the modern pentathlon.

Bob's work ethic has carried over into his coaching. He has helped to develop five Olympians and numerous national champions. He has achieved the following awards for his coaching accomplishments: ASCA Coach of the Year in 1973, ASCA Hall of Fame in 2011, and Coach of the Year in Washington, Florida, and Oregon. Bob continues to swim 3,000 yards a day and still competes in masters swim meets.

Bill Pilczuk is a three-time NCAA All-American and five-time USA National Champion. He was also a 1997 Pan Pacific Champion, a 1998 World Champion, and a former American record holder in the short course 50-meter freestyle.

As a coach he was worked with the best, including David Marsh, Dave Durden, Kim Brackin, Cathy Sursi, and Ralph Crocker at Auburn University. He was the national sprint coach for Great Britain, under Bill Sweetenham and took over the National Youth Coach for Great Britain. Bill currently lives in Savannah with his wife Davana who works at Gulfstream. He has two young children and spends time helping with the Savannah Swim Team, coaching a summer swim league team at the Savannah Golf Club, and performing clinics and consultations with teams.

Jan Prins is currently on the faculty in the department of kinesiology at the University of Hawaii and the director of the aquatic research laboratory. He was "Doc" Counsilman's head assistant coach at Indiana University from 1975 to 1978. During that time he completed his PhD in human performance. From 1978 to 1987, he also served as head men's swimming coach.

During his tenure, his teams placed in the top 20 at the NCAA Division I Championships and in the top 10 at the USS Senior Indoor Championships. For the past 30 years his research interests have combined competitive swimming and aquatic rehabilitation. His current research centers on the use of multiple high-speed cameras in the biomechanical analysis of stroke mechanics.

Bill Rose began his career at the University of the Pacific (1968-1974), where his team won two PCAA championships. He then built the DeAnza Swim Club into the nation's largest club during his tenure (1974-1976). After that he coached the Canadian Dolphin team of Vancouver, before taking the head women's coach position at Arizona State University in 1979. Coach Rose has served as U.S. national team coach in Bremen, Germany and head coach of the Canadian Pan-American women's team, the Canadian world championship team, and the Canadian Commonwealth team. Rose served as a coach for the United States team in the 1995 Pan American Games in Mar Del Plata, Argentina, and was named to the staff of the U.S. World University Games team competing in Sicily, Italy, in August 1997 and again on the 1999 WUG team competing in Palma de Mallorca, Spain, as head women's coach.

In August 2001, Rose was a coach for the Philippines in the Southeast Asian Games held in Malaysia. In 2003, he was the U.S. head coach for the Pan American Games in Santo Domingo, Dominican Republic. Rose was named to the staff of the U.S. World University Games held in Turkey in August 2006, where his protégé swimmer, Justin Mortimer, earned a gold medal in the 1,500-meter freestyle. In 2007, Rose was the head coach for the U.S. open water team at the world championships in Melbourne, Australia. At the same time, he held a position on the swimming staff for the Melbourne events. In 2008, Rose was named to the U.S. Olympic team coaching staff and was the head coach for the Olympic debut of the 10K; one of his swimmers, Chloe Sutton, was the first American woman to compete in this Olympic event. In 2009 he was appointed to USA Swimming's world championship staff in Rome. In 2004, Rose received the highest honor that can be bestowed by his peers: induction into the American Swim Coaches Hall of Fame. In 2006 and 2008, Rose was named the Developmental Coach of the Year by the United States Olympic Committee.

Richard W. Shoulberg was the first aquatic director and head coach of the Girls and Boys swim teams at Germantown Academy and established the Germantown Academy Aquatic Club. He has served as head coach for U.S. national and junior national teams, men's and women's Pan American and Pan Pacific teams, and women's Goodwill Games team; Richard was an advisory coach for U.S. women's 2000 Olympic team, and he has received many professional awards including the USA Swimming Award—the highest award given by United States Swimming—as well as awards from NISCA, ASCA, and the PA Hall of Fame. During his career, Shoulberg has coached several Olympians and world record holders including Dave Wharton and Dave Berkoff and has published numerous articles in various swimming magazines.

Bob Steele retired after coaching all skill levels of competitive swimming during a 46- year career. His collegiate teams won five NCAA Division and two championships in his seven years at California State. His Southern Illinois University teams won the National Independent Championships six times. He served as the Director of Athlete and Coach Development for USA Swimming for nine years, and he served as a member of the USA Swimming Master Coach/Consultant program by visiting teams with a high school swimmer in the world rankings. He operates the Winning Spirit Racing Camps and is the author the highly successful book, *Games, Gimmicks, Challenges for Swimming Coaches*.

Bill Sweetenham grew up in the mining towns of Mount Morgan and Mount Isa, Queensland, Australia. He has held the positions of head Olympic coach for three countries as well as the national performance coach of British Swimming. Bill has coached numerous world-record holders, world champions, and Olympic champions. He was named a member of the Order of Australia and awarded a Churchill Fellowship. He continues to play a role with the Australian Sports Commission through chairing the Head Coaches Podium Group for all Olympic and world championship sports and works with Swimming Australia Ltd in assisting and mentoring its 12 top Olympic coaches.

Gregg Troy has brought the University of Florida swimming and diving program back to the national spotlight after winning the women's second NCAA title in 2010, its first since the Gators won the inaugural NCAA title in 1982 in Gainesville. As a result, Troy was named the 2010 USA Swimming Coach of the Year, 2010 and 2011 ASCA Coach of the Year, 2010 NCAA Women's Swimming Coach of the Year, and 2010 SEC Men's Swimming Coach of the Year. A top 10 NCAA contender in his 13 years at the helm, Troy has created an atmosphere of consistency and excellence in both the men's and women's Gator swimming and diving programs. The result has been the elevation of one of the most storied collegiate programs to even greater levels of success. In his career, Troy has tutored more than 75 Olympians and more than 240 All-American swimmers, and he has coached athletes to more than 155 U.S. and international records.

Troy earned his bachelor's degree in history and government from Texas Christian University in 1972. In 1987, he earned his master's in history education from Jacksonville University. Troy and his wife, Kathleen, have three sons.

Jon Urbanchek is currently the head coach at the Post-Graduate Center of Excellence in Fullerton, California and has years of coaching experience under his belt. He coached at the University of Michigan from 1982-2004 and at Club Wolverine from 1982-2009. His philosophy on the Senior level has always centered on the middle distance training (200-400 meter events) because it is simple to move up or down in training to fit the needs of most swimmers. Since middle distance training requires close to equal amounts of aerobic and anaerobic training, this gives rise to great variety, which swimmers enjoy.

Jon's coaching has yielded great success in middle distance events on the NCAA and Olympic level. He has coached Olympic gold medalists and World Record holders, including Mike Barrowman (200 Breaststroke, 1992); Tom Dolan (400 IM, 1996/2000); Tom Malchow (200 Butterfly, 2000); Peter Vanderkaay; Dan Katchum; and Klete Keller (800 Free Relay, 2004). He has also had great results in sprint events (Brent Lang and Gustavo Borges with 7 NCAA titles) and in the distance events (Tom Dolan and Chris Thompson with numerous NCAA titles in the 1,650).

Stephan Widmer was born in Switzerland and swam internationally for 10 years. He completed an MS degree in Zürich, Switzerland, aiming to become a high-performance swimming coach. In 2001 Stephan was appointed as a coach at Queensland Academy of Sport. Since then, his swimmers have achieved 20 world records, 3 Olympic gold medals, and 16 world championship gold medals. His coaching concept is based on a process-driven and race-pace-specific training model that employs people-management skills and explores human behavior and a complex understanding of swimming techniques.